TESS READ grew up in London where she went to stage school until it was realized that she might need a proper education. After graduating from Cambridge University, and then being permanently on the point of finishing a PhD at Oxford, she took to travelling to far-flung places known for their interesting and exotic cuisine. In between travelling, studying and organising French cake-baking competitions in Hanoi she works as a journalist specialising in politics, finance and travel. She covered Vietnam on the BBC's *From Our Own Correspondent*.

She lives in Oxford surrounded by cats – despite being allergic to them.

Vietnam by Rail
First edition 2001

Publisher
Trailblazer Publications
The Old Manse, Tower Rd, Hindhead, Surrey, GU26 6SU, UK
Fax (+44) 01428-607571
info@trailblazer-guides.com
www.trailblazer-guides.com

British Library Cataloguing in Publication Data
A catalogue record for this book is available from the British Library

ISBN 1-873756-44-5

Editor: Anna Jacomb-Hood
Series editor: Patricia Major
Proof-reading: Honor Jones
Typesetting: Anna Udagawa
Layout: Anna Jacomb-Hood
Cartography: Nick Hill
Index: Jane Thomas

Printed on chlorine-free paper from farmed forests by
Star Standard (☎ +65-8613866), Singapore

VIETNAM
BY RAIL

TESS READ

TRAILBLAZER PUBLICATIONS

Acknowledgements

So many people make travelling such an enjoyable experience and help to bring a book together that it would be impossible to list them all, but my special thanks go to Ty, Phi, Ha, Hai, Tu, Quynh, Binh, Andrew, Dr Le Van Chau, Richard Cox, everyone at Netnam for managing to keep me in touch despite the huge obstacles, Xavier Callard, Bryn, Ba Nguyen Thi Thu, Ong Truong Vinh Thinh, Madame Dai, Tran Thai Nghiep, Rukmini Callimachi, Nguyen Doan Minh, Do Dinh Tho, Do Duy Toan, Tran Tien Dat, Hanh, Hong, Thi, Ivo Vasijiev, Lien, Thomas Debourse, Jeff Richardson, Didier Corleau, Clare Kelbrick and Fuji film, Barry Street, Chris Lines, Mike Popham at the BBC, Tara Winterton for her magnificent hospitality, Glendra Read, Graham Read and Freda Lupton for their tireless support and frequent inspiration and all my travelling companions – most especially the incomparable Rupert Read and Daniel Davies.

A request

The author and publisher have tried to ensure that this guide is as accurate and up to date as possible. However, things change: prices rise, rail services are extended or cut back, hotels open and close. If you notice any omissions or changes that should be included in the next edition of this book, please contact Tess Read at Trailblazer (address on p2) or email tessr@trailblazer-guides.com. A free copy of the next edition will be sent to persons making a significant contribution.

Cover photo: Surveying the paddy fields from a convenient mount: water buffalo and owner outside Kep.

CONTENTS

INTRODUCTION

Vietnam is much more than the scene of a war. It is a tropical country of striking contrasts rich in cultural heritage where conical hats linger in the luminous green paddy fields of the countryside, while motorbikes and cyclos stream down the French-style boulevards in the cities, and brightly-dressed hill tribespeople lead lives steeped in tradition in the mountains. Between Saigon with its heady pleasures and the charming elegance of Hanoi, the Paris of the Orient, there lies a beautiful country of historical towns, an ancient imperial city, long sweeping beaches and some very visible left-overs of that war which made Vietnam well known. Through the strip of land between the blue of the South China sea and the coffee-growing slopes of the central highlands runs Vietnam's railway, and the train they call the Reunification Express.

In the 25 years since the Communists won what they call here the American war, Vietnam has lived through years of re-education camps and international isolation, but it has emerged blinking into the light of global capitalism. The railway system holds the history of the last turbulent century in its tracks. Built by French colonialists, it has been attacked by the Japanese, bombed by the French and Americans, booby-trapped by both north and south Vietnamese, and then rebuilt both to symbolize and create some kind of unity in this country so divided, north versus south, by war. The bright red engines of the trains still connect people and places as they travel through the lovely countryside in a cacophony of chatter and eating in hard-seat class, or in the peaceful comfort of soft sleeper class.

In Vietnam today you can see cities which are bursting with life, where smart executives rub alongside peasants selling their produce from shoulder panniers. You can seek out the remains of war, from vast networks of tiny underground tunnels to battle sites and discarded tanks; you can also observe traditional country life, rich in rituals and hard work, where the ways of working the rice fields have not changed for centuries. Vietnam has successfully repelled many invaders but has kept influences from each and the result is a heady combination. Nowhere else in Asia can you buy freshly-baked baguettes accompanied by 'La Vache Qui Rit' cheese, then stop for a delicious foamy mug of draught beer, then perch at a streetside stall over a mouth-watering bowl of hot noodle soup brimming with the scent of freshly cut lemongrass and basil, before taking in an evening at the opera. Or you can spend your time trying to find an answer to the question that has always fascinated me in this land where every one of these friendly, generous people has a story, a tragedy, to tell: whether Vietnam now is one country or two.

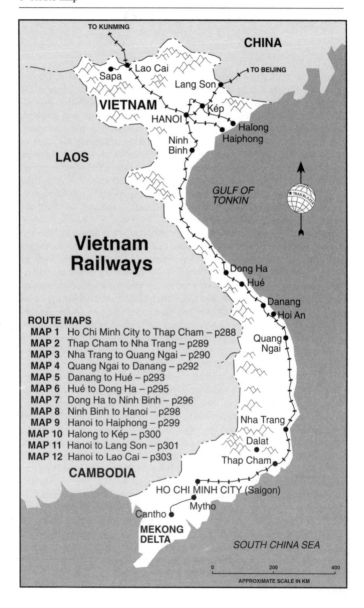

TO KUNMING

CHINA

Lao Cai

Sapa

TO BEIJING

Lang Son

VIETNAM

Kép

HANOI

Halong

Haiphong

Ninh
Binh

LAOS

*GULF OF
TONKIN*

**Vietnam
Railways**

Dong Ha

Hué

Danang

Hoi An

Quang
Ngai

Nha Trang

Dalat

Thap Cham

CAMBODIA

HO CHI MINH CITY (Saigon)

Mytho

Cantho

**MEKONG
DELTA**

SOUTH CHINA SEA

0   200   400

APPROXIMATE SCALE IN KM

PART 1: PLANNING YOUR TRIP

Routes and costs

ROUTE AND STOPPING OPTIONS

Covering Vietnam by rail is a joy in itself, but it can also comprise the first or last leg of the world's longest train journey reaching all the way between Ho Chi Minh City (Saigon) and Seville – nearly 10,000km.

This epic train journey would take you from the southernmost tip of Spain, through Eastern Europe, on to Russia, then China, and finally you would head south to reach Vietnam, travelling the length of this beautiful country on the evocative Reunification Express. Not forgetting, of course, to stop off to explore the charming back streets and tranquil lakes of Hanoi, the fabulous scenery of Halong Bay and Hoa Lu, the 19th-century capital Hué, the great beach and town of Nha Trang, and the capital of the country – bustling Ho Chi Minh City, with the delights of the Mekong lying just to its south. On the way you will find the many sights and sounds of the wars this country has seen – from tunnels to tanks, from the bamboo stakes which repelled the Mongols in the 13th century to statues of Ho Chi Minh. And there are many relics and reminders of the war which made this country famous, known throughout the world as the Vietnam war, though in Vietnam it was called the American war.

This guide covers the country from south to north as this is the direction Vietnam is most usually travelled, but of course the information is just as valid the other way round.

Vietnam's 2600km of railway line runs along the country's coastline through all the major centres from Ho Chi Minh City (HCMC) up to Hanoi where it forks into three. The north-west fork grinds up the **Red River valley** to Lao Cai (from where you can make a further hour's ascent by road to the lovely hill station of Sapa) and then continues on into China's Yunnan province through stunning scenery. The middle fork heading north-east toils up through beautiful Vietnamese landscape to the town of Lang Son and then continues into **China** and on to Beijing. The third fork of the railway heads directly east to Haiphong, the stopping-off point for the divine **Halong Bay**, often called one of the wonders of the world.

In deciding your route a vital fact to be aware of is that there is no such thing as a railway ticket enabling you to break your journey. This means that you have to buy tickets at each station to each new destination.

If you get off a train before your planned destination don't expect to be let back on a later train without buying a completely new ticket.

If your budget or time is limited you may want to consider not attempting to cover the whole country (see p12), but if you do, taking overnight trains can be the best way to do it in reasonable time and spirits. If this is your plan it is important to realize that stations in small towns often have a small daily allocation of tickets for foreigners so you should try to **buy a ticket in advance**. Additionally small stations often do not have an allocation for sleeper tickets – hard or soft – though this generally does not matter because unless the trains are full (such as during the lunar new year festivities of Tet in January or February) it is almost always possible to upgrade on the train and is often cheaper to do so. Also beware that if you want to go only a short distance you will not be able to buy a ticket for an express train, even though it stops there! The lack of any computerized ticketing system is dealt with by limiting places on express trains to long-distance stops – such as HCMC– Nha Trang, Nha Trang–Danang, or Danang–Hanoi. The actual process of buying a ticket is usually very easy; either from a railway station, there are rarely queues, or from a travel agent or hotel.

COSTS

Hotels, transport and food

Vietnam is a very poor country so costs are lower than in most of the rest of South-east Asia, and certainly travelling here is much cheaper than in Europe, America or Australasia. But some costs are much higher than the market price due to the simple fact of government control.

The Vietnamese government essentially operates as an international Robin Hood – raising money from the rich first world to give to the poor third world, or at least Vietnam's part of it. So foreigners are free to roam the country but they are charged several times more than Vietnamese for all transport costs, and a foreigners' tax is levied at hotels making accommodation more expensive than for Vietnamese. But the prices for transport and hotels for Vietnamese are so low that the foreigners' price is still reasonable; and you can see the government's point. An average hotel costs $15 for a double room per night and an express train journey of 500km in good comfort costs $18. In comparison with the communist days of Russia, the expense is usually worth it – hotels at $10-20 are good clean enjoyable places and you can travel in comfort on the trains.

The third major expense of any trip – food – is of course not subject to any government control so can be had astonishingly cheaply yet is often

---

❏ **Dollars**
Unless specified, prices quoted in dollars are given in US dollars.

❏ **Upgrading**
Whatever ticket you buy it is almost always possible (except during Tet) to upgrade to soft sleeper once you are on the train, or even just when you are on the platform waiting for the train. Conductors know how expensive it is for foreigners to buy train tickets and they can make it cheaper for you to travel in a good class. This means that the cheapest way to travel in soft sleeper is always to buy a ticket for the cheapest class you could bear to risk if upgrading went horribly wrong and then upgrade on the train. How much you pay will depend on your bargaining skills, but as a rough guide you could upgrade to soft sleeper air-con on a journey such as Saigon–Danang for around 150,000d per person.

delicious. A succulent ham and chilli sandwich in French bread from a street vendor costs less than $0.20 and a tasty streetside bowl of vegetable noodle soup keeps you going for hours for around $0.30.

Prices in restaurants go up from here – a full meal with drinks costs around $5-8. In Hanoi and Ho Chi Minh City (HCMC) you can find smart restaurants, but still you are unlikely to pay more than $20 a head and here the quality is so good that you are getting great value for money.

Daily budgets
It is hard to say what the minimum daily budget is for travelling in Vietnam, because it depends not only on how much of the country you wish to see and your minimum required comfort level, but also on your bargaining ability and whether things such as imported soft drinks or beer are important to you or not. Assuming a modicum of transport, food, sights and basic accommodation $8 is probably a basic daily minimum. The average foreign visitor probably spends upwards of $10 a day. If your budget is higher than this, the extra expense all goes on quality – luxury hotels, super berth with air-con on the train, and tipples of whisky or gin can all be yours.

❏ **Everyday prices**
To ease your travels these are the real prices for a few everyday items:
● Large bottle of mineral water $0.15
● Plain cup of coffee $0.20
● Can of coke $0.30 ($0.40 if cold)
● Can of local beer $0.25
● Can of imported beer $0.50
● Baguette $0.03 (small)
● Coconut $0.25
● Three or four bananas $0.10
(These prices have been quoted in US dollars in case of a changing dollar/dong exchange rate, but the prices would normally be payable in local currency, the Vietnamese dong.)

The best advice on costs for goods at any level of luxury is that if you don't know what something should cost you can expect to be overcharged for it – potentially heinously. This is partly because hard bargaining is de rigueur for many transactions amongst the Vietnamese and partly because the official price discrimination for foreigners encourages private individuals to follow suit. One traveller said: 'When in doubt, bargain, bargain, bargain.' (Anna from Norway)

Expenditure so much depends on your personal taste in souvenir and gift buying as well that it is hard to suggest appropriate budgets, but here is a rough guide. An absolute shoestring budget of around $6 a day would be broken down as $3 for the cheapest accommodation (always sharing), $1 for bicycle hire, and $2 for food plus souvenirs/necessities. In addition you would need to add the cost of travel to Vietnam plus insurance, long-distance travel for which you could allow perhaps $100 to cover the length of the country, plus you need to allow for the extra $10-15 cost of the cheapest tourist accommodation available in some towns.

A more comfortable way to see Vietnam would have you spending $7-10 a night on accommodation, $5 for cyclos/sight entrance fees, and $3-4 a day on food and drink (amounting to $15-19 a day). In addition you should allow $200 in order to travel the length of the country and a few sidetrips, plus perhaps $100 for some tailor-made clothes and souvenirs. Spending more than this will allow you to stay in some fabulous hotels, eat in fantastic restaurants, be chauffeured around in taxis long distance, kit out your entire wardrobe/house, or make meaningful contributions to the worthy local charities – or all of the above.

Highlights

The diverse beauty and charm of Vietnam rarely disappoints first-time visitors or those who return for more. There are so many things to see and do that it is hard to pick out only a few – what you choose really depends on what kind of trip you want.

Perhaps the country's single most unmissable sight is the majestic beauty of **Halong Bay** described, amongst many others, by a 1926 Thomas Cook guide to the region as 'one of the wonders of the world', and it hasn't changed since then. The scenery is best admired by taking a boat out into the azure waters of the bay, but you can also enjoy it from the comfort of the beach.

For simple beach pleasures visit **Nha Trang,** Vietnam's most-developed resort; it still has a pleasant town and with its fresh coconut and seafood vendors strolling along the beach it has a lot to recommend it.

Those interested in the arenas of the American war, and those keen on vast beaches of white sand and smashing rollers alike, may prefer to visit **China Beach** near Danang. There are many such sites of **historical interest** worth visiting, from the American bases in the demilitarized zone (DMZ) to Viet Cong (VC) headquarters in the Mekong Delta.

The **Mekong Delta** is certainly worth an excursion to experience the delights of gliding through small fertile waterways amidst the daily life of the Vietnamese and other ethnic groups who live there. **Sapa** in the north is the perfect springboard to see the brightly-coloured dress and traditional way of life of many montagnard ethnic tribes, as well as being a beautiful mountain holiday location.

Of all the cities in Vietnam the one-time capital **Hué**, with its beautifully-preserved tombs of emperors, draws many en route between charming lake-filled **Hanoi** and the cosmopolitan city of pleasures **Ho Chi Minh City** (formerly Saigon, also known as HCMC). This guide follows the route of the railway through Vietnam making stops which take in all these highlights and many more.

But to see all these sights without being in a permanent lather you need to spend at least a month in Vietnam. If you are lucky enough to have more time than this you can take in the additional excursions detailed in this guide or have the chance for a real adventure, such as living on a boat and exploring the thousands of islands and caves in Halong Bay, or trying to climb Vietnam's highest mountain, Fansipan.

If your time is more limited you might consider focusing on one area, so cutting down travelling time which is significant unless you fly. A two- to three-week trip starting in the **south** could have you spending a few days in HCMC, visiting the Mekong Delta for three days, travelling to Nha Trang and spending a few days at its great waterfront and on nearby beaches, then continuing up to Danang and catching a glimpse of real Vietnamese city life before stopping at Hoi An for a few days of oriental and Cham culture and buying silk clothes and then taking an overnight train back to HCMC (or to Hanoi and even through to China).

❏ **Particular highlights**

● Witness the Vietnamese taking exercise at dawn en masse in a choice location such as Hanoi's Hoan Kiem Lake or HCMC's Cong Vien Van Hoa Park is a must for everyone once.

● If you are would like to have silk clothes tailor-made then you are in for a treat in Hoi An.

● Those interested in the history of the American war shouldn't miss the sights, sounds and tunnels of the DMZ.

● If you like coffee don't pass up the chance to try the rich strong taste of Buon Ma Thuot coffee beans which are roasted in butter before being added to boiling water (you don't need to go to Buon Ma Thuot to try or buy some).

On the other hand, a two- to three-week trip starting in the **north** could have you spending a few days in and around Hanoi sampling Vietnamese life and visiting the Perfume Pagoda, travelling to Halong Bay for its stunning scenery and beaches, then making your way to the mountainous north-west and spending some time at Sapa before returning overnight to Hanoi from where you could take the train to China, or overnight down to HCMC stopping for a day or two to see Hué or the DMZ.

A great one-week trip would be to visit HCMC and the Mekong with an excursion up to Nha Trang if you felt ambitious, or a week in the north would be perfectly spent between Hanoi and Halong Bay with the option of the return to Hanoi via Kep.

Wherever you choose to go in this fascinating country you can expect to come across delicious food and delightful people. 'The paddy fields are as green as any in South-east Asia, but the friendliness of the people – that's something unique.' (Danny, London)

When to go

There is no good or bad time to visit Vietnam, because it has such a diverse climate that when one part of the country is too hot or cold or dry or rainy somewhere else will be sunny and warm.

The whole country is in the tropics or subtropics so hot weather can be expected for much of the year, though mountainous regions are much cooler, even temperate.

Beware that if you travel to Vietnam between November and February you should be prepared for a real winter in the north, and heavy rains and cold north of Nha Trang. Rain and chilly or cold weather are brought to all of Vietnam north of Nha Trang by the north-east monsoon blowing polar air between October and March – average winter temperature in the north is 16°C (61°F). But this monsoon also brings dry warm weather to the south during this time.

The south-western monsoon meanwhile brings warm and humid weather to the whole country from April to October but the south can be very hot during this time. The upshot is that April to September is the best time to see the north, although coastal regions are often struck by typhoons during this time, while you may want to avoid the south in April and May if you find very hot weather unpleasant.

There are also regional subclimates: for example Hué is often truly deluged in October. Having said all this it is as well to remember that there is always room for good and bad luck with weather and that getting soaked in the heat by a sudden downpour isn't the end of the world.

Visas

All foreigners need a visa to enter Vietnam. In theory you can now buy one on arrival, but in practice you may be unable to board a plane if you are without a visa because the authorities abroad may not know the new regulation and because it has only been officially decreed, rather than actually implemented on the ground.

A standard **tourist single-entry visa** is easy to obtain, costs £40/$40-60 (depending on how you obtain it) and lasts for 30 days. It is cheapest to obtain a visa direct from a Vietnamese embassy. The process takes three to ten days. In order to apply for a visa you have to submit two application forms (available from the embassy), two passport-sized photos, your passport and the fee. Your passport must be valid for at least a further six months and there must be an empty page in it for the visa stamp.

The visa is valid for all international entry/exit points and the 30 days begin from your stated arrival date, even if you don't actually arrive until a later date. When your visa is issued, a copy of your application form with space for a photo will be returned to you; this needs to be given to customs' officials on arrival. (These days they don't seem to mind if your photo isn't attached.) Visa service companies can get a visa in about ten days – Trailfinders (UK ☎ 020-7938 3848) charges £18 for this service. Travel agents in Bangkok charge less and take only four to five days.

Even if your purpose in visiting Vietnam is tourism it may be possible to obtain a **business visa**. These are valid for three months and can be multiple entry on request but will cost at least $150. If you want to try to obtain one you are best off talking to travel agents in Bangkok (Khao San Road) or to visa service companies in other countries. You are unlikely to have much success approaching a Vietnamese embassy for a business visa unless you have a letter of sponsorship from a Vietnamese company.

❏ **Vietnamese embassies**
Australia (☎ 02-6286-6059) 6 Timbarra Crescent, Canberra; **Belgium** (☎ 02-374 9133) 130 avenue de la Floride, 1180 Brussels; **Canada** (☎ 613-236-0772) 226 McLaren St, Ottawa, Ontario; **China** (☎ 010-532-1125/1155) 32 Guanghua Lu, Jinguomen Wai, Beijing; **France** (☎ 01 44 14 64 00) 62-66 rue Boileau, Paris 16ème; **Germany** (☎ 228-357-021) 37 Konstantinstrasse, 5300 Bonn; **Italy** (☎ 06-854-3223) 12 Piazza Barberini, Rome 00187; **Laos** (☎ 21-5578) 1 Thap Luang Rd, Vientiane; **New Zealand** – contact the Vietnamese embassy in Australia; **Thailand** (☎ 2-251 7201) 83/1 Wireless Rd, Bangkok; **UK** (☎ 020-7937 1912) 12-14 Victoria Rd, London W8; **USA** (☎ 202-861-0737) 1233 20th St NW, Washington DC 230036.

Getting there and away

BY AIR

Most visitors arrive and leave Vietnam by air, and this certainly is the most hassle-free way to get through customs. Ho Chi Minh City's (Saigon) Tan Son Nhat airport is the country's busiest, though many airlines also fly in and out of Hanoi's Noi Bai airport. Danang has now become a truly international airport and it is possible to fly directly from Singapore and Bangkok to Danang. More direct connections can be expected. A number of airlines offer the chance to fly into one airport and out of another and although the price increase for doing so is often near the $170 cost of a one-way air ticket between the two cities, there is still a significant convenience factor.

There are no direct flights from the UK (though BA has now opened an office in Hanoi so this may not be far off) and only one airline flies direct from the USA or Canada but while changing planes increases the time spent travelling it also often means you can stopover at no extra cost. It is expensive to fly from Australasia to Asia, including to Vietnam. There are regular flights between nearby centres such as Bangkok, Hong Kong and Phnom Penh and availability is generally not a problem except around the lunar new year in January/February when all flights to and from Vietnam (and China, Singapore, Hong Kong) are very heavily booked.

Ticket types

The cheapest ways to fly long-haul to Vietnam are either by a cheap airline, such as Aeroflot, or by buying a ticket from a travel agent offering special deals – buying a ticket to Bangkok and then buying a ticket on from there can be the cheapest, although not quickest, way. Beware though: not only can tickets from 'bucket shop' travel agents include certain restrictions (such as that dates cannot be changed) but it is even possible for particularly dodgy travel agents to go out of business before you fly and for you to find that your ticket is not valid. For this reason it is often best to book with reputable travel agents (listed below) and, in Britain, ensure that they are ABTA authorized.

APEX (advanced purchase) tickets can also prove a cheap way to fly, but they have to be booked at least a few weeks ahead of departure and have restrictions. Round-the-world (RTW) tickets can be a cost-saving way of getting around, starting from around £700/$1000 for a one-year ticket. But if you do go for this option make sure it has sufficient flexibility for your needs and check whether putting Ho Chi Minh City (Saigon) or Hanoi on the itinerary isn't more expensive than buying the extra from Bangkok would be.

From Europe

Britain and France are by far the cheapest places to fly to Vietnam from Europe, even though there are no direct flights from Britain. Air France and Vietnam Airlines fly direct to Ho Chi Minh City (HCMC) and Hanoi from Paris; Vietnam Airlines also flies direct from Berlin.

A good peak-season return fare from Britain to HCMC would be around £600 inclusive of tax (the cheapest fare would be about £460). Airlines which fly to Vietnam from Britain in rough ascending order of price include Aeroflot (via Moscow and Bangkok), Alitalia (via Rome and Bangkok), KLM (via Amsterdam), Lauda Air (via Vienna and Bangkok), Air France (via Paris), Thai Air International (via Bangkok), Emirates Air (via Dubai), Lufthansa (via Frankfurt), Malaysia Airlines (via Kuala Lumpur), Kuwait Airlines (via Kuwait City and Bangkok), Singapore Airlines (via Singapore) and Cathy Pacific (via Hong Kong).

Three of the most reputable discount travel agents in Britain which also offer student discounts are Campus Travel (☎ 020-7730 8111), STA Travel (☎ 020-7361 6262) and Trailfinders (☎ 020-7938 3366). Numerous other travel agents offering special deals are listed in the major newspapers.

From North America

Northwest Airlines is the only airline yet to fly direct to Vietnam from the USA or Canada but many airlines fly via stopovers. A good peak-season fare from the west coast would be around $1000, rising to $1200 from the east coast. Airlines which fly to Vietnam from several major cities in the USA and Canada in rough ascending order of price include China Airlines (via Taipei), Asian Airlines (via Seoul), Korean Airlines (via Seoul), EVA Airlines (via Taipei), Thai Air International (via Bangkok), Air Canada (via Hong Kong), Canadian Airlines (via Hong Kong or Bangkok), Malaysia Airlines (via Kuala Lumpur), Singapore Airlines (via Singapore) and Cathay Pacific (via Hong Kong). Council Travel is the largest student travel operator in the US offering good discounts through branches in many cities; CUTS is the Canadian equivalent. Other special deals are best found by shopping around travel agents.

From Australasia

Flying from Australasia to Vietnam is expensive given the distance. A good peak-season fare would be A$1500 from Sydney and A$1300 from Perth. Airlines which fly to Vietnam include Vietnam Airlines, Thai Air International (via Bangkok), Malaysian Airlines (via Kuala Lumpur), Singapore Airlines (via Singapore), and Quantas (via Bangkok). STA Travel has offices in most major cities in Australia and offers student discount travel. To find other special deals your best bet is to check travel sections of the major newspapers.

From South-east Asia

It is quick, easy and reasonably cheap to fly between Vietnam and nearby Asia. Bangkok stands out as the major air gateway: Air France, Vietnam Airlines and Thai Air International fly daily to HCMC for $150 one way, or $300 return ($180 return to Hanoi). The flight to HCMC takes only 80 minutes. Check out travel agents on the Khao San Rd in Bangkok for any special deals.

Vietnam Airlines and Cambodia Airlines fly daily between Phnom Penh and HCMC for $60 one way, $120 return; Hanoi is a lot more expensive at $220 one way. However, the Hanoi–Vientiane connection ($90/$180 one way/return), flown by Lao Air and Vietnam Airlines is cheaper than the HCMC–Vientiane route ($250 return).

Cathay Pacific flies daily between Hong Kong and Vietnam for $300 one way, $540 return: it is best to check out travel agents in Chungking Mansions for good deals.

Vietnam Airlines and Singapore Air/Malaysian Airlines respectively fly between Vietnam and Singapore and Malaysia for $200-300 one way, a high price given the short distance. Garuda Airlines flies between Vietnam and Indonesia from $450 one way.

It is also possible to fly direct to Danang on Singapore Airlines from Singapore, and from Bangkok on Thai Airways.

BY LAND

To/from China

There are two border crossings into China; one in north Vietnam via Dong Dang and the other in north-west Vietnam via Lao Cai.

There are train routes from Hanoi to destinations in China on both these routes, though at each of them you need to walk across the border and change trains. Equally you can take buses, or shared taxis to the towns of Lao Cai or Dong Dang and ride a *Honda om* (riding pillion on the back of a motorbike; also known as *xe om* or *xe Honda om*) to the border, cross on foot and pick up transport on the other side where train tickets are cheaper – though bear in mind that on the Chinese side from Dong Dang the nearest town (Pinxiang) is 15km from the border. Also bear in mind that you can expect significant delays crossing the border from China into Vietnam on grounds of suspected smuggling, and in the other direction on grounds of bureaucracy.

❏ **Dollars**
Unless specified, prices quoted in dollars are given in US dollars.

The railway line from Dong Dang leads to **Beijing**, a total of 2966km between Hanoi and Beijing. There are two direct international trains per week running between Hanoi and Beijing. The other train journey into China crosses the border at Lao Cai and leads to **Kunming** in Yunnan province of China; this line passes such stunning scenery in China that it was known when built by the French as 'la ligne acrobatique' (see p131). (Additionally, from Lao Cai it is only an hour by motorbike to the beautiful hill station of Sapa.)

Tickets are more expensive when bought in Vietnam than in China despite the fact that Chinese trains are more luxurious than Vietnamese! So if you can face the hassle the cheapest way to get by train to Beijing is to buy a ticket from Hanoi to Dong Dang, make your way independently to Pinxiang and buy a ticket to Beijing from there. Tickets for all international trains are payable in dong but, bizarrely, are quoted in Swiss francs! Rumour has it that this is because the Vietnamese government wanted the railways to be quoting prices in a stable currency, but were not prepared to give official credence for the almighty dollar.

Timetables for the international trains between Hanoi and Beijing change, but currently they leave Hanoi each Tuesday and Friday at 2pm arriving in Beijing 53 hours and 40 minutes later on Thursday and Sunday respectively at 7.40pm. This includes a three-hour delay at the border, known as Friendship Pass (Huu Nghi Quan in Vietnamese), a two-hour wait at Pinxiang and around a three-hour wait at Nanning. Trains leave Beijing for Hanoi at 8.30am each Monday and Friday arriving in Hanoi at 11.30am on Wednesday and Sunday respectively. The full timetable is given in Appendix B, pp311-13.

The route from Hanoi to Kunming is 765km and takes around 43 hours, passing through stunning scenery on the Chinese side, though the views from Hanoi to Lao Cai are rather ordinary. So it is best to take the overnight train from Hanoi to Lao Cai (train number LC1). For details of train times see Appendix B, pp311-13.

To/from Laos and Cambodia

There are two official crossing points for Laos and one for Cambodia. Beware that customs guards at land borders are much more officious than those at airports. Be sure when entering Vietnam overland to check the length of time the guard has validated your visa for, as it may be less than the standard month. If so you could try subtle bribery, but if this fails you may just have to reconcile yourself to obtaining a visa extension before your current term expires. Also beware that you will be lucky to find any banks or travellers' cheques changers at the crossings on the Vietnamese side so ensure you are carrying some US dollar cash with you.

There are two border crossings for **Laos**: one at the small village of Lao Bao on Highway 9, 80km west of Dong Ha, and the other at Cau

Treo, 110km west of the industrial city of Vinh. The border post at Lao Bao is 3km beyond the village. Direct international buses depart every two or three days in the very early morning from Danang or mid-morning from Dong Ha straight to Savannakhet, costing $15 for the journey from Dong Ha. Alternatively Dong Ha is served by local buses to Khe Sanh and then to Lao Bao. But this way even if you take a Honda om from Lao Bao to the border you will still need to walk the 1km between the border posts.

The border at the suspension bridge of Keo Nua pass, known in Vietnam as Cau Treo, can be reached by local buses from Vinh or from Tha Khaek in Laos, or by a new luxury coach which leaves Danang every other day for Vientiane; the journey takes 30 hours and costs 230,000d. The coach leaves from outside Dien Bien Hotel at 35 Dien Bien Phu St in Danang.

Beware when travelling in Laos that the route between Luang Prabang and Vientiane is considered dangerous as is the area to the east of Luang Prabang.

The border crossing for **Cambodia** is at Moc Bai, 60km north-west of Ho Chi Minh City (Saigon) and 12km west of the town of Go Dau. A variety of buses run every day between Ho Chi Minh City and Phnom Penh via Moc Bai. They vary in comfort and cost (up to $12 for air-con) but all are stopped at the border while everyone on the bus is cleared for customs. It is possible to prevent this delay – although it is likely to engage you in others – by taking a tour bus ($4) or local bus to Tay Ninh but jumping off at Go Dau and then taking a short Honda om to the border and walking over yourself. Shared taxis usually wait on the other side of the border in order to take you to Phnom Penh for a few US dollars.

TOURS

Many tour companies operating regionally and worldwide offer tours to Vietnam. Tours can give you peace of mind and differing amounts of independence and companionship. But do bear in mind that a tour is a much more expensive way to see Vietnam even than if you pay a travel agent to buy first-class train or air tickets and use relatively expensive car-hire companies. Doing things this way is fairly hassle-free – particularly if you follow this guide! – so you may consider the extra expense of a tour not worth it.

Many of the operators listed below also offer tours of the region, usually combining a stay in Bangkok with sightseeing in Vietnam and Cambodia. Details of other companies offering tours to Vietnam can be obtained by searching on the Internet.

Escorted tours
● **Kuoni Worldwide** (head office ☎ 01306-740888, 🖳 www.kuoni.com/co.uk), Kuoni House, Dorking, Surrey RHY 4AZ, operates week-long

locally-escorted tours from £1199/£1371 (low/high season) or four-/eight-day tours (£215/£779) starting in Bangkok.
● **Thomas Cook** (head office ☎ 01733-418450, 🖳 www.thomas cook.com/co.uk), PO Box 36, Thorpewood, Peterborough, has a good-value 16-day tour covering the length of the country for £1300.
● **Asian Journeys** (☎ 01604-234855, 🖳 www.asianjourneys.com), 32 Semilong Rd, Northampton, NN2 6BT, UK, has long specialized in tours to Vietnam and offers the best around in cultural sensitivity and culinary delights. Their 16-day tour includes a trip to the central highlands where you ride on elephants and in dug-out canoes.
● **The Imaginative Traveller** (☎ 020-8742 8612, 🖹 020-8742 3045, 🖳 info@imaginative-traveller.com, 🖳 www.imaginative-traveller.com), 14 Barley Mow Passage, Chiswick, London W4 4PH, offers a range of tours including a comprehensive and very good value 21-day tour for £890, taking you round the country by bus, rail etc.

Tailor-made tours
A tailor-made tour is a good option if you want a hassle-free but independent trip – you decide where you want to go and when and the agency books all the hotels (five-star when possible) and travel arrangements. You can also specify which sections of your trip are to be covered by train, road etc.
    Some operators offering tailor-made tours are:
● **Kuoni Worldwide** (☎ 01306-740500, 🖳 fareast.sales@kuoni.co.uk) see p20 for full contact details.
● **Thomas Cook** (see above for contact details)

❏ **Specialist steam tours**
There are several companies and individuals who organize steam tours of Vietnam by chartering a steam train from Vietnam Railways. Prices of the tours vary so you should certainly get a few quotes from different providers for the precise itinerary you are interested in before booking.
● **Regent Holidays** (☎ 0117-921 1711; 🖹 0117-925 4866, 🖳 regent@regent-holidays.co.uk, 🖳 www.regent-holidays.co.uk), 15 John St, Bristol BS1 2HR. This highly recommended travel agency can offer individual tailor-made tours covering the whole Indochina region and can organize specialist steam tours of Vietnam.
● **Warwickshire Railway Society** (☎/🖹 01564-826143), 145 Fulford Hall Rd, Tidbury Green, Solihull, West Midlands, can organize steam tours, generally in the first few months of each year.
● **Enthusiast Holidays** (☎ 020-8699 3654, 🖹 020-8291 6496, 🖳 info@train-seurope.itsnet.co.uk), 146 Forest Hill Road, London SE23 3Q, has a very good reputation for organising railway tours to Vietnam.
● **Hugh Valentine** (☎ 01785-850052), 3 Redhills, Eccleshall, Stafford, ST21 6JW, has organized several steam tours of Vietnam and knows the country and its steam trains well.

● **Progressive Tours** (☎ 020-7262 1676, 🖹 020-7724 6941), 12 Porchester Place, Marble Arch, London W2 2BS.

● **Steppes East** (☎ 01285-810267, 🖹 01285-810693, 🖥 sales@steppeseast. co.uk, 🖥 www.steppeseast.co.uk), Castle Eaton, Cricklade, Wilts SN6 6JU.

● **Bales Worldwide** (☎ 01306-732718, 🖹 01306-740048, 🖥 www.balesworldwide.com) offers tailor-made tours to Vietnam/Indochina and can arrange a package on the Victoria Express to Sapa from £150.

❏ **Vietnam on the Internet**

The World Wide Web is a great resource for finding out all sorts of odd pieces of information about Vietnam and hooking up with a large number of veterans from the American war. Unfortunately, as yet, there is not a great deal of useful information for the traveller such as train timetables or hotels; certainly there are sites with hotel details on them, but few are equipped to offer online booking. Although there are a number of sites which encourage you to buy fully organized tours in Vietnam it seems unnecessary to buy them in advance because companies, such as the Green Bamboo organization, offer precisely the same tours once you are inside the country (which you can usually book with one day's notice). Furthermore, the message of this guide is that for most people buying such tours is not necessary.

The most useful online resource for finding out about recent news in Vietnam and cultural features is **www.destinationvietnam.com**. This site lets you read the current, usually excellent, edition of the magazine and search through their archives. For more city-centric travel-oriented information, probably the two best sites at the time of writing are **www.vietnamonline.com** and **www.vietnamadventures.com**, but neither are particularly good. The site **www.vietnamtourism.com** is currently blocked – this could mean that the Vietnamese Tourist board is about to launch a marvellously useful site detailing train, air and bus timetables and prices not to mention hotel and restaurant details, but I doubt it. For details of travel agents in Vietnam try **www.1000traveltips.org**. A government-run site with information on many government-run hotels, restaurants and other information is **www.saigon-tourist.com/hotels/hotels_info.htm**; this site enables you to book rooms in Saigon's finest hotels, including the Continental, Rex and Majestic.

At the time of writing there was little information on the web specifically on the railway. You can find several personal stories of trips to Vietnam and photographs of the trains but little else. Vietnam Railways now has email but it is certainly not equipped to deal with queries by this means. The good news is that they say they are working on producing a website, which might end up having timetables posted on the net; the bad news is that there is no official target date for completion.

The best way to search for information on particular areas, cities or major hotels in Vietnam is to use keywords in a search on the major search engines such as **www.google.com**, or **www.altavista.com**. Yahoo.com has a division which covers only Asia, which you can locate through their main site and search for Vietnam. Searching like this is also the best way to find stories about veterans of the American war or about boat people made good in the States. Some of these sites make interesting reading.

Adventure tours
● **Exodus Expeditions** (☎ 020-7675 5550), 9 Weir Rd, London, SW12 offers a 19-day tour of Vietnam by bicycle with back-up bus.
● **The Imaginative Traveller** (see p21 for contact details) organizes cycle and adventure tours.
● **VeloAsia** (USA ☎ 415-664-6779, 🖳 veloasia@aol.com), 1271 43rd Ave, San Francisco, CA 94122, USA, offers cycle tours.
● **Global Spectrum** (USA ☎ 202-293-2065), 1901 Pennsylvania Ave NW, Suite 204, Washington DC, USA, runs hiking as well as cycling tours.

Ecological or cultural projects
● **Earthwatch** (☎ 01865-311600) at 57 Woodstock Rd, Oxford, OX2 6HJ, UK, runs fascinating ecological and cultural projects and take volunteers who pay for their own travel and help raise sponsorship funds. Currently they have no projects running in Vietnam, but future work is possible.

What to take

The golden rule is: keep your luggage to a minimum bringing no large supplies of things that can be bought on your travels, but omitting nothing which you cannot buy out there. Very few travellers bother with suitcases – they are unwieldy, make you look rich and wheels don't roll smoothly on broken-up pavements and roads. Rucksacks are the baggage of choice for most, though shoulder bags are also popular. Many opt for one large rucksack with one very small one which often fits on the large. My preference is for two, or three if necessary, medium-sized rucksacks because these are much easier to take care of on trains or buses, easier to fit on cyclos and it's easier for other people to carry your bags for you! A moneybelt worn next to the skin is very useful protection against the theft of your most essential items, but it does get uncomfortable in hot weather so you may find yourself wanting a small rucksack or bag for back-up.

CLOTHES

Your optimal choice of clothes to take to Vietnam depends very much on the time of year and where in the country you are visiting. If you are travelling in the summer months and are not planning any serious expeditions in the mountainous regions, bring less rather than more. Not only will you not need any warm clothes but also clothes in Vietnam are very cheap, whether it be T-shirts, or tailor-made cotton or silk clothes which you can design to suit your travelling (or elegance) needs (see p217).

Shoes are a different matter as it is difficult to find good-quality shoes, trainers or sandals in Vietnam, particularly for large Western-sized feet, so it is advisable to bring such shoes with you. Unless you plan to stay only in high-quality accommodation, flip-flops are a wise purchase (before you come or in Vietnam) to keep showers clean and comfortable.

If you are travelling to Vietnam during its winter but are intending to visit only the south you still don't need to prepare to wrap up as it is always warm. But in the north of the country the temperature drops significantly in winter: at this time Hanoi averages 16°C (60°F) while the mountain regions are much colder. You will need warm clothes for this and should be prepared for even easy-to-dry fabrics such as silk never to dry fully in the cold dripping humidity. Don't expect to find heating anywhere. One traveller, Mark from Australia, said 'Hanoi in winter was a serious shock to the system – no heating, no hot baths and not even a change to the culture of outside eating on the street.'

Whenever you travel to Vietnam you should consider your bed linen arrangements – see box on p87. A final essential item you'll never regret having is a small towel – the new super-absorbent towels on the market are a fantastic investment. If you are planning any extended hill- or mountain-walking be aware that you can't obtain the highest-quality specialist clothes (such as fleeces and Goretex) and equipment in Vietnam, so you need to bring them in from the West, or from nearby centres such as Hong Kong or Singapore. Berghaus' website (www.berghaus.com) can tell you where to find the nearest stockists of their quality equipment.

MEDICAL SUPPLIES

Even if you plan to stay in luxury hotels and ride in taxis you should take a small medical kit with you. Making one up rather than buying a pre-prepared one will generally give you better-quality bandages and so on, as well as being better value for money.

A basic first-aid kit should include essentials such as a bandage and/or joint support tubigrip, some elastoplast or plasters, several sterile syringes and swabs, insect repellent, suntan lotion, something for an upset stomach, a needle and thread, and if you have ever had allergic reactions you should bring an adrenaline shot or two and syringes.

Trekkers intending to explore far from civilization should certainly take a more extended medical kit including supplies of emergency treatments for tropical diseases (see p32).

If you have a medical condition it is clearly advisable to bring sufficient supplies, but bear in mind that you can buy many prescription drugs over the counter in all the major centres in Vietnam and often for a great deal less than you would pay in the West. For example, antibiotics and asthma treatment are readily available at all pharmacies as well as treatments for the tropical diseases that you might contract out there (see pp32 and 34). These 'prescription drugs' are often of perfectly good quality and are made in countries like Australia – but do be aware that they should not be past their sell-by date.

GIFTS

If you arrive in Vietnam armed with photos of your family and a little map of the world (inflatable plastic globes are the best) you won't find it hard to make friends wherever you go.

If you want to be generous to all those countless Vietnamese people who'll make your trip such a delight then a small memento 'from your country' will be very much appreciated. This could be anything like postcards or a pen with London written on it or just foreign coins – anything so long as it clearly looks foreign. Western-brand cigarettes are often popular with smokers (555 especially) and can be very useful in a potentially nasty situation with people in authority, such as bus conductors (though be aware of the thin line between acceptable gift and bribery). Whisky is also popular with men, though cognac has a higher status value.

Do bear in mind, though, that in Buddhist Vietnam the etiquette of gift-giving differs from the West – in Vietnam gift-giving is to the benefit of the giver who gains merit by their action. The result is that you should not expect effusive thanks on receipt of a present and should not expect it to be opened, if it is wrapped, while you are present.

OTHER EQUIPMENT

Those who want to keep a diary, will find it remarkably difficult to get hold of simple **writing books** anywhere other than in big department stores in the main cities. Finding little notebooks is not a problem and these can be very useful as address books (taking yours from home is not advisable if you don't want to lose it). It is advisable to bring **sunglasses** so that you can be sure they provide protection against UVA and UVB rays, though glasses' wearers who can't find clip-ons of an exact fit should

---

❏ **Meaningful flowers – colours for giving**
If when you are in Vietnam you find that you want to buy a gift for someone Vietnamese, note that flowers are always a good choice, but certain colours and types have specific meanings – here's a brief guide: red is a good warm colour, but pink roses are for lovers, purple is also a romantic colour, green is associated with youthfulness, blue with freshness and hope. Black and white are gloomy colours associated with death though white is also associated with purity and white flowers are the perfect gift for a young girl's birthday, but always avoid the flower called *hué,* which has hundreds of tiny white buds on the top of tall stems, as these are used at altars.

know that the opticians in the tourist areas of Ho Chi Minh City (Saigon) and Hanoi can usually oblige for $7-10. A pair of spare **glasses** or **contact lenses**, or at least a copy of the prescription, is a wise precaution, as is a tiny optician's **screwdriver set** which can prevent a loose spectacle arm turning into broken glasses. You should certainly wear a **hat** in the sun but provided you are happy with standard designs you can pick one up fairly easily in Vietnam.

It is an extremely good idea to bring a good-quality **torch (flashlight)** in order to deal with the combination of poor streetlighting and severe pot-holes, as well as frequent power cuts and variable hotel lighting. Maglite torches are the best around with their spare bulb in the back, and their abil-ity to act as a candle can make you popular in restaurants and clubs during power cuts. A **padlock** and **chain** is useful both for chaining rucksacks up in trains or buses and in case you wish to double lock your hotel door.

If you are purifying your own water you will want a **water bottle**; you are likely to find more durable specimens outside Vietnam. You can buy iodine in Vietnamese pharmacies, but the more sophisticated **water purification tablets** should be brought with you.

A **pocket compass** is a travellers' mainstay and is particularly useful in cities such as Hanoi for correctly negotiating the north/south or east/west boulevards.

Earplugs are a good idea even for the sound sleepers of this world, because you never know when a hotel is going to start construction work at the most unlikely hours (many Vietnamese get up around dawn).

Finally, the question of phrasebooks: while this book aims to provide you with many of the essential language skills, a **phrasebook** enables you to get even more out of your trip, not least because it helps non-English speakers communicate with you. Vietnamese is a tonal language which makes it very difficult for Westerners so you seriously need guidance. The Rough Guide phrasebook is the best around; beware in particular of an old edition Lonely Planet phrasebook (readily available in Vietnam from street sellers) which is apparently full of intriguing mistakes.

MONEY

There are two key questions about bringing money to Vietnam: how much to bring and in what form? The second question is much easier to answer than the first (for which see p11).

Travellers' cheques are a must for their security and ease of exchange; the easiest to access are denominated in pounds sterling or US dollars. Credit or debit cards on which you can withdraw money are a good back-up, though it is wise to check the charges your credit card company will make. Cirrus and Delta card-holders and customers of ANZ Grindlays Bank will find accessing funds from the cashpoints in Hanoi and Ho Chi

Minh City (Saigon) extremely easy and cheap – it may not be long before the same facilities are available elsewhere in the country.

Dollar cash (US$) is generally exchangeable in even the tiniest of banks, or at the reception of many hotels, many shops or traders also accept it and it is useful in an emergency, so it is advisable to bring plenty. For travelling through the most rural areas of Vietnam, however, you must ensure you have sufficient Vietnamese cash. Wherever you are it is always wise to have a reasonable amount of small denomination Vietnamese notes in order to pay for a cyclo or buy a streetside meal.

READING MATTER

It was quite by chance I fell in love with Indo China. The spell was first cast, I think, by the tall elegant girls in white silk trousers, by the pewter evening light on flat paddy fields, where the water buffaloes trudged fetlock-deep with a slow primeval gait, by the French perfumeries in the rue Catina [today's Dong Khoi St], *the Chinese gambling houses in Cholon, above all by that feeling of exhilaration which a measure of danger brings to the visitor with a return ticket.* From Graham Greene's *A Sort of Life, Fragments of an Autobiography*

Available in Vietnam

In general the best books on Vietnam are available outside the country only, and indeed other than the few books which are widely on sale in the book exchanges in Hanoi, Ho Chi Minh City (HCMC/Saigon), Nha Trang, Danang and Hoi An it is almost impossible to get hold of any books in English. The exceptions to this are the following books on Vietnam which are available from the many street sellers in Hanoi and HCMC.

Graham Greene's novel *The Quiet American* is a finely-written and fascinating tale of murder and intrigue set on and around the streets of Saigon during the period of French rule in the 1950s; Greene's typically anti-hero hero is brought to appreciate the dangers of supposedly innocent foreign involvement.

Another piece of essential reading is Bao Ninh's *The Sorrow of War* which is a beautifully-told autobiographical vision of lost innocence and transient camaraderie as the youth of North Vietnam go to war to preserve their land and life and return to find what little is left. It also contains vivid scenes on the 'Peace train' – the packed train which, at the end of the war, took 48 hours to take the soldiers from the North back home; this train route would shortly be named The Reunification Express. This tale is also strikingly reminiscent of one of Vietnam's most prominent works of literature which if you are lucky you can find sold in English. This is the lyrical and touching love-story poem of Kim Van Kieu, or *The Tale of Kieu*, written at the end of the 18th century by Nguyen Du. The poem also has a more serious message as the stress on the importance of the purity of women is thought to be an allegory for political allegiance (see p77).

The other books readily available in Vietnam are historical works which are generally unfeasibly-long treatises on Vietnamese culture often with an added dose of propagandic fiction, such as *Vietnam, a Long History* by Nguyen Khac Vien, or *Vietnam, Civilization and Culture* by Pierre Huard and Maurice Durand.

Two books, however, stand out: one is Stanley Karnow's interesting account *Vietnam, A History* which focuses on recent history, particularly the American War, from a communist's viewpoint and which seems to be available only in HCMC, and General Vo Giap's account *The Battle of Dien Bien Phu* which is an extremely interesting and readable account of how and why the numerically inferior and less well-equipped Vietnamese forces beat the French in 1954.

Other than these there are a number of special interest but rather dry books available on certain topics, such as *Ethnic minorities in Vietnam* or *50 Vietnamese recipes*.

Available outside Vietnam only

There is a vast array of books on Vietnam in English published and available outside the country. The following list includes those considered to be the best or the most interesting works. On Vietnamese history it is hard to beat Joseph Buttinger's long and worthy but comprehensible account *The Smaller Dragon* which is particularly good on early history.

The American War has spawned thousands of works of fiction, non-fiction as well as cinema fodder. Taken together, *Into the Quagmire* by Brian VanDeMark and *Lyndon Johnson's War* by Larry Berman provide a believable account of why America's involvement in the war escalated and its effect on the political apparatus of the USA.

There are numerous accounts of the progression of the war from the attempt at objectivity in Jonathan Schell's *The Real War* to the involved accounts by fighting Americans such as Robert Mason's *Chickenhawk* and the extraordinary story of how the war came to the villages of Vietnam in the life of one Vietnamese girl told by Le Ly Hayslip in *When Heaven and Earth Changed Places*. Graphic portrayals of aspects of the war can be found in the remarkable tales of *The Tunnels of Cu Chi* by Tom Mangold, or in the harrowing and abhorrent narrative of *Four Hours in My Lai* by Michael Bilton and Kevin Sim.

A unique account of the war is Richard Nixon's perspective as president in *No More Vietnams*; this deserves a read even if you dismiss the arguments justifying the principles of American involvement. John Pilger's excellent book *Heroes* is a worthy counterbalance to Nixon's defence of the war.

The most fascinating account of the end of the war and of the lead up to America's/South Vietnam's final defeat is *Decent Interval* by Frank Snepp. However, this book is very difficult, although not impossible, to obtain for extremely interesting reasons. Snepp was a CIA operative in Saigon during the war and his thrilling account of the bungled process of the war is as extraordinary an inside story as you will read. However, on its publication in America in 1977, two years after the war had ended, the Justice Department attempted to ban the book in an unprecedented lawsuit, claiming Snepp had violated the CIA's secrecy agreement. The courts finally upheld the government, but not until over 100,000 copies had been sold. Some can still be found in libraries or second-hand bookshops.

A book which is really worth a look is the Pulitzer Prize-winning *Fire in the Lake* by Frances Fitzgerald. This is a well-considered account of the reasons and results of the American War, based on a visit to Vietnam in 1966. The book traces deep cultural differences between East and West and is heavily critical of America's role in the war.

Two recent and extremely good books which discuss Vietnam's changing relationship with itself and the rest of the world in an informative and readable way are *Vietnamerica* by Thoman A Bass, which looks at the experience of Amerasians, and *Shadows and Wind, A view of modern Vietnam* by Robert Templer, an extremely well-respected journalist who creates with interest and clarity a picture of this complex country.

There is some excellent travel writing on Vietnam. Indochina was a popular exotic location for wealthy, nostalgic and fairly adventurous travellers in the 19th and early 20th century. Most of these accounts, however, are unreadably jovial, and the travel guides of the time are mostly concerned with where the best hunting was to be had; though they are interesting for their universal recommendations of either the Continental or Majestic hotels in Saigon. But there are two excellent works, written in the 1950s and 1960s respectively, by Norman Lewis, *A Dragon Apparent*, and by Paul Theroux, *The Great Railway Bazaar*; the latter has the advantage of taking you on some of the journeys offered by the truncated rail service of the South in wartime.

Health

Vietnam has at least its fair share of tropical diseases as well as the usual travellers' diarrhoea. But the Vietnamese are more hygiene-conscious than many of their Asian neighbours so provided you take sensible precautions you needn't expect to contract any illnesses while in Vietnam. Sensible precautions include having relevant vaccinations, protecting yourself against malaria, avoiding tap water and ice, and equipping yourself with a reasonable medical kit (see p24). It is also always a good idea to have your teeth checked before travelling.

If you do become ill, Hanoi and Ho Chi Minh City have by far the best medical facilities in the country, but if your condition is serious you should get yourself flown out to Bangkok or Hong Kong. But as Pascale from France said 'If you get really unwell here, you're unlucky. It's *nothing* like India'.

VACCINATIONS

The diseases you should be vaccinated against before you go are polio, tetanus, typhoid and hepatitis A. At some surgeries in the UK these vaccinations are available free on the NHS; elsewhere you may have to pay, in which case visiting a travel clinic may prove to be more convenient. British Airways has a travel clinic (☎ 020-7439 9584) at 156 Regent St, London W1.

For up-to-date information on vaccinations in the USA call the Center for Disease Control and Prevention (☎ 404-639-3311) in Atlanta, Georgia. Try to plan ahead as some injections have to be staggered. If you fail to get vaccinated before going it is possible to have the injections at medical centres or even large pharmacies in the main cities, but you probably run a greater risk of infected needles by doing this.

No vaccinations are compulsory to enter Vietnam, except for **yellow fever** if you are entering from a yellow-fever infected country.

Immunization from **polio** takes the delightful form of a sugar cube; one dose protects you for 10 years. The **tetanus** vaccine needs a renewal jab every 10 years to protect you from contracting the disease.

Typhoid is transmitted through contaminated food and water, and epidemics do occur in tropical countries. Vaccination lasts for three years, but if an epidemic is reported in a region it may be wise to avoid that area, or at least be very careful what you eat and drink.

Hepatitis A is a disease of the liver which isn't fatal but can lay you out for several months and is easily transmitted by contaminated food or water so is well worth being vaccinated against. Gamma globulin protects you for two to six months; Havrix Mondose protects you for one year and a booster shot given at the end of the year extends protection to 10 years.

Other possible vaccinations

As well as the vaccinations listed above there are others you can choose to have depending on your likely level of risk. You are at risk of contracting **Japanese encephalitis** only if you intend to spend time on farms which have pigs because the disease is spread by mosquitoes which breed around pigs. The disease is not treatable and can be fatal so if you think you might be exposed to this risk you should be immunized.

Rabies is contracted through the blood or saliva of infected animals, principally dogs. The vaccine which is available does not protect you fully from the disease – you still need serious medical treatment – but it buys

you time (four to five days) in getting that treatment. Avoiding stray animals and mad dogs is my preferred strategy. This is actually much easier
in Vietnam than in the rest of South-east Asia where packs of dogs roam
the streets at night and their endless howls and fierce fighting bark prevent
any night-time quiet. This does not happen in Vietnam – stray dogs are
rare and when encountered are obeisant. This wonderful state of affairs is
due to just one thing – the Vietnamese eat dogs.

Hepatitis B is transmitted through infected blood or bodily fluids.
Risky activities include sexual contact, blood transfusions or having a tat-
too. If these sound appealing then you could consider vaccination, especially as the disease can be hidden, in that carriers of Hepatitis B do not
necessarily have the disease, although Vietnam is not a high-risk country.

POTENTIAL HEALTH PROBLEMS

Malaria
South Vietnam is a high-risk region for malaria, particularly around water
such as in the Mekong Delta, though the risk is low in the large cities.
Malaria is potentially fatal and although it is curable relapses can occur
later in life. It is carried by some mosquitoes, so you are potentially at risk
from every mosquito bite; since there is no comprehensive protection
against malaria preventing mosquito bites is the best protection. Locals
have some immunity against the disease, but Western travellers do not.

● **Prevention** Some travellers take Mefloquine, also known as Larium,
as it is the most effective preventative medicine against the strains of
malaria found in Vietnam; it is certainly useful to carry this with you as it
can be used as a cure.

Larium is available on prescription in the West and can't be found
over the counter in Vietnam. However, many travellers fight shy of using
it because it often produces severe side effects such as headaches, dizzi-
ness, vomiting and even hallucinations. In any event it should not be taken
by women who are pregnant or planning to become so within three
months.

The alternative to Larium is the antibiotic Doxycycline. The dose is
100mg daily starting one week before entering the malarial area and continuing until four weeks after leaving the area. But be aware that it should
not be used for more than three months and shouldn't be taken while
pregnant or by children aged under 12. Users may become susceptible to
sunlight. The drug has not yet been licensed in the UK. For more advice
on malaria a useful number in the UK is the Malaria Reference laborato-
ry (☎ 0891-600350), but note that a call is not cheap at 39p per minute
cheap rate.

Because of potential side effects many visitors decide not to take preventative medicine, just preventative action against the mosquitoes. Insect

repellent (it must contain diethyl-toluamide, 'deet', to be effective) is widely available in the West but more cheaply so in Vietnam; the quality of the bottle not the contents is likely to be the only difference.

Mosquito coils which burn like incense but produce stronger smoke are effective if you're stationary and can be bought cheaply in Vietnam. Most hotels have mosquito nets – even basic rural homes often have sheets of muslin around the beds – but they need to be sprayed with Deet to be fully effective; buying a net in Vietnam is much cheaper than in the West. Mosquitoes come out particularly at dusk and during the night so legs and arms should be covered in the evenings.

● **Treatment** If you should be unlucky enough to develop malaria you need medical treatment; so if you develop a high fever you should seek medical attention urgently. But if you are miles from anywhere treating yourself may be your only option. If you have Larium take 750mg (this usually means three tablets) initially, followed by 500mg 8-12 hours later and another 500mg 8-12 hours after that. Quinine is the drug more commonly used for self-treatment: take 600mg three times daily for three days, followed by three tablets of Fansidan a day until symptoms recede. Quinine is available from pharmacies in Vietnam and trekkers going far from towns should certainly take it with them.

Sunburn/heatstroke

The sun is so strong in Vietnam that you can get sunburnt even on cloudy days. Also remember that the sun's rays are reflected off water so you can get sunburnt under a hat if you are by water. This means you should be permanently armed with suncream. Standard makes of suncream are readily available in Vietnam, but certain specialized products are only available in the West. For example, Clinique offers a sun-protection cream (factor 15) specifically for the face (Face Zone) which is extremely effective as well as acting as a good moisturizer (and is pleasantly tinted too).

Sunglasses are another must to protect you against the sun. They are on sale everywhere in Vietnam but you have to go to a very smart shop to be sure of getting UVA and UVB protection.

In any tropical climate, such as Vietnam's, Westerners are at risk of developing heat exhaustion or heat stroke. Symptoms include severe headache, giddiness, extremely flushed (red) skin, and the victim may sweat profusely then very little. Headaches act as an early warning symptom and should be reacted to by getting the person out of the sun, giving them lots of cold water to drink and cooling the skin with a wet towel or sheet. The problem may then be avoided by keeping water intake high to prevent dehydration and taking salt tablets to replace the salt lost by sweating.

(**Opposite**) Soon after dawn, in parks across the country, local residents congregate for their early morning exercises.

Diarrhoea

The most common illness afflicting travellers is diarrhoea. To avoid contracting this potentially-debilitating irritant the most important thing is to avoid tap water. The bottled mineral water which can be bought in Vietnam is safe, and in general the water used to make tea, fill thermos flasks in hotel rooms, or cook food is well boiled. Tap water in HCMC and Hanoi is chlorinated but it is still best to avoid drinking it unboiled.

Avoiding tap water also means avoiding ice, huge chunks of which are commonly put into cold drinks as a little luxury. The best alternative if you want a drink cooled down quickly is to get hold of a bucket or large bowl and fill that with a mixture of ice and cold water and put the bottle or can into the bowl. Turning the bottle round and round speeds up the cooling process significantly. Avoiding tap water also means avoiding raw vegetables; unfortunately this rules out all salads which you may not wish to do, preferring instead to take a calculated risk based on the view that the smarter the restaurant the less the risk of poor hygiene.

Seafood in general is safe to eat if cooked, but if you are eating prawns do ensure the darkly-coloured nerve running the length of the spine has been removed otherwise you are likely to become ill. You will probably have to perform this operation yourself if you are buying from a beach vendor. Even if you stick to all these precautions diarrhoea sadly is common enough, but it may well just be your body's natural reaction to a change in diet so is not worth worrying over.

● **Treatment** If you develop diarrhoea the best treatment is rest and intake of fluids (or rehydration solutions). There are medicines you can buy, such as the brand-named Immodium, which claim to stop diarrhoea within hours, but all they actually do is clog up your system. While this can be a relief it can also prevent your body from really recovering, and certainly postpones you discovering that the illness is in fact more serious than simple diarrhoea.

Dysentery

There are two kinds of dysentery – neither is pleasant and both can be serious if untreated, but they can be cured completely with a prompt course of medicine. Bacillary dysentery is distinguishable from amoebic dysentery by adding fever and vomiting to serious lower abdominal cramps and bloody diarrhoea. But amoebic dysentery is the more serious as it will certainly not go away if left to itself and can recur even if treated. You need a stool test to confirm which type you have: bacillary dysentery is treated with a seven- or ten-day course of antibiotics; amoebic dysentery requires a seven- to ten-day course of the anti-amoebic drug

---

(**Opposite**) **Top**: Snake alcohol: said to enhance virility. **Bottom**: Dragon fruit is one of the many delicious and unusual varieties of fruit available in Vietnam.

Flagyl, which is available from most pharmacies in the country. (Note that drinking alcohol while taking Flagyl or within a few days of taking it makes the patient feel worse than ever.)

Giardia

Giardia is another type of parasite causing severe but intermittent diarrhoea, nausea, bloatedness (including belching), weakness but no fever. Seek medical supervision if possible, but be aware that the anti-amoebic Flagyl is the only cure. Take the drug for a week to ten days and keep monitoring the situation after that. Again, avoid alcohol while taking Flagyl or within a few days of taking it. You can buy Flagyl from pharmacies in Vietnam.

Meningitis

Meningitis is a fast-acting disease which attacks the brain and is potentially fatal. It is not common in Vietnam but cases do occur in the remote northern mountains. The disease is spread through the coughs and sneezes of carriers or through saliva present on, for example, food left over by carriers of the disease. The first symptoms are the sudden onset of a scattered rash, fever, severe headache, sensitivity to light and a stiffness of the neck preventing bending of the head. The disease must be treated within a few hours by large injections of penicillin.

PART 2: VIETNAM

Facts about the country

GEOGRAPHICAL BACKGROUND

Vietnam forms the rugged eastern part of the Indochinese peninsula. It borders China in the north, Laos and Cambodia to the west and it looks out onto the South China Sea to the east and the Pacific Ocean to the south. The land is a variety of tropical forests, rugged mountains, mangrove swamps, fertile plains and wide-sweeping beaches.

Vietnam stretches 1650km from north to south, from 23°20' to 8°33', but is only 600km at its very widest and less than 50km at its narrowest. It's a long thin country shaped like an 'S' which the Vietnamese liken to an upended bamboo pole supporting a basket of rice at each end. An apposite image this, as three quarters of the country's 330,000 sq km is mountainous down the country's narrow spine but the other quarter consists of rich alluvial plains, real rice baskets, where most of the people live. The country's two biggest cities are built on these fertile plains – Hanoi on the Red River delta in the north, and Ho Chi Minh City (often still called Saigon) on the Mekong Delta in the south.

Much of the north of Vietnam is founded on limestone. Erosion over time has resulted in hundreds of fissures, caves, underground rivers and rocky crags often to fine effect, such as the Marble Mountains around Danang. In the South China Sea off the north-east coast of Vietnam is a huge sunken plateau of limestone crags which now appears as over 2000 tall jagged cliffs rising out of the sea, this remarkable scenery in Halong Bay is often used by the Vietnamese to symbolize Vietnam. Similar but less impressive effects are produced off the south coast of Vietnam around Ha Tien. The central highlands are known for their fertile red volcanic soil covering the high flat (and unfortunately not very scenic) plateau linking the centres of Dalat, Buon Ma Thuot and Kontom.

CLIMATE

The climate of Vietnam varies significantly from north to south and from season to season, but the country is essentially a tropical one with a humid monsoonal climate. Vietnam lies in the South-east Asian intertropical monsoon zone and is subject to two monsoons; the north-east monsoon brings a vigorous mass of polar air blowing south during the winter months, causing a real winter in the north above the 18th parallel – a much colder winter than that of any other region at the same latitude. But additionally there is a strong expansion of an equatorial mass of air to the north which brings humidity. But for this humidity, large parts of the country would remain arid, as in other regions of this latitude in east Asia. The summer is dominated by the south-western monsoon which brings warm and humid weather to the whole country. The upshot is that there is no good or bad time to visit the country (see p14).

The climate in the mountainous regions is colder and wetter with intense direct solar radiation. By far the most elevated centre in the central highlands is Dalat at 1471m, while Sapa, in the north, is 1650m above sea level. Vietnam's highest mountain, Fansipan, is near Sapa and is 3143m high. Above 2000m the climate is temperate. In the mountains, for every 100m increase in altitude, the temperature decreases by an average of 0.5°C. From 600m upwards tropical characteristics disappear and a sub-tropical mountainous zone emerges.

FLORA AND FAUNA

Vietnam is a tropical climate with a diverse geology supporting many varieties of wildlife living in the dense rainforests or vast mangrove swamps which used to be widespread in the country. With the stresses of population growth and the ravages of the American war, the extent and diversity of Vietnam's flora and fauna has fallen dramatically.

The country still has some areas of wilderness; it is one of the last countries in the world which has some three-tier rainforest and in 1992 a new species of mammal, called the Vu Quang Ox, was found here – the first such find anywhere in the world for 50 years. It's the forests near the Vietnam/Laotian border where these riches and others like the shy honey bear, leaf monkey, clouded leopard and tigers are found, but without making a special excursion you are unlikely to see much wildlife beyond the humble water buffalo or Vietnamese pot-bellied pig, though elephants can be seen in the central highlands – Buon Ma Thuot being the best place to arrange a ride on one. If you wish to explore the forests you will need to talk to a wildlife agency.

Exotic and rare birds are more accessible and a visit to Nam Cat Tien National Park (280km north-east of Ho Chi Minh City) could well result in you spotting great slaty, heart-spotted woodpeckers, or red-breasted parakeets. Cuc Phuong National Park near Ninh Binh in the north is also home to many different exotic birds (see p243).

There are two main reasons for wildlife not being more plentiful. One of the explicit aims of the American war was to defoliate the country; this resulted in 72 million litres of herbicides known as Agents Orange, Blue and White, being sprayed on the country revealing trails and communist encampments by stripping the land bare. Secondly, pretty well everything which lives in the wild and can be eaten has been. Even when the government releases birds into Hanoi's parks to repopulate them, the show is accompanied by pleas for restraint, asking Hanoi's population not to 'disturb' the birds ie not to trap and eat them.

Vietnam's diverse climate also supports a variety of vegetation. Many kinds of fruit and vegetable are grown in the deltas, while tea, coffee and rubber, all major exports, are grown in the highlands. These areas are also well populated by the pretty and sensitive mimosa plant. The dense forested areas are also thought to be home to over 12,000 plant species, of which as yet only 8000 have been identified. Coconut trees, bamboo and, of course, the ubiquitous rice are found throughout the country.

HISTORY

Legendary beginnings

According to an Adam-and-Eve-like legend the beginnings of the Vietnamese people can be traced to two original ancestors and accurately located in time. For non-believers the origin of the Vietnamese as a race is a more prosaic and uncertain story involving the movement of people from China and Thailand, but every Vietnamese knows the legend of how a man wandered south from China and found a beautiful land ruled by a dragon lord. He married the dragon's daughter and they had a son called Lac Long Quan – Lord dragon of the lake. Lac ruled the land and married an immortal princess of the mountains, Au Co. Together they ruled in peace and love and when Au Co became pregnant they awaited the arrival of a son or daughter; but Au Co gave birth to 100 eggs which hatched out into 100 fine sons.

The lord and lady decided to part company taking half each of their splendid brood with them because Au Co pined for the mountains and Lac for the sea. Au Co and 50 of her sons settled in the mountains near present-day Hanoi, while Lac and his 50 sons settled in the Waters Palace on the South China Sea.

So the legend has it that the Vietnamese are descended from a dragon, a symbol of good luck and fortune, and from an immortal princess. The legend also says that all Vietnamese are related to each other and shows their concern with uniting the hill people and the lowlanders. Anthropologists have seen in this and other legends evidence that early Vietnamese society had matriarchal elements.

The first kingdom and the first Chinese rule in the north

A more realistic tale of the origin of the Vietnamese people is that of a gradual movement of people from China and Tibet (the Thais coming later) settling in northern Vietnam during the paleolithic age, 500,000 to

300,000 years ago. Over hundreds of millennia these hunter-gatherers evolved into people of 'polished stone', then around 300BC saw the invention of bronze, and the bronze age then led to the iron age. The whole period is called the Dong Son culture, after a village in the centre of Vietnam where evidence of the bronze industry was first discovered. During this time the people developed systematic methods of agricultural cultivation – dykes to control the flow of water from the Red River to prevent alternating droughts and floods depending on the season.

Around the first millennium BC archaeological and legendary versions of history come together. The system of building and maintaining dykes required a body with overall control; this came in the form of the first kingdom of north Vietnam – the Hung Kingdom, from which came the Au Lac Kingdom which was the first to unite the lowland people and the hill people. But, around 200BC, after only 50 years of unified Au Lac rule and after the formation of the Nam Viet Kingdom, the country for the first time suffered defeat at the hands of invaders as the Han Dynasty in China came south and conquered. They held onto power for 1000 years.

The Funan Empire in the south

But Chinese rule didn't extend to the south of the country. Here, kingdoms of a very different orientation ruled the land. The Funan Empire extended out from its still spectacular centre at Angkor Wat in east Cambodia encompassing much of south Vietnam. To its north was the Champa Empire. This originated in Quang Nam, just south of Hué, and soon extended 300km south to Cam Ranh Bay and into the Mekong valley of current Cambodia and Laos.

Our knowledge of these empires is not great but we do know that both came about because of Indian cultural penetration of the peninsula which brought Indian customs, religious practices, art, Sanskrit as the sacred language, and civilization. The earliest Chinese account of Funan is in the 3rd century AD recording that the Chinese were amazed to find great walled cities, palaces and archives. However, the mass of the land was peopled by peasants engaged in primitive agriculture.

The Funan Empire lasted until around 600BC when it was engulfed by the Chams. The Chams themselves ruled the region until they too were pushed aside by the Viets from the north. But that didn't happen until after the end of the first period of Chinese rule.

Confucius and the plough

The Chinese brought intellectuals, Confucianism and the plough and these were the tools which they used to attempt wholesale sinicization. Waves of Chinese scholars and state officials travelled south, all were political refugees who were previously high up in the Han dynasties. With them was brought the liberating instrument of the plough (hauled by animals also brought in from China) as well as huge technological advances such as writing and silk weaving, and the often repressive social force of Confucianism. The teachings of Confucius (551BC–478BC, Khong Tu in Vietnamese) almost wholly concerned social rather than spiritual matters. His work set in place a highly-structured hierarchical feudalist system governed by mandarins which allowed for almost no social mobility. He squared the circle of justice, however, by stipulating that rulers were to lead and retain authority by example of good behaviour not by force, and scholars obtained their position only by passing rigorous examinations. Sinicization was successful in certain ways but was a total failure in its main aim – both in the short term and ultimately in the long term (though Confucianism lives on today, counter-intuitively, in Vietnam's communist structures).

Sinicization was highly successful in that the people of the Red River delta immediately latched onto the new agricultural tools and better irrigation methods – indeed the natural condition of the very fertile alluvial soil meant that there was much to gain from the Chinese methods. But sinicization was a failure in that Vietnamese culture was not so much assimilated, rather it adapted and developed while the people retained their own sense of identity from the Chinese rulers. So when Chinese rule was harsh they retained the desire to repel it, and still saw their rule as foreign imposition. Rebelliousness came especially from the upper classes who were driven out of their positions of power by the influx of Chinese state appointees.

Hai Ba Trung

The first outright rebellion was the celebrated uprising of the two Trung sisters (Hai Ba Trung) in AD39. After the murder by the Chinese of Lady Trung Trac's nobleman husband, she and her sister rallied the local lords and peasants and led an attack on the Chinese forces at the governor's residence and defeated them. The Chinese fled and the Trung sisters were proclaimed queens of the territory between Hué and the land north of Hanoi.

But their kingdom lasted only two years, until the Han Emperor dispatched a larger, better army and thoroughly defeated the new rulers. The sisters are thought to have thrown themselves into a river, committing suicide rather than submitting to Chinese rule. One of their comrades, Phuong Thi Ching, led the army in the centre of the territory, despite being pregnant. Surrounded on all fronts, she delivered her baby, strapped the newly born infant on her back and, brandishing a sword in both hands, opened a bloody route through the enemy and escaped. Later, hearing that the vanquished queens had committed suicide, she did the same.

The sisters are venerated as the first national heroes of Vietnamese independence, and Vietnam has two pagodas celebrating them – the Hai Ba pagoda in Hanoi has a statue of the sisters which the Vietnamese say depicts them about to throw themselves into the river. The victory, however, was short lived, while the defeat lasted a further 750 years – because the insurrection was almost entirely the work of the feudal class, not the mass of the population, and in defeat the Chinese eliminated almost all that class, by death or by exile to China. All the local lords were replaced by Chinese ones and, crucially, these administrators were not to be independent feudal rulers over the territory, but rather to be servants of a centralized state. Under this system, genuine conquering rule began and the Chinese called the territory of Vietnam under their rule Annam – the 'pacified south'.

One thousand years of Chinese rule

But in the long term sinicization still failed. Chinese culture brought much in the way of technological advancements and the beginnings of the establishment of a state made for effective rule but the seeds were still sown for revolt in both the elite and the peasants. Revolt that wasn't successful for another thousand years but was still harboured in the different levels of society for all this time.

The Chinese administrators, the elite in Vietnam, were permanently stationed there so they began accumulating Vietnamese cultural traditions and notions just as much as they infused Vietnam with Chinese cultural practices. The result was a group of people who worked with what was left of the old aristocracy and became believers in independence for the country from Chinese rule. So, for example, 500 years after the Trung sisters' revolt a rebellion was led by Ly Bon who tried to expel the Chinese from the country, even though he himself was Chinese.

Meanwhile the peasants had continued the customs and traditions they had held before the Chinese invaded and this notion that their rulers and oppressors were also invaders led to a strategy, carried out over centuries, of passive resistance to Chinese rule. This meant that cultural sinicization happened very little at the peasant level, not least because the peasantry and the agricultural structure was the only reliable and permanent source of wealth. Once the elite tapped into the peasants' desire to shake off the Chinese yoke revolution was born.

Military victory brings independence at last

After a thousand years of Chinese rule, Vietnam was reborn. In AD939 one of the bloody encounters between Chinese and local soldiers in the Bach Dang river of the Red River delta resulted in defeat for the Chinese thanks to a brilliant military scheme by the Vietnamese leader, Ngo Quyen.

The Vietnamese lured the Chinese ships out into the estuary and engaged them in battle until the tide began to come in. They then retreated upriver and watched as most of the Chinese armada were left impaled on upturned bamboo stakes which the Vietnamese had planted in the river-bed in the previous low tide. The Vietnamese then returned in smaller boats and burned the broken and stranded ships and the battle was won.

The victors couldn't have known that it would lead to a long period of independence for the country. That it did so, was to the credit of countless descendants of these warriors in defeating Chinese and Mongolian invaders time and again, such as the attempt by Emperor Ly Thai To in the charming legend around the naming of Hoan Kiem lake (see p247).

The first emperor in this period set the tone; Dinh Bo Linh called his state Dai Co Viet – the kingdom of the Watchful Hawk. China agreed to recognize Vietnam's independence, although in return for a substantial annual tribute. Then began 900 years of independence (interrupted briefly in the middle of this time by a short period of Chinese rule) until the French succeeded, in 1883, in concluding their 25-year struggle to win Vietnam. In the meantime much outside of politics had happened in the country.

The march to the south – straight through the Chams

For a start the Vietnamese began to venture south to try to find more land which was fertile. There were no other directions they could try, being bordered to the north by China, to the east by the sea, and to the west by mountains. So they gradually moved south, coming upon fertile land most of the way, but also coming across the Champa civilization. This civilization was very different with its Indian roots and heritage (as can be seen from the Cham remains). It is Vietnam's geographical and cultural location between India and China that has defined its geopolitical position as well as shaping much of its culture; from this the name Indochina is derived.

But if some of the Indian spirit of the Champas lives on, in for example the cooking of the south, their civilization did not. It was wiped out by the Vietnamese people pushing ever further south for land. Fixed battles were rare, but the climax of the Vietnamese victory over the Chams was in 1471 when they destroyed the Cham city of Indrapura, killing its 40,000 inhabitants. The historian Joseph Buttinger has said that the nature of this 'march to the south' which was done so gradually by small groups of peasants, gave Vietnam a unity 'like the unity of a chain'.

Dynasties rise and fall

The history of Vietnam's 900 years of independence is a history of great dynasties, rivalries, repulsions of foreign invaders and progress. It's best seen divided into four periods. The first period from AD938 to AD1010 was a time of successive crises as institutions tried to evolve without the back-up support of Chinese garrisons. In these 72 years Vietnam used up three dynasties. But change gradually came about – Emperor Le Hoan was the first to make the highly symbolic act of launching a Vietnamese currency to replace Chinese money.

The second period was a stable one of 400 years lasting until 1400. There were only two dynasties during this time – the Ly and the Tran, each lasting roughly 200 years. In the Ly Dynasty each individual emperor ruled for a long time, one reigning for 55 years, astonishing longevity for that time. But the later Ly rulers were feeble; the last was a psychopath who abdicated in favour of his seven-year-old daughter. So the wheel spun round, the dynasty fell and another took its place, in 1225.

Kublai Khan's Vietnamese adventure

It was fortunate for Vietnam that the Tran Dynasty consolidated political power so effectively because 60 years later the country had to face a much more violent threat than mere internal crises – the Mongol invasion.

At this time the Mongols under Kublai Khan were ruling ever-increasing parts of the world from the backs of their little Mongolian ponies – the invention of stirrups (enabling them to throw spears from horseback), and a willingness to use utter terror were their crucial innovations. But Kublai Khan attempted to take Vietnam three times in the 13th century and three times was repulsed. In the final battle in 1287 Kublai Khan led an army of half a million men down through China to the Vietnamese land, but the mountainous terrain wasn't ideal Mongol territory and the Vietnamese army succeeded in repulsing them back into south-west China. They returned by sea and the armadas faced each other in the Bach Dang river in the Red River delta, ready for a bitter struggle.

Bamboo stakes defeat the Mongols

But in the end the fight was monumentally one-sided, turning into a rout of the Mongol fleet as General Tran Hung Dao remembered Ngo Quyen's trick of 350 years earlier of planting sharpened bamboo stakes in the estuary and luring the fleet onto them when low tide came. The invaders' ships were fatally impaled on the stakes and as the ships were captured or sank Vietnam's victory was total. The history museum in Hanoi claims that the bamboo stakes it holds are the self-same stakes that put paid to Kublai

---

❏ The conical hat

Historical documents first show the palm leaf conical hat, *non la*, appearing in Vietnam in the 13th century, during the Tran dynasty. In those 800 years the Vietnamese conical hat was traditionally made from palm leaves for the cone, bamboo for the frame, and tree fibre for the stitching. Many hats are still today made from these materials, although some have definite elements of plastic.

The non la can be worn by any age, sex or class, and photographs of ceremonies during Emperor Khai Dinh's reign, 1912–1916, show the Emperor himself wearing a decorated non la. But as the conical hat has increasingly come to symbolize a romantic notion of Vietnam – to Vietnamese as well as to foreigners – so the rich and successful have abandoned it, leaving its usage to young girls who wear it coquettishly, and to the poor of the cities and countryside who wear it to keep off the sun.

The best conical hats come from Hué. Huéan non la are embroidered with poems or pictures on the inside to really lay on the nostalgia.

Khan's Vietnamese adventure. In a victory poem the Vietnamese General proclaimed that 'this ancient land will live forever'.

But Chinese invaders are harder to repulse

The Tran Dynasty ruled for a further 150 years, but increasing state involvement in the push south to quash Champa and an increasingly decadent lifestyle among the rulers was bleeding the country dry and as the 14th century turned into the 15th the Tran Dynasty was overthrown by an ambitious court official Ho Qui Ly. He stamped his authority on his new office and looked set to emulate his long-lasting predecessors, but seven years later in 1407 the expansionist Ming Dynasty in China turned the country's army south again and attacked Vietnamese territory.

The Chinese succeeded where the Mongols had failed because the ruling elite in Vietnam had been weakened by extravagance and disunity, and because of a clever psychological campaign waged by the Chinese. They claimed their only aim was to restore the Tran Dynasty and got through to the masses by putting up posters across the country proclaiming their cause and even inscribed the message on pieces of wood which they floated down rivers. The first multi-media campaign was successful – many Vietnamese simply laid down their arms.

Le Loi's gleaming sword defeats the Chinese

But the restored Chinese rule was brief – mercifully so because it was undoubtedly harsh. Intellectuals were deported to China, ancient archives were destroyed, outrageous taxes were demanded from the poor peasantry, identity cards were even issued to all families and the beloved betel nut was outlawed. China was attempting the sinicization it had so signally failed to make lasting before – this time through pure violence. The country was ripe for rebellion and needed only a leader.

Leadership came from the province of Thanh Hoa south of the Red River in the form of the man called Le Loi who would become known as Emperor Ly Thai To and revered as a patriotic hero second only to Ho Chi Minh. He led and organized ten years of national resistance against the Chinese which finally led to defeat for the foreign army, again thanks to clever military tactics.

In the narrow pass of the Chi Lang Gate, or Ai Chi Lang, (which the modern-day road between Hanoi and Lang Son/Dong Dang runs through) he lured the Chinese army into a massive, and devastatingly effective, ambush. The legend surrounding Hanoi's Hoan Kiem lake also has it that he defeated the Chinese with a gleaming sword retrieved from the depths of the lake. The Chinese invasion was over.

Nation building

Ly Thai To's rule marked the beginning of the greatest dynasties in Vietnam's history, the Later Le Dynasty – great in terms of political stability and progress. This third period of independence lasted three and a half centuries, from 1427 to 1787. The emperors of this time built on the state-building projects of previous rulers – the creation of a national postal system in 1044, the establishing of a training college for civil servants in 1075, the creation of a fixed hierarchy of state officials in 1089 and the establishing of an officers' training school in 1225. The great Le monarchs set in train reforms with more widespread societal impact; as Le Loi's adviser Nguyen Trai had described the Vietnamese strategy – 'Better to conquer hearts than citadels'.

It was Le Loi's successor, the revered Le Thranh Ton, who lifted Vietnam into a golden age with the formulation of a new criminal and civil code designed to produce central power and local flexibility which lasted right until the 19th century. Under this code, women were given equal rights to men in many important areas such as inheritance, and marriage was legal without parental consent. Social mobility was even possible; attainment of the rank of officer in the new conscripted army could be achieved by passing exams, as could advancement to the position of mandarin. Le Thranh Ton also founded many hospitals where treatment was free and organized a service to fight epidemics. Other aspects of his Confucianist doctrine are less palatable though; adulterous women were trampled to death by elephants and, in accordance with Confucianism, crimes threatening order and by implication the emperor's divine authority were highly punished. Nevertheless, under his rule Vietnam became the most modern and advanced of all the Indochinese states.

But despite all this Vietnam very rarely had a time of inner peace when it wasn't necessary for the monarchs to fight against local men with ambitions to power. This is essentially because of a contradiction in Vietnamese society – its survival against foreign invaders required a progressive and centralized state, but its agricultural economy meant that the ruling class would always have feudal economy interests and feudal political aspirations. Replacing defeated nobles with members of a monarch's own family didn't always prove to be an effective solution, as the Later Le Dynasty found out in the civil war between the family factions that ensued.

Division – North and South

In the early part of the 16th century the fading Le Dynasty increasingly succumbed to two such powerful feudal lords, the Trinh clan ruled the north from Hanoi and the Nguyen clan ruled the south from Hué. Both claimed nominal allegiance to the Le Dynasty but by the late 16th century all genuine power was wielded by the rival feudal lords and in 1620 the country was formally divided into two.

The Nguyen family in the south was the weaker of the two, but they managed to prevent defeat by building miles of huge walls along the narrow coastal plain north of Hué. The southern rule also resisted the northern threat by expanding westwards and reaping the riches of new lands for peasant and lord alike in the Cambodian-controlled area of the Mekong Delta. Between 1650 and 1770 south Vietnam fought 12 wars with Cambodia. The regime also retained dynamism thanks to the influx of economic and political refugees from the northern regime.

A nation of provinces

But expansion promotes disunity: the larger the country became the larger became the expanses far from the centralized control in Hanoi or Hué. This was especially because the various local economies were such that they could prosper no matter what happened 20km away. So provincial separatism grew at the same time as pressure grew for reunification.

The desire of local mandarins and lords was always to accentuate local economic autonomy, thus holding back possible greater centralization and the development of a more powerful class. This is why the Vietnamese economy didn't rise from the village level despite its growth. So there was no economic necessity for a national transport system and so on. This means that nothing developed to block the continuation of the semifeudal societal structure. Vietnam could even be split in two and life hardly changed for its people – apart from anything else, the country still had one nominal head.

Rebellion and the first Nguyen emperor

However, trouble was brewing thanks to the reward the peasants received for this unthinking loyalty – a hard, miserable life. Despite legal codes, the laws protecting the peasants against their lords were highly ineffective because the central state would always give the lords the power to press-gang the peasantry for military purposes, and this led to the creation of many landless peasants once the fighting was over. So the rebellions became more and more driven by the peasantry rather than aggrieved aristocrats and eventually one such rebellion was successful, that of the Tay Son brothers.

In 1771 the three brothers from Tay Son village led an insurrection against both the Trinh and Nguyen regimes and defeated them both. They ruled the country for 30 years, including kicking out yet another Chinese invasion in 1789, and looked set to establish a new dynasty. But instead they gave way to a lone survivor of the Nguyen family who styled himself Emperor Gia Long and set up court in Hué in 1802 from where he ruled the whole country. But although the Tay Son rule was brief, the reunification it brought survived the overthrow of the last of its rulers.

France stumbles in

But this unity came at a price and the price was foreign influence. For Nguyen Anh who became Emperor Gia Long only attained this position with French military and financial support, so ultimately the unity was but a short-lived and pyrrhic gain.

Vietnam had had contact with other countries for many centuries as a trading centre – indeed the little town of Hoi An was the most important trading post for Portuguese, Japanese, Chinese, Dutch and English merchants between India and China at the peak of its activity during the 16th century. Some merchants from China and Japan stayed on during the non-trading months and eventually settled but not the traders from the West. The first Westerners to settle in Vietnam were missionaries, officially classified by the Vietnamese authorities as 'red-haired barbarians', such as Jesuit Borri depicted by Norman Lewis (author of *A Dragon Apparent*) and Alexandre de Rhodes who codified the romanization of the Vietnamese language.

Missionaries increased in number from the 16th to the 19th centuries and increasingly were French Catholics all of whom were given favoured access to Vietnam's territory and governance in the court of the French-supported Gia Long. But his successor, Emperor Minh Mang, was not eager to retain French influence and began an anti-French policy, directed particularly against the missionaries.

At the same time, from the mid-19th century onwards, France began to revive its military expansionist aims. Nonetheless, France didn't so much plan to acquire Indochina as a colony as stumble into it through a series of military actions, often by French adventurers more interested in looting than ruling but responding to the anti-Catholicism of the emperors who were sanctioning the execution of missionaries.

France takes Danang and Saigon

The first move was an attack on Danang (then called Tourane) by two French naval vessels in 1847. But it wasn't until 11 years later in 1858 that a full-scale attack on Tourane was launched by a large naval fleet and even then it's not clear that there was a plan to take the whole country. Rather this arose as a goal once the French had expended a considerable financial and military cost in taking the key centres of Danang and Saigon – which fell in 1858 after two months of hard fighting.

Tu Duc hands over the Mekong

The organized armed struggle against the French didn't last long and was signally hindered by the ruling emperors' extreme Confucianism which had not only led to an attitude of indifference towards the West resulting in ignorance of France's military abilities, but also imbued the ruling elite with a conservatism unsuited to quick battle responses.

In 1862 Emperor Tu Duc astonished the French military forces by signing a treaty handing over to France the three eastern provinces of the Mekong Delta and granting limited trading rights for the rest of the country. But, in reality, Tu Duc had little choice because France's seizure of Saigon and the surrounding area was starving his armies and, given his previous anti-Western policies, he couldn't count on any outside power to assist his country in fighting the French. This didn't stop him sending Abraham Lincoln a last-minute appeal for help on the eve of surrender, but in vain.

Tu Duc's appeal to his people also yielded little result: the French were hated, but so were the corrupt and despotic mandarins of his rule. The problem, which recurred during the American war, was that under Tu Duc's rule the archaic feudal structure had so decayed that the traditional ruling classes couldn't call on any support to defend their existence.

France takes the country

From this moment on resistance against the French was bottom-up or rather middle-up – guerrilla forces organized by the scholar/gentry class. But the back of the resistance movement was broken by a major French offensive in 1867 when France took the whole of the delta region and occupied it as a French colony which it named Cochinchina. The 1870s were a time when the rest of the country was nominally ruled by Tu Duc from Hué while France led serious skirmishes in the north. In 1883 Emperor Tu Duc died and in the midst of a succession crisis the French arrived in force in Hué, in August, and the new emperor saw no option but to hand over the reins of power.

At one fell swoop France both deprived Vietnam of its independence and its unity; the country was split not into two as it had historically been, but into three – Tonkin in the north, Annam in the centre and Cochinchina in the south. By 1896 the whole subcontinent had fallen and the French colony of Indochina was born.

The riches of the poppy

Once France had a foothold in the region it was not slow to see the potential economic advantage it could reap from gaining the whole country. The issue was primarily not to gain a sphere of influence, but to derive economic gain: some historians have argued that the appeal of the region to France can be summed up by one word – opium.

Opium brought riches, as the British had found in China, and France was anxious to ensure the British didn't have sole claim to the substantial supplies in north Vietnam and southern China. Undoubtedly, France also wanted its own 'place in the sun'; concurrent with its annexing of Indochina was the European 'rush for Africa' in which the empire-building countries of Europe competed for colonial control of the continent.

The failures of the French

But the beginning of French rule in the region was not marked by success. Ten years after annexing Indochina, only Cochinchina in Vietnam had any effective civil government; Tonkin and Annam were still in a state of considerable unrest. France had also failed to make much of an impact on trade in or with the region. In short, Indochina was a national disgrace for the French.

The main problem seemed to be that French society was not organized in such a way as to encourage immigration to colonies (as, for
example the English system of primogeniture did) so those who did make
the expedition generally did so as a last resort. As Bismarck said:
'England has colonies and colonialists, Germany has no colonies but has
colonialists, France has colonies but no colonialists'. This all changed
with the appointment of Paul Doumer as first Governor-General of
Indochina in 1896 – by the start of World War I Indochina was France's
richest colony.

Enter Doumer and the railways

Doumer's principal means of reaping riches from the colony was by
building railways. By building a network of railways, troops could be
transported to the northern mountainous regions to restore order to
regions awash with bandits, peasants could be transported from one
region to another to work on the plantations, and freight could be transported to the ports and shipped out. Doumer created official monopolies
to produce and market alcohol, salt and opium. Before this only the
Chinese residents in Vietnam had smoked opium and in very small quantities. But Doumer had a refinery built in Saigon, whereupon Vietnamese
addiction rose greatly – opium eventually counted for one-third of
France's entire revenue from Vietnam.

Meanwhile France effectively dispossessed the Vietnamese peasantry,
who had always previously owned their land, by the new policy of export-
ing surplus rice rather than keeping it back for lean years as previous governments had allowed the peasants to do.

By the start of World War II Vietnam was the world's third-largest rice
exporter (as, ironically, it is today). This had meant the expanding of
acreage to stimulate production and this encouraged French speculators
and rich Vietnamese families to grab land at the expense of the peasants.
So, by the 1930s, around 70 per cent of Vietnam's peasants were tenants,
or farmed uneconomically small plots. But of course landless peasants
suited Doumer because they were available to work in the mines or on the
vast and harsh rubber plantations, or to build roads or railways. Thus, for
example, the Hongay coal mines saw production quadruple to two million
tonnes between 1913 and 1927.

Doumer also embarked on an obsessive building programme at the landless peasants' expense: from opera houses, roads and railways to the remarkable bridge across the Red River at Hanoi that bore his name until the
Communists took power – but at least these projects have a favourable legacy.

Heavy-handed rule

To run the more modernized country France overhauled the administrative system, and gradually the dominant Confucianist doctrine gave way

to a less authoritarian system of government. But France chose to rule by direct rule rather than by 'association' as the British did in India. This meant that by 1925 it took as many French officials (5000) as English to rule over one-tenth as many Vietnamese as Indians. In the early part of the century the French appointed as prime minister a naturalized Frenchman who could barely speak Vietnamese. In 1903 the highest ranking Vietnamese official earned less than the lowliest French official. Plus, when the French first took over, most mandarins abandoned their positions, while some joined the resistance. The result was that there were no rooted bases for support. A French admiral, Rieunier, is reported to have said 'On our side we have only Christians and crooks'.

China and Japan battle for control of Indochina

France continued to hold onto Vietnam and Indochina during WWI, but WWII was a different matter altogether. And change came quickly.

Following the fall of France to Hitler's Panzer blitzkrieg in 1940 and the establishment of the Vichy puppet regime, the French administration in Indochina also changed over to German-friendly rule. Meanwhile, there was another major aggressor power in the region – Japan. In the few years in the lead-up to WWII Indochina managed to stay clear of the intensifying Sino-Japanese conflict despite increasing clashes over the trains in northern Vietnam transferring supplies from China. But after the free French regime fell in France and so in Vietnam, the country was left helpless against Japan and capitulated to effective Japanese rule after heavy bombardment by the Japanese, particularly on the railway lines.

Vietnam was now Japanese ruled and was exploited for the economic benefit of Japan, but there was resistance. This resistance was most effectively led by groups with communist leanings, but despite this these resistance movements had significant American military support in terms of weapons provision and military training. Resistance was prolonged, but ultimately it was only America's H-bombs dropped on Hiroshima and Nagasaki which brought about Japanese surrender. Japan finally surrendered on 14 August 1945 – Ho and his Communist Vietminhs wasted no time. The very next day he called for a national uprising.

The August revolution

This Vietminh revolt, known as the August revolution, generated widespread popular insurrection, especially in the north, and, most importantly of all, brought about the abdication of Emperor Bao Dai. Bao Dai's resignation in favour of the Vietminh was a key factor in their success because it raised their profile and gave them credibility. Ho said the gesture gave the Vietminh the 'mandate of heaven' – ie it gave Ho the legitimacy that in Vietnamese eyes had resided in the emperor.

Bao Dai handed over 'sovereign power' to the Vietminh; he gave up the royal seal and sword as well as his regal title and became plain

❑ Ho Chi Minh

The hero of Vietnam's liberation from the French and then the Americans led a dramatic life which started in humble origins. He was born Nguyen Sinh Cung in 1890 in a village in a central province in Vietnam, the son of a low-ranking mandarin who had been ejected from the court of Hué for his anti-colonial attitudes. He attended the high school in Hué until he himself was expelled for involvement in a student protest. But he cut his political teeth during his years of wandering the world which began in 1911 when he climbed aboard a freighter bound for Europe, signing on as a stoker and galley boy. Thirty years passed before he returned to Vietnam. During all this time he kept no diaries, nor did he ever write his memoirs so details about his movements or motives are sketchy. A later communist comrade explained that his hope had been to learn from the West how to fight the West.

He spent three years at sea travelling around India and Europe. In 1913 he crossed the Atlantic – visiting Boston and stopping in Brooklyn where he worked as a dockyard labourer and was dazzled by Manhattan's skyscrapers. After a year in America he sailed to London where he worked in the kitchen of the chic hotel, the London Carlton, as a pastry chef. In London, now known as Nguyen Tat Thanh, he began to flirt with politics – in the city where Karl Marx wrote *Das Kapital* he met Irish nationalists, Fabian socialists as well as Chinese revolutionaries and Indian anti-colonialists.

After the end of WWI he travelled to Paris where he stayed for six years. Here he took the name Nguyen Ai Quoc – Nguyen the Patriot – and combined conspiratorial activities with highly eclectic cultural pursuits. He later said that he was convinced both of France's 'mission civilisatrice', and of the need for revolution in Vietnam. He made an appeal to Woodrow Wilson in 1919 requesting recognition for Vietnamese independence. No such recognition was granted and Nguyen seems to have increasingly turned to communism, but he later said that 'It was patriotism and not communism that originally inspired me.' He saw his mission to restore independence to Vietnam because 'the figure of Justice has had such a rough voyage from France to Indochina that she has lost everything but her sword'.

In 1924 he journeyed to Moscow where he met Stalin, Trotsky, Zinoviev and the other leading communist figures. He found them uninterested in Vietnamese revolution, but his time there transformed him from a propagandist to a political organizer. Activated by tales of rebellion and revolt in Vietnam in the 1920s he thought it time to launch the communist movement.

Nguyen Vih Thuy. He announced that he felt relieved and unburdened of ruling over a subjugated people. He declared that he appreciated that the Vietminh reflected Vietnamese aspirations for independence rather than for communism. He appealed to France's ruler, General de Gaulle, to understand the 'yearning for independence that is in everyone's heart'. He also prophesied that if France were to restore colonial rule in Vietnam 'it will not be obeyed. Every village will be a nest of resistance, each former collaborator an enemy, and your officials and colonists will themselves

Ho Chi Minh (cont'd)

He went to Hong Kong to try to form a communist party out of three rival factions. In June 1929 he got together different factional leaders at a football stadium during a match to avoid detection. They launched the Indochinese Communist party, the name reflecting the ambition to extend Vietnam to include Laos and Cambodia. Their programme called for Vietnamese independence and a proletarian government – a big change from the moderate proposals he had made to Woodrow Wilson in 1919.

Then one of the many adventures in Ho's dramatic life occurred: the Hong Kong police arrested him – as an insurrectionary – but a local British lawyer arranged his release, and his decision was upheld by Sir Stafford Cripps, solicitor-general of the Labour government. A British doctor diagnosed him with TB and had him sent to a sanatorium in London, but the Hong Kong police charged him with illegal departure and had him extradited from Singapore where his ship had docked. He was put in a prison infirmary, but managed to escape to China having persuaded one of the hospital employees to report him as dead. His obituary appeared in the French press, and the French and Hong Kong authorities closed his file.

For the rest of the 1930s he was a perpetual traveller crossing many countries in Asia and east Europe. But he was now an ill man of nearly 50 – a French communist agent recalled 'He was taut and quivering, with only one thought in his head, his country, Vietnam.'

Amidst the tumult of WWII he slipped across the mountainous border into Vietnam from China, his first return in 30 years. He met confederates who called him uncle. They formed the Vietminh Independence League to fight against the Japanese and the French Vichy puppet regime. He took on the pseudonym Ho Chi Minh, Bringer of Light, and was nick-named Bac Ho – Uncle Ho. Still it took another foreigner to save his life before it was time to make history – a young American, Paul Hoagland, had parachuted behind Japanese lines in America's campaign to support the Vietminh against the now Japanese-ruled Vietnam, and had found Ho seriously ill and very near death. He treated his malaria with the quinine he carried and nursed him back to health. Ho admitted this young American saved his life. Only a little time later Ho entered Hanoi and called for a national uprising; on 2 September 1945 he proclaimed the independence of the Democratic Republic of North Vietnam from Hanoi's Ba Dinh square, flanked by two American advisers, and quoted America's Declaration of Independence. Then the real battle began; it began well.

seek to leave this atmosphere, which will choke them'. Ho appointed him 'supreme advisor' to the new Vietminh government in Hanoi.

Potsdam divides Indochina

But just at the moment when Vietnam had rediscovered its independence, on the other side of the world at the Potsdam conference the major world powers were deciding Vietnam's fate. The era in which Vietnam would above all be treated as a pawn in the contest between the major world powers had begun.

In July 1945 one month before Japan surrendered, the Allies met at Potsdam and came up with a scheme to disarm the Japanese in Indochina. It was decided that the British would quell the Japanese in the south of Vietnam, the Chinese nationalists would take the north. The country would be divided at the 16th parallel. But when the British arrived in Vietnam they found that not only were the Japanese troops running riot, but also amid the chaos there were a number of nationalist groupings including the Vietminh who had set up impromptu workers' cooperatives – these had been gradually accumulating power until the Vietminh had set up an infant administration. So the British disarmed the Japanese troops but then restored order by delegation – back to the Japanese and French troops.

Re-armed Japanese soldiers set about putting down the nationalist forces by violence. French troops, armed with military equipment provided by the Americans then followed their instructions to send the Japanese packing, joined the Japanese in quashing the competing nationalist groups.

The French took to it with alacrity: French General Leclerc returned and on arrival in Saigon proclaimed the French had returned to 'claim their inheritance'. The governor released 1400 French foreign legion troops interned by the Japanese who embarked on an orgy of violence. The Vietminh responded in kind and the first step in the Indochinese war began in the south.

Ho loses ground; the French do a deal with Chiang Kai-Shek

Meanwhile, in the north, 200,000 Chinese troops arrived as a horde of 'human locusts' – ragged, starving peasants and officers. This was no army but a populous mass who conquered by pillaging the villages and occupying the land. Ho's first strategy was to placate them. He dissolved the Communist party as a gesture of appeasement and made a deal with the Chinese general that elections would be held putting both Vietnamese and Chinese in power. But in the meantime Chiang Kai-Shek, who had seized power in China, offered the French a deal – on 28 February 1946 the two powers signed an accord. China would withdraw its troops and allow the French to return to Tonkin in exchange for France returning Shanghai and other Chinese ports.

Ho's appeal to America to defend Vietnam's independence against these invading threats had fallen on deaf ears – in contradiction to America's previous position it had now fallen in behind France. Now Ho was trapped between the French, backed by American support, and the Chinese. He chose to take the French, as his famous quote explains why: 'The white man's rule in Asia is over. Last time the Chinese came they stayed 1000 years. I would prefer to sniff French shit for five years than to eat Chinese shit for the rest of my life'.

But the deal is rotten

The deal was that Vietnam would be a 'free state' within the French Union (ie empire) and Ho would allow 25,000 French troops to be stationed in

Vietnam to replace the Chinese troops there. This was agreed in the Treaty of March 1946, and with each side placated it seemed that war had been averted. But this was but the first of many agreements in Vietnam's recent history which was so vague in parts (what was a free state within an empire?) that it was easy to disagree as to whether it had been implemented or not. Also instructions were certainly clear in other areas and it was equally clear that these were not implemented by all parties. So the Treaty stated that the ruling French in the south would hold a referendum to establish whether Cochinchina wished to join the new northern state or remain a French colony independent of the north. The French never held such a referendum.

As 1946 wore on and no referendum was held so the number of French troops stationed increased. The Vietminh began to lose patience and in September the talks broke down. Skirmishes between Vietminh and French troops grew more frequent and more serious, until an obscure customs dispute in Haiphong escalated in November 1946, resulting in France bombing the city and the port. Full-scale war began.

The Franco-Vietminh war begins

France became dragged into war through a number of diverse forces. Firstly, there were certainly many elements of French political society which wanted to salvage something of the 'gloire' of France from postwar devastation – the rise of de Gaulle and his party as a political force perhaps epitomized this aim. At the same time the political instability in postwar France created an environment in which many issues became just pawns in political power games and Indochina was one such. So left-wing governments felt the need to act as aggressively internationally as their right-wing opponents.

❏ **Bao Dai – the reluctant ruler**

Bao Dai lasted one year as Ho's supreme adviser. Then, in 1946 on the pretext of representing Ho in China he fled to Hong Kong. But it wasn't just the communists who wanted him on their side – everyone wanted a piece of him, including the French. They made contact with him and he was offered the chance to be emperor again – of South Vietnam but of course with prospects of expansion to take in the North too.

But Bao Dai was a reluctant ruler, and evading his would-be kingmakers he hightailed it to Paris and spent a frantic month eluding them by hiding in cinemas by day and cabarets by night. Eventually the comic scene came to an end as the French who had followed him back to France finally caught up with him and he succumbed to the inevitable.

The unwilling ruler returned to South Vietnam and after being restored to his position of seeming power he spent most of his time at his hunting lodge at Dalat ordering new tracks through the jungle to be built with better and better elephant-hunting possibilities.

Enter America

American involvement was more of a considered response, but it was a response to questionable evidence. In the aftermath of WWII the French increasingly managed to persuade the Americans that the Vietminh represented a part of potential world communism and in 1947 Truman's officials agreed that Ho's communism might serve the Kremlin's purposes. Two years later three things happened – America 'lost' China to communism, China and Russia both recognized the Democratic Republic of Northern Vietnam and military aid began flowing across the Chinese border to North Vietnam. Truman put financial muscle behind his words of support and authorized $15 million to help the French forces recapture north Vietnam. The rival opponents for Vietnamese affection had staked their claims, taken their places on the stage. The scene was set.

The first conflict was a pitched battle in Hanoi in December 1949 when Vietminh troops attacked French troops installed there. The fight claimed 6000 men, according to France, or 20,000 according to the Vietnamese. While the resistance forces held Hanoi for a few days Ho and an army entourage slipped away to their jungle HQ, there to begin the war in earnest.

An ideological nationalist war

It was to be a fight of several years. The Vietminh were backed by Russian and Chinese military aid, but in the end it was their strategy, and pure staying power, which did for the French. Conflicting goals among the French and the Americans didn't help – tensions soon emerged. The aim of the Americans was to show global presence and to make a stand to stem what they saw as the flood of world communism. The French, meanwhile, had a far more parochial aim – to restore colonial power.

The disparity between America's broad aim and France's narrow goal meant that France knew that America was prepared to go to greater lengths not to lose. France used this as a lever to gain increasing amounts of military assistance (by the end of the war the Americans were paying 78 per cent of the colonial war supporting the same colonials they had previously castigated). And yet the French did not accede to American requests to conduct the war more effectively by promoting nationalists who could be a credible anti-communist force, or even by cutting Bao Dai's allowance.

The emperor's personal allowance claimed a huge slice of the American money – this was not mostly spent on a lavish lifestyle, but in amassing cash in Swiss bank accounts to prepare for a more uncertain future. Meanwhile, Bao Dai's government was different from previous regimes in being rather more dishonest, according to a US consul who claimed it was composed entirely of 'opportunists, nonentities, extreme reactionaries, assassins, hirelings and finally men of faded mental powers'.

This hardly seemed a good return for American money, or French blood, and there was much being shed. France lost 50,000 men between 1945 and 1950. A French General claimed that 'officers are being lost at a faster rate than they are being graduated from officer schools in France.' Much Vietminh blood was being lost too, but heads are rarely counted reliably when the struggle is ideological and about the survival of a nation. 'If you are prepared to put all your population into fight', as Ho said to a French general 'You can kill ten of my men for every one I kill of yours. But even at these odds, you will lose and I will win.' And in a nationalist struggle the French could never win, for there weren't enough who would stand up to support its stunning combination of fading majesty in Indochina and oppressive colonial rule.

Castries vs Giap at Dien Bien Phu

The end came, of course, where the French least expected it. In 1954 the French army parachuted in men and equipment establishing a strong and growing battalion in an isolated valley in north-west Vietnam near the Laotian border close to the town of Dien Bien Phu. Here they established a 16,000-man garrison and by having bulldozers parachuted in they created two airstrips which they bounded with nine heavily-fortified positions on the valley floor (named after the mistresses of the French Colonel de Castries).

The French chose to group here in an attempt to cut the Vietminh's supply lines through Laos and force them into open battle which they believed they would win. The French also chose the location not least because they thought that General Giap's Vietminh couldn't respond here in strength. But Giap proved to be the greater tactician – he had deliberately created the impression of having little force in the region by staging diversionary actions around the rest of Vietnam. General Giap recalled to the historian Stanley Karnow that at that point he had no idea where – or even whether – a major battle might take place but he was intent on retaining manoeuvrability in case, because as Ho said 'the art of war is flexibility'. As they realized the French were pouring troops into Dien Bien Phu the decision was taken – this was to be the scene.

The odds that this would be the decisive battle of the war increased as the confrontation grew nearer because it was really decision time for both the French and the Vietminh. Ho had already signalled that he might be prepared to negotiate, while the French were becoming very war-weary and likely to become more so under a recently-changed sceptical leadership in Paris. And as a US official said 'You don't win at the conference table what you've lost on the battlefield' and both sides had agreed to meet over the Geneva Conference in May 1954.

An impregnable stronghold?

On the face of it the French looked far more likely to win a pitched battle in open country. Their supply of the latest American military equipment was not only more plentiful than the Chinese and Russian equipment which flowed to the Vietminh but also more technologically advanced and the French were well ensconced into what they thought to be an impregnable stronghold. But in his compelling account of the Dien Bien Phu conflict (available at bookstands throughout Vietnam and well worth a read) General Giap tells how the invulnerable stronghold turned into a nightmare 59-day siege for the French forces trapped in the narrow valley surrounded by ever-encroaching Vietminh forces.

Or a modern-day Waterloo
From the start of 1954 General Giap began smuggling 50,000 troops and an estimated massive 300,000 civilian workers into the mountainous territory around the valley. Between them they hauled, at night, and on foot or by bicycle, tonnes of military hardware to the steep sides of the valley. The French positions were very well defended and from their airstrips they also had air capacity. They could only be reached by the longest-range shells which were too massive to be hauled along jungle tracks – or so the French thought. In fact Giap's great victory was to enlist substantial support from the local hill tribes in manoeuvring these huge guns into position. The French were shocked out of their complacency on 10 March 1954 when the first shells rained down. Two of the French positions (Beatrice and Gabrielle) were knocked out in five days and the siege began.

But the French were not to be starved out – they still had planes which flew over the rest of the country several times a day and made parachute drops. But this could only keep them in business, not bring them victory. To do this they had to break through the Vietminh positions – and with their massive geographical disadvantage they never got close. Instead the Vietminh closed in further and further – now the parachute drops were as often as not discharging their load behind enemy lines. As the Vietminh neared the valley floor they approached victory but also faced potential annihilation, had it not been for their final ace – a network of some hundred kilometres of tunnels dug in the valley from which they emerged and took the French positions totally by surprise, surrounding them.

On 7 May 1954, just one day before talks were due to begin in Geneva, General Giap's troops finally took de Castries' bunker and the French leader surrendered. After two months of hard fighting and heavy losses on both sides the north Vietnamese flag flew in this secluded valley that had suddenly come to mean so much. The French had met their Dien Bien Phu and the Franco-Vietminh war was over.

The so-called peace
But the peace was a sham. The upshot of the talks in Geneva was the Geneva Accords. These committed both sides to a number of obligations – most of the important ones were broken and at least one of the others

was not quite what it seemed. The country was to be split in half, at the Ben Hai river along the 17th parallel, but only as a temporary measure pending nationwide elections to be held in July 1956. Until elections were held there was to be an 8km demilitarized buffer zone on either side of the river. During this time there was to be a free passage of people across the border in either direction. But elections were never held and the movement of people was heavily engineered, for while the Geneva talks had been going on there had been some significant power changes in the south – Bao Dai demoted himself to president, his new prime minister being the virulently anti-communist Ngo Dinh Diem – thanks largely to the CIA.

Step forward the CIA

The CIA presence in Indochina was not a recent thing; its predecessor, the Office for Strategic Studies, had long carried out secret work there. But the result of the CIA's work had started to become more obvious.

The evidence is that the CIA engineered Diem into office, organized scaremongering propaganda to persuade Catholics to leave the north in order to establish a strong Catholic constituency for Diem in the south, and encouraged Diem in his view that Ho would win elections if they were held. Nearly a million (Catholic) northerners travelled south, aided by US Navy ships, to escape supposed communist oppression. It was proved in the Pentagon Papers that the Catholics had been propagandized into leaving. One US leaflet dropped at that time read 'Beware! The virgin Mary has fled south. Follow her or be slaughtered.' In fact there was no Catholic bloodbath, although Ho's rule was not a model of a free society. The communists reserved their worst for the landowning classes – their campaign against private property in agriculture was very reminiscent of Stalin's campaign 'collectivization of the kulaks' as were the bloody consequences.

Gerrymandering north and south

But there was no free government in the south either. Elections were never held in the country – on either side of the Ben Hai river. Ho and his troops had already claimed power in the north and they held onto it. Diem, meanwhile, in the south held a so-called 'referendum' for support for his continued rule – so-called because vote rigging was so extensive that his victory of over 98 per cent of votes cast included a third more votes than voters in Saigon. Diem then booted Bao Dai out of power altogether (rather to the latter's relief), proclaimed himself president and with the creation of a CIA-trained secret police force set in train a purge to get rid of Vietminh sympathizers. This turned into a witch-hunt of dissidents, liberals, journalists and so on – the regime passed a law conferring the death penalty on anyone who spoke out against or 'spread rumours' about the government. The free press was strangled, replaced by government-approved newspapers, and nearly 50,000 people were killed.

Strategic hamlets?

In the decade between the Geneva Accords in 1954 and America entering the war in August 1964 the country was supposedly at peace, albeit divided. But what was really going on was rather different – in both halves of the country those who weren't being rallied for war were having their villages taken away from them so they were forcibly mobilized into war.

The south of the country was the real battleground during this time. Some North Vietnamese troops were allowed to remain in the south after the Geneva Accords and they spent their time regrouping in this '3rd Vietnam' and indulging in nightly skirmishes. The result was that the villages were thought to be loyal to the south by day but were overrun by communist forces by night. (This daily changeover was brilliantly described in Graham Greene's *The Quiet American.*) To counteract this, America launched its famously-doomed 'strategic hamlets program'.

The idea of this project was to establish safe areas, ie villages which would be free of communists and subject instead to American protection. In fact the result was a sordid, squalid mess. Encampments were built away from original villages, surrounded with barbed wire and villagers were forced into occupying them. Moved out of their houses and away from their land the peasants were forced into ramshackle huts which not only left their animals abandoned and traditional rhythm and way of life shattered but soon were fantastic breeding grounds for a variety of virulent tropical diseases. The old and infirm generally did not last long. The Americans were winning few friends for their involvement, nor for their puppet-ruler Diem.

Diem condemned by religious fire

Meanwhile Diem himself was going out of his way to make his rule more unpopular with a series of anti-Buddhist measures – religious tolerance had obviously not fled south with the Virgin Mary. Thus, for example, villagers were told to vote in the presidential referendum of 1955, the cost of doing so was being issued with an identity card after having voted. The problem for Buddhists lay in the fact that each card was marked with a small cross. Buddhists had no wish to be associated with this so threw the card away. This created grave problems when the same Buddhists were stopped by the police and asked for their papers. Then, suddenly, with a single act, the world grew to learn of the oppression.

On 15 August 1963 a monk from the Thien Mu pagoda in Hué drove to Saigon and set fire to himself in protest. A Western journalist-photographer happened to be nearby and the world's press had the picture on the front page of every newspaper the next day. On top of the allegations of cronyism, incompetence and brutality of Diem's regime there was too much bad publicity for 'Asia's George Washington', as Diem styled himself, and on 1 November 1963 the American-organized coup against him was launched.

America chooses the seemingly-pliant Thieu

The CIA claim, believably, that they did not want Diem killed, just deposed. If this was their aim, it certainly failed. Both Diem and his brother were murdered, within hours of publicly agreeing to hand over power. The coup was also made to look as if it was an inside job – generals pitted against the top man. But the lie to this was given when three months later the Americans overthrew the generals in favour of their own choice – Nguyen Van Thieu.

Thieu's principal contribution to the proceedings was his absolute conviction, popular with the Americans, that the South Vietnamese should not negotiate with the successor force to the Vietminh in the south – the NLF (National Liberation Front). Many, including the generals who replaced Diem, regarded the NLF as non-communist and sufficiently free from Hanoi's control to make it a force for the liberation of South Vietnam from foreigners into a non-communist state. This was the primary reason for the Americans removing the generals. Subsequently, all South Vietnamese pretenders to power knew the position they had to adopt to keep popular with their rich benefactors – opposition to the NLF and to all Vietnamese forces promising national liberation.

Vietnam's Pearl Harbor brings America in

Then, suddenly, in August 1964, these benefactors, the Americans, turned into outright protectors. America military-might entered the war – thanks to the Gulf of Tonkin incident. This led to the Gulf of Tonkin Resolution, the nearest the American Congress ever came to declaring war on Vietnam.

The actual events which occurred during the incident have been heavily debated (a precedent to the British debate over the sinking of the *Belgrano* which led to the Falklands war). It is thought this is what happened: A US spy ship, called the *Maddox*, patrolling in the Gulf, thought it picked up enemy torpedoes so cabled the president of the US, Lyndon Baines Johnson (LBJ), to this effect. But the ship then cabled doubts about this. LBJ urgently asked his military staff for clarification and advice, for he was about to go on television to give the presidential State of the Union address. Defence secretary, Robert McNamara, advised that there seemed to be a genuine report of an attack. Further reports then came from the *Maddox*, expressing further doubts; these were ignored as LBJ went on TV and announced that America was going to war. Congress then passed the Gulf of Tonkin Resolution which enabled the president, as commander-in-chief, to deploy as much military machinery and manpower as needed in Vietnam, in order to 'prevent further aggression'.

Or was it just an excuse

The Pentagon Papers were a later investigation of the war. They were released in 1971. They made clear that the Resolution that had been passed to Congress had been drafted two months prior to the incident. Either the *Maddox*'s observations had been used as the pretext for entering war, or, perhaps, the *Maddox* was also complicitous and there had been no observations. At any event, it is clear that by this stage certain high-ranking decision-makers in America wished to engage Vietnam in war and found a means to do so. They wished to enter the war because increasing political stability in South Vietnam led to a change in strategy – away from the policy of stability in the south before escalation, to stability through escalation.

The Vietnam war – an American invention

Now began the war which became synonymous with the word Vietnam, but which the Vietnamese called the American war. LBJ sanctioned the first attack – on 14 December 1964 American bombers ravaged the Vietnamese–Laos border, searching for communist infiltration groups. It was codenamed Operation Barrel Roll. The first television war also began. The first American troops stormed the beaches in Danang on 6 March 1965; they were bemused to find no dug-in Viet Cong (an abbreviation of Vietnamese Communist) troops lying in wait to attack them. Instead there were Vietnamese girls in flowing white *ao dais* welcoming the troops and offering them posies of flowers – supplied by American 'military advisers' for the benefit of the video cameras of the waiting world's press. The chess game between the great powers, with Vietnam acting as the pawns, had started and the cameras were rolling.

Lyndon Johnson's war

So the war was 'Americanized' – LBJ announced an immediate increase in American troops in Vietnam from 75,000 to 125,000 with a further increase just seven months later to 429,000 troops by the end of 1965. March 1965 also saw the launching of 'Operation Rolling Thunder' – a three-and-a-half-year long carpet-bombing campaign which replaced the strategic hamlets program with the even more vilified 'search and destroy' strategy. During these years twice the total tonnage of bombs dropped during the whole of WWII was unleashed on North and South Vietnam. But the North Vietnamese, the VC, were not defeated – the destroying was done rather more effectively than the searching.

Search and destroy

Above all, the result of America's strategy of 'search and destroy' was to tear villagers away from their lives, their roots, their land. Leaflets picturing destroyed villages were dropped by air and villagers then had between one and six hours to decide to stay and fight the artillery fire or to go with the Americans.

The scale of the operation was enormous: in the late 1960s an average of one million leaflets was dropped every day on Quang Ngai

---

❏ **Why did Lyndon Johnson escalate America's involvement?**

'This is a war I inherited' Lyndon Johnson (LBJ) said to Walter Lippman, 'I don't like it, but how can I pull out?' By all accounts, LBJ was reluctant to try to hit the North until the South was stable. He believed that political problems required political remedies, not bombs. But, whatever his lingering doubts, he did agree to the programme of escalation put before him. It was he who sanctioned the bombing of North Vietnam rather than just supporting the Southern government, because he was convinced by the domino theory.

The concern with Vietnam was that the strength of the communists was borrowed from the USSR thus it was not native. Global containment of communism was the issue. Or was it? Perhaps for him it was above all about domestic political issues – about enabling him to carry out his Great Society reforms. As LBJ said, in his truly inimitable fashion: 'I knew Harry Truman lost his effectiveness from the day the Communists took over in China. I believed that the loss of China had played a large role in the rise of Joe McCarthy. And I knew that all these problems, taken together, were chickenshit compared with what might happen if we lost Vietnam.'

The point is that LBJ 'Americanized' the war believing otherwise that South Vietnam would be lost and that this would lose him the political potential to carry out the Great Society Program. Thus he said: 'If I left the woman I really loved – the Great Society – in order to get involved with that bitch of a war on the other side of the world then I would lose everything at home. All my programs. All my hopes to feed the hungry and shelter the homeless. All my dreams to provide education and medical care to the browns and the blacks and the lame and the poor. But if I left that war and let the communists take over South Vietnam there would follow in this country an endless national debate – a mean and destructive debate that would shatter my Presidency, kill my administration and damage our democracy.'

The tragic irony is that the Vietnam war did destroy his presidency and his Great Society project never recovered from the vast clefts cut through society by 'Lyndon Johnson's war'.

---

province alone. When the warning leaflets designed to scare were dropped, the inevitable happened – the VC left the village, so the raid destroyed a village devoid of military targets. But B52 logic found a way round this – to drop leaflets and then destroy the village immediately so as to hit at least a few genuine VC targets. Thus the village had to be destroyed in order to save it. Vietnamese effectively came to be judged as VC or not by what had just happened to them – if a village or villager had just been shot at by an American then it was judged as VC. When American troops entered a village and rounded up the inhabitants it would be registered as 100 per cent VC, but when the same villagers were removed to a camp they were categorized by the Army as refugees.

A camp is not a home

The leaflets dropped by Americans offered the Vietnamese the opportunity of abandoning their village and gaining the security of American protection – ie resettling. But the 'resettling' of so many Vietnamese was a bad joke. The deal was meant to be that if a Vietnamese family was made homeless they were to be given 5000 piastres so they could build a new house. But in fact what happened is that the Americans built them a house (in a camp) said it was permanent and was now theirs and therefore did not pay them the money. Another solution was to bring in a village chief and thereby the area could be called a village which took it out of the hands of one American administrative unit, which dealt with resettling and the handing out of the money and into another, which didn't.

Conditions varied enormously from camp to camp – in newly-built ones the conditions were terrible. One American doctor wrote that several deadly diseases were rife in the camps in one province and that on average two to three people would die per week from the diseases and lack of food.

At the start of 1967 the Americans were saying these refugees were an unfortunate, inevitable result of war. By August they were saying it was a helpful useful military strategy to deprive the VC of support – by then 70 per cent of the villages in South Vietnam had been destroyed. Two-thirds of the population of South Vietnam by 1968 were refugees. It is hard to see how Americans can have expected to build up support for the South Vietnamese regime under these conditions.

Khe Sanh, 1968
Meanwhile the communists exploited the consequences of the disastrous structural impact of the war on these Southerners. Their strength remained solid in the north, despite the shelling of B-52s and the privations of war, and was still significant in the '3rd Vietnam', northern strongholds in the south. Then came the siege of Khe Sanh base in mid-Vietnam near the Laos border.

When on 21 January 1968 the surrounding North Vietnamese troops started raining down artillery shells on the US base the American military became convinced they were facing a potential Dien Bien Phu. There was confusion in the leadership – massive ammunition and other military hardware supplies were diverted there; the siege must be broken. From the North Vietnamese point of view; success – they had fallen for it. Ten days later the actual big push came. The Tet offensive began in a great push southwards on 31 January 1968.

The Tet offensive brings in the heavy gun – public opinion
The North Vietnamese troops plunged southwards taking the Americans and South Vietnamese alike by surprise. They met with early success – taking control of over a hundred cities and towns for several days. Hué was the largest and most symbolically important victory. Though when the red flag flew over the imperial citadel it meant death for around 20,000 residents who were anti-communist. Hué was held by the VC for 25 days. Eventually South Vietnamese and American troops began fight-

ing back effectively. The vicious hand-to-hand fighting left Hué's priceless treasures decimated and pushed the North Vietnamese back north. But if the VC lost the battle (and lost their attempt to win the war before Ho died) it nonetheless marked a crucial turning point in the war which ended in their victory. Not because American or the South Vietnamese military machine had been ravaged, but rather because a more subtle weapon had been brought in, and it worked to the North Vietnamese's advantage. The weapon was American public opinion.

A government out of step with its people

The biggest shock of the Tet offensive was to the American public, who were suddenly made aware that the war was not under control as their leaders had been telling them. The war became a huge issue in America, uniting at a stroke liberal intellectuals, disaffected youths, pacifists and anti-racist agitators. This was the year of radical demonstrations all across America and Europe – from the *soixante-huiters* in France to the devastation of the Watts riots of Los Angeles. LBJ's mistakes were that he chose not to mobilize America for war; chose to paint optimistic scenarios for the American public of the process of the war and even chose to hide the enemy build-up before Tet – perhaps because in an election year he hoped for a military miracle.

And it's one, two, three, what are we fighting for?

Ultimately, the American public's growing and voluble distaste for the war taught the lesson that in democracies the populace has to be involved in a nation's decision to go to war, or the leadership must be prepared for a potential backlash. The Vietnam war became unpopular in America when American boys next door started dying – when the draft and body bags which didn't just belong to volunteer troops started hitting home. The anti-war movement all but disappeared as a political issue when Nixon's 'Vietnamization' had set in and American troops were all but absent from the war scene again (as seen by McGovern winning only one state in his presidential bid standing as the only candidate committed to unilaterally ending the war). And ultimately, LBJ not seeking re-election showed that the Vietnam war had become interwoven with his presidency – it had become LBJ's war.

Nixon and Vietnamization

After the Tet offensive, the Vietnam war was deeply unpopular in America and was not being won on the ground. Enter Nixon. Richard Nixon took office as president of the USA in January 1969.

By now America's war effort was going badly wrong: Congress had repealed the Gulf of Tonkin Resolution giving rationale to America's involvement and the army was unravelling from within. It was divided into 'lifers' – trained combat soldiers – and those who were there because

❑ Great powers and small

America always operated the war under three key restrictions: LBJ forbade invading North Vietnam because that could trigger the mutual assistance pact between the North and China; he equally forbade mining the harbour at Haiphong because a Soviet ship might be sunk by mistake; and he forbade expanding war into Laos and Cambodia because it would expand the war politically and geographically, possibly to no discernible advantage. But this last did not hold – while no formal declaration of war was ever made against Cambodia or Laos, because of America's belief in the VC hype of the Ho Chi Minh Trail they by no means escaped the conflict, or indeed the carnage.

In the late 1960s the US launched a massive bombing campaign of Laos and Cambodia. The campaign had two purposes: to attempt to block the Ho Chi Minh Trail (which went through Laos and Cambodia and which US intelligence thought carried most of the military hardware from North to South Vietnam) and to prevent the Pathet Lao turning Laos communist by blocking the route along the Plain of Jars that they would need to take to march on Vientiane, Laos's capital. But this war was kept entirely secret from the American public. The location of the country where America lost the lives of many handpicked volunteers was classified information. Laos was simply referred to as 'the other theatre'. The military pilots flew into battle in civvies – wearing jeans and T-shirts, no Airforce wear. Yet as many bombs were dropped on Laos as had rained down on Nazi Germany during WWII.

of the draft, many of whom did not believe in being there. They showed it with their long hair, peace signs and drug-taking. According to the journalist John Pilger, by this time it was unusual to find a drafted GI who wasn't getting stoned. Nixon was elected, promising to 'end the war and win the peace'. His policy of Vietnamization was meant to achieve the former, the Paris Peace Accords which were finally signed in January 1973 were meant to achieve the latter.

Dependence fosters weakness

Vietnamization was a double-sided coin: withdrawal of American troops and beefing up of the South Vietnamese army. The first part got underway quickly – the number of American troops fell from a peak of over 500,000 in early 1969 to nearly half this number by the end of the following year. But the attempt to turn the South Vietnamese army, the ARVN, into a formidable fighting force on its own was less successful after so many years of dependence. The whole American effort in Vietnam foundered on the contradiction that if you do things for others it makes them weaker not stronger. So the war became about time, not space. The day the Americans

(**Opposite**): The legacy of the Hindu Champa civilization is the numerous Cham Towers still to be seen in the south of the country. This is the central tower at Po Klong Garai Cham towers (see p182).

arrived it was clear they would leave some day – the North Vietnamese just had to wait. So they waited and waited, and while they waited they negotiated.

The war before the peace

In 1971 and 1972 Kissinger was conducting secret negotiations with the North Vietnamese and through them with the Russians. He believed the assurances he was receiving that the VC were negotiating for real and were not about to attack again. Nixon, meanwhile, had secretly travelled to Peking where he negotiated with the Chinese. As far as American intelligence was concerned, all was set fair for genuine peace negotiations. Meanwhile, the president of the Southern regime that the Americans had installed after the generals' coup, Nguyen Van Thieu, was not so sure. From his intelligence in the field, which he often kept secret from American intelligence operators, he grew increasingly uneasy and became convinced that the North Vietnamese were about to attack.

On Good Friday, 31 March 1972, four NVA divisions charged south across the demilitarized zone, just as Thieu had predicted. Six weeks later Nixon announced that US bombers were to fly north again, extensively bombing North Vietnam above the 20th parallel for the first time since late 1968. The US public was shocked, but the bombing continued – Vietnamization or no Vietnamization. The Communists did not waver from their demand for a coalition government in the south with no place for Thieu and the B52s did not stop bombing. Each side was anxious to gain as much as possible on the battlefield before sitting down at the conference table. Nixon flexed his military muscles one last time in his Christmas bombing raids on Hanoi – the first time B52 raids had been launched on the city – before the Peace Accords, for what they were worth, were finally agreed.

Sign in haste, repent at leisure

The Accords which were signed in Paris in January 1973 guaranteed one thing, American withdrawal. That was really all they could guarantee since that was the only outcome that depended on American actions alone.

In all other areas the Accords were a mess. The explanation CIA officer Frank Snepp gives (in his acclaimed and classified book *Decent Interval*) is that the US was so keen to withdraw that the negotiations were conducted with such haste that imprecise drafting left key loopholes which were exploited by both sides. Thus it was specified that North Vietnamese troops would withdraw from Laos and Cambodia, but no timetable was given so withdrawal never began. Also, it was specified that

(**Opposite**) **Top**: A bunker in the demilitarized zone (see p235). **Bottom**: Graves of Vietnamese war martyrs at Truong Son National cemetery (see p236).

some North Vietnamese troops could remain in South Vietnam but no more military hardware would be brought in after the ceasefire, but as the ceasefire never came, the fighting never stopped, neither did the communist war machine. And then there was the really fudged question of how South Vietnam was to be run.

A 'decent interval'

The country was to be run by a Council of National Reconciliation and Concord made up of Thieu, his government and the North Vietnamese government, and all votes were to be unanimous. A Joint Military Commission was also to be formed made up of South and North Vietnamese figures and again all decisions were to be unanimous. These arrangements were entirely unworkable. Soon the structures existed in name only. Some have argued that these Accords, the result of Kissinger's finalising of Nixon's policy of Vietnamization, showed that the basic aim of the two men was not so much peace as to create a 'decent interval' between America's withdrawal and Vietnam tearing itself apart – probably ending in a North Vietnamese victory.

The war after the peace

At least Kissinger is thought to have been serious in trying to get some kind of equilibrium between the two sides. Behind the scenes he had persuaded China and Russia to lessen their support in return for a promise of $4.25 billion in reconstruction aid to North Vietnam (only cursory mention was made of the need for Congressional approval, although in fact the money was never paid). But such moves to calm down the military situation can have been little consolation for the escalation which actually occurred – after Nixon had announced the 'peace with honour' the war was no longer news and the correspondents began to filter back home, but the conflict actually intensified. More bombs were dropped after the Accords than at any time before, although most were on Cambodia and Laos. In 1974 the Senate Refugee Committee noted that an average of 141 people were being killed per day.

Watching like hawks

And still the North Vietnamese did not leave Laos or Cambodia so the B52 raids continued. But when Congress got to hear of it they saw it as a clear indication that the Paris agreements were meaningless. They dug in their heels and thwarted presidential attempts to re-introduce American involvement – whether military or just aid. Finally, a resolution was passed, on 15 August 1973, prohibiting any further American involvement in the whole of Indochina. Thieu simply couldn't believe this – he could not understand that Nixon wasn't master of his house as he was of his. But as the Watergate scandal deepened Nixon was increasingly master of nothing. Even when Gerald Ford finally took over in 1974, Thieu still did not grasp that America wasn't going to reverse its position and start bombing the North again. But the North Vietnamese did understand. They watched Congress take its decisions, they watched Nixon leave the White House and they waited.

A single spy

The communist offensive began in late autumn of 1974. The strategy Hanoi took in the offensive was determined by the receipt of a report from a single spy (whose identity is still secret) in Thieu's government which set out how and where the South Vietnamese government thought the North Vietnamese would attack. Thus as an attack was expected in Tay Ninh they would strike in Phuc Long province, and as no push was expected in the central highlands that was where they would launch an assault which would turn out to be devastating.

Would the Americans hit back?

At the turn of 1974 VC divisions attacked Phuc Long province and in the space of just two weeks took and held the town. Now both the North Vietnamese and Thieu received the initial answer to the question of whether America would step in. The answer was no. In the communist-ruled Politburo it was Le Duan who had pressed the strategy of acting on the espionage intelligence and he now pressed for a bolder one – to liberate all of South Vietnam over the next two years, with the possibility of victory by the end of 1975 if conditions arose. No one believed defeat for the South could come before then.

Russian guns, superpower politics

The reason for the change in strategy was external to North Vietnam. It came from the USSR. For the first time since the ceasefire the USSR seemed prepared to sanction a more aggressive policy and granted a four-fold increase in supply of military hardware to the communists. Big power politics was again the root cause. Now that the USA was comprehensively limited in its actions in Indochina the USSR used this arena to punish the US for linking human rights issues in Russia with trade: Congress had taken a decision to withhold trading benefits without human rights improvements. Le Duan's aggressive stance was also gaining converts in the Politburo because those in favour of reconstruction first were finding little joy in negotiating with the South. This in turn was because olive branches which were proffered were consciously ignored by Thieu and by American Ambassador Graham Martin as they tried to present an increasingly doom-ridden view to Congress in an attempt to screw more money out of them. This attempt signally failed.

Strike quick, strike hard, strike the Highlands

Then came the key North Vietnamese military success. And the key to the success was surprise. The North Vietnamese managed to move an entire division south of the 17th parallel without anyone noticing and manoeuvre two whole divisions from their usual positions of targeting Kontom and Pleiku to targeting Buon Ma Thuot without alerting the enemy. They then planned to take Buon Ma Thuot by use of the 'blossoming lotus' strategy, comprising a deep strike at the heart of the objective followed by explosive waves outwards to mop up the outskirts. Thanks to these secret manoeuvres, when General Dung set up his HQ to the west of Buon Ma Thuot he had an advantage of 5:1 to attack it and no-one in the South Vietnamese government or army even knew he was in South Vietnam. So strong were the North Vietnamese that the battle for the centre was extraordinarily quick – the attack was launched on 10 March 1975 and Buon Ma Thuot was won by 10.30am on 11 March. Pleiku and Kontom fell soon after.

Thieu orders secrecy and creates disaster

The victory came as a profound shock to Thieu's government, and to Martin's embassy. They set about formulating a strategy of damage limitation, but Thieu didn't share his conclusions with the Americans who were nevertheless the ones who had to pick up the pieces. He decided on a strategy of 'light at the top, heavy at the bottom' – meaning abandoning the northernmost centres under attack and concentrating troops on protecting the main centres of Hué, Danang, Nha Trang and ultimately Saigon. After the Buon Ma Thuot victory the southern General Phu moved his HQ to Nha Trang in what was the only orderly part of the new strategy. Then followed a disastrous mistake – the movement of troops from the abandoned highlands to the coast. The problem was that all major roads to the coast were shut down, leaving only Route 7B, an old logger's road, which extended eastwards to the coast. This route was therefore chosen by Thieu.

A river of mud

But no-one had bothered to survey the route or to provide for the thousands of civilians who were bound to follow the units out. As Frank Snepp reports: 'Troops and civilians soon became hopelessly intermingled, tank commanders and battle-hardened rangers bullied their way to the head of the column, and as the heavy armour and *caissons* pulled out in front, the road broke and rutted under the weight. The 2,000 cars, jeeps and trucks strung out behind quickly became mired in a river of mud.' Once the VC realized the route the South Vietnamese forces were taking they swung into action to cut them off. Two days after the fall of Pleiku they had captured the town of Cheo Reo, which lay directly on the retreating troops' line of march. Frank Snepp: 'With that stroke, the evacuating column was cut in half, part of it trapped west of the town, the rest strung out along Route 7B to the coast. Its destruction was now only a matter of time.' The rot and the panic quickly spread.

Hué in frenzy

'Nearly 150,000 inhabitants of Quang Tri City and the surrounding hamlets were now stumbling south towards Hué, army stragglers and provincial militia strong-arming their way to the front of the column. As the first of them streamed through Hué itself, many of the city's own population were caught up in the frenzy and soon a monstrous tidal wave of honking jeeps, Honda riders and overloaded buses was rolling south toward Danang, along Highway 1. From the outset, the flight of the civilians had a devastating impact on the morale and effectiveness of the army. Not only did the surging masses on each road and airfield hopelessly disrupt troop movements and supply lifts, but their mood, the panic itself, soon became infectious. Thanks to an old army tradition, many of the refugees...were in fact military dependents. Years before, the high command in Saigon had decided the troops would fight better with their wives and children at their side and had chosen to base dependents wherever the army made its home. ...The only exceptions were the Marine and Airborne Divisions...The difference would tell dramatically in the next few days, for as Hué, then Quang Ngai and finally Danang came under direct Communist attack, the ARVN troopers in each of these cities would fall prey to family commitments. ...Only the Marines, with their dependents safely in Saigon, would finally be left to fend off the attackers.' (Frank Snepp)

The terrible flight south, but is Saigon safe?

In a nutshell, the withdrawal was a disaster. Well-disciplined army divisions fell apart, there was little organized military response, only a flight south. Panic-stricken civilians followed. Within weeks there were over two million displaced people and the cities fell like ninepins. Hué was abandoned on 25 March. Nearly all the South Vietnamese forces around the city had been destroyed, or had simply disappeared thanks to the 'family syndrome' which Snepp described above. The North Vietnamese General Dung proposed a push for total victory, taking Saigon. The Politburo agreed. The next target was, therefore, the death of Danang. The total disarray of the retreat from Danang comprised a human tragedy (see p200). Suddenly even Saigon looked in danger. It was. As Embassy and CIA officials under Kissinger's instructions used up time manoeuvring Thieu out of office and replacing him with a compromise figure in the hope of a last-minute negotiated settlement North Vietnamese troops were thrusting south and tightening the net around Saigon.

Panic

On 28 April 1975 for the first time since 1971 North Vietnamese rockets hit the city. Finally on the morning of 29 April Kissinger authorized the mass evacuation that some CIA and Embassy figures had been planning for weeks, largely on their own initiative. But much too late. And Kissinger had stipulated that the evacuation must be completed that day.

Since the airport lay within range of North Vietnamese rockets American choppers were taking off from every roofpad and courtyard. But it soon became evident that the Americans were not going to live up to their promise that if the worst ever came they wouldn't leave behind anyone whose help had been such that their lives would be endangered if captured by the communists. Even highly-classified documents naming undercover Vietnamese agents were left around unincinerated, or scattered by helicopter back drafts and left sprayed over bushes and trees.

Utter panic, chaos and confusion spread – and escape now depended more on force or luck than merit. Halfway through the day the mood among the mass of humanity desperate to be evacuated was already turning volatile and dangerous; 'rumours of abandonment and betrayal whipped through the crowds like random sparks, and time and again, to add to the tension, the sound of gunfire wafted in over the walls as looters and army stragglers rampaged through the abandoned British Embassy across the street' (Snepp).

According to Ambassador Martin's aide, Kenneth Moorefield 'some explosive problems had already developed. You'd find one Vietnamese inside the fence [of the Embassy compound], the rest of the family on the other side, and they'd all be weeping and pleading with you to open the gate. But you knew there was no way to let one or two in without having to beat back hundreds more.'

The airlift and the end

Many were left behind when President Ford ordered the Ambassador's departure and an end to the airlift at 4.20am on 30 April. But the Americans, although some more than others, had done their level best and even North Vietnamese General Dung acknowledged in his memoirs that the airlift was a spectacular achievement, the largest helicopter evacuation in history. At the final count a rescue force of only 70 choppers had flown over 630 sorties in 18 hours and evacuated 1373 Americans and 5595 South Vietnamese.

For those who were left behind, 30 April saw VC troops smash through the gates of the Presidential Palace and declare victory. Saigon was renamed Ho Chi Minh City. The war was over.

A war of one-sided will and conviction

Throughout the war the will of the North Vietnamese was solid, while that of the South Vietnamese was non existent – only the will of the USA was changeable. Therefore the crucial contests of the war would take place in the arena of public opinion, just as elections are decided by the floating voters. The American public was never asked to rally behind the effort – rather it was hidden from what was actually going on.

The Tet offensive, then, showed the American public that it was America that could not win the war, because the Saigon regime was weak and American-dependent, while the North Vietnamese were resolute. Ultimately it was only when American boys next door started dying that the American public involved itself in this war and forced the decision-makers to become accountable for its consequences.

It was this forced openness that led to Congress' restrictions on presidential and military actions which eventually brought about the end of the war. Robert Kennedy said 'We have sought to solve by military might a conflict whose issue depends on the will and conviction of the South Vietnamese people. It's like sending a lion to halt an epidemic of jungle rot.' So, as Jonathan Schell has said, when the end came the retreat showed only too vividly that South Vietnamese society had no inner cohesion – it was merely held together with foreign arms, money, will. The only 'plan' the South Vietnamese had for defeating the North was the re-intervention of America. When this did not arrive, they gave up.

How did tiny North Vietnam defeat mighty America?

Looking back, it seems remarkable that such an insignificant country as the former Democratic Republic of Vietnam should have held off for so long the world's most powerful superpower the United States of America, and of course it is extraordinary that they should have defeated the US. As the American colonel said to the North Vietnamese colonel 'You know, you never defeated us on the battlefield.' 'That may be so, the other replied, but it is also irrelevant.' Political problems required political, not military, solutions. Vietnam was not so much lost on the political front in the US, as Nixon argued, but on the political front in south Vietnam.

The legacy

The war left behind its legacy of scorched earth, an estimated 1,250,000 dead Vietnamese (58,022 dead Americans), thousands of amputees and a deeply-divided society. Saigon's residents feared a dreadful bloodbath when the communists arrived. This in fact never happened, but the thousands who were sent to 're-education camps' for years after the war and the many thousands who attempted to escape the country during the 1970s and 1980s, the 'boat people', found reason enough to hate communist rule.

Old enemies prevent peace

Still Vietnam had not found peace. In 1979 China launched an attempted invasion over the mountains in north Vietnam. They were repulsed quickly, but left a trail of destruction. In the same year, after continued infractions of Vietnam's southern border with Cambodia, Vietnamese troops marched into Phnom Penh and ousted Pol Pot and his Khmer Rouge from their barbaric, vicious rule. Pol Pot escaped to the jungle with many of his generals where he died in 1998. He was never brought to trial for his crimes against humanity, but equally Vietnam was never thanked for lifting the yoke of his rule. Indeed, as a punishment for this act President Reagan spoke of 'bleeding Vietnam white'.

❑ **Was the American war justified – were Ho and his colleagues communists or nationalists?**

President Richard Milhous Nixon effectively took responsibility for ending the Vietnam war by his policy of 'Vietnamization' – ie taking the Americans out of the war by making the South Vietnamese instead of Americans fight the war against the North Vietnamese. But he was a staunch defender of America going into Vietnam and of doing likewise again and again. But even Nixon made a crucial admission in his book *No More Vietnams*. He stated that if Ho and his colleagues were primarily fighting a civil war, a war of national liberation, America should not have been there. Many influential people thought this was indeed the case.

Major Archimedes L A Patti of the Office of Strategic Studies (the forerunner of the CIA) studied Ho's activities and his inaugural speech and as a result produced a paper entitled 'Why Vietnam? Prelude to America's albatross' which was ready to be published in 1954. But by this time McCarthyism had taken hold in America and Major Patti was threatened with disciplinary action if he went ahead and relayed his version of events in Vietnam because, according to him, Ho and his colleagues, far from being communists were pro-America and its way of life, believing Americans to be different from Europeans, from colonialists and to be in support of the Vietminh's primary aim – national liberation.

The VC preached 'Why should outsiders divide the country? A nation can't have two governments any more than a family can have two fathers.'

Keeping the world order

The contrary view is worth a look – the world looked very different when the Americans entered the war. There was a genuine fear in America and much of the Western world of a world communist take over. The role of global policeman is always a hard one in which successes are often hidden, while failures are all too public. Criticism of America is justified, but no-one else has stepped up to take the floor.

Today – a new Hanoi Hilton

Vietnam today is a country that the rest of the world has largely come to terms with, while it still struggles to come to terms with itself. It opened up to the outside world in 1986 when the Politburo launched its version of perestroika, called *doi moi*. Several years later, in 1994, the US lifted the trade embargo it had slapped on the country at the end of the war. With trade relations normalized, the usual signs of globalization slowly followed. Nowadays imported Honda motorbikes are increasingly replacing the more traditional bicycles, Coca-Cola is everywhere, jeans have started to replace ao dais, people are marrying later, and the government is becoming more open.

At the start of 1999 America appointed its first-ever ambassador in Hanoi, and the first in the country since Ambassador Martin was air-lifted off the roof of the embassy in Saigon in May 1975. The old prisoner of war camp in Hanoi, nicknamed the 'Hanoi Hilton' by GIs, has been razed to the ground, while next door to the Opera House the actual Hilton chain has opened a new hotel.

But much remains the same; traditional rural life is still there to be seen and the fading grandeur of Saigon and Hanoi is still captivating despite the roar of motorbikes. Certainly the people's love of good food and good company seems to be an historical constant.

The quest for identity must be never ending

But now in the era when the Vietnamese government is welcoming marketization of the economy the question is whether it can fight off some of the pressures of globalization and stay unique.

Thus, having defeated the world's most feared historical conquerors – the Chinese, the Mongols, the Japanese, the French and the Americans can Vietnam truthfully embody its own proverb, that Vietnam is like a house with windows through which the wind may blow from all directions, but at the end the house remains intact.

VIETNAM TODAY

The people

Vietnam is home to 72 million people who are very unevenly distributed across the country. The majority live on the flat coastal plains which run the length of the country, and especially in the Red River delta in the north and Mekong Delta in the south, while the inland mountainous areas are sparsely populated.

Ethnic divisions run very much along the same lines, with the majority Viets, or Kinh, living along the coast while the hill tribe minorities live in the mountains – and this in turn echoes the Vietnamese legend of the origins of the Vietnamese people which has them split into coastal and mountain people (see p37).

There are 54 ethnic minorities in Vietnam who comprise 13 per cent of Vietnam's population. The biggest minority are the ethnic Chinese, followed by the more numerous hill tribes, such as the Tay, Thai and Muong, while further down the scale are Khmers and much lower down the Chams. The smallest distinct ethnic hill tribe in Vietnam, O'-du, numbers only a hundred members. The most colourful hill tribes in the country live in the north, many live around the charming hill station of Sapa (see p278).

Religion

Most Vietnamese that you are likely to come across are Viets and most Viets are Buddhist. Many are devout and most observe at least some of the religion's rituals, many of which are particular to Vietnam and focus especially on ancestor worship. But although some rituals may be different, Vietnamese Buddhists believe in the fundamental tenets of Buddhism

❑ Traditional Vietnamese Buddhist death rituals

Elaborate rituals are traditionally conducted after there has been a death in the family not only to ease the grief of those left behind, but more importantly to ease the passage of the soul to the spiritual world.

The body and casket of a dead person is prepared outside the house and then it is carried in, feet first, through the middle door, which is only used during funerals and festivals. The person's worldly goods are lined up between the bed and the wall. A ball of sticky sweet rice is mixed with three coins and a hard-boiled egg and placed in the deceased's mouth so the person doesn't go into the spirit world poor or hungry.

The body lies in state for two days and a night while relatives and friends are alerted of the death and given time to get to the funeral. Prayers are spoken during this time for the dead person to encourage the soul not to grieve for those left behind or for leaving behind worldly possessions. If someone is by the bedside while the person dies a particular silk known as *cao vong* is used to catch the person's spirit. Otherwise the *cao to* ceremony is performed which tells the soul not to worry and that the body will be buried properly.

Then the coffin is carried to the graveside. Leading the procession are the youngest children who carry a scroll of the name of the dead person and of their dead ancestors, then follow male relatives who throw paper money from side to side to pay the old ghosts to look after their newest member. Next come village men, carriers of sweet rice, cooked pork and tea, followed by altar carriers and drum players. Then come the pall bearers carrying the body feet first in its coffin, followed lastly by all the womenfolk. At the graveside all those present clasp hands and give three bows, thus recognising the new spirit life of the person which will now return to occupy their old home.

Three days after the funeral the 'open grave' ceremony occurs whereby all family members bring incense and flowers to decorate the grave. For the next 49 days the family puts an extra serving of food at their table and every seventh night prays with the Buddhist priests so that the soul will find the nearest temple.

including that one's deeds in life create karma which becomes realized through reincarnation and that by earning merit in life the spirit can eventually transcend to nirvana.

Almost all Vietnamese pay attention to the lunar calendar, and the greatest celebration of the year comes at the time of the lunar new year (see p101). Also, most Vietnamese are suspicious, favouring certain numbers and therefore certain dates or numbers of people (see p103).

Vietnam has pagodas and temples, many of which are delightful; the Perfume Pagoda is perhaps the most enchanting. But don't expect temples to match those of, for example, Thailand. Of course, all this religion takes place in a communist country and it is notable that the Vietnamese government has never tried to quash religion as the purist Soviet or Chinese regimes did. This must be largely because the assault on Buddhism by the Southern regime was clearly very unpopular. It resulted in the suicide by burning of Buddhist monks as protest to worldwide condemnation. Key

❑ **Traditional Vietnamese Buddhist death rituals (cont'd)**

On the hundredth day after the death the family hold the 'stop crying' ceremony at which Buddhist monks perform a three-day mass to celebrate the soul's release from fear and want and to entice the soul back to the house with continuous chanting. Then on the first anniversary of the death the family hold a memorial service in which they burn a paper bed, paper clothing and paper funeral money.

The anniversary of a person's death is remembered each year while there are still people alive who knew them. For such an occasion the family would cook a great meal and invite all the extended family over. When all have arrived, the food and some water is placed on the altar with three joss sticks; the joss sticks are set there to invite the spirit of the dead person to come back. When they have burned down it is assumed that the spirit has eaten and drunk so new joss sticks are lit to keep the spirit there and the food is taken down and the family eat; eating this food is thought to bring luck. If the relation is more distant there will be a smaller family party and only one joss stick will be set to burn alongside, at the minimum, a bowl of rice, an egg and a glass of water. Then again, once the joss stock is burned the food is eaten by the assembled family.

If a person dies without leaving a will a medium who must be a stranger to the family is invited to communicate with the dead person and announce the desired distribution of property. The medium is put into a bamboo cage covered by a blanket and family members walk past it until he correctly identifies them. He is then thought to be in the trance state of the departed soul so can announce the departed's will.

If the head of the house, the father, dies and there is no son to take over, he must still be consulted on many things. Two coins are used, painted white on one side. A question is asked of the spirit and the coins are tossed in the air. If they land with one white side showing, the answer is yes; if with two or no white sides showing the answer is no. Interestingly this biases the answer towards the negative and this feature is certainly used when deciding which questions to refer to the spirit and which not.

features of Buddhism relating to the importance of relatives and family were also used by the communists as a tool against the Southern regime and the Americans, as the following song which the VCs made up and taught to villagers shows (related by Le Ly Hayslip):

Americans come to kill our people
Follow America and kill your relatives!
The smart bird flies before it's caught
The smart person comes home before Tet
Follow us and you'll always have a family
Follow America and you'll always be alone.

The difference between temples and pagodas is that temples are places where believers come to worship Buddha and pagodas are buildings erected to celebrate a particular person who did notable things in the area; thus every pagoda has a meaning, such as being for parents without sons. Inside every pagoda there will be a gateway leading to the most important altar. This will be guarded by two bodyguards – one good, one evil. The evil one is painted a violent red.

● **Cao Daism** Cao Daism is unique in two ways – not only is it exclusive to Vietnam but it also has the distinction of claiming to fuse all major world religions and the philosophies of East and West. It is the ultimate fusion of ideas in an attempt to prescribe the good life. Followers worship the supreme being, represented by the Divine Eye, but also regard as his underlings such diverse figures as Jesus, Buddha, Lao-Tse, Confucius, Mohammed and Moses.

Cao Daism holds that the truths of the supreme being were communicated to humans through history by these agents but that the revelations were limited in scope and became corrupted over time. But the teachings of the founder of Cao Daism, the mystic Ngo Minh Chieu, hold that this phase is over and that Cao Daism represents a new alliance between God and man in which God communicates directly with man through spirits who live as men. Such spirits include Joan of Arc and Victor Hugo (though not Charlie Chaplin as some guidebooks have claimed!). Mediums communicate with the spirits and their messages are transcribed and pass into official doctrine. Rumour has it that Graham Greene seriously considered converting to Cao Daism.

Ngo Minh Chieu founded Cao Daism in the 1920s after receiving a series of revelations from the supreme being. This mystic and member of the French colonial administration then evangelized in the area surrounding Saigon and quickly gathered followers. By the end of the decade the temple at Tay Ninh was built. The religion and its community went from strength to strength and by the mid-1950s it was virtually established as an independent state in the Tay Ninh region within the French colony of Cochinchina. The French courted this independent power base and successfully won over the Cao Daist private militia who agreed to fight with the French against the Viet Minh. But at the moment of most extreme danger for the French regime the Cao Daists turned neutral. The eventual Viet Minh victory owed something to this reversal. But Cao Daism did not convert to the VC cause, which cost them dear in confiscated lands after the eventual VC victory. Today the cult is tolerated by the Communist regime and it thrives here in its centre in Tay Ninh, 100km north-west of Ho Chi Minh City. The spectacularly colourful and decorative temple in Tay Ninh is well worth a visit.

There are also significant religious minorities in the Cao Daists and the ethnic minorities who have their own religious beliefs and customs (see p280).

Culture

● **Traditional arts** Vietnam is rich in traditional arts from singing to water puppetry. Vietnamese **music** played on traditional instruments can be heard in hotels and restaurants and is well worth the effort. Singing is usually the task of young women who have through the centuries used the combination of melody and a tonal language to produce songs of a haunting quality. Traditional instruments include bamboo xylophones, mandolins and an instrument unique to Vietnam – the 'one string' – *doc huyen*. It is a real art to be able to play this extraordinary instrument to good effect as its limited range of notes are produced only by bending the one string. **Silk painting** is almost ubiquitous in South-east Asia but the subjects in Vietnam will be typically Vietnamese, while another art – water puppetry – is unique to Vietnam (see below).

Vietnam's tradition of **literature** is also well established. Today, just as Shakespeare stands tall above other literary figures for the British, so Vietnam has one writer who is prized above all others; Nguyen Du. He was an 18th-century scholar and author of one work beloved still today by many Vietnamese, *The Tale of Kieu*, or *Kim Van Kieu*.

This great poetic work (which has been translated into English) tells of a girl called Kieu who agreed to leave her home and marry a man for a handsome sum in order to save her father from ruin. But she is betrayed and trapped into a life of prostitution far from the help of her family or friends. Eventually she escapes and begins wanderings which lead her through years of happy marriage with a warlord and finally leads her home and to her childhood sweetheart.

It is the story of one woman's life of sacrifice and betrayal but it was very much written as an allegory characterising the shifting political allegiances during the Tay Son revolution which occurred during Du's lifetime. But the poetry is so exquisite that it can be read just for this and indeed is by many Vietnamese who can recite hundreds of lines of the work. It resonates to today's readers and the themes find echoes in Bao Ninh's *The sorrow of war*.

To an outsider its portrayal of suffering, sacrifice and sorrow helps an understanding of how the Vietnamese seem to bear their serial misfortunes. As Kieu says:

'I've had my ample share of wind and dust –
and now this double load of mud and ash.'

It's thought that Vietnamese **water puppetry** began in the 11th century when a ritual puppet show to celebrate the spring rice festival in North Vietnam found itself performing in flooded fields. This then became a tradition in itself. A typical performance has 10 water puppeteers, male and female, who operate a complicated system of strings and pulleys to swish puppets through water in a retelling of ancient Vietnamese stories. With a remarkable display of mastery of physics, top of the range performances include golden dragons who spout first water and then fireworks. There is also wonderful live music accompaniment on traditional instruments. During the winter cold the puppeteers used to operate from vats of *nuoc mam* (fish sauce) to keep warm – these days more convenient diving suits are used.

● **Traditional Vietnamese thinking** The **growing of rice** dominates the life of all who live in the countryside. The rhythm of life is set by the cycle of its cultivation and legends surround its origin on earth.

Ong trang ba hung is the story of the spirit messenger who had been entrusted by God to bring rice, the heavenly food, to earth for humans to enjoy. God gave the messenger two magic sacks. 'The seeds in the first' said God, 'will grow when they touch the ground and give plentiful harvest anywhere with no effort.'

'The seeds in the second sack, however, must be nurtured, but if tended properly will give the earth great beauty.' The first sack was meant to contain rice, the second grass. But the messenger mixed up the two sacks so grass sprang up everywhere, while rice was difficult to grow. On learning of this God punished the spirit by expelling him from heaven and instead sent him to earth as a hard-shelled beetle, to crawl in the ground and dodge the feet of the people he had harmed.

God then saw the trouble the mixing up of the sacks had caused and as compensation he commanded the rice to 'present itself for cooking' by rolling up to each home in a ball. So the rice proceeded to do so and arrived at the first home. But the housewife was frightened of the apparition and hit the rice with a ladle, scattering it into a thousand pieces. The rice grew angry and said 'See if I'll come back to let you cook me. Now you'll have to come out to the fields and bring me in if you want your supper!' The legend does not record what happened next but presumably God gave up.

Traditional Vietnamese thinking holds that the human world is divided into the **microcosm** and the **macrocosm** – this is to say that animal, vegetable and mineral are in substance epitomes of the wider Universe.

Reciprocally, the Universe is endowed with elements and a soul identical to that of man, the animals, plants and minerals. So a constant relation binds the behaviour of the macrocosm and man, as a part of the microcosm. Thus there is thought to be a correspondence between these different elements of the macrocosm and the microcosm (see the box).

Another part of traditional Vietnamese thinking which persists to the present-day is the ancient skill of **geomancy** (or feng shui, as the Chinese call it).

❏ **Microcosm and macrocosm**	
Microcosom	**Macrocosm**
Vessels	Rivers
Skeleton	Mountains
Hairs	Vegetables
Head (round)	Heaven
Foot (square)	Earth
Menstrual cycle	Lunar cycle
Breath	Wind

It was brought to Vietnam by a Chinese governor in the 9th century and is thought of as the science of natural laws – wind and water. It depends on the belief that a spiritual end is attached to all material goods and the Vietnamese system has developed differently from the Chinese. So in building a house or a boat, numerous rites must be observed before, during and after the performance of the work. For example in the siting of a house the geomancer must use the geomatic compass. This points out the distribution of the two great breaths of substance, the Blue Dragon, or beneficent breath (*thang long*), and the White Tiger or pernicious breath (*bach ho*). The closer one is to the neck and the mouth of the dragon the more favourable the site; it is important to keep the White Tiger on the right and the Blue Dragon on the left.

Finally, only a virtuous person can make use of geomancy. As the saying goes 'First, be engaged in good actions, then look for the dragon's vein'.

● **Contemporary attitudes** In these changing times many traditions still persist while others are changing. You will find that many men in Vietnam follow the Asian practice of growing at least one fingernail very long in order to show that they do not do manual labour. It's still considered vital for Vietnamese families to have sons; if a family has only daughters it is considered they have no children because only sons can lead the prayers for the parents after they die. Meanwhile in Hanoi and Ho Chi Minh City there are some Vietnamese people who, amongst their friends, are fairly openly gay. There are no specific outlets in terms of gay nightclubs or newspapers yet, but being gay is gradually becoming more acceptable.

● **Lifestyle** In Hanoi, 'curfew' for young girls used to be 9pm – when the radio signalled three beeps it was time to rush home. So girls always had to be near a radio when out. These days it's more like 11-11.30pm, because that's when the television shuts down. It's important not to be home later than that without having the whole neighbourhood thinking you're a 'bad girl'. Of course it's different for boys – they can return home at any time – because no-one expects them to be obedient.

Almost everyone who can lives with their parents and extended family, and even in the city few married couples live on their own. Most city

---

❏ **Toenails are sacred?**
Some Vietnamese collect their toenail clippings in jars and have them buried with them when they die because animists regard the fingernails as similar to the tiger's claws and therefore holy. But most Vietnamese never get the chance to grow their fingernails because they are committed to a life of manual labour, so they grow their toenails instead.

❏ **A typical week for a young Vietnamese**

Monday to Friday:

8am	Gets up, has breakfast with the family
9-9.30am	Arrives at work
12-1.30pm	Has lunch at home
5.30pm	Finishes work
6.30-9pm	Attends university evening classes
9pm	Goes home for dinner
11pm	Bedtime

Works every Saturday morning and some Saturday afternoons.

Sunday is free! Spends the day at home relaxing or goes out for a picnic; may go out in the city on Sunday evening.

residents who do not do manual labour do early morning exercises; traditional tai chi and other sports remain popular among the young because the early morning sorties are seen as a great way to socialize. But not everyone has the time for dawn exercises. The box shows the daily schedule of one Hanoi resident – a young working woman.

● **Attitudes to foreigners**

Everywhere you go in Vietnam you will hear the word *tay*. It sounds like 'die' but it only means foreigner, or rather it explicitly means a foreigner with a white face. Part of the explanation for children's fascination/fear of whites is that they are told from a very young age that if they are not good they will be given to the foreigners! So foreigners are elevated to the status of universal bogeymen; such figures hold an extraordinary fascination for children across the world.

Travellers often wonder why it is that so many Vietnamese are so friendly to foreigners, when historically white foreigners especially have so often brought conflict and oppression to the country. Apart from inherent humanity it seems that the answer may also lie in the permanent threat from the greater dragon to the north – China. With China always so close Vietnam is always looking to other parts of the world for allies.

Names

Vietnamese names are ordered in the opposite way to Western names so the family name comes first, this is usually followed by two first names. A very popular surname is Nguyen – this name was adopted by around 55 per cent of families when the first Nguyen emperor decreed that people could take his name as a surname instead of their own.

In general women's first names evoke rivers, flowers, birds or precious things, while men's first names refer to abstract virtues. Examples of women's names are mother-of-pearl (Trai), phoenix (Loan), willow (Lieu), autumn (Thu); examples of men's names are virtue (Duc), and modesty (Khiem). A typical name would be formed in this way:

Chi	Nguyen	Thu	Ha
Miss	surname	autumn	river (first name)

Most Vietnamese are also given a name which is a number, corresponding to the order they come in the family – ie oldest child etc though the systems for this vary in the north and south. In the north, Hai (two) is the second child's name, in the south, Hai is the name given to the oldest child, Ba to the second child and so on. In the north the Chinese name for four is used for the fourth child – Tu – while the south uses Bon (though of course this is the name given to the third child). The youngest child is given the same name in both north and south – Ut. Thus if Nguyen Thu Ha was the youngest child she would be known by her family as Ut Ha.

POLITICS

Vietnam is ruled by a Communist government which sits in Hanoi. Elections for the national assembly are held every five years but Vietnam is only a quasi-democracy, though a changing one. There is only one party – the Communist party – but a percentage of non-party delegates is permitted, though these must first be approved by the Fatherland Front. This percentage was increased from 8 to 20 per cent in 1997, but a disparate collection of around 50 individuals cannot represent much of a power bloc against 400 Communist party members.

Additionally, the voting procedure for members of the National Assembly is a vexed issue. Vietnam has one of the highest turnout rates of any country in the world, averaging around 99 per cent. This is due in part to likely deliberate vote-miscounting but also because trouble can be caused for those who do not vote and because the elder member of a family usually block votes for the whole family. This means that the younger voices which are often more in favour of reform are not heard. But cries for reform from a different quarter have just started to be heard; in 1997 for the first time Vietnamese living abroad were allowed to vote (in person only) in the election.

Some have seen in these changes signs that the country is moving ever closer to full-blown democracy with an increasingly powerful national assembly able to challenge the government. But others think that the key issue is whether the changes in leadership in 1997 when the 76-year-old president and 74-year-old prime minister were replaced with younger men are reining back power for the government. If so, the question is power for what? These men are certainly reformers, anxious to continue the country's drive to modernization and Westernization, but neither are advocates of substantial political change, change which would inevitably challenge their positions.

So Vietnam looks set to continue its path of moderate political change against the background of major economic change. Perhaps they, like Gorbachev in Russia, will discover this path is not sustainable, or maybe they'll find some miraculous way to square the circle.

THE ECONOMY

The economy of Vietnam has undergone a remarkable transformation since the government launched a policy of economic 'renovation' (doi moi) 10 years after communism won the war against capitalism.

It's still a very poor country and has not achieved anything like the development of its neighbours, the 'tiger economies', but a lot has been achieved to relieve the poverty of its people through embracing the market and decreasing central planning.

Direct foreign investment really took off in the early 1990s, helped by the US finally lifting its 20-year trade embargo with Vietnam in 1994. But Vietnam still has some central planning, as the economy is dominated by state-owned enterprises – the government keeps trying to privatize them but no-one wants to buy. Still, the closed state of the economy compared to the rest of South-east Asia meant that Vietnam was somewhat insulated from the effects of the Asian crisis in late 1997.

Doi Moi

Torn apart by 20 years of wars against foreign powers and 10 years of attempting to implement dogmatic socialism in the face of economic isolation put Vietnam's ruling Communist party in a tough position in the mid-1980s to launch a programme of economic liberalization. But the initial moves to reform were far-reaching and the entry into the world market of the last untapped emerging market of the Indochina sub-region meant that foreign interest grew quickly. The early 1990s were heady days when interest from the outside world grew and grew.

Since then Vietnam has failed to enter the same league as South-east Asia's tiger economies and foreign interest has slackened. The launching of foreign investment projects is often mired in bureaucratic delays and the need to pay the right amount of sweeteners to the right people, and doubts have emerged about some parts of the Communist party's continued commitment to reform.

The legal basis of capitalism

In 1995 Vietnam enacted a civil code, so it took a big step towards the establishment of a framework for sound business practice. In the legal sphere, since liberalization was launched in 1986, laws have been promulgated governing accountancy standards and bankruptcy procedures and there have been several attempts at tax reform and simplification. These developments are not only attempts to establish a sound legal footing for economic activity, but also represent attempts to improve efficiency in business.

Corruption

But these measures have not been enough to foster efficiency because of the amount of fraud in business which the government is probably only scratching the surface of, and because of widespread corruption in government which is being tackled but with measures which are unlikely to have a significant effect. Fraud cases in business are common and some found guilty have been sentenced to death. By these means the government is trying to show it is getting tough on fraud – but cases continue and it's not clear how much is really changing.

Additionally, government suspicions that local administrative units are the chief culprits in discouraging foreign investment by bureaucratic delays and costly corruption money have led to the government taking decision-making power away from the regions for the four 'first class urban areas' of Ho Chi Minh City, Hanoi, Haiphong and Danang. However, this measure does not prevent foreign companies having to go through an average of nine levels of signatures for the approval of a project, and each level requires a stuffed brown envelope. One foreign investor has estimated that 10 per cent of the total cost of their deal was dispersed in this way. It seems unlikely any changes in the law will bring about a change is this situation, as the problem can go right up to the law-makers.

The real issue is the attempt by the Communist party to implement capitalism in half measures and then generally discovering that this is just not possible.

The current situation
Where does this leave Vietnam's economy? Vietnam has been the fastest growing economy in ASEAN since its entry in 1995. Its growth rate has since dipped from the 1995 high of 9.5 per cent, but was still within the 9-10 per cent target range for the 1996-2000 development plan.

According to the IMF, Vietnam's high output growth was due to increases in productivity and was led by the industrial sector which grew at an average rate of 13 per cent during 1991-5. During this time inflation was brought under control, dropping from 70 per cent in 1991 to a steady three per cent by 1996.

Recent government statistics suggest that Vietnam is 20-25 years behind its successful neighbouring economies. This makes it equivalent to Malaysia in the early 1970s or Thailand in the early 1980s. This is a substantial advance from the 50-year gap it was mired in when economic liberalization was launched in 1986. But the government's aim of 9-10 per cent GDP growth for the next few years rests on what would be an impressive 14-15 per cent growth rate for industry, and a 12-13 per cent growth rate for services. The long-term catch-up aim, the government has announced, is for Vietnam to be an industrialized country by 2020.

Natural advantages
The IMF reported in 1996 that Vietnam had two distinct natural advantages: untapped natural resources and an enviable geographical location.

Through the 1980s and early 1990s reserves of oil, coal, minerals and metals were continually being discovered. However, recent reports from the country indicate that these resources are nearing the point of being fully exploited.

Vietnam's unique geographic location at the centre of South-east Asia, flanking major trade routes is less ephemeral. Two new developments are underway which will increase the attraction of Vietnam's location. Perhaps the most important of these is the building of a deep sea port at Haiphong, enabled by a $60m investment by Belgium, which will mean that Vietnam will have the potential to import and export directly to the rest of the world via deep sea-going vessels without first having to dock at Singapore. The taxes involved in a transfer at Singapore generally double the cost of the goods. A project is also planned to build a grand Trans-Asia highway, which will link Bangkok with Vietnam's major southern port Vung Tao via Cambodia. The highway is targeted for completion in 2010. This could increase the volume of traffic between countries in the region six-fold.

The problem with all this is that especially after the Asian crisis investment is hard to come by. Vietnam is a very poor country – recent figures from the Ho Chi Minh City Statistics Department show average domestic consumption standing at $34 a month, of which 65 per cent is spent on food. But there is a lot of money slooshing around for people in the right places as, for example, a number of newly-forming mobile phone companies in Vietnam are discovering to their satisfaction. The problem in Vietnam, as the name 'emerging market' implies is that the market is still in its infancy and indeed is still barely crawling towards a financial system which enables the wealth which does exist to get round the economy and create more wealth.

But one place where wealth can come from is from Vietnamese returned from overseas – people called the Viet Kieu. Now that the Vietnamese government is looking ever westwards for its economic inspiration it's also looking to the knowledge and skills of overseas Vietnamese. Returning boat people are now welcomed, not rebuffed, so the economy is further helped along and also in this way past divisions begin to be relegated to the past where they truly belong.

How to measure time

Vietnamese history has it that in the days before clocks were invented time was measured according to how long certain everyday activities took. So, three or four minutes were expressed by the time it takes to chew a mouthful of betel leaves. A quarter of an hour was how long it takes to cook a rice pan for three or four people. And half an hour was expressed by the time it takes to cook a pan of rice for ten people.

Practical information for the visitor

DOCUMENTS

If your visa was issued directly by a Vietnamese embassy it will be stamped into your passport, so provided you don't forget that you're all set. Except, that is, for a tiny blue piece of insignificant-looking paper which you complete on arrival, called your **departure card**. You don't absolutely need this to depart – if you lose it you are generally just asked to fill in another one – but every hotel will want to take it from you in order to register you with the police and you will want them to do this because it prevents you having to hand over your passport.

Only rarely in rural backwaters do hotels demand that you leave your passport with them, but in this eventuality handing over photocopies of the visa and key pages of the passport may still leave you with passport in hand. Saying that you need the passport in order to change money at the bank can be a way of ensuring this.

Allowing and issuing **visa extensions** to the standard 30-day tourist visa has gone in and out of fashion with the Vietnamese authorities in recent years so it is best to check with a travel agent when you arrive. The latest situation seems to be that a visa can be extended only by the same amount of time as it was originally granted for ie a one-month visa can be extended for one month, a six-month visa for six etc.

Currently, in Saigon, Hanoi, Danang (and therefore Hoi An), a one-month visa can be extended four times but elsewhere a one-month visa can only be extended one time. It costs $25-35 for the first extension (tending to be cheaper in Saigon than anywhere else) and more for each subsequent extension. The immigration police of any provincial capital can issue you with one but it is best done either at a travel agent in a tourist area or, if you are elsewhere, through a trusted intermediary.

You will need a passport-sized photo of yourself and the process should take only three days. Failing this if you only want to stay on a few days more you can try outstaying your visa – often the worst that happens is that, on leaving, you pay a late-stay fee of $1-2 a day. But it is probably not worth trying to run on empty like this outside of a touristed centre. If you sign up for a 'full time' (minimum ten hours a week) language or other course you can then apply for a six-month renewable **student visa** from the immigration police.

A standard **tourist visa** is single entry, but for a fee, usually $20, plus passport photo and a wait of one or two days travel agents in the main centres can arrange for the immigration police to make your visa double entry.

TRAVEL PERMITS

Until 1988 travel for Vietnamese even within Vietnam was restricted to those who had friends in high places who could obtain the obligatory travel permits. Travel permits for tourists were abolished in 1993 and these days everyone can travel the country freely, with only a very few, changeable, exceptions. The exceptions are changeable because the requirement for travel permits is generally an invention of the local police of an area which lasts until the tourists stop coming or the national government intervenes, whichever is the earlier.

Places which have recently required 'travel permits', costing around $10 a day, include some minority villages around Dalat, the Mai Chau area and Ba Be National Park. It is best to check with travel agents in a tourist centre before heading off to one of these areas, but always be prepared to play it by ear.

ENTERING AND LEAVING THE COUNTRY

Customs procedures are quick and easy if you enter Vietnam by air without carrying guns or drugs and provided you have the same number of receipts for baggage items stuck onto your airline ticket as pieces of baggage. If you fall foul of any of these conditions things are likely to get a little harder. So, for example, if you enter Vietnam overland be prepared for a rigorous search through your baggage to take the place of the airport X-ray machines. It is only likely to be through this procedure that potentially seditious materials will be rooted out and confiscated. In theory this could include certain foreign music and videos etc.

In practice you are unlikely to experience much trouble with customs unless you lose a baggage receipt (this causes a lot of difficulty), are gun-running or are bringing in vast quantities of gold or diamonds. In any event you must fill in a (yellow) customs form when you enter Vietnam, which you keep and need to produce again on leaving, declaring foreign currency and expensive items in your luggage. There is no harm in listing your property on this form and it may ease the passage of your baggage out of the country, though probably it makes no difference. Upon entering you have a duty-free allowance of 200 cigarettes, 1.5 litres of alcohol and perfume and jewellery for personal use.

ACCOMMODATION

Accommodation is likely to be a major component of the cost of your stay in Vietnam, but the good news is that at least it is generally worth it. As more and more hotels have become licensed to take foreigners standards have improved and prices have fallen.

Hotels

Most hotels are friendly and clean, and there is often a charming family-run aspect to the small hotels which can even extend to preparing a meal for you (home-prepared food is generally delicious). It is the influx of small private hotels (mini hotels) into the market that has changed matters, so it is only in small towns with just one newly-built government hotel that prices are exorbitant. Elsewhere you should generally have the choice of a range of hotels and prices.

Bearing in mind that, in general, price depends on occupancy not size of room, and assuming a certain amount of bargaining a clean basic single with fan should cost $4-5, a standard double with shower and fan $10, a double with shower, air-con and IDD telephone around $15-20, and the sky is the limit for luxury hotel rooms and suites. You can normally negotiate a discount for 'long stay', which means anything more than one night.

Every town has its grimy, dingy and generally foul hotel, but even if you wanted to stay there and were permitted as a foreigner to do so (which is often not the case) because of the taxes levied by the government on foreign visitors these are often little, if any, cheaper. Instead, the cheapest accommodation is in dorm rooms in travellers' guest-houses and cafés – $3-4 a night – or in out of the way places not designed for foreigners but where they cannot be refused a bed – such as the rooms at Kep railway station which are $0.30 a night.

Budget hotels generally congregate in a particular area of any town; this guide points the reader towards this area as a first step. Most hotels which can accommodate foreigners advertise it with the word hotel or guest-house in English, but it is worth knowing that the Vietnamese for hotel is *khach san*, and *nha khach* or *nha nghi* means guest-house.

Advance reservations are possible though generally not necessary outside the Tet season (see p101). However, it is worth ringing in advance it you would like to be met at the station and taken to the hotel. Most hotels are happy to do this and it can be very handy if you are due to arrive in a town in the middle of the night; you will not be expected to pay much more of a tip to the driver than the cost of the motorbike or cyclo ride.

❏ Sleep easy

Bed linen in most hotels is clean enough but if you want to ensure good clean cloth next to your skin every night sleeping inside a duvet cover brought from home is my tip for cool clean portable comfort.

Alternatively you can buy silk sleeping bags for around $8 from any tailor in Hanoi, Ho Chi Minh City or Hoi An, but beware that the dye has a habit of colouring your skin whenever you sweat. Primary coloured sleeping bags produce particularly alarming results.

Staying in people's homes

If you are out walking through a rural area, such as in the mountainous region around Sapa, you may be invited to stay in the homes of local people. In theory this could land you, and them, in trouble with the police, but in practice very little is likely to happen.

If you come across a dwelling and are angling after a bed for the night try to be discreet about it; the general rule is that if you are still taking tea or conversing with a host or family by the time night falls they are likely to convey the message that you are welcome to stay for the night.

If you are invited to stay be prepared to rise when the sun does and try to pay particular attention to which water supply is for washing and which is for cooking. A small useful gift such as soap is often sufficient to show appreciation for the hospitality, though a few dollars (US) worth of Vietnamese dong left discreetly will be much appreciated. Such a stay can be a rewarding cultural experience all round though it can have its limitations as most mountain people are likely to know no English or French and speak Vietnamese as a poor second language if at all.

Camping

Camping officially is all but impossible in Vietnam: there are no designated camping sites and because in the last analysis the police have the responsibility for finding accommodation for foreigners they feel the need to prevent you choosing to stay in your own 'thousand star hotel', as the Vietnamese term sleeping on the street.

But sleeping on a beach is unlikely to get you in trouble with the police, though robbery would be a different matter. If you are nevertheless desperate to go camping your best bet is to talk to travel agents in Ho Chi Minh City.

LOCAL TRANSPORT

For information on **trains** within Vietnam see Part 3.

By air

Vietnam Airlines flies all over the country regularly and fairly efficiently, though at a cost. Pacific Airlines also flies between the large cities. Cities which have airports include Hanoi, Haiphong, Hué, Danang, Nha Trang, Dalat, Ho Chi Minh City and Cantho. Many of the airports are fairly close to town centres and easy to get to (though Hanoi is a notable exception).

Flight frequency varies from two or three times a week for out of the way routes to two or three times a day for popular routes, such as

---

❏ **Departure tax**
The departure tax when flying out of Vietnam is $8, payable in US dollars or in dong. The domestic airport service fee is 20,000d.

❏ **Domestic flights**

Vietnam airlines	Frequency (daily)	Cost (one-way foreigner fare)
HCMC–Hanoi	Several flights	1,900,000d
HCMC–Nha Trang	Twice	650,000d
HCMC–Danang	Twice	1,000,000d
HCMC–Hué	Twice	1,000,000d
Danang–Hanoi	Twice	1,000,000d

Other routes such as HCMC–Buon Ma Thuot, HCMC–Pleiku, Pleiku–Danang, Nha Trang–Danang operate three to four times a week, for 400,000-650,000d.

For the latest, somewhat indecipherable, timetable check out 🖥 www.vietnamair.com.vn.

Pacific Airlines flies between HCMC and Hanoi for the same price as Vietnam Airlines (1,900,000d one way). The booking office in HCMC (☎ 08-823 1285) is at 2 Dong Khoi St, opposite Majestic Hotel. The office in Hanoi (☎ 04-733 2159) is at 36 Dien Bien Phu St.

HCMC–Hanoi. Note that although prices are quoted in dong (see box above) you can pay by credit card or in cash.

Thanks to computerization, booking a flight is fairly easy; you just need to show your passport and a valid visa. You can book at a travel agent but it is safer, generally just as efficient, and you avoid a fee if you book in person at a Vietnam Airlines office. They can also tell you over the phone the availability for a particular flight. But beware that although overbooking is no longer a chronic problem it can still happen, especially on holidays and at weekends when flights tend to be busy. For this reason it is always wise to confirm your flight, and turn up early at the airport.

All the airports are fairly basic with not much in the way of comfortable seats or places to eat and drink; HCMC's is probably the best. The flights are comfortable enough and this is where you get fed and watered. Vietnam Airlines has a reasonable safety record and increasingly so as the old Russian planes are replaced with Boeings or Airbus models.

By road

Put simply, travelling by road, in particular long distance, is something you should think carefully about; you are putting your life in the hands of a thousand and one unqualified drivers (there is no driving test) of unsafe vehicles who are in a hurry.

Within towns there are few traffic lights, junctions instead are crossed by an ad-hoc dance of death, but because there is little heavy traffic in towns most moving obstacles are avoidable so you are unlikely to have any serious trouble. Main trunk roads connecting cities are a different matter, however. And quite apart from the endless vicious potholes and constant noise of horns the danger alone of a long journey by road might be enough to make you hesitate. Add to this single-lane trunk roads with a lot of very slow heavy traffic which people drive like lunatics to try to get around and you have a deadly combination. Night journeys are truly perilous and you can count yourself lucky if you have a trip of a few hours by night without at least one near miss.

There are more horror stories of tourists killed or seriously injured in road accidents than by the much better publicized danger of war. You have been warned, but here are the best options.

● **By cyclo** The various forms of bicycle are by far the best way to travel around in a town or city. Vietnam's unique *cyclos* (pedalled rickshaws with the driver positioned behind the comfy double seat for the passenger) provide a wonderfully unencumbered view of the scenes all around you.

Unless you are supremely confident of the correct price always negotiate the fare in advance (even though the driver will try to persuade you not to). This is best done by holding up the amount of money you will pay – this prevents any dollar/dong confusions arising. Cyclos cost about 2000d per km, after good bargaining. They can also be hired for the day. Cyclo drivers are very keen on this because it means guaranteed business all day – offer the multiplication of the kilometre rate plus a little for the waiting times. Cyclos are used by the Vietnamese for transporting everything from unfeasible numbers of people to vast pieces of furniture.

● **By bicycle** Alternatively you can rent bicycles from travellers' cafés, travel agents or hotels for around $1 a day. Usually a small deposit is required and you may even get a rental agreement. Such bicycles are generally bone-shaking no-geared pieces of literal rubbish but they are a great way to get around and do give you independence. You can often buy one for as little as $10. Most will have a built-in lock but this provides almost no protection from theft which is very common. So if you stop at a restaurant or café let them know you have a bike and they will look after it for free. Or park it at one of the many designated parking spots seen around markets etc (around 1000d), but try not to lose the ticket you are given or getting your bike back can be a real task.

❏ **Horses for courses**
To soak up the local colour and to live at least a little like the Vietnamese, bicycles are the best way to see towns, motorbikes the best way to make short excursions, shared taxi (called 'minibus' by the Vietnamese) the pick of transport modes between towns, and local bus the cheapest, most authentic but most gruelling way to make long journeys.

Regular tourist bus services run between most tourist centres, they are efficient, fairly cheap and offer a great deal more comfort than local buses. But the significant downside is that you are cocooned away from Vietnamese life. Very few buses run in some rural areas and only 4WDs are safe in the northwest mountainous regions, especially if it has rained recently.

If you want to do any long-distance biking you are advised to bring your own bike; the state of the roads means that a mountain bike is strongly recommended. It is possible to buy reasonable mountain-style bikes in Hanoi and Ho Chi Minh City; from around $70 for a good Chinese bike to $200 for a Taiwanese make, or around $300 for a Japanese bike. But you may have to shop around a bit and could still be left with doubts about quality.

If you do use the bicycle as a way of seeing the country, repair kits are cheap and easy to find and there are also numerous street-side bicycle repairers in towns. It should cost only around 500d to have a tyre pumped up and 5000d to have a puncture repaired. Noticeboards in travellers' cafés are probably your best bet for selling the bike afterwards.

● **By moped/motorbike** Mopeds and motorbikes are increasingly becoming the most popular form of transport in Vietnam. Whole families get around on a single motorbike. If you don't want to be left out you can either hire your own or you can ride pillion; this is called riding *Honda om* or *xe om*, which translates as 'motorcycle hug' – but you can hold onto the back of the bike and avoid the hug element. Anywhere you see ranks of bikes on a street they are likely to offer xe om – the words may be scrawled on a sign or tree. Bargaining is de rigueur, and you should aim for around 5000d for a five-minute ride, or around $5 for a day.

On roads with little traffic outside towns **motorbike hitch-hiking** is perfectly acceptable; you can flag someone down with a gentle wave of the hand pointing downwards, as if shooing away a brood of ducks, and then negotiate a price into town. A lot of Vietnamese women who ride pillion do so side-saddle which it is not as crazy as it looks. It is surprisingly easy and very comfortable – although you do occasionally see gracefully-positioned girls slide off at low speeds and ungraciously fall to earth!

Renting a moped – a 50cc or less scooter – is easy in any town used to tourists and costs from $3 a day. Any hotel that doesn't have scooters to rent should be able to tell you who does. Bear in mind though that you will not be covered by most standard holiday insurance policies and it may take you some time to be used to the roads. But if you want to take the plunge don't let the lack of experience or a licence hold you back. Scooters are extremely easy to master and most can't go over around 60km/hour.

Renting a motorbike (above 50cc) is meant to be more difficult, requiring a valid international driving licence endorsed for motorbike use. However, this is often waived – although it does mean that if you are stopped by the police without an endorsed international driving licence you are breaking the law.

Motorbikes are readily available for rent in tourist areas from around $10 a day; in non-touristy towns, however, it is often more difficult to find

---

❏ **Petrol**
Petrol is very cheap and readily available. You can buy petrol for around 4000d per litre from official filling stations selling quality-assured petrol or from roadside stalls (where it has usually been watered down).

---

a place to rent any kind of bike and if you do, it is likely to be an old Russian model with rusty gears which are so difficult to drive that even their owners stall them regularly.

In theory you need to be a bona-fide foreign resident to **buy a motorbike**. In practice it is possible to get round this by registering it to a Vietnamese friend, or to the shop where you bought it. The Japanese Honda Dream is a great way to travel (around $2,200 second-hand) but as it is the nation's favourite motorbike it is very susceptible to theft. A lot cheaper is a Russian Minsk 125cc ($350 second-hand). Truly a Russian bike consumes petrol like mad, instantly gets filthy spark plugs and is very easy to stall – but it never gives up. Except when it does.

● **By car** Although it is not possible to rent a car to drive yourself, hiring a car with driver is easy and not too pricey. You can rent from a travellers' café or a mini travel agent – prices start from $30 a day, with no guarantee of quality of car, though they are generally big old comfortable cars – or from a reputable company such as Avis, which has an office in HCMC, or Vietnam Tourism which has offices all over the country. For around $80 a day you will get a plush air-con stereo-equipped car and possibly even a driver who speaks English; a guide, more or less helpful, is usually an obligatory part of the deal.

It is possible to hire either type of car for several days but it is much more of a deal than for only one day. For a trip of several days the price will depend not only on the kilometres, and on the nights spent but also on the terrain, and on whether the driver wants to go there anyway or not. For a few days travelling it is always wise to see the car, meet the driver, agree a (flexible) itinerary, and establish who is to pay for petrol and food. It is best to let the driver pay for his own accommodation as it makes sure he is charged the Vietnamese, not tourist, price. If you are going to mountainous areas make sure the car is a 4WD and looks as if it would make the journey.

● **By taxi** The major cities have good well-run **meter taxi** companies, with new cars, air-con and stereo. But only HCMC is really large enough to warrant travelling within the city by car, unless you are in the middle of monsoon storms. For most meter taxis the way to tell if they are for hire is if there is a red light on, on the dashboard.

Shared taxi (minibus) is in many ways the best road vehicle to get about the country. They are generally easy to find, fast, fairly comfortable and have you journeying with Vietnamese people while keeping your luggage safe and your costs reasonable. Shared taxis are small modern Japanese people carriers with room for around 6-11 people.

Many towns have a particular spot where the shared taxis congregate in the mornings until around 11am, often around the bus station. They can also be flagged down on main roads between towns. The driver's henchman is the one whose eyes you want to catch. He is also the one who will set the tone for the car and makes it recognisable as a shared taxi by leaning out of the window announcing its arrival or its town of destination.

Shared taxis are faster than buses, in better state of repair, far more comfortable (although they too can fill up), and may not be much more expensive than a tourist-priced bus ticket, depending on your bargaining ability and how full the vehicle is when you get to it. A good price is $2 per 100km, although you may often be asked to pay much more than this. Some people get dropped off directly at their homes and you can negotiate to be taken to your hotel.

● **By bus** Vietnam has a huge range of **local buses** and **'express' buses** connecting towns and cities at often dirt cheap prices. But 'you have about as much comfort as sardines that have been overpacked into tins and put into an oven to slow roast' (Jo from England). And about as much roadspeed. Plus if your luggage isn't preventing your every move it is up on the roof away from your protective gaze. One traveller was caught helplessly trapped inside a bus as he watched someone take his luggage from the roof, inspect it, and remove his camera. Some buses making long journeys run to timetables but others don't and in any event be assured that almost all buses will leave in the very early morning – from 5.30am onwards. As a last resort you may be able to flag down a bus along a main road out of town.

Irrespective of when or where you buy your ticket the price can vary: in some areas you may be asked for the Vietnamese price, in others the price charged is often about five times this. The Vietnamese pay about 12,000d for a journey of 50km. You are often able to get a better price if you flag down a bus rather than buying the ticket in the bus station, but be aware that if the conductor realizes you are desperate – eg if you are miles from anywhere – you can be ripped off right royally. One of my fellow travellers reported 'We were once asked for $50 each for a 50km trip and were manhandled and threatened we would be thrown off if we didn't pay!' (With the help of some Marlboros and a great many smiles we weren't and didn't.) For connections between major cities you can pay a little more and get an express bus for a little more comfort, but not much more speed.

❏ **Dollars**
Unless specified, prices quoted in dollars are given in US dollars.

❏ **You can't be chicken if you want to cross the road**
Many visitors find the experience of crossing a road chock-a-block with all manner of bicycles, cyclos, cars, carts, trucks and buses a surprisingly difficult and even rather terrifying experience. But there is a secret to it – don't make death-defying leaps to cross the whole road in a single bound as the other occupants of the road will not be expecting this and will have trouble reacting to avoid you in time. Instead, begin walking slowly across the road, not stopping, moving ever forwards, just as if you literally do own the road, until hey presto you're at the other side. Well, it feels that simple sometimes – after practice.

If your first taste of the experience is on Ho Chi Minh City's huge boulevards, then good luck. The alternative, of course, is to go everywhere in a cyclo, in which case you will find yourself being swept forward into the full flow, propelled from behind with nothing between you and the traffic. Enjoyable enough if you're up to it but you may find it even more terrifying than the pedestrian approach.

There are a number of dedicated **tourist bus services** running around the country. Hotels, travellers' cafés, and travel agents offer mini tours around Vietnam (see p95) and 'open tickets' enabling you to get on and off the bus in major centres where and when you choose.

These buses let you travel in comfort, if not style, with cushioned seats and air-con. The downside is that you are shut away from all Vietnamese life. But if you can stand the caged-in environment the services are regular, friendly and very good value at $32 between HCMC and Hué, and $22 between Hué and Hanoi. Several different companies offer these tickets and their services differ a little, though not much. The most reliable providers are Kim Café and Sinh Café (HCMC), Lac Thanh restaurant (Hué), and Old Darling Café and Real Darling Café (Hanoi).

By water
There are a number of ferry routes in Vietnam such as along the waterways of the Mekong and out to the island of Cat Ba and connecting Haiphong with Halong Bay. The crossings are cheap but generally very slow and often crowded and hot.

A far more pleasant way to travel is by smaller boat; it is usually possible to hire a small boat in areas such as Hué, Nha Trang, Ninh Binh, Halong Bay and the Mekong Delta where there is stunning scenery. But apart from on the Mekong and its charming narrow tributaries it is sadly very difficult to hire living, working, Vietnamese-style boats such as reed sampans rather than more showy tourist boats. The topography of Vietnam means that rivers are not of much use in getting around the country, except in the Mekong where they are the main mode of transport as well as the focus of life.

TOURS

Ho Chi Minh City and Hanoi are well equipped with travel agents and travellers' cafés offering mini tours from a day to a week long of the surrounding areas such as the Mekong and the Cu Chi tunnels in the south and Halong Bay, Cat Ba Island, and the mountains of Sapa or relics of Dien Bien Phu in the north. Hué is full of places offering DMZ tours, and Nha Trang's speciality is boat trips. Prices and itineraries vary considerably from travel agent to travel agent so it is worth shopping around. Vietnam Tourism rates are always the highest, which is only partly due to the quality of hotel you will be put up in.

Travellers' cafés advertise their tours heavily with photos of sights on the trip and comments by satisfied customers. The tours are popular because from as little as $35 all inclusive for a five-day tour they are good value and provide instant companionship for a trip which usually only has to be booked the day before. Taking such a tour can be a good value way of being shown around the sights and it may enable you to see things you wouldn't otherwise have access to – such as a rice husking factory or paper mill.

Tours of the Mekong make the inevitable boat trips bargaining free experiences, and also deserve to be popular because many of the guides used by the travellers' cafés were associated with the South Vietnamese regime and the interesting stories they tell are brought alive when they point out bomb craters or show you round VC jungle headquarters. But think hard before you hand over your money about whether a tour is likely to be your cup of tea.

Whoever you book through, it will consist of being cooped up in a minibus for hours every day with a load of tourists driven to sights and then herded around them. You have very little flexibility and if you are unsatisfied and wish to leave the tour half way expect no refund. Unless you are in a large group already there are often better ways of seeing the country. And how many factories do you really want to see round? Nonetheless the tours are often tempting because they are so cheap; a two-day tour including accommodation may cost as little as $20.

GUIDES

It is generally easy to find someone to guide you round an area ($5-10 a day) by asking at your hotel or in cafés before 10am or after 6pm. More often than not guides will find you rather than vice versa. Having someone show you round can be a great way to get more of an understanding of local sights and sounds, although it is rather the luck of the draw as you can never really be sure who you are getting. The DMZ is the area in which you will most benefit from having a guide (named guides for this area who charge around $10 a day are listed in this book). Bear in mind that if you eat together you will be expected to pay.

In theory it is illegal for a Vietnamese to be paid for being an unofficial guide but you are unlikely to have any problems provided you reassure the police if stopped that the person is just a friend. Of course an alternative is to hire an official guide from Vietnam Tourism. For around $15 a day any government tourist office will furnish you with an English-speaking guide.

In the past part of the job of these guides was to keep tabs on tourists and report back, but this is unlikely to happen unless you do particularly strange things. If you want a guide for a long-distance ambitious trip (such as Buon Ma Thuot to Nha Trang by pedallo) you should forget about the official tourist agencies and prepare yourself for a long process of asking around.

ELECTRICITY

The electric current in almost all buildings is 220V/50Hz (cycles), but some old buildings run on 110V/50Hz. Sockets use American-style two-pin plugs; adaptors are readily available in all cities and cost around $1 (much less than in the West).

Power cuts frequently occur, especially during the dry winter season in the south because of the reliance on hydro-electric power. In the event of a power cut businesses will often have diesel generators which will kick in, but it is always wise to have a torch (flashlight) with you. Rural areas often rely wholly on diesel generators. Power surges are also common in Vietnam. Hardly any electric connections are earthed, so be very careful when you plug something in if you want to avoid an electric shock. More seriously, beware of live connections made by open wires in low-grade hotels and open areas providing some shared electricity points, such as on pillars at quays.

TIME

Vietnam is seven hours ahead of GMT. There is a single time zone for the country and it does not operate a 'summer time'. So at 6pm anywhere in Vietnam it is 7am in New York, 11am in London and 9pm in Sydney. These differences will be an hour reduced during countries' summer time: so, for example 6pm in Vietnam will be noon in London under British Summer Time. China also operates summer time meaning that it is an hour ahead of Vietnam between April and October.

Apart from China, Vietnam's neighbours share the same time zone.

(**Opposite**) **Top**: Rice piled high in Hoi An market. **Bottom**: The French colonial period has had a strong influence on food in Vietnam; local bakeries produce crusty baguettes and a range of pastries fresh each day. The cakes at Hanoi's Kinh Do Café (Café 252), pictured here, even come with a recommendation from Catherine Deneuve.

MONEY

The Vietnamese currency is the dong. Prices in some hotels and shops are quoted in US dollars, but it is always possible to pay in dong, and often the Vietnamese prefer dong, quoting dollars only for ease. Indeed, in north Vietnam you can use the dollar/dong exchange rate as a tool in bargaining negotiations by agreeing a price in dollars but then paying in dong at the rate the vendor suggests – it will often be a bit lower than the official rate. The south Vietnamese are much more savvy, however, and if you try it with them you are likely to find yourself on the wrong end of the deal.

❏ **Exchange rates**		
Australia	$1	7570d
Canada	$1	9423d
Europe	Euro 1	12,290d
New Zealand	$1	5660d
UK	£1	21,000d
USA	$1	14,000d

For up-to-the-minute exchange rates visit **www.xe.net/currency**.

Dollar cash can be exchanged at a more or less preferential rate almost everywhere, except in rural areas where it is essential to bring enough dong cash to see you through. Cash in other currencies can be exchanged at banks.

ANZ has brilliantly hassle-free and cheap ATM facilities for Cirrus and Delta card holders in HCMC and Hanoi, and HSBC also has an ATM in HCMC. There are also branches of other foreign banks in Hanoi and HCMC. You can withdraw money on credit or debit cards in banks all over Vietnam for two to four per cent commission. This is fairly cheap, but the charges your credit card company will lay on you are not – interest is chargeable daily and at a high rate. If you have a Visa debit card, and funds in a bank account, you can withdraw cash for only the cost of this commission.

Travellers' cheques can be exchanged at most banks; dollar American Express or MasterCard ones are the easiest to exchange. Vietkom banks generally offer the best rate, although different branches charge different levels of commission.

POST AND TELECOMMUNICATIONS

Vietnam's postal and telecommunications system is fairly reliable and efficient, though expensive. Be aware that all communication links are monitored by the government so it is sensible to be careful what you say if you want to avoid problems and ensure your communication gets through.

(Opposite): Ethnic minorities make up some 13 per cent of Vietnam's total population. The Black Hmong people (see p282), pictured here, migrated to the Sapa area from southern China about 300 years ago.

Post

A post office (*buu dien*) is to be found in every city, town and even village. Main post offices offer express post, fax, telegram, telex and international telephone services, and most tend to be open from around 7am until at least 8pm. It is only at a centre's main post office that you can witness the stamps on your letters being stamped; a sensible precaution as it ensures they are not removed by underpaid postal workers. The staff in post offices are generally friendly and helpful and almost always speak some English. So post offices are often a good place to turn if you have a problem in a small town and cannot find English speakers.

❏ **Addresses**
Addresses in Vietnam are written as follows:

Chi Nguyen Thu Ha
43 Le Duan
Quan 1
T.P. Ho Chi Minh

meaning

Miss Nguyen Thu Ha
43 Le Duan Street
District 1
Thanh Pho (City) Ho Chi Minh City

While sending domestic letters is fairly cheap at 400d, the rate for international post is relatively high. Sending a postcard to Europe costs 7000d, to USA 8000d, to near Asia and Australasia 6000d. Posting a letter costs 10,500d to Europe, 12,500d to the USA, and 9000d to near Asia and Australasia. This seems expensive to foreigners but is unaffordable for many Vietnamese, which is something to bear in mind if you write to any Vietnamese you have met; buying extra stamps and sending them back is one solution. Items over 20kg must be shipped out. Shipping is much cheaper than air mail, but takes three to four months. The first kilogram costs $10-15 (according to the destination), and each additional kilogram costs $1-2.

Mail sent from Vietnam is a little quicker to arrive in Australasia than Europe or America and can take as little as ten days, though it can take up to a month and indeed is likely to if sent from a small town or village. Stamps and envelopes are not adhesive on the back, hence the pots of glue in all post offices.

Poste Restante services at the main post office in the major cities are organized and it is easy to receive letters here. You need to show your passport to pick them up. Receiving parcels is much more of a deal. They are opened and inspected in front of you and offending items – which include political material and can extend to videos, compact discs and cassettes – may be confiscated. Federal Express has an office next to the main post offices in Ho Chi Minh City and Hanoi.

Telephone/fax

Vietnam is one of the most expensive countries in the world to phone to and from, though phoning into the country tends to be half the price of phoning out. Thanks to Vietnam's move to digital technology international calls are at least easy to make: international direct dialling (IDD) is available from all main post offices and from most medium-priced hotels.

The cheapest way to make a call is to reverse charges from a post office, or call IDD from a post office. Operator-assisted calls are around 10 per cent more expensive and you are automatically charged for three minutes; hotel charges are variable but rarely negligible. Standard-rate charges apply from 7am to 11pm Mondays to Saturdays. Charges at other times and on public holidays are around 15 per cent cheaper. After the first minute the length of calls is count-

> ❏ **Useful numbers**
> Police 113
> Fire 114
> Directory enquiries 116 or 108
> (Hanoi 04-108,
> Saigon 08-1080)
> International operator 110

ed in six-second chunks, though be warned that most hotels count one second as one minute. See the box below for details of the standard-rate charges for IDD calls from a post office to the rest of the world.

Local calls, for example within towns and cities, are free up to a certain limit per month, after which they cost a miniscule 65d per minute. As a result, bars and restaurants are often happy to let you use the phone to make a local call. Calling from area to area is not particularly cheap, however: Hanoi to Ho Chi Minh City (HCMC) costs $0.33 per minute. Both Hanoi and HCMC have yellow pages equivalents and directory enquiries services (at which there is always someone who speaks English).

Directory enquiries within Hanoi or HCMC costs only 300d per minute.

Email
Vietnam is well and truly joining the computer age – despite substantial government censorship. More and more businesses are getting connected,

❏ **Phone charges** Country groups	**$ per minute first minute**
Cambodia, Laos, Thailand, Malaysia, Hong Kong, Singapore	$2.45
China, Taiwan, Australia, South Korea, Indonesia, Philippines, Myanmar, Brunei	$3.32
USA, Canada, Japan, Eastern Europe, Russia	$3.28
Western and Northern Europe, India	$4.01
Southern Europe, New Zealand, Pacific Islands	$4.20
Middle East, South America, Africa	$4.23

Fax rates for the same country groups ascend from $4.50 for the first page and $3.60 for each additional page, up to $6.75 and $5.25. The cost per word on a telegram rises from $0.23 to $0.65.

and cyber cafés are springing up everywhere. If a town does not yet have a cyber café you can almost always get online at its main post office – for only 250d per minute. Cyber cafés usually cost more, from 300d per minute, to 1000d at swanky hotels.

While email is great for contacting hotels and reserving rooms, and for keeping in contact with home, beware that government surveillance is constant and real and messages do go astray, simply for containing a controversial word such as corruption. This is especially so for addresses run by the governmental ISPs – including endings vnn.vn and netnam – but the government controls access to the whole of the web including hotmail and yahoo addresses. Emails also seem to go undelivered entirely unaccountably. However, it is fair to say that most emails get through, eventually.

FESTIVALS AND PUBLIC HOLIDAYS

Brightly-coloured flags and banners lining the streets, prettily-packaged gifts of flowers or food filling the shops are the hallmarks of many Vietnamese festivals. They are often colourful and noisy events, reaching a zenith in the famous Tet festival bringing in the lunar new year. Many are regionally based and some are primarily private family affairs.

As well as traditional festivals timed according to the lunar calendar there are a number of national holidays based on fixed dates in the Gregorian calendar. Christmas and New Year's Day have recently been reinstated as public holidays.

The most notable holidays and festivals are listed below. Lunar dates have been converted into dates on the Gregorian calendar for the years 2001 and 2002.

1 January New Year's Day, a public holiday.
6-13 February (25 February to 3 March 2001, 24 February to 2 March 2002) Tet (Tet Nguyen Dan). The welcoming of the lunar new year is Vietnam's most important religious festival and the most dazzling (see box on p101).
11 February (1 March 2001, 28 February 2002) Tay Son festival to commemorate the victory of the Tay Son brothers over the Vietnamese rulers with Chinese assistance. Mock battles and colourful marches are staged in Tay Son district.
21 February (11 March 2001, 11 March 2002) Ha Loi festival celebrating the Trung sisters' victory over the Chinese army in AD41. Each year in Den Citadel (Cu An Hamlet, 40km north of Hanoi) there is a day of games and entertainments.
22 March Merian festival at the Po Nagar Cham towers in Nha Trang celebrates the lady protectoress of the city symbolized in statue form in the Cham towers – rituals surround the bringing of gifts and the cleaning and decorating of the statue.

❏ Tet festival

The Tet festival celebrates the lunar new year and is Vietnam's biggest festival by a long way. The celebrations can be a glorious spectacle, though be prepared for endless noise (to drive evil spirits away) and closed museums. Even more important to note; Tet is a time when most Vietnamese visit relatives. This means that flights and hotels may well be full, and roads and trains very busy. The whole country used to take three months to prepare for it but in a productivity drive the government has managed to whittle the revelry down to a few weeks and only three days of public holiday. Still, every family will stretch their budget to the maximum, and often beyond, so as to partake in a mass spending spree, and then will take as much time off as possible in order to spend time with the family, honour ancestors, welcome spirits and let off the noisiest fireworks they can find.

While many of the festivities are just family occasions there is also a lot of socialising in public and a continual air of excitement, and sulphur. The most private day of the festivities is the first day of the new year, immediately followed on the second day by the start of the public shows such as dancing, buffalo fighting and wrestling.

While the celebration of the lunar new year originates from Vietnam's adoption of the Chinese calendar, and fireworks are often imported, most of the traditions of Tet are Vietnam's own. For example, much of Tet focuses around the kitchen god, or *tau quan*. The Vietnamese believe (or these days keep up the tradition as if they did) that every kitchen hosts a kitchen god which watches over the household through the year and then, on the 23rd day of the 12th lunar month goes to heaven to report to the Jade Emperor on the worth of the family. But they are not infallible – offerings of whisky as well as food and incense are given in the hope that the god will get drunk and remember only the good things about the family.

It is because the kitchen god is in heaven away from the house during Tet that the family loses their protection against evil spirits so instead a constant barrage of noise and light must be kept up, hence fireworks are the perfect solution. On the first day of the new year the kitchen god is thanked for their care during the year and a new kitchen god is welcomed for the next year. Only good things should be said during this day and the first visitor of the new year to a home brings all their good, or bad, luck with them which stays in the house for the rest of the year. So this encounter is rarely left to chance. If you should be honoured with an invitation be on your best behaviour.

Special foods and gifts are on sale in the lead up to Tet and are thought to bring good luck for the new year. If you want to give a gift fruit, plants, flowers, crystallized ginger or candied lotus seeds are all good. Peach (for the northerner) or apricot (for the southerner) tree branches are also good as they are thought to ward off evil spirits for the new year.

Tet is also very much a time to worship ancestors. A sacrifice for ancestors is held on the last afternoon of the old year to welcome their souls back to earth for three days to share the Tet celebrations. As the official Vietnamese history of the Tet tradition states: 'The first day is reserved for the cult of ancestors; the second to near relatives, and the third day is also consecrated to defuncts.'

22 March-25 April (9 April to 13 May 2001, 1 April to 3 May 2002)
Huong Tich festival of the Perfume Pagoda. During this time many thousands of Vietnamese make a pilgrimage to the beautiful mountain and river scenery of Perfume Pagoda (60km south-west of Hanoi, see p263). There is more chanting by monks than usual but the waterways and paths are almost overrun with people and stalls.

10 April (28 April 2001, 18 April 2002) Thanh Minh, Festival of the Dead is a day of private ancestor worship; gifts are offered to the dead in solemn visits to graves.

12 April (30 April 2001, 20 April 2002) Thay Pagoda festival celebrating the life of To Dau Hanh, a revered Buddhist monk, with music and water puppetry at the pagoda 40km south-west of Hanoi in Ha Son Binh province.

30 April Liberation Day is a public holiday commemorating the day on which North Vietnamese tanks burst through the gates of the Presidential Palace in Saigon and the South surrendered. Flags are flown everywhere and many cities see evening parades.

1 May International Labour Day is also a public holiday making this a long weekend of celebrations.

13 May (30 May 2001 and 21 May 2002) Phat Dan festival celebrating the birth of Buddha. Celebrations are held at pagodas throughout the country and in peoples' homes.

8 June (25 June 2001, 15 June 2002) Tet Doan Ngu summer solstice festival. At this time when the sun is at its peak people offer gifts to the Gods to ward off ill-health and death. They also make symbolic gestures like dropping lemon juice into their eyes to make them shine, or burning human effigies.

17 August (2 September 2001, 24 August 2002) Vu Lan festival, or Wandering Souls Day is a day of worshipping for dead relatives. It is important religiously and offerings of exotic fruits to the dead are made in pagodas and homes. Special prayers are also made to all the dead who have no living descendants. After the festival, the food prepared for the dead is often distributed to poor children.

15 September (2 October 2001, 23 September 2002) Trung Thu or Moon festival celebrates the peak of the fullness of the moon. It is a festival for children in the days before which adults buy them colourful toys or differently-shaped illuminated lanterns and sweet banh, or mooncakes, made of sticky rice, eggs and lotus seeds; beware, these tend to hang around in the shops long after moon day while the eggs inside steadily go off. In some towns there is an evening procession on the day itself.

2 September National Day is Vietnam's most important secular public holiday celebrating the anniversary of Ho Chi Minh's founding of the Republic of Vietnam in 1945. Flags fly in even the smallest of towns and the major cities host parades and outdoor celebrations.

3 September This day is often still celebrated as the anniversary of Ho Chi Minh's death even though the government has admitted that he died on 2 September and the announcement was postponed because the date collided with National Day.

7 October (26 October 2001, 16 October 2002) Tet Trung Cuu or Double Nine festival – the coming of winter is celebrated all over the north by children flying kites.

10 November (30 November 2001, 21 November 2002) Welcome the Moon festival is celebrated in Khmer minority areas in the Mekong Delta. There are dances and entertainments and the stunning climax is the noisy colourful spectacle of the famous Ghe Ngo boat race. The beautifully-carved long wooden boats with 40-50 men apiece racing against each other down the swift flowing river is an unforgettable sight. The race is held near the Soc Trang Khmer temple, 65km south-east of Cantho.

25 December Christmas is a public holiday celebrated more in the south than north because of the greater number of Catholics.

There are also many other small regional festivals, religious events or celebrations of historic events, plus lucky and unlucky days throughout the year – which may affect the desire of some Vietnamese to do business on a particular day. The number 13 is unlucky as in the West, but here three is also an unlucky number. So it is considered bad luck to take photographs of three people. But nine is a lucky number, as in China.

TOILETS AND TOILET PAPER

If you haven't been to Asia before and are unaccustomed to the insalubrious toilets in France and Italy, be prepared. While almost every hotel or mini-hotel is equipped with Western toilets all more primitive places to stay, bia hoi stalls, eateries and trains specialize in the squat loo. These can take a bit of getting used to – the key thing is to plant your feet firmly on the two pedals (affectionately known as clutch and brake) and, well, aim.

The usual system is that there is a supply of water nearby to sloosh down the hole. Toilet paper is generally not provided in such establishments, but even if it is note that you really mustn't send it glooping down the hole too – because the cesspit systems are just not equipped to deal

---

❏ **Affection not urination!**
In August 1998 Vietnam's official government newspaper, the *Ten Phuong (Vanguard)*, made an attempt to turn the older conservative public away from traditional values and instead embrace more youthful values. Specifically: 'It's time for the older people to have more tolerance and less prejudice about the youth. It is ironic that people say it is awful to kiss in public when men are unashamed to urinate in the streets.'

with it. Instead a bucket is usually to be found next to the toilets and it's in here that you should put your used paper. Often Western toilets in hotels have a bucket which means that even this seemingly-modern system cannot deal with toilet paper; if you were to flush it down the loo the problem would go away only for you.

FOOD

Whether you dine in the smartest restaurants or at tiny streetside stalls, travelling in Vietnam can be gastronomic heaven. Sumptuous food sizzles and steams on every street corner; the florid bouquet of lemongrass and garlic sends an olfactory message about the culinary delight that awaits you.

Vietnamese food is best described as oriental but with distinctive characteristics of its own. Some say it's like a fusion of Chinese and Thai food but this is not the whole story. Vietnamese cuisine has certainly been highly influenced by Chinese cooking techniques, and in the south especially, it shares Thai methods but Vietnam has the added influence of French cuisine, plus its own traditions.

Flavours and texture

Vietnam shares with China the concept that dishes should be a harmonious combination of the 'five flavours' – salty, sweet, sour, bitter and hot tastes. Stir frying is also the dominant cooking technique, but the Vietnamese use only a very little oil, less than most regions in China do, making it in general very healthy food. Also, more vegetables and herbs are eaten raw. And this makes for one of the unique aspects of Vietnamese cuisine – every single dish must have contrasting textures as well as contrasting and complementing tastes. Shallots, sesame seeds or roasted peanuts are quick fried and added to the top of noodle dishes or salads, while crisp raw vegetables and/or fresh herbs or small squeezes of lime are added to a dish just before it is served, or are added in between bites giving a greater dimension to the food.

Judicious splashes of rich *nuoc mam* (fish sauce) are also an invaluable adornment to most dishes. The result is a lightness and freshness in the cuisine balancing often rich flavours with an exquisite subtlety.

Western influences

The French influence is visible in the light airy baguettes sold from street stalls after being heated lightly on grills, or carried along the streets in sack cloth balanced on girls' heads. The bread is best eaten with half an avocado as a filling or as part of the delicious ubiquitous ham sandwich – *banh mi kep thit hun khoi*. The French influence is less visible but is discernible in the tenderness of meat, and in the south many dishes are sautéed in a frying pan rather than stir-fried in a wok.

If you find coming across 'La Vache Qui Rit' cheese in street stalls incongruous, bear in mind that it is because of the French influence that Vietnam is unusual for non-Western countries in its consumption of dairy products. Here you find butter – *bo* from the French *buerre*; cheese – *pho mat* from *fromage*; yoghurt – pronounced ya waw – and even café au lait, even if the milk used is sweetened condensed milk.

Also, because of its trading history with other European countries such as Holland, Vietnam has known corn, potatoes and snow peas almost as long as seafaring European countries like England have.

Regional variations

Food in Vietnam varies, particularly from north to south. Southern food is very aromatic, most dishes contain sugar, and many travellers prefer it, but there are also some very fine dishes particular to the north (see p259). Needless to say most southerners and northerners hate each others' style of food; northerners saying they can't stand the sugar in southern food and southerners saying northern food is just so unsubtle.

Southern food has been more influenced by French cuisine, while the north shows a greater Chinese influence – more congees and stews. The town of Hoi An is in many ways the food capital of Vietnam; with its cosmopolitan influences through the centuries the town has developed several wonderful dishes, of which *cao lau* (a dish of soup, noodles, ham and herbs topped with crumbled biscuity rice paper producing multi-layered textures and tastes) perhaps epitomizes Vietnamese cuisine. Good food is cheap everywhere in Vietnam (see p11) but in Hoi An it is fantastically so – a filling dish of cao lau in a smart restaurant will set you back a mere $0.30. Nha Trang does the best 'fast food' in the quick fried eggy pancakes called *banh xeo*, literally meaning noise pancake.

Hué is another contender for the top food spot of the country – in theory the city boasts more than 2000 possible dishes, developed because every meal for the emperor had to consist of 50 dishes. Hué's fabulous seafood specialities are famous throughout Vietnam. Hué makes its own extremely-pungent version of the fish sauce found everywhere, nuoc mam, made with prawns instead of fish. Also, many areas have their own specialities; this book describes them and tells you how to find them.

Ingredients

Most of the ingredients used in Vietnamese cuisine are found in other Asian cooking; rice, noodles, bamboo shoots, beansprouts, Chinese cabbage and water spinach feature in many meals. Water spinach is ideal for Vietnamese cuisine because the colours of the leaf and stem are different and so too the textures because the leaf becomes soft in cooking while the stem remains crunchy.

Vietnamese cuisine also uses the common herbs and spices of Asia – chilli, ginger, basil, coriander, lemongrass and garlic. But everywhere you will find that the emphasis is on using raw vegetables or herbs on the top of the dish to complement the herbs which have infused the food during cooking and to add varieties of texture and colour.

Vietnam's long coastline means that seafood is eaten everywhere but in the highlands. In any centre near the sea you will usually come across several different types of fish, including cuttlefish and abalone, and other seafood including lobster, king prawns, squid, eel and crab. There are also excellent freshwater fish to be found including types of mud-fish.

Chicken is a staple meat dish, while duck is a little rarer. Pork is probably the most common meat served after chicken, and pork paté and pork fat are used to great effect in the delicious ham sandwich served at the tiniest street stalls.

Beef is more common in the north than in the south because there is more suitable land there for cattle to graze upon. Freshwater frogs (the whole creature, not just the legs) are served in most of the country and are often delicious.

Rice and noodles

Rice is the staple of most Vietnamese meals, whether as grains, rice noodles, or rice paper. The vast stretches of luminous green rice paddies in the Vietnamese lowlands shows that rice is an integral part of the Vietnamese economy, it covers three-quarters of the cultivated land. It also forms a major part of the Vietnamese diet – the average person eats 340g of rice a day.

Grains of rice are bound together to make sticky desserts or sweet breakfast snacks or are plainly served to accompany a meat or vegetable dish; rice noodles are added to soup to make bowls of filling *pho*, and rice paper wraps spring rolls when fried to make a crisp golden-brown casing.

There are literally dozens of kinds of rice, each varying a little in flavour and texture but a lot in colour, aroma, gluten and expense, as you can see from any market stall. Rice noodles can be round, *bun*, flat and thick – *mi* or *pho*, or thin and clear vermicelli, *mien*.

❏ Wild food

In Vietnam you can also sample several different kinds of 'wild food'. Southerners eat field mice and several kinds of snake (see p157), in the highlands north of Hanoi game and dishes such as roast squirrel are common, while dog is considered an extremely nutritious and even virility-enhancing food and is commonly consumed in much of the country, especially in Hanoi and the highlands.

In case you decide to sample it, be aware that hot dog is much better than cold dog. Roast dog tastes somewhat like beef. In case you think the practice of eating dog a dubious one, remember that it's largely because of it that Vietnam is free of the packs of dogs frighteningly common in some other Asian countries.

Salads

Vietnamese salads are wonderful combinations of raw vegetables and meat or seafood topped with lotus seeds, roasted peanuts or sesame seeds. A salad is intended to accompany other dishes rather than as a meal in itself. You will generally only find salads in good restaurants rather than at street stalls, which is just as well as the more confident you can be of the cleanliness of the water the raw vegetables are washed in, the better.

Some of the ingredients of salads are common to Western salads – such as carrot and cucumber – but instead of the vegetables being cut directly before eating they are left to stand in salt and after being washed are squeezed thoroughly to ensure the salad is truly crunchy.

Snacks

There are several kinds of filling snacks that can be picked up from street stalls, street vendors or sellers on buses or railway platforms. They do not all tend to be to Western tastes, though. *Gio* is a strong-tasting snack of lean sliced or pounded meat tightly wrapped in banana leaves and boiled.

Glass cabinets on the streets often contain large white balls of dough, *banh bao*, which are Chinese-style pastries filled with a heady mixture of meat and vegetables or with more palatable sweet shredded coconut and sugar. Something that makes a fabulous snack when served with different sauces and chutneys is *banh da* which are huge poppadum-like crisps covered with black sesame seeds. But beware of eating these from beach sellers because they're not great without the sauces.

Banh xeo which at its best is served with crisp raw vegetables, which you wrap yourself in rounds of starchy rice paper and then dip into nuoc mam, makes a great snack. (The ability to wrap the rice paper neatly and produce a strong structure for dipping tends to become a matter of unreasonable pride.)

Banh xeo are similar to the ultimate in Vietnamese snacks – spring rolls. Although these share some characteristics with Chinese spring rolls they are also distinctively different – most notably Vietnamese spring rolls are served with fresh coriander and mint leaves which are wrapped into a whole crisp lettuce leaf and dipped into nuoc mam, so giving the dish variety in texture as well as in flavour. Spring rolls are called *nem*, and there are many different varieties depending on whether the filling is beef, pork, prawn, crab or just vegetables.

Condiments

As well as having unique dishes, a unique stress on variety in texture as well as flavour, and unique historical influences, Vietnam also has a unique condiment – the orange-coloured fish sauce called nuoc mam. It is different from the fish sauces used in other Asian countries, and is used compulsively in dishes much as soy sauce is in China.

Nuoc mam is made by salting fish heavily and leaving them to ferment for months in wooden or steel barrels. (It's probably best not to think too much about the implications of fermentation for fish – as it involves successive generations of maggots.) Although it may seem unlikely the flavour is good and it strengthens over time, but as with olive oil the liquid produced from the first draining is considered the finest. Different spices and species of fish are used by the many nuoc mam makers along the coastline to produce a variety of flavours but the strong odour seems fairly universal.

Condiments that you are likely to find on a restaurant table or streetside stall are chillies (often in the form of chilli sauce which is usually bright red in colour), and thin, pale but strong nuoc mam, or a nuoc mam with added garlic, chilli, sugar and lemon or lime juice according to the chef's taste. Soy sauce is also often offered and the salt-like substance put on tables is usually not salt but monosodium glutamate (MSG) *(bot ngot)*. Foreigners are often wary of MSG which can cause headaches, hyperactivity and other symptoms but it is worth remembering that it needn't be feared as a chemical additive as it is in fact a plant extract.

Desserts and fruit

The Vietnamese have a very sweet tooth and their **desserts** have been influenced by the conquering French and the visiting Americans. The French influence can be seen in numerous pastries, doughnuts and cakes, *banh* and even crème caramels, although all tend to be slightly heavier and stickier than their Parisian counterparts. Meanwhile the Americans left behind a love of ice cream *(kem,* from the French *crème)* and the ice cream you find in smarter cafés comes from a number of flourishing kem factories.

Vietnam also has a number of traditional sweets, such as the sticky egg cakes eaten during the Moon festival. Yoghurt is common, sweetened or natural (the finest home-made variety comes from Café 252 in Hanoi, see p261). The milk from the national milk company Vinamilk is sweetened (Vina derives from the first two letters of Viet and the first two of Nam to produce, ironically, a very non-Vietnamese-sounding name), and very sweet condensed milk in coffee or the blended avocado drink is almost obligatory.

Vietnam has a wonderful range of **fruit**. The fertility of the southern delta means this is where the greatest variety grows so you can be sure of finding markets full of wonderfully-fresh ripe avocados, pineapples, watermelon, jackfruit, rambutan, lychees, papaya, green banana (ready to eat and flavoursome despite its colour), yellow banana, sharon fruit, apricots, grapes, mangos and mangosteen.

Dragon fruit, *thanh long*, so called because the leaves of the creepers are pointed like dragon's scales and which has a deliciously-soft white flesh peppered with tiny black seeds wrapped in soft shocking pink skin is grown in the Mekong Delta.

The delicate flavour of soft gooey custard apple flesh, *qua na*, also known as sugar apples or sweetsops, can be enjoyed everywhere – but whatever you do, don't risk squashing a custard apple – the resulting mess is legendary. More seriously, never consume the incredibly strong-smelling durian (*sau rien*) with alcohol as the combination has killed people. Blended avocados or the milk of young coconuts, which is delicious and nutritious, make fine cooling drinks. Meanwhile, in the highlands of Vietnam, such as in the cool hill station of Dalat, you can feast on apples, pears and even strawberries.

Meals and meal times

The Vietnamese in general eat three meals a day. A breakfast, usually before 7am, of sticky rice, a ham sandwich on freshly-cooked bread, or a filling bowl of hot pho keeps people going until lunch, which is usually before noon. Lunch is likely to consist of pho, or barbecued meat and rice, eaten at home for a rural family, and eaten at home or from a street vendor for urban people.

Families try to be together for the evening meal which is the main one of the day. This is likely to consist of a soup with a little meat in it, plus a filling dish of meat, fish, eggs or tofu served with vegetables and rice. The richer the family the more dishes there are. Since the evening is a time when families eat together, street vendors are likely to pack up after dark; so for a meal after around 8pm you will need to look for a restaurant. Also because the day starts early few restaurants serve after 10pm.

Cooking traditions

The cook in a rural family is traditionally the youngest daughter, but cooking is more shared out for families living in cities, where there are usually several demands on everyone's time. Because it is still considered important to bring all the family together for an evening meal a daughter would not regard it as extreme to spend several hours preparing dinner. And this is how long it takes – although the actual cooking time for most Vietnamese dishes is short, there is usually lots of preparation needed. So, for example, spring rolls are fried in oil for five minutes, but it takes around an hour to soak the vermicelli, marinate the meat such as pork with a panoply of herbs and spices and then carefully roll warm damp rice paper around the mixture.

To make pho, an ox bone is put into water and salt for an hour to draw out the blood, then the meat will be stewed for around five hours with fresh ginger and an assortment of spices which always includes salt, pepper, garlic, and sugar. The broth is then strained and ready to have a bundle of crisp noodles, vegetables, chillies and squeezes of lime put in just before eating. Despite the six hours of preparation the broth is kept for only that day.

The bill

Whenever dining in a small restaurant or at a street-side stall which does not have a menu with prices, be sure to ask for the total cost of the meal you are ordering, or be prepared for a shock later. This is the accepted practice and Vietnamese people will do so without embarrassment. Be aware that the price of a street-side bowl of pho or banh xeo, for example, will vary according to how much meat you ask to be added, while the cost of a meal of previously-made spring rolls, for example, will depend solely on how many you order.

In smart restaurants you may find a cover charge added to your bill, as in the West, for things such as hand wipes or peanuts. As in the West if you object to paying for these you need to refuse them as they arrive, as quibbling with their appearance on the bill is not very seemly.

Tips are not generally expected in eating places, but always appreciated – as are sincere thanks and signs that you have truly enjoyed the food. If a service charge is added it is not assumed you will leave a tip as well.

Hospitality

You may find while travelling that you are invited to dine in the home of Vietnamese people you meet. If you are it will be appreciated if you try to observe the manners of the Vietnamese (see p116). In any event, whether you eat dinner in someone's house or are merely offered a banana by someone on a train or bus it's hard to miss the Vietnamese desire to share food, which they see as a unifying and healing social agent. As an old Vietnamese proverb says 'In food, as in death, we feel the essential brotherhood of man.'

See Appendix A, pp304-10, for phrase lists covering many Vietnamese dishes, snacks, fruit and vegetables.

DRINK

Tap water is chlorinated in Hanoi and Ho Chi Minh City but it is still wisest to boil it before drinking. The hot water provided in thermos flasks in every hotel room has always been found to be boiled and therefore is safe to drink. In these two cities problems have not been encountered in consuming ice, but elsewhere you should beware of tap water and therefore of ice. Mineral water is freely available almost everywhere and other soft drinks such as Coca-Cola, Fanta and so on are also easy to get hold of.

Beer is also readily available, whether it's cheap and excellent *bia hoi* (draught 'beer of today'), cheap and less excellent local beers, such as 333 (*ba ba ba*), foreign beers brewed locally such as San Miguel, or imported beers.

It is possible to buy local bottled rum, gin, vodka and so on in every town, often from the tiniest roadside shacks. These local products are of dubious quality – you will need to be in a large centre to find better imported options. There will always be somewhere in towns which is wised up to tourists, such as Hoi An or Nha Trang, doing a great line in cocktails.

Exotic soft drinks are also popular such as delicious freshly-squeezed fruit purée (*sinh to*), intriguing bean drinks with many possible different combinations (generally costing around $0.25), and pureed avocado drinks.

Finally, Vietnamese coffee is a must for any coffee fan. The best beans (usually considered to be those from Buon Ma Thuot) have an astonishingly rich flavour which derives from the unique Vietnamese tradition of roasting the beans in butter. The coffee is then brewed directly above the cup through a small drip-feed device – which incidentally makes an excellent small cheap present.

LANGUAGE

Vietnam is unique among the tonal languages of Asia and the Orient in that it uses Roman script – ie it does not have its own alphabet nor use Chinese-style characters. This means that all place names, signs, menus and so on can be easily read – a fantastic boon for travellers and for those trying to learn the language. The Roman script exists even though the language is tonal, as Chinese is, so words are spelt the same way but different accents on the letters can give entirely different meanings – it all depends on the way you say the words. How, you might ask, did Vietnam develop Roman script given its geographical location. Of course it didn't of its own accord – the French developed it for them; this radical change is one of the developments the colonials brought which the Vietnamese embraced.

Up until the middle of the 17th century Vietnamese was written using Chinese-style characters, though it was (and is) a different language from Chinese; in pagodas and temples you can still see inscribed Chinese characters. But one particular Frenchman had other ideas.

Alexander de Rhodes was a tenacious French Jesuit missionary who spent many years in Vietnam during the latter part of the 17th century. Earlier Christian missionaries had made forays into phoneticising the Vietnamese language based on the pronunciation of Portuguese which was the trading language of the time. But it was de Rhodes who codified and systematized the transcription of Vietnamese into the Roman alphabet, plus he invented the system of tone marks which indicate vowel pronunciation. The new language was called *quoc ngu*.

Use of this romanized script was, however, restricted to foreigners and traders until the early 19th century when the ruling French colonialists saw the great practical value of literally supplanting the old system with the new. They also thought this would be a vital stepping stone to converting the Vietnamese to Catholicism which they thought was being held back by the inherent Confucianism in the use of Chinese characters. Unlike most other aspects of colonialization the Vietnamese educated classes took an active interest in promulgating quoc ngu. The legacy of this interest today is possibly evident in the high literacy rate (88 per cent in the 1989 census) and it is certainly true that those Vietnamese who try to learn Western languages, or indeed use a computer keyboard, have a much easier time than they would have had.

Although Vietnamese is a tonal language, and therefore difficult to learn, it's well worthwhile picking up a few key phrases, such as hello and thank you, and worth bearing in mind that you are unlikely to get a fair price in street transactions if you can't bargain in Vietnamese. For an easy guide to the tones and key phrases see pp304-10.

SPORT

If you stay for any length of time it is hard to miss the people's love of sport and fitness. The most fascinating sight of mass exercise at dawn rewards an early riser. Everywhere in the country hundreds of people gather at first light or earlier, in parks or on the beach or just round the streets, to run, play badminton, or do Tai Chi. Participants are of both sexes and all ages and form into large groups swaying and moving in time with an instructor or even a loud disco beat, or into smaller groups running in a jovial mob or playing badminton cheerily, or just individually stretching and swaying as the sun comes up. Young women can be seen each morning practising slow motion shadow boxing believing it to keep their bodies beautiful, while many young men are serious about fitness and run competitively in the mornings or work out in gyms.

In Ho Chi Minh City the best place to see this is Cong Vien Van Hoa Park, in Nha Trang near the northern end of the beach, and in Hanoi Hoan Kiem lake and West lake are hard to beat, though Lenin Park has the best display of group Tai Chi. It's an unmissable event if you can handle such an early start. If you can't, the chances are you might still get to see sporting matches. Many businesses have large forecourts which get used for work matches in badminton or *da cau* – a game using a shuttlecock which has the rules of volleyball but using the feet like football.

Water sports

With so much beautiful coastline **swimming** is popular. Young men can be serious swimmers but most others tend to spend their time in the water either laughing and splashing or bathing leisurely in the English Victorian manner. Swimwear fashion is also reminiscent of Victoriana for women who generally go into the water almost fully clothed, as bathing costumes are considered immodest, except at well-developed beach resorts such as Nha Trang, Vung Tao or China Beach where they are more accepted.

Water sports for tourists are most accessible at Nha Trang where there are highly-recommended **diving** schools and some **snorkelling** possibilities. The variety of tropical fish and coral is not bad, though not exceptional. Snorkelling is not exceptionally rewarding because the best areas are in waters which are several metres deep, though the water is beautifully clear if it is not the windy season. Diving is an alternative but there have been reports of faulty equipment, so it is best to deal with a highly-reputable centre, such as the PADI centres on the waterfront in Nha Trang.

Other activities

In any of the main cities expat communities organize various sports events. If you want to take part ask at one of the expat run bars or cafés about forthcoming events. One of the most long-standing groups is the **Hanoi Hash House Harriers** running group (nothing to do with marijuana). A bus leaves each Saturday at 2pm from Sofitel Metropole Hotel, 15 Ngo Quyen Street, for the weekly Hash House Harriers run, but note that the Hash group does not particularly welcome short-stay tourists, and nor do other expat sporting team events. The Asia-wide expat running group of the **Saigon Hash House Harriers** meet on Sundays at 2.30pm at Caravelle Hotel.

NIGHTLIFE

Few Vietnamese have much time for relaxation. Working hours are long and family commitments heavy for all ages and those who are not struggling to make ends meet are striving for a better life. Plus the notion of bars, pubs and nightlife in general has negative memories for many Vietnamese because of the growth of such places in the American era in South Vietnam and the resulting explosion in prostitution. After reunification the bars were all shut down and other expressions of immorality such as ballroom dancing and disco dancing were banned. But since doi moi the situation has relaxed a lot. Western-style bars have re-opened, Vietnamese-style coffee or beer bars are common, discos have reached the border of acceptability and the Vietnamese have discovered karaoke in a big way.

The south still has a livelier nightlife scene than the north – despite the authorities being stricter on southern lapses of morality than northern. Vietnam has not felt the need to establish out of town entertainment centres so the chance of finding any evening entertainment in non-touristy areas is basically nil. Since the Vietnamese get up early many bars and restaurants, even in cities, close around 9pm.

Bars

The words *bia hoi*, literally meaning the beer of today and referring to draught beer, can be seen scrawled by street-side cafés in every city and town. The beer is often good and you can't beat the relaxed atmosphere. You won't find Vietnamese women here, but it is OK for foreign women to have a drink.

Coffee bars, however, are frequented by both sexes and are much livelier for it. Young Vietnamese go there in groups to chat above the music sipping hot or cold soft drinks. These bars are most popular in Nha Trang but can also be found in other cities, usually away from the tourist trail, advertised by the words *ca phe* (a phonetical version of the French word café).

Western-style bars are growing in popularity among the Vietnamese and both Hanoi and Ho Chi Minh City have examples of very up-market bars that would not look out of place in New York or London. This is where to go if you find yourself craving a gin and tonic, but expect to pay at least $3. Because of their expense, going to these bars is a real status symbol for Vietnamese. Expat bars pepper the major cities. These range from swish bars to English- or Irish-style pubs; most are friendly and can be a welcome haven. At the top of the scale, cocktail bars in the best hotels can mix you the finest cocktails from around $8, but these venues will take you almost entirely out of Vietnamese circles.

A different way to enjoy evenings in the cities is to stroll around the streets as the young Vietnamese do, astride their bikes or motorbikes – out and about to see and be seen.

Discos
In Vietnam these are places which combine Western pop music, popular Vietnamese songs and ballroom-type dancing to a disco beat. It can be quite a combination, until there is a power cut.

The best discos are in Ho Chi Minh City. Here you can find nightspots which have fairly recent if not the latest in fluorescent lighting and techno music. The dancing style is often frenetic and free. Everywhere else,

---

❏ **Cinema**
According to official history, Vietnamese cinema began with a film of the proclamation of Vietnam's independence on 2 September 1945. The film 'pioneers' had only a 16mm camera and a few hundred metres of film which had to be developed 'in incredible conditions – inside an earthenware jar and on a boat taken secretly to a town where it was possible to get ice'. Since then the subject matter of Vietnamese cinema has not changed much; most films are nationalistic drama/documentaries about the American war. Such films can be seen in the cinemas which are dotted around cities.

Not surprisingly imported foreign videos are fast taking over in popularity. Indeed, there has been such an influx of foreign films in video form that the censors are unable to keep track. It may be that the authorities will be forced to accept a relaxation in the formal rules giving Vietnamese cinema a chance to regain popularity; but there are no signs of it yet.

however, it is very conservative, consisting of couples or groups of girls swaying gently to the fast and furious beat. Some of the girls in discos are prostitutes which it is best to be aware of if you enter as a single man or in a group of only men.

Karaoke

Karaoke has almost become an obsession with the Vietnamese. Every city has literally hundreds of karaoke bars – whether they are swanky affairs in top hotels or tiny lounge bars in the front rooms of people's homes. The Vietnamese love karaoke and if you make Vietnamese friends they will likely as not take you to a karaoke bar.

Most of the songs in are popular Vietnamese love songs accompanied by soppy videos, though some bars also hold some Western songs and you will be encouraged to take the microphone and start crooning. Going to a karaoke bar with a group of Vietnamese can be great fun and is a good way of getting to know people better. The Vietnamese owners are also likely to be amused by hosting a group of Westerners keen to sing their hearts out.

Often even in very small towns in rural areas there will be one house with a karaoke set and a lone singer blasting out renditions of the latest tunes into the peaceful night air. Many Vietnamese are very fine singers. It is unfortunate that these never seem to be the ones singing karaoke, but note that it is extremely bad manners to point this out.

EMERGENCIES

If you have a **health** emergency and you are in Hanoi or Ho Chi Minh City (HCMC/Saigon) go straight to one of the English-speaking hospitals or clinics listed in this book (see pp154 and 256). Elsewhere try the local hospital bearing in mind that the most important thing will be to find a good interpreter. Be prepared to move quickly to Hanoi or HCMC where conditions are better, and even to fly out to Bangkok or Hong Kong if surgery is required, where more modern equipment is available.

If you suddenly find yourself short of **money** and know someone outside the country who could help you out, the best option is to make a reverse charge call from a post office and ask for money to be transferred by Western Union which has offices in almost every country in the world. This can be done through a cash payment or by credit or debit card. Western Union operates out of bank branches in almost every large town in Vietnam and money can be collected only 15-20 minutes after it has been sent. Western Union's head offices are in HCMC on ☎ 08-835 6605 or 08-829 1834 and are open Monday to Saturday, 7.30am-5pm.

If you get in trouble with the **police** either as a victim or perpetrator of a crime contact your embassy straight away and ensure you get an interpreter (you are entitled to one). If you are a victim of theft and intend to claim on an insurance policy be certain to obtain a police report otherwise your claim will automatically be invalidated.

ETIQUETTE

Avoiding offence

There are a few golden rules for avoiding offence in Vietnam: always be polite, don't cause people to lose face, show respect for authority and age, don't even jokingly question a woman's propriety and watch your eating habits. Of course, there are other important customs as set out below.

Losing face, ie being humiliated over something or showing excessive emotion such as an outburst of anger, is something Vietnamese strive hard to prevent. If you become angry over something you will often find others smiling or laughing. This is not out of humour, but because they are embarrassed for you because you have displayed a weakness and poor manners. Causing someone else to lose face is an even more serious offence.

Eating etiquette is important to observe, especially if you are invited to a Vietnamese home. Some norms are universal, some have a definite north/south split. The most important north/south difference is that it is polite to refuse an invitation to eat at a northerner's house a couple of times and accept only if it is again repeated, whereas it is rude to refuse an invitation to eat with a southerner's family, even if you are not hungry. Historical food shortages in the north explain the difference.

Most Vietnamese meals are eaten by putting small amounts of food at a time in individual bowls from dishes in the centre of the table – southerners put food only into their own bowls, whereas in the north your hosts will put food directly into your bowl. This creates a real hazard of eating more than your fair share, so you need to be especially aware of how much food there is to go round.

In anyone's home beware about asking for drinks your hosts might not have – tea or water are the only safe bets. Whatever you drink your host will be obliged to refill your cup if you empty it.

Everywhere in Vietnam you should lie chopsticks across the top of a dish rather than leaving them sticking out because not only is this potentially messy, but more seriously it represents the death symbol.

Never put a half-eaten piece of food into a communal dip as it is thought to 'contaminate' the food. If you do not like the food which has been cooked for you it is impolite to eat none of it, but perfectly acceptable to try a little and feign fullness. However, rice is traditionally seen as so precious that it is insulting to leave any in your bowl.

Public nakedness is not encouraged. Thus women often wear clothes over bathing costumes when swimming, though the sight of a bare-chested man, particularly if adorned with a Sean Conneryesque rug of chest hair, is more likely to cause amusement rather than shock.

Appropriate dress is something both sexes need to think about; you may feel most comfortable in T-shirts, shorts and desert boots and although this doesn't offend the Vietnamese it doesn't please many and marks you out as a seemingly rich Westerner.

Blending in a little is easy enough and the Vietnamese do notice and appreciate the effort. Long trousers for men are more acceptable than shorts, and women can easily get ideal clothes (such as long baggy trousers and flowing top) made up very cheaply in good cotton or silk (see p126).

Public displays of affection between different sexes are also frowned on (although this is becoming more acceptable in the main cities); indeed it is impolite to touch anyone of the opposite sex. However, don't be surprised if almost complete strangers of the same sex touch your arm or even pinch or grab you – it is almost always meant as a friendly gesture.

As with all countries in Asia if you are a travelling gay couple it will generally not prove a problem because a lot of touching and affection is common between friends of the same sex. Indeed, you can see this as a sign of continued de-Americanization – men are to be seen everywhere holding hands. This practice all but disappeared during the American war from Danang southwards, because of the hostility they received from Americans who thought Vietnam was a nation of homosexuals.

Feet, heads and shoulders Avoid pointing your feet at people and especially at statues of Buddha as it is very rude. Be careful never to touch someone's head as it is believed their spirit resides there. A different genie lives on the shoulders so avoid touching people there too.

How to get things done

The combination of Buddhism and Confucianism fosters a contract of maintaining social harmony meaning that it is seen as well mannered to respect authority and tradition and to have self-discipline. This means that you rarely see people arguing or raising their voices and bad news is generally skirted around or avoided altogether. This lack of directness can be very frustrating if you are trying to sort something out, but losing your cool will not help. Instead be patient, polite, assume that if an issue is being avoided it is probably for good reasons, and be aware that a smile can often work wonders.

Avoiding questions demanding direct 'yes' or 'no' answers is the key. As in most of Asia, nodding the head and saying 'yes' is more often a gesture of support or understanding rather than agreement (Vietnam also has the added difficulty that questions are always phrased in the 'are you not OK?' form to which a yes answer would mean that one was not OK). So open-ended questions are always a better option if you want real answers.

How to avoid getting into trouble

If a situation looks as if it might get nasty two tactics are particularly useful: distraction and presence. If there is more than one of you a very good diversionary tactic is suddenly beginning to talk animatedly amongst yourselves thus creating valuable time for things to cool down. If this isn't possible or doesn't work remember that the Vietnamese are generally small. If you are not, the sheer act of drawing yourself up to your full height can create a big impression. This physical intimidation can be very useful.

It is wise to avoid behaviour that could bring you in contact, let alone get you in trouble with, the police. Corruption is not unknown and in a dispute you may find they will side with the Vietnamese rather than with you, although this is not necessarily so. The regulation of life and of tourists is nothing like as heavy as it used to be so, on an average trip, you are unlikely to find the police presence oppressive and probably won't notice it at all. If you have to deal with the police, be calm, measured, patient and get your own interpreter.

If a Westerner is involved in a road accident with a Vietnamese a rowdy, even ugly, crowd scene can develop. It is because of this that although it is contrary to practice in the West, it is officially recommended by the British Consular in Vietnam, among others, that if you are involved in a road accident you should not hang around afterwards. If someone is hurt they recommend you stay put until they are being looked after but then leave. Do report the incident at the nearest police station, but wait until several hours later. This gives you the best chance of avoiding huge compensation claims. Insist on an interpreter and request that extended family or friends are not invited to the station. You will probably find that a fair request for compensation is made, and if the injured was a child, you may even find that the parents are apologising to you for their child's irresponsible driving.

❏ Women travellers

Women should be aware that most Vietnamese women refrain from activities which are associated only with prostitutes; that is to say, drinking alcohol, smoking and dancing wildly. However, that is not to say that Western women enjoying these pleasures are necessarily judged accordingly. Much depends on the manner adopted and, if you are unmarried, it depends on how you announce this.

If someone asks if you are married, the best answer is 'not yet' – *chua, chua den* (pronounced joo-a dayn). Unmarried women aged over about 30 are considered strange creatures and divorce is a scandal. However, the Vietnamese find it very difficult to judge Westerners' ages, so if you choose deception the task is usually easy.

Asian women travelling with Western men are sometimes given a hard time because they can be assumed to be Vietnamese prostitutes. Talking volubly in a language that is not Vietnamese and, ironically, consciously avoiding clothes that blend in are the best ways to dispel this conclusion.

THE MEDIA

Newspapers

Vietnam's only English-language daily newspaper is *Vietnam News*. Almost purely an instrument of government propaganda, it makes rotten, sometimes risible, reading, except for a few cultural features. The weekly *Vietnam Courier* is little better. If you want to know what is going on in Vietnam try the weekly *Vietnam Investment Review* which also has a very useful supplement on entertainment as well as some interesting cultural articles, or the monthly *Vietnam Economic Times*.

For uncensored news you can find foreign newspapers on stands and in the best hotels in Hanoi and HCMC but at a price. Papers available include *The Bangkok Post* and the Hong Kong edition of the *International Herald Tribune* in Hanoi, and the Singapore edition in HCMC.

Many UK expats subscribe to the extremely good overseas weekly version of the *Guardian* newspaper called the *Guardian Weekly*.

Radio

There are numerous Vietnamese-language radio stations broadcasting a mixture of music and news throughout the day on both AM and FM; but all English-language stations are on short-wave frequencies.

Vietnam receives the BBC World Service for which you can try a number of frequencies: 15,360 kHz, 17,760 kHz, 21,660 kHz are best during the day, and 6195 kHz, 9740 kHz, 11,995 kHz are best during the night. If the signal fades on one frequency try another.

Other stations which can be received include Radio Australia, and even the Voice of America. The Voice of Vietnam, founded at the time of the proclamation of independence in 1945, and the Voice of America were both propaganda instruments during the war. These days the ideological battle on the airwaves is more subtle.

Television

Since Vietnamese television began in 1970 it followed the precedent of communist leaders by going through years of hiding in the jungle, before exploding onto the cultural scene with one channel, now three, of dull news, sport and cultural programmes.

Apart from the (few) establishments with satellite, Vietnamese families have little incentive to spend their lives slumped in front of the television.

FINDING WORK

In theory you need to have a business visa to work in Vietnam, but it is often possible to do language teaching or work in expat bars unofficially, meaning just on a tourist visa. To continue working you may be able to renew your tourist visa or, once you are more established, you may be able to persuade a company to 'employ' you as a 'consultant' and so get a business visa.

There are a great many foreign-aid non-governmental organizations (NGOs) which employ appropriately-skilled foreigners for one or two years. To get such a job you should apply from outside Vietnam – the USA, UK, France and Japan generally have the most positions advertised. The same applies for any other type of jobs from hairdressers to high-technology experts, though Australia and New Zealand are the best countries for job adverts for South-east Asia.

Language teaching

Language teaching is the most common job held by English-speaking foreigners, apart from working in bars in Nha Trang. Jobs range from official work with public universities or through voluntary service overseas (VSO), through private language schools, to ad-hoc and unofficial private tutoring. VSO work is probably the hardest to get from inside Vietnam and indeed is difficult from outside the country because the Vietnamese operation is still very small (and currently deals only with English-language teaching). Approach VSO headquarters in your home country, or in London, to find out about opportunities. Asking around for jobs once you are in Vietnam is the best way to find other teaching work. Hanoi and Ho Chi Minh City are the best bets, but there are also opportunities in other cities or smaller towns. Having a teaching certificate helps, but isn't essential, even to get a job in public universities.

Universities pay around $2-3 per hour, but free accommodation is often thrown in and visa extensions should be no problem. If you do get offered a job here be aware that you may have to sign a long contract before you are able to check out what your teaching and living conditions will be like. So meeting other foreigners working there and asking them about it before you sign any contract is a very good idea.

Private language centres are bursting onto the scene all over Vietnam. Work here can be easier, because of the smaller class sizes, and better paid, though without the free perks. You are likely to get the best pay from private tutoring ($5 an hour) which is also the easiest work to pick up. It can be rewarding but isolating and difficulties with visa extensions might make this only a short-term option.

LEARNING THE LANGUAGE

Whether you intend to be a serious student of Vietnamese or just learn enough to get by for a short trip the Vietnamese around you are likely to be your best tutors. Spending a little time with a Vietnamese one-to-one (or paying for a private tutor) gives you the time you need to master crucial aspects such as the tones and avoids the rote learning and grammar emphasis of most universities and language centres.

If you just want to pick up a little, a combination of this and following the initial steps in the language section of this book (see pp304-10) or a phrasebook should be enough. To learn more, dictionaries and phrasebooks are a good resource, but radio programmes teaching Vietnamese are regularly broadcast, private tutors are easily arranged, or you can enrol on a language course.

Western-produced dictionaries and phrasebooks are the most useful. All such books are much cheaper when bought outside Vietnam. Of the phrasebooks on offer, the best is the Rough Guide *Vietnamese phrasebook*. You are unlikely to be able to find this in Vietnam – instead the old edition of the Lonely Planet phrasebook which is riddled with mistakes is commonly sold by street vendors. Also available in the West, but not recommended, is the comprehensive book and tape set by Tuan Duc Vuong and John Moore, published by Routledge; it can't be recommended because the pronunciation on the tapes is so unclear as to make the tones indistinguishable. Vietnamese is taught on FM frequencies two slots a week at varying times.

Arranging private tuition is generally easy once you have located a good English speaker. Paying a few dollars for a lesson is as acceptable as paying in kind with some English teaching. The largest official language-teaching centres are at the General University of Ho Chi Minh City at 12 Binh Hoang, District 5, Hanoi National University at 90 Nguyen Trai St, or at the Hanoi Foreign Language College, Vietnamese Language Centre at 1 Pham Ngu Lao St. Tuition averages two hours a day at around $5 an hour.

CRIME

Vietnam is in general a very safe country to travel in – despite what the Vietnamese say. They are convinced that their cities are crawling with criminals who won't miss an opportunity to rob you or worse. It is surprising how untrue this is. While incidents do happen, crime is not rife and violent crime is rare. It is sensible, however, to take precautions against the most common forms of crime: motorbike drive-by theft and pick-pockets.

Drive-bys are a potential danger everywhere and although few occur outside Ho Chi Minh City, a lot do occur here. To protect yourself when on cyclos or bicycles, always wrap your rucksack or bag straps securely around an arm or leg. The hold has to be strong enough to withstand a severe yank with no warning. Keeping your spare cash, travellers' cheques etc in a hidden moneybelt is always a good idea and in particular prevents pick-pockets being anything more than a nuisance even if they do succeed in picking your pocket.

A less common form of theft is inside jobs by hotel staff; if this happens it is likely many travellers will be hit so, unless you are unlucky enough to be one of the first, you can hope to have been warned by others – either by word of mouth or from noticeboards in travellers' cafés. Most English speakers who act as guides are honest – but beware anyone who offers you things for free the moment you meet them.

Theft on trains can also happen. Luggage near open windows can be vulnerable, as can any of your luggage while you sleep (except in soft sleeper). But in fact incidents are rare, possibly because, unlike on buses, enforcement is never far away – conductors are a power unto themselves on trains and they can almost always call on army passengers to help them out. Still, it is always wise to keep track of your luggage and if you want to be sure the bottom bunks of soft sleeper provides entirely safe storage.

All Vietnamese are convinced there is a more extreme train hazard – children throwing rocks at open windows. For this reason, after opening the window there is still a protective (removable) metal grill which conductors and passengers alike often encourage you to keep shut. The problem, insofar as it exists, is almost entirely confined to the north and seems to be less believed than it used to be. But of course it would only take one incident, so the judgment is yours.

DRUGS

The small green bundles seemingly of grass peddled especially by the Red Dao and H'mong in Sapa are indeed just that. Marijuana in mountainous regions is accessible and cheap, but be aware that it is illegal. The rest of the country has potent tobacco as its strongest drug, except for Ho Chi Minh City, which has something of a heroin problem.

Users and dealers tend to be the socially excluded of Vietnam – associated with the past South Vietnamese regime. This scene is not a pretty one and Westerners who get involved not only have to deal with the dangers of AIDS but also of dealer/police kickback deals which the Westerner would very much get the bad end of. It is also not advised to try taking drugs out of the country.

UNEXPLODED BOMBS

Vietnam has been a theatre of war for many years and most who plunged weapons of mass destruction into its soil could not or did not return to remove them. Hundreds of thousands of Vietnamese have been maimed or killed through accidental impact with fatal metal and now even though most hostilities in the country stopped over 20 years ago, discoveries of devices continue to be made, to deadly effect.

Take particular care when walking around the demilitarized zone (DMZ) or anywhere off the beaten track. Be sure never to touch any bombs or artillery you find lying around – if they haven't been picked up by scrap metal merchants there's usually a good reason. They could contain, for example, white phosphorus which burns into flesh the instant it comes into contact with air. Be careful for the danger is real – don't become a statistic.

❏ Little creatures

The averagely adventurous tourist would be highly fortunate to come away from a stay in Vietnam without a few encounters with cockroaches, which often grow to immense sizes, and with the ubiquitous mosquito. But you can consider your self unlucky if you come across other little creatures such as bedbugs, rats, scorpions, snakes, tapeworms or leeches.

Mosquitoes are most prevalent during monsoon seasons but even then they can prove little more than a nuisance if you take reasonable precautions – it is always best to avoid being bitten by mosquitoes rather than resigning yourself to the consequences, not least because of the risk of malaria (see p31). Mosquitoes come out particularly at dusk and during the night, so covering legs and arms is a good idea for the evenings. These days most hotel rooms which are at risk of mozzies (ie with no air-con) have mosquito nets.

Sadly air-con is no protection against **cockroaches**. These can even be found in clean, well-kept hotel rooms, usually in the bathroom. Avoid leaving food or drink around so as to minimize their numbers (the same goes for ants) and bear in mind that squishing them is a nasty experience – try catching them instead. Sprinkling boric acid liberally around kills them, but it first attracts them to the powder and then leaves them dead scattered around the room.

It is rare to come across hotel rooms with **bedbugs** but if they do it is easy enough if you have your own bedding to prevent the insects getting their jaws into your flesh. Spots of blood on a sheet mattress are a tell-tale sign of bedbugs – if you see these spraying the bed with insecticide and then sleeping in your own sheet should kill some off and keep the others away.

It is not much of a joy to share a room with a **rat**, but if you do hear these creatures scurrying around don't be too alarmed. They are unlikely to come near you and will probably disappear altogether if you do not have any food lying around.

Scorpion bites are very unpleasant, **snake bites** potentially deadly, but you are only likely to be at risk if walking in areas of jungle, such as on Cat Ba island. If you are bitten by a snake try to remain calm (to slow down absorption of the venom) while seeking medical attention fast. Identifying the snake is important for treatment purposes so try to kill it and bring it along to the hospital if possible, or at least get a good look at it.

If you avoid walking through mud or muddy water without shoes you should avoid **tapeworms** and other intestinal worms.

Leeches are likely to be a hazard only in stagnant water and while walking through wet undergrowth. Leeches do not actually infect you but the sight of them sucking your blood is so unpleasant that panic is an understandable reaction – but also the most dangerous. If you pull them off infected suppurating leech wounds are likely so resist; instead burn or salt them off, or just grimace as they have their fill.

WHAT TO BUY AND WHERE

You can come away from Vietnam with a veritable treasure trove of goodies. From beautiful tailor-made silk clothes, stunning traditional lacquer dishes, unique handmade musical instruments, traditional or nouveau art, to of course the ubiquitous postcard. The problem is narrowing your purchases down to manageable proportions. Posting non-breakables home is one option – by ship takes a long time but is generally reliable and much cheaper than by air.

Bargaining is almost always the order of the day and where you do find a shop with prices marked they are likely to be a little higher than the post-bargaining price you could get elsewhere. The elusive non-touristy shop or factory with fantastic-quality goods is indeed rare, but if you happen to see a factory in the middle of nowhere do check out whether it has a showroom/shop.

Fabric

There are certain exceptions to the rule that clothes are best bought in Hoi An: the best-quality imported wool for men's suits can be found only in HCMC – at Dong Kanh or Ben Thanh market (or occasionally in Hanoi). Embroidered silk is most readily found in Hué (upstairs in the Dong Ba market), and silk is painted only in the south – designs can be bought but not commissioned in Hanoi. HCMC and Hoi An are the only places where you can buy patterned cotton fabrics, though plain cotton is available elsewhere. Embroidered cotton is most easily found in Hanoi.

Lacquer work

Painstakingly-crafted and beautifully-designed lacquer work is one of the gems of Vietnam. Introduced from China in the 15th century lacquer work took off as exquisite objects d'art inlaid with mother-of-pearl or ivory for Vietnamese emperors. Traditional designs are still seen, but charming bird or flower motifs are now more common.

The traditional method of honing the wood to derive a perfect shape for a dish or vase hasn't changed at all. The result of the craftsmanship is not only a pleasing artefact but also a finish which enables you to distinguish between good work and shoddy work.

A lacquer dish is traditionally made from hundreds of tiny strips of porous wood coiled around each other by hand from the middle out and sealed together with the milk-like sap obtained from lacquer trees (*cay son*) which grow in the north. The edges of the wood are then finely planed and polished with pumice stone until perfectly smooth. Lacquer

---

Not two for tea, but...
A Vietnamese proverb goes: Four for alcohol, three for tea, and two for opium.

and colour (vermilion or cockroach's wing colour) are then assiduously applied in multiple layers until the perfect smooth gloss finish is reached. A pattern is drawn by hand on top and a final gloss layer is added.

A good lacquer piece should reflect and shine evenly and the coils of wood should not be visible. If the colour of the dish is gold or silver a blocking effect of the colour should be seen. The price can also be a marker: expect to pay around $10 for a good-quality medium-sized fruit bowl. Lacquer is now ubiquitous in the Pham Ngu Lao St area of HCMC, but the most hassle-free place to buy good lacquer is from the reasonably-priced government shop in Hanoi at 13 Hang Gai St.

Silk paintings
Traditional Vietnamese silk paintings can be found everywhere that is touristy across the country, but you have to know where to look if you want art which is a little different.

Hoi An is chock full of small shops selling oil paintings or watercolours of traditional village scenes. At $5-20 a painting these are not expensive but the fairly uniform style can pall after a while. This is not so for the varied offerings in the many nouveau art shops and galleries in Hanoi and HCMC where you can find a vast range of styles and pick up paintings by named artists for around $100.

Alternatively, in the tourist areas of HCMC you can pick up a pretend Renoir, Matisse or da Vinci. Famous paintings are copied to a high standard as are photographs if you care to bring one along. But beware – you may be pleased with the result at first only to find later that you are staring at a picture of yourself, or the Mona Lisa, with Vietnamese eyes!

Animal products
Some parts of the country specialize in making goods from particular animal products. Some make entirely legal, if rather peculiar, objects d'art – such as the vast array of intricately-designed artifacts made from cow and buffalo horn in Lang Son. But trade in some other goods such as ivory has been internationally outlawed.

Pottery
Chinese-style blue-and-white patterned pottery is available from most town markets. For more original pottery designs you are best off looking in the markets in Hanoi or, better still, checking out the shops and showrooms in Bat Trang, the pottery village outside of Hanoi. The quality of the goods here is high, yet the prices are also good – you can buy a full dinner set for around $30. But transportation is a nightmare; the pottery is heavy and highly breakable.

Musical instruments
Vietnam has many traditional musical instruments which are easy to play at a rudimentary level and as their sounds are reminiscent of Vietnamese

❑ **Tailor-made silk clothes**
Having clothes tailor-made is something that few who visit Vietnam pass up
the chance to do. Tailors' shops crowd the streets and indoor markets of every
city and town, but the quality of work and fabrics varies considerably. There
are good tailors and a wide range of materials available in Hanoi and Ho Chi
Minh City, but the tiny touristy town of Hoi An is still likely to be your best
bet for your clothing needs. The vast number of tailoring shops here produce
the kind of competition which keeps prices low and quality high. Also, Hoi An
is still a trading port, so it gets the biggest range of good-quality Japanese and
Chinese silks in Vietnam, at the best prices.

In all but the swankiest tailoring shops in HCMC and Hanoi the cost of a
piece of clothing depends on the quality of the fabric plus only a little for
labour. Beware that sometimes the word silk is loosely and metaphorically
applied to fabrics, but artificial, often Japanese, 'techno-silk' is still a good fabric and can make excellent clothes. Vietnamese cotton or fake silk is the cheapest at around $1 per metre. Vietnamese ribbed silk and most Japanese 'silk'
should cost $1-2 per metre. (Japanese 'silk' is hard-wearing, non-crease and is
machine washable at low temperatures.) Exquisite Chinese brocade is more
expensive, but should still cost only $2.50 per metre. Soft velvets are the most
expensive at around $5 a metre. Using Chinese brocade as the benchmark fab-
ric, a top should cost $4, trousers $9 and a man's suit $20-25. Shirts should cost
$4 for simple cotton, $6 for good cotton, or $8-10 for good silk.

While you can expect the quality of tailoring for these prices to be good,
be prepared for accessories such as zips to break and don't expect the sewing
to last too long. Take care how you order the clothes too – see p217 for tips on
how to avoid that fantasy dress turning into a shapeless bag.

celebrations they make good souvenirs. In Hanoi or HCMC you can pick
up a well-made bamboo xylophone for around $12, a 16-string zither from
around $20, or a wooden mandolin from $20. You can even buy reduced-
size replicas of the metre-long 'one string' instrument, doc huyen, as
unique to Vietnam as are its haunting wailing tones.

Other goods
For the ultimate in tacky souvenirs look no further than the Vietnamese
conical hat. Those made in Hué are decorated on the inside with poems or
pictures; but they are prohibitively heavy and awkwardly shaped to make
ideal carrying. Chopsticks inlaid with pearl or fake pearl make more convenient gifts.

The railways

Vietnam has 2600km of railway, designed by French colonialists, built by Vietnamese labour, attacked by Japanese invaders, sabotaged alternately by North and South Vietnamese troops and finally rebuilt by postwar Vietnam – a symbol of reunification and an attempt to foster that unity. A single railway line runs the length of the country transporting both passengers and freight, and connects Vietnam with its huge neighbour, China, on tracks stretching to Beijing and Kunming.

The railway was built for economic and military reasons – in fact only the Yunnan line destined for Kunming ever made real money for the French, but has resulted in a picturesque tour de force. Railways are a vital means of communication in any country – in Vietnam with its history of invasion and war they have meant much more.

BUILDING THE RAILWAYS

In the late 19th century, Indochina was, for the French, a national disgrace. In 1893 Tonkin (the north) was still in a state of disorder despite being regularly patrolled by military columns, in Annam (the centre) the French protectorate was merely nominal, and Cochinchina (the south), the only province in which any effective civil government had been established, was beginning to agitate for separation from the rest of the colony. Moreover, the stagnant local trade was almost entirely in the hands of foreigners, and France's share of Indochina's external trade was a miserly one-fifth. But by the start of WWI France had turned this situation around completely: the value of trade from Indochina increased from 162,000,000 French Francs (FF) in 1893 to FF400,000,000 just ten years later, and France's share had increased to one-third. This achievement was largely the work of one man – the industrious first Governor-General of Indochina, Paul Doumer, appointed in 1896. The principal reason for his success was the building of railways in Vietnam and China.

A French government decree of 18 February 1878 masterminded by Paul Doumer from his position in the French government codified a decision to begin building a rail network in Cochinchina. Doumer's achievement was substantial, particularly as his predecessor governor, Monsieur de Lanessan, had failed to gain approval for his proposal for a Trans-Indochina railway which would go from Hanoi to Saigon, but via the inner plateaux of Laos. This would have enabled some migration from the Tonkin delta to underpopulated Laos. But the plan came to nothing, as it was decided there was insufficient economic or demographic reason to justify building 500km of tracks across a very underpopulated region.

In 1881 the government of Cochinchina decided on a 71km railway between Saigon and Mytho. It is telling that this earliest line has fallen into disuse today because it was not until the lines connecting with China were built that the Indochinese railway brought real economic or military strategic gains to France and, ultimately, to Vietnam.

Why were the railways built?
The Lang Son to Phu Lang Thuong line (which nowadays extends to Hanoi) was built for military reasons. The colonialists had great difficulty keeping control of northern Tonkin – installing troops in a region rife with malaria without any paved roads and infested with bandits was a nightmare task. So it was decided that a railway would solve the problem. Meanwhile, France was desperate to penetrate the market and territory of Yunnan in China. There are three theories why.

Some historians argue that France wanted to access the produce of China's rich interior and that rail would be an improvement on the current boat route. As it was, the Yangtse river in China was only navigable by heavy tonnage boats as far as Hankow, which was 1000km from the river's mouth. It certainly seems that it was because of this that the Haiphong to Hanoi section of the line was built. Other historians believe the key reason for building the line to Yunnan was simply to try to prevent Britain from gaining all the access points to the region – this relies on the proverb that says that whoever is master of Yunnan is master of Indochina.

The third theory is a combination of the previous two, with an extra heady element – opium. This seems to be the real reason why France wanted access to China; they didn't want to leave the riches of the opium trade solely to the British. But even if this was why this railway was built and even if one reason for building a line linking Hanoi and Saigon was to enable Vietnamese labour to be brought from the north to the south to work on French plantations, still the railways served to develop the country in lasting and beneficial ways. And the story of their construction is a remarkable one.

THE PHU LANG THUONG TO LANG SON RAILWAY

The building of this railway was begun in 1880. Work was extremely slow because when malaria and mountainous terrain weren't hampering proceedings, workyards were raided by marauders who carried off the white

(**Opposite**) **Top**: The Reunification Express at a level crossing in Hué. **Bottom**: A steam engine in Hanoi. Steam is still sometimes used for freight transport.

foremen for ransom. However, these obstacles just made the reasons to build the line even more clear – a better way had to be found to resupply troops or evacuate the sick and wounded who had been stationed at Lang Son than the eight-day journey on foot across mountain trails. These obstacles were eventually overcome as sufficient local labour was found, and the railway was built. But it took five years of hard grind and FF20 million (FF1.8 billion in today's money) to build a line of a mere 101km. The railway opened in December 1894

After its completion the military objectives were forgotten and as the line failed to reap economic benefits it was highly criticized in France. The railway was built with a 0.60 metre gauge, earning it the name 'petit chemin de fer', and this too was criticized for being too small.

Under Doumer, the gauge was converted to metre gauge from 1896 onwards, a task which was completed in 1902. In the same year, the line was extended to Hanoi; the famous 1.68km bridge which was constructed to cross the Red River in the city was named after Doumer. The bridge still stands despite being repeatedly bombed by Americans, because the Vietnamese just as repeatedly patched it up so the trains could still run.

Raising construction funds for Doumer's grand project
To build the line between Lang Son and Phu Lang Thuong (which was later extended to Hanoi in the south and Dong Dang in the north) millions of French Francs had to be borrowed. But Doumer and his associates thought that the chambers of government in France would not agree to the raising of such funds for his foreign exploits, so he decided to ask the government purely for emergency funds, which were less well scrutinized and could be more easily renewed.

The strategy worked. Disguised loans were agreed to, which were in theory reimbursable from the colony's finances. The debt had risen to FF40 million by the end of 1885. As so often seems to be the way with large public projects the loan had to be rescheduled. The Law of 10 February 1896 packaged railway debts with other debts and commitments totalling FF80 million, of which FF20 million went towards the Lang Son to Hanoi line.

Following the success Doumer had in raising money for this section of his project he went on to elaborate the whole grand plan. He presented to a commission in France a proposal to build 3200km of railway right across Indochina and into China. According to the usual principle of asking for more than you would actually be content with, he was satisfied with the agreement by the French government to build 2000km. This was made concrete by an agreement which formally passed into law on

(**Opposite**) **Top:** The dramatic scenery of Halong Bay (see p268): the eighth wonder of the world. **Bottom:** Paddy fields near Hoa Lu. Rice, the country's staple, covers three-quarters of all cultivated land in Vietnam.

Christmas Day 1898 which authorized a loan of FF200 million to go exclusively towards the building of railways in Indochina.

The money was to be disbursed in three tranches. First, FF50 million was to be dispatched by 110,000 bonds of FF500 each at 3.5 per cent, reimbursable in exchange in 75 years' time at FF452; note that this makes a commission for the broker of FF5 million. The bonds were to be free of all taxes. Secondly, a decree of 25 July 1902 authorized the release of FF70 million which was to be funded by 155,000 bonds of FF500, each at three per cent, including a commission of FF7.5 million. A final tranche of FF80 million was raised by a decree of 7 October 1905.

After the funds, the plans for three lines

The lines were originally conceived as being in three parts: the Trans-Indochinois line from Hanoi to Saigon, a section connecting Haiphong with Yunnan via Hanoi, and an extension of the Saigon to Mytho line reaching further south to Vinh Long and Cantho. The Hanoi to Saigon line was to be constructed in several stages; first the section from Hanoi to Vinh, via Nam Dinh. This was built as planned, with the result that there is a kink in the line as it juts out east to Nam Dinh, leaving the path of Highway 1 for a 59km excursion. The second section was to begin around 180km south of Vinh at Quang Tri and cover the 100km to Danang via Hué, alongside the beautiful Cau Hai lagoon and over the difficult Hai Van pass. Then the southernmost section of the line would be built, connecting Saigon with Nha Trang. This was all the French government would agree to plan; the gaps would have to wait to be filled, in fact until after WWI (see p133).

With the Hanoi to Lang Son section of the line already opened, only the tracks between Haiphong and Yunnan, conceived as a single line, remained to be built. The line was begun at Haiphong, because it makes more sense to build inland from the port where all the materials arrive, than the other way round. All materials which could not be found, or had not yet been manufactured in Indochina but were needed for construction had to be shipped in from France.

The first section to be completed was from Haiphong to Hai Duong, 45km east of Hanoi. Then this line was to be connected with Hanoi, while a track stretched out eastwards from Hanoi to Viet Tri and onwards to Lao Cai and then to Yunnan. The original plan for the section between Hanoi and Lao Cai would have taken the railway line 20km to the east of the Red River and along the path of modern-day Highway 70, near the banks of elegant Thac Ba lake. But it was concluded that hugging the eastern bank of the Red River would be an easier task than tracking behind the Con Voi mountain range. It is a shame this caution in planning was abandoned for the Yunnan section of the line, with the disastrous consequences of the 'mistake of 500 metres' (se p131).

At the time of the law of 1896 a railway line had already opened, on 20 July 1885, between Saigon and Mytho. This had been an expensive enterprise, costing FF135,000 per km. But still there were plans to extend the line to Vinh Long and Cantho for political reasons – Doumer had a pressing need to satisfy local interests, because his only power base lay in Cochinchina.

At a much later date a railway line was also built connecting Saigon with Loc Ninh, 130km north-west of Saigon on Highway 13, and a branch of the Trans-Indochinois was opened to Dalat in 1933 from Thap Cham, two sections of which were rack railways.

Sadly all three lines fell into disuse, the result of damage from several wars and also because these lines were built to connect unpopulated areas, or in the case of Dalat mainly to enable Indochina's elite to escape easily to the cool of the hill station. This was a great pity, given the amount of money, effort and indeed creativity involved, as the still surviving Art Deco railway station at Dalat shows.

THE HAIPHONG TO YUNNAN RAILWAY

The railway line running between Haiphong and Yunnan via Hanoi was one of the most costly colonial feats ever. The line was constructed in seven years – between 1903 and 1910 and stretched 849km, of which 465km were in China. It traversed such incomparably difficult land that it became known as the 'ligne acrobatique'.

In June 1895 France obtained agreement from China for a private French company to build a railway in Yunnan province, opening up many Yunnan towns to foreign commerce. Agreement having been reached, planning for the line was done with vertiginous speed, taking only four months. Just two engineers and assistants then drew up plans for the line in only one year. As a result vast errors were made in planning which were compounded by a lack of local technicians. When technicians had to be brought over from France they were newcomers to Indochina and pretty quickly fell prey to the malaria which was rife in the area and which no-one had considered. As well as the technical obstacles there was an acute local labour shortage. So 'coolies' had to be imported from China at great expense, and not to the delight of the Chinese.

Material and supplies were transported to the site on the backs of men and mules over narrow tracks which ascended up steep slopes. Negligence in planning soon became apparent. Workers found themselves building on unstable ground amidst falling rocks. The death toll rose, reaching its peak with the debacle of the Nam Ti valley. Not only was this valley so infested with malaria it became known as 'death valley', it was also known as 'the mistake of 500 metres', because its perpendicular sides were traversed only because one engineer far from the scene of action had marked with his pencil a line on a map which happened to go straight through the valley!

❏ **Building the railways – who gained and who lost**

Building the railways in Vietnam was the most expensive of all France's colonial railway ventures, costing FF384 million (roughly equivalent to FF3.2 billion in today's money). This compares to FF179 million to build railways in French East Africa, and a mere FF75 million to equip Madagascar with rail.

The building of the railways in Indochina did profit the contractors, if not, in the beginning many others. At first, contracts were drawn up in which the contractors charged implicit interest rates of 12 per cent – ie charged 12 per cent more on completion of the project than they would have done at the beginning. It was not until the financial distress which hit France in 1908 that the French government ordered the Indochinese administration to limit interest in contracts to five per cent. Due to their extreme cost, the projects became very unpopular back at home in France, which along with the interruption of wars was another reason why construction slowed down significantly, such that from 1889-1910 200km of line was built, but 1911-28 saw only 350km built.

● **The benefit to France** Historically, the Indochinese railways were not very important for freight transport. This was because the country's primary export commodities, rice, corn and coal, were usually shipped by river or loaded directly onto ocean-going vessels. Inter-regional trade was not of great importance because the coastal plains, which were connected by rail, almost all produce the same thing. When revenue costs are compared with operational costs, only the Yunnan line shows a steady favourable balance from the time the service began and yielded a reasonable return on the capital invested.

The rest of the network is hardly profitable at all up until WWII, especially if accrued interest from government borrowed funds is taken into account. When the railway was at its peak in 1936-7 the profit made per km (in piastres) amounted to 1164 for all lines, but 3480 for the Yunnan line on its own. This was because passenger and baggage accounted for 71 per cent of all revenues on the Hanoi to Saigon line, but only 49 per cent of revenues on the Yunnan line, which carried 321,000 metric tonnes of freight – nearly one-third of all freight carried on Indochina's railways.

The legend grew that 100,000 local labourers died in the line's construction, but the truth is probably more like 25,000 – still a dreadful statistic. Of the 300 Europeans at the scene, 40 are reported to have died. But, despite everything, the first train reached Yunnan on 1 April 1910 connecting Hanoi with the Chinese interior and with the sea.

In all, the Chinese section needed 5000m of bridges, viaducts, and aqueducts, and 155 tunnels were built. The highest part on the line is the Chonei Tang pass at 2030m which the train reaches by a gradient of over 2.5 per cent in some places.

THE TRANS-INDOCHINOIS RAILWAY – SAIGON TO HANOI

The jewel in the crown of Doumer's public works project was to be the building of a railway which would connect Hanoi with Saigon, and Saigon with the capital of Cambodia, Phnom Penh, then continuing on to

---

❑ **Building the railways – who gained and who lost (cont'd)**

● **Private profit** It was a private company, not the French government, which reaped the benefit of the profitability of the Yunnan line. This came about because of the need for political sensitivity – the railway line was to be built on foreign, Chinese, land. It was decided in top French government circles that it was diplomatically easier for a private company to carry out the project than the French state itself. The result was that, to the French government's displeasure, a private company was reaping the rich rewards of penetration into the Chinese fertile, and opium-growing, lands.

● **Public loss** The French planners including Doumer made a theoretical distinction between building railways in colonies for penetration to open up new lands and eventually reap the rewards this may bring and for the transportation of readily-available goods for export and instant economic exploitation. The difficulty was that the planners believed they were carrying out the second of these in Indochina, whereas in reality apart from the opium trade, they were in fact undertaking the first.

● **The benefit to Vietnam** Immediately the railway was built, trains were hugely popular with the population. Each train had four classes of travel, but the first three were usually accommodated into one carriage, while the rest of the train was the basic and cheap fourth class – reserved solely for natives. Rail use increased steadily until the 1920s, and then in the 1930s when the network was finally completed, fares for the lowest classes halved. Rail travel shot up while the average distance travelled increased gradually from 39km in 1913, to 46km in 1936 and finally rose to 100km in 1980. As people travel further the railway becomes a greater source for unity, as well as reaping for the country the economic benefit the French colonisers originally hoped to reap for themselves.

Bangkok in Thailand and Vientiane in Laos. But the later parts of the project were never completed (and indeed it is only now that there are renewed plans for this cross-border project) so Doumer had to make do with a railway between Saigon and Hanoi. Even this took some doing, for as the project wore on so France railed against the unexpectedly high costs of the lines connecting with China.

So, by 1905, the 300km of railway track between Hanoi and Vinh were laid and in 1906 a difficult second section from Tourane (Danang) to Hué was opened, across the dramatic Hai Van pass, the pass of the clouds as the French called it (see p293). This was so that the then Vietnamese capital (Hué) had access to the sea.

By 1908 the railway lines extended to Quang Tri, at the foot of the Ai Lao pass just south of the 17th parallel. Then construction of the southern line began, stretching northwards from Saigon to meet the lines reaching south. By 1913 the section between Saigon and Nha Trang was opened. So, on the eve of WWI Indochinese Railways had 2012km of working track, of which 465km was in China. But even so the route was not complete.

Due to the interruption of WWI only 52km were built between 1913 and 1922 until new loans were forthcoming from France in that year and

❑ Technical details

Vietnam currently has 389 1000mm locomotives, of which 326 are described as usable, and 18 1435mm locomotives, of which only 11 are usable. Engines are Belgian-built BN Cockreills, French-made Alsthoms, or US-made diesels imported in 1969. Vietnam has 4087 1000mm wagons, of which 3412 are listed as usable, and 567 1435mm wagons, of which 431 are usable. In addition there are 610 1000mm coaches and 18 1435mm coaches all of which are thought to be railworthy.

Throughout the whole network of railways in Vietnam there are 1767 bridges, making a total of 52.16km, and 39 tunnels making a total of 11.468km. In all there are 250 stations, which communicate with each other by aerial wire (iron wires covered with copper), two-way radio, telegraph and the more down-to-earth telephone and fax. The signalling system is in some stretches a token system with a semaphore signal and in others a semi-automatic block system using coloured light signals.

The railway's importance in shipping freight has drastically increased over the years: 450,000 tonnes were carried in 1913, rising to 1,118,000 in 1929, and 1,171,000 tonnes in 1937. This had tripled by 1988 (the next year for which reliable figures are available) to 3,927,000 tonnes which in turn had increased to 4,580,000 by 1998.

The gauge for the main line running between Saigon and Hanoi and extending from Haiphong to Yunnan is one metre, for which the minimum radius of curves is 100m, and the gradient of the track is rarely more than 1.5 per cent, except in the Chinese section where it rises to 2.5 per cent.

The tracks which run between Halong and Quan Trieu via Kep are 1.435m, while those between Hanoi and Dong Dang via Kep, and those between Hanoi and Quan Trieu run on mixed gauge – meaning there are two outer rails so the track can accommodate rolling stock of either width. Ties were usually made of metal and 30kg rails progressively replaced the previous lighter ones.

Vietnam Railways was, in the spirit of doi moi, released from a strait-jacket of government control in 1989. Since then it has reduced its staff levels by one-third and, largely as a result of this, managed to break even for the first time in 1995.

Now it has ambitious plans for the railways of Vietnam including linking with Cambodia, Laos and Thailand as was originally planned for the region. Within the next 10-15 years it aims to increase the maximum speed of a passenger train to 100km/hour compared to the current maximum of 80km/hour (which is, in fact, more theoretical than real), and increase the speed of freight trains to 80km/hour (compared to the current 50km/hour).

Feasibility studies are also being carried out for new lines between Ho Chi Minh City, Dalat, Buon Ma Thuot, Kon Tom and Danang; between Ho Chi Minh City and Vung Tau; and reviving the old lines between Thap Cham and Dalat and between Ho Chi Minh City and Can Tho. Above all, Vietnam Railways hopes to double track the route of the Reunification Express, believing that this would make an unimaginable difference to the efficiency of the railways. Anyone who has waited in sidings for a train to pass the other way will agree.

in 1927 the section between Vinh and Dong Ha was opened up, connecting the north and central sections.

The construction work on the Indochinese coast was highly expensive. Deltas provided good sandy beds, rocky sub-soil, especially where granite provided good ballast, and labour supply was generally abundant and manageable, but crossing wide estuaries was a different matter. These required costly engineering work, especially to navigate flooded plains which required endless embankments. And still there was no line between Danang and Nha Trang. This was because this section was technically very difficult as spurs from the Truong Son mountain range had to be dealt with. Between Qui Nhon and Tuy Hoa the track could be routed through internal valleys, but south of Tuy Hoa the granite range of 'la mère et l'éléphant' made it necessary to cut several tunnels – one of which, the Babonneau, was 1,175m long. This section was opened in 1936. Thus on the eve of the most violent 40 years in Vietnamese history the country finally had an operative railway network stretching the length of the country. Enter WWII.

World War Two

With the outbreak of WWII Indochina found itself a small insignificant country at the mercy of international events and decisions taken by the great powers.

When the Sino-Japanese conflict bubbled its way to the surface in 1937 Indochina and its railways managed to stay clear of the conflict. But as the Yunnan line began carrying an ever-increasing portion of China's supplies Japanese protests were eventually heeded and the Indochinese authorities stopped all transit to China over the railway in December 1938 including Red Cross supplies and US-owned petrol and planes all awaiting shipment. When the Japanese went on from this to occupy China's Hainan Island which commands the Shanghai–Hong Kong and Singapore shipping lanes and blocks the port of Haiphong, the French responded by reopening the Yunnan line on 20 March. The Japanese bombarded the line but it kept running. However, the following year the fortunes were reversed.

In 1939 Indochina battled desperately but inadequately against the Japanese invasion. The sudden German victory and fall of France in 1940 left Indochina helpless against Japan. After heavy bombing of the line

---

❏ **Made in India**
The first air-conditioned railway coaches came to Vietnam in 1995 and were stamped Made in India. The ten air-con coaches were the first to be exported from the Integral Coach Factory in Madras. Vietnam Railways also bought five non air-con coaches from Madras. All are now in use on the Reunification Express. The total cost to Vietnam was Rs10.75 crores.

during June 1940, and despite French capitulation too, the Indochinese section of the Yunnan railway fell under Japanese control while the Chinese section fell into disrepair. Meanwhile the rest of the network was still reasonably operational despite Vietnamese sabotage of Japanese use; although US bombing of Japanese positions at the end of the war did inflict damage.

After the war was over and the Japanese troops had been sent packing, a Franco-Chinese accord of 28 February 1946 handed over control of the Chinese section of the Yunnan line to China. The accord wasn't popular in France but it was a crucial bargaining tool for encouraging Chinese troops to leave Tonkin (the north) which they did.

The Franco-Viet Minh war

The rail system was a vital means of transporting supplies for both sides in this war. Consequently both committed hundreds of acts of sabotage. France's main targets were the northern branches of the railway – from Haiphong to Lao Cai via Hanoi, and from Hanoi to Lang Son. Their methods were simple – massive air bombardment such as Operation Swallow in July 1953 which ravaged the line from Hanoi to Lang Son.

The methods of the Viet Minh were, of course, simpler, relying on pure manpower. Nonetheless their efforts on the main Trans-Indochinois Hanoi–Saigon route were so successful that the French attempted to solve the problem by building two armoured trains. Armoured trains are still no defence, however, against the enemy simply removing kilometres of track overnight. All in all the network was pulverized into a dreadful state by the time of the Geneva Accords in 1954. The rebuilding that followed was just about enough to get most of the system operational again (with some exceptions, such as Dalat–Thap Cham) when the bombing and sabotage started all over again, in the American war.

The American war

Once again the importance of the rail network was not lost on either side in the war. Sabotage by the Viet Cong grew more and more sophisticated and effective – as well as the usual explosives placed at night on bridges, which were possible to spot with care, there are tales of VCs infiltrating workyards and loosening crucial nuts and bolts when their masters took them to be carrying out repairs. But the trains kept running. As Paul Theroux relates in his book *The Great Railway Bazaar* 'as the Deputy Director of Vietnam Railways [in the south], Tran Mong Chau, a short man with thick glasses told me: "We can't stop the railway. We keep it running and we lose money. Maybe we do some repairs. If we stop it everyone will know we've lost the war."'

Meanwhile, American B-52 bombers swooped in over the northern rail system rendering it unusable again and again. The Americans also realized that while the delicate power situation might mean they couldn't mine Haiphong harbour or bomb too near the Chinese border, they could bomb the rail routes which connected these places with the rest of North Vietnam.

Meanwhile the North Vietnamese became expert at quick repairs – it was estimated that during the war a railway bridge could be repaired during only three nights. Night working was in fact so common, in an attempt to use the cover of darkness to escape detection, that in the north the railway was called the 'ghost railway' – trains ran only at night emerging as apparitions on tracks which were covered by leaves during the day to disguise the line.

The final use the train was put to in the war was to be the so-called 'peace train'. *The Sorrow of War* by Bao Ninh wonderfully describes the painfully slow but joyous progress of this train, packed with North Vietnamese soldiers finally returning home, victorious.

Rebuilding the railway – launching the Reunification Express

Soon after a North Vietnamese tank smashed through the gates of the Presidential Palace on 30 April 1975 and Vietnam was declared liberated and united, one of the first major economic reconstruction plans was launched: to rebuild the railway.

A mammoth repair programme was carried out; in all over 1300 bridges were replaced (totalling three-quarters of all bridges), 28 tunnels rebuilt (including one over 1km long) plus over 150 stations. Just over a year and a half later the first 'Reunification Express' train left HCMC for Hanoi on 31 December 1976. It was a remarkable achievement.

But despite the vast reconstruction, the legacy of destruction the railway had suffered was such that the trains in 1976 made the run between the two cities in around 40 hours – this was no faster than the fast service launched in 1936, and today the journey still takes 36 hours, at its fastest.

LIFE ON THE TRAINS

Vietnamese trains have a maximum of six classes – hard seat, soft seat, soft seat with air-con, hard berth, soft berth, soft berth with air-con. All trains operating between Hanoi and Ho Chi Minh City have hard seat, soft seat, hard berth and soft berth, while the fastest trains S1, S2, S3 and S4 also have soft seat with air-con, and their soft sleeper carriages are all fitted with air-con.

Carriages with air-con are appealing in this tropical climate, but have a tremendous disadvantage – the windows are fixed shut except for a small gap at the top, and are filthy. This means that in the best class of travel you can see almost nothing out of the window and are totally deprived of the wonderful experience of lying full length on a soft sleeper gazing directly out on to the beautiful countryside. There are two ways to avoid this – take a class without air-con, such as hard sleeper or soft seat with no air-con, or take soft sleeper in trains S5, S6, S7, S8, and avoid the soft-sleeper class in the fastest trains S1-4.

Hard seat

Hard seat has the wonderful advantage of plunging you amongst Vietnamese who are likely to be considerably interested in you especially on remote lines and always generous with their food, but has the disadvantage that it is terrifically uncomfortable. By day it is bearable and there are often empty spaces on the wooden benches allowing you to spread out and keep a good eye on your baggage, but conditions become so cramped by night as everyone tries to stretch out that the heat rises and sleep becomes virtually impossible. There is also a tendency for luggage to become strewn around the floor if the overhead racks are full, or if your luggage is too big to fit – there are difficulties with a very large rucksack.

You don't get fed in hard-seat class but on the remote lines such as Halong–Kep or local trains Hanoi–Lang Son a man goes up and down the train offering slugs of tobacco from a large pipe mechanism.

Note that if you are on a train in hard seat but the train has other classes you are very likely to be able to upgrade after a bit of judicious dealing with the conductor – this method can even give you the better class for less than it would have cost if you'd bought the ticket at the station.

Soft seat

Soft seat as its name implies certainly has more of an element of luxury about it – the seats are covered in a softish plastic cover and each individual seat reclines (unless it's broken). Because the seats are split off into pairs a soft-seat carriage is nothing like as friendly as a hard-seat carriage, but the main problem with any soft-seat journey is again the heat which besets you if the carriage is full.

Soft seat is still not the most sleep-inducive environment – the bright lights left on in all the carriages don't help, nor do the occasional bits of metal which stick out of the chair into your back.

Having soft towels or clothes handy is a godsend; some Vietnamese resort to the drastic solution of stretching out on the floor, amid nutshells and other detritus. At night particularly do beware of mosquitoes. But in the daytime you do get rather nice food which varies from soup, mineral water and yoghurt around lunchtime to a fuller meal in the evening. Once again, as with hard seat, you can usually upgrade classes if need be once on the train.

Hard sleeper

Hard sleeper is a significant step up in price and in comfort for an overnight journey. With hard-sleeper class you are in an enclosed compartment with its own light switch and six hard berths each covered with a length of rush matting. The berths are hard but are reasonably comfortable – except when the jolting of the track is too much for the train's primitive suspension, which is sadly all too common.

The prices of hard-sleeper class vary according to which bunk you take – top is cheapest, bottom most expensive. The way the compartments work is that the middle bunk folds up during the day giving enough head-room for people to sit on the bottom bunk while the top bunk is only really used to lie down on as there is not enough space to sit up.

❑ Tips for top train travel

1. The best soft seats by far are those in the very middle of each carriage where there are four seats facing each other. You can ask to buy a ticket for these with the following Vietnamese phrase – *gho ngri mem giua ton theo huong tau chay* – but they do tend to get booked up quickly.

2. Whatever class you are in, be prepared for speakers at the end of each carriage which blast out music and invocations in Vietnamese each morning.

3. Being at the back of the train is better than being at the front in one simple way – you aren't so near the endless noise of the engine's horn being honked to warn peasants and animals off the line.

4. Every carriage has several levels of windows and grilles. Locking the grille in the up position gives the best view but provokes grim warnings from Vietnamese about children's habits of throwing rocks at train's open windows. Insofar as this problem exists it is confined almost entirely to the north and seems to be believed less and less. But it would only take one incident so the judgment is yours.

5. Almost any station the train stops at, no matter how small, there will be sell-ers of fruit, dried fish or meat and good instant meals, cold drinks and poten-tially other miscellany such as newspapers. You can usually buy fruit and drinks through the window of the train – the sellers know better than you whether there is time to get off the train or not. On non-express trains the sell-ers sometimes come onto the train.

6. A fabulous way to spend time on the trains is to stand by an open door sur-veying the scene as it rolls by, but beware not to draw attention to yourself or the conductor may close the door – apparently because the train company isn't sufficiently insured to cover a foreigner's death!

7. Don't leave your carriage within 15 minutes or so of the train's final desti-nation if it's an express train because the connecting doors get locked and you'll have to run back along the platform to collect your luggage.

8. Don't lose your ticket as you won't be able to leave your destination station without it, or without buying an entirely new ticket.

9. It is very wise to bring toilet paper with you for a long train journey, or buy it at a station stop. Trains often start their journey with toilet paper but rarely end with any. There is almost always running water (certainly not for drinking) in the small bathrooms at the end of every carriage but there are no showers, baths or even hot water. The toilets are fairly clean if somewhat basic – a direct hole onto the track approach. The tall pole above the hole is for hanging on to and it has a silver mechanism for flushing half way up it.

10. Given the above arrangements it is pretty essential that you don't use the toilet while the train is in a station.

If you are travelling on your own the top bunk is often a good choice as it enables you to leave your luggage safely out of reach during the day during which time no-one will object if you sit on the bottom bunk. But if there are two of you the bottom and middle bunks are good ones to fill so that there aren't two of you occupying someone else's bottom bunk during the day and so that you can choose when the middle bunk is folded down for sleep. The compartments can become hot unless you can persuade your fellow occupants to leave the window open – but if you do this beware mosquitoes. The food brought to each compartment is usually acceptable.

Soft sleeper

Soft sleeper is indeed soft and does encourage sleep. Soft-sleeper class has you in a compartment of four berths; at each end of the carriage there are even compartments with two berths, the phrase for which is *phong ngu hai gi long*. Each berth has a soft-covered mattress around 5cm thick and the conductor provides everyone with a white cotton sheet, pillow and duvet.

Each compartment also has a small table and occasionally a washbasin or one or two chairs or stools. The bottom bunk is definitely the best option (you have to ask for it specifically when buying your ticket) because not only is it the most pleasant for sitting on during the day but it is also a fully-enclosed wooden box such that you can put all your luggage inside, underneath the mattress, and be sure of its safety. Here you meet fairly well-heeled Vietnamese but the atmosphere is still friendly and you might even come across someone who speaks English. The food brought round is usually good.

Soft sleeper with air con, the ultimate in luxury on Vietnamese trains, is provided only on the fastest Reunification Express and only really necessary if you are very sensitive to heat on long journeys because ordinary soft sleeper does not tend to get too hot. Of course the superiority of rail travel over air is not questioned, but there is a great difference in the time taken and at this class little difference in price, plus beware of the significant disadvantage of air con – you cannot see out of the window (see p137).

STEAM TRAINS

The first trains to run on all the Vietnamese track were French-made steam locomotives, but all these wood-burning steam engines have been steadily phased out. Today you can often see the old French 4-6-2 or 2-8-2 steam trains lying in the yards of major stations – Hanoi always has one or two about. However, steam is still sometimes used for freight transport which you either may be lucky enough to see, or you can arrange a steam tour with Vietnam Railways, or with foreign tour operators (see p21).

PART 4: THE SOUTH

Ho Chi Minh City and the south

Ho Chi Minh City (HCMC), or Saigon, is Vietnam's biggest city and it is a great place for food, drink and entertainment, and has many interesting historical sites – from the Reunification Palace where the war was won to the American embassy where it was ignominiously lost.

Outside the city are the fascinating war-time tunnels of Cu Chi which, if visited, must be combined with a trip to the extraordinary Cao Dai temple at Tay Ninh. You can live very cheaply in HCMC or enjoy the finest luxury the country has to offer amongst elegant colonial villas or the swankiest new bars.

HCMC is also the gateway to the fabulous Mekong Delta – the experience of phut-phutting through these lush waterways surrounded by waving smiling children is one that should not be missed.

Stretching out of the huge metropolis that is HCMC is the coastline of Vietnam where the Cham Towers of Thap Cham provide an interesting cultural diversion before reaching the beach culture of Nha Trang. Here you can enjoy the huge crashing waves on the stretch of sandy beach, great weather all-year, excellent seafood and still be on the doorstep of a genuine Vietnamese city.

CLIMATE

The south of Vietnam enjoys year-round hot weather with temperatures ranging from 22 to 32°C (70-90°F). The hottest and most humid times of the year are the months before the summer monsoon which brings warm rains from June to August. The summer rains bring heavy downpours – but they are rarely bad enough to spoil your day.

Ho Chi Minh City (Saigon)

Ho Chi Minh City (also known as HCMC) used to be called the Paris of the Orient for its wide sweeping boulevards and pleasures of the night.

Despite this reputation, when North Vietnamese troops finally entered the city triumphantly in April 1975 they were amazed by the affluence and luxury they saw there. The regime of austerity which the north enforced began in the renaming of the city and still continues today in the occasional closing of nightclubs denounced as 'social evils'.

The two cities of Hanoi and Ho Chi Minh City couldn't be more different – where HCMC is dominated by cars, then motorbikes, Hanoi is full of motorbikes and bicycles; where Hanoi encourages the opening of new discos, the much more vibrant scene in HCMC is often disrupted by their closure; and finally where Hanoi is the political capital of the country, HCMC is very much the economic capital accounting for one-third of Vietnam's GDP. As this would suggest HCMC is a very Westernized city where most people you meet speak at least some English and where you can enjoy the most luxurious accommodation in the country and sample the finest Vietnamese, and Western, food.

There is a lot to do in the city in terms of shopping, eating, nightlife, visiting pagodas (though none are truly remarkable), and especially viewing sites from the American war such as the Reunification Palace and the Rex Hotel where the press briefings were held at 5pm each day and were so notoriously works of fiction that they became known as the 'Five O' Clock Follies'. But the most Saigonesque way to enjoy this hot city is to stroll out in the evening to see and be seen.

The big bustling city is still officially called Ho Chi Minh City (or, in Vietnamese, Thanh Pho Ho Chi Minh) but many southerners and even some northerners have returned to calling it Saigon. It's divided into 11 districts – District 1 is the central district containing most places of interest (all shop fronts mark their location with D1/D2 etc). HCMC also has a large Chinese area, known as Cholon, where you can eat great Chinese food and visit many of the city's pagodas and from where, less visibly, the entrepreneurial spirit of the Chinese is bringing them, and the region, to greater economic prosperity.

HISTORY

It is over 300 years since Vietnamese fleeing from the violent rivalry between families vying for rule of the country first settled in the Mekong Delta. Despite the abundance of the land, life was not easy at first as the resident Chams had to be dealt with.

Gradually during the 18th century lands were cleared (and the Chams on them gave way in what became a monumentally one-sided clash), and on a bank of the Ben Nghe river an urban centre sprang up including a big market, the literal meaning of Cho Lon, and a street, Sai Gon.

In 1790 the citadel of Saigon was built, but after an unsuccessful rebellion against the ruling emperor was launched from there it was razed to the ground. It was rebuilt and in the next most important rebellion, against the invading French in 1859, the invaders were successfully resisted for two months, until the city fell. A few years later it was made the capital of Cochinchina and was the largest urban centre in the whole of Indochina.

The French set about making it a city to be proud of. In the era after Haussmann had redesigned Paris, building a network of connecting boulevards, the resulting beautiful effect was mimicked in Saigon (and on a smaller, but these days more concentrated, scale in Hanoi).

French impact on Vietnamese life was felt nowhere more strongly than in Saigon – where Vietnamese men were recruited into the civil and military administrations and where education in French became widespread among the reasonably affluent. Still today many elderly people around Saigon and in the Mekong Delta speak fluent French and will tell you of the glories of pre- or post-war Paris where they were sent for their education.

During the Franco-Viet Minh and American wars Saigon continued to offer a heady existence for its resident Westerners – most journalists who lived in Saigon to report on the war never left the city, nor did the last American Ambassador to the country. Because it symbolized for Vietnamese all that was luxurious it also represented much that was economically successful about the country – and the North Vietnamese were not about to win the country and lose this prize. At the same time as North Vietnamese troops reached ever closer to Saigon in 1974 and 1975 the South Vietnamese government under President Thieu hatched a plan to retain only Saigon and some of the Mekong Delta and give up all the rest of the southern territory to the North.

The plan failed miserably – attempted concentration of troops resulted only in their fatal weakening and suddenly as the rest of the country fell to the communist troops the ultimate stronghold of Saigon was quickly under real and massive threat.

The first bomb within the city limits fell on 28 April, the first troop skirmishes within city borders came the next day as a huge and chaotic evacuation was attempted before troops finally entered the city, stopping their tanks only to consult maps to try to find the way, and smashed open the gates of the Reunification Palace on 30 April 1975.

The evacuation left behind an estimated 65,000 Vietnamese who had at some time been on the payroll of the embassy or CIA and there was intense fear among the populace of a bloodbath on a scale to make the purge in Hué in 1968 seem petty. But for several days nothing happened. The streets were quiet, deserted. Then began the careful process of revenge. In June all bank accounts in the south were frozen and in October all citizens were given exactly 12 hours to convert their old currency for new, thus reducing many lifetime savings to a few US dollars in a stroke. Shortly after, began the widespread 're-education programme'. This saw an unknown number, reaching certainly into the hundreds of thousands, of leading and minor supporters of the southern regime or of the American effort incarcerated into camps of hard labour for years and then relegated to 'new economic zones' – ie barren unfertile land on which survival depended on a great deal of ingenuity and a greater amount of luck.

Over the years, and especially since Vietnam launched market reforms in 1986, the lucky ones have trickled back to Saigon (HCMC). The city now officially has four million residents – but in fact perhaps another three million live here unofficially, illegally returning to relatives or just to scrape a living often as an overeducated cyclo driver. There is still no love lost between HCMC and Hanoi, but although Hanoi holds the political whip HCMC is the country's primary economic driver and Hanoi knows it.

As is typical of thrusting Asian cities HCMC seems to hold all human life within itself. The roads fill with city slickers – a smart female office worker glides to a halt on her Honda dream with a high-heeled shoe on the brake and removes her elbow length gloves which prevent her arms tanning too much. The bars fill with businessmen supping Western beer on draft. At night persistent prostitutes cruise for business in white ao dais on motorbikes. Meanwhile amputee beggars, children selling postcards in pidgin English wearing 'I Love the USA' baseball caps, and rows of empty cyclo drivers all push themselves towards you and remind you where you are.

SIGHTS

Ho Chi Minh City is mostly a city of great and vital economic activity – not a city of museums and great buildings to look around. The finest way to spend time in this city is tasting its pleasures of food, drink, nightlife and just cruising around the streets stopping for a snack and a cold beer whenever you fancy between the shops. You can take in the evening air at one of the places where youngsters meet and chat, such as in the piazza around the Municipal Theatre, or on the dappled shade of the lawns in Cong Vien Van Hoa Park (the northernmost corner of which used to be home to the wartime expat social club, the Cercle Sportif). However, there are several sights which are well worth a look.

Perhaps the most visited sight is the **Reunification Palace** – previously known as the Presidential Palace. It was here, on 30 April 1975, that North Vietnamese tanks burst into the compound, the VC flag was raised above the building and the city, and thus the whole country was claimed by the North Vietnamese. The tank which first burst through the gates, a T-54 tank, No 834 of the 203rd Armoured Brigade, is on display in the Army Museum in Hanoi.

James Fenton wrote about this dramatic incident in his book *All the wrong places;* he was a journalist in the city at the time and was ensconced in his hotel with the few other journalists who were still in the city when he realized from the noises of the streets that the North Vietnamese had arrived. He grabbed his bag and dashed out into the open to find a tank rolling towards him adorned with young, uncertain but happy North Vietnamese soldiers debating the route. They looked at him, a Westerner, and he instinctively looked to find his passport and papers from his bag then realized this was the last thing the soldiers were thinking of; in fact he saw one of them grinning at him and motioning him on. He clambered aboard and amidst the gaggle of chattering voices and tension of expectation he found himself on the back of the first tank of many lumbering towards the Presidential Palace compound.

The building appeared ahead of them and now only the wrought-iron gates lay between them and victory. The tank rolled forward and smashed into the gates. They didn't budge! Just a small shard of twisted iron flew off, but nothing more. Then a soldier already inside the gates reached for the catch and opened the gate inwards. The tank stole through and the jubilant cry of victory was raised. Theatre was to be all – but pragmatism won the day.

The Reunification Palace is worth seeing for its symbolic value and the interior has been preserved in all its glorious 1960s and 1970s kitsch, adorned with numerous presidential objets d'art and books which the guides think to be rather more thrilling than they actually are. The Reunification Palace, 106 Nguyen Du St, is open daily from 7.30 to 10am and 1 to 4pm and costs $4.

In terms of significant symbolic value and unexciting contents the **former US Embassy** ranks high. This large building to the north of central HCMC was where so many of the American operations in Vietnam were decided on and planned. It was from here that the coup against Diem was launched and when it was all over it was from here that hundreds of Americans were evacuated from the courtyard and the helipad on the roof in the dying hours of the Southern regime. The red spot marks the point where Ambassador Martin was airlifted to safety in the early hours of 30 April 1975 while hundreds of Vietnamese were left behind (see p70 for more on the evacuation).

Museums

The **War Crimes Museum** (previously called the Museum of Chinese and American War Atrocities) is by far the most visited museum in Ho Chi Minh City. But be prepared – the displays are just as grisly as you might expect from a museum with such a title, perhaps even more so. The courtyard's display of US military hardware is acceptable enough, although the French guillotine is more graphic. But it's indoors that the true horror begins, from the frightful photographs of tortured victims, burnt, mangled and mutilated bodies, to representations of the 'tiger cages' in which

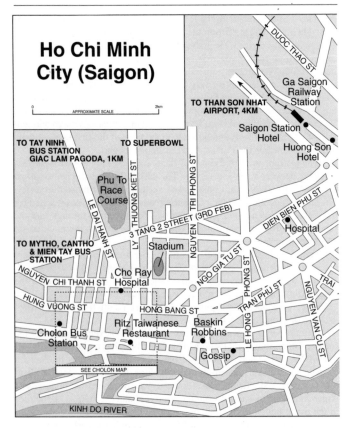

Ho Chi Minh City (Saigon)

APPROXIMATE SCALE
0   2km

DUOC THAO ST

TO THAN SON NHAT
AIRPORT, 4KM

Ga Saigon
Railway
Station

Saigon Station
Hotel

Huong Son
Hotel

TO TAY NINH
BUS STATION
GIAC LAM PAGODA, 1KM

TO SUPERBOWL

LY THUONG KIET ST

TRI PHONG ST

Phu To
Race
Course

LE DAI HANH ST

3 TANG 2 STREET (3RD FEB)

NGUYEN TRI PHONG ST

DIEN BIEN PHU ST

Hospital

TO MYTHO, CANTHO
& MIEN TAY BUS
STATION

Stadium

NGO GIA TU ST

NGUYEN CHI THANH ST

Cho Ray
Hospital

HUNG VUONG ST

HONG BANG ST

TRAN PHU ST

LE HONG PHONG ST

NGUYEN VAN CU ST

TRAI

Choion Bus
Station

Ritz Taiwanese
Restaurant

Baskin
Robbins

Gossip

SEE CHOLON MAP

KINH DO RIVER

North Vietnamese prisoners were kept for years on remote islands – their only comfort being that the vile conditions were grist to their revolutionary mill. It's a shocking display of the consequences of war.

Given the above it comes as heaven-sent respite that across the courtyard from the museum is a small building housing a display of Vietnamese traditional musical instruments. Performances are held regularly through the day and are hauntingly soothing.

The War Crimes Museum is appropriately enough housed in the former US information service building at 28 Vo Van Tan St, a block north from Cong Vien Van Hoa park. It is open daily from 7.30am to 12 noon and 1 to 4.30pm.

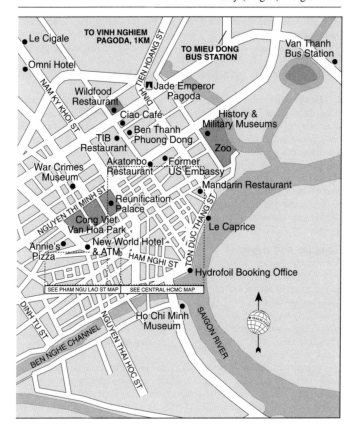

There are several other museums but probably the most worthwhile is the **Revolutionary Museum**, not least for the building which is an elegant white colonial structure which used to be known as Gia Long Palace and was home to Diem when he was president of South Vietnam. Indeed underneath the palace is a network of interconnected bunkers and tunnels which in theory stretch all the way to the Presidential (now Reunification) Palace (bring a torch and you may be allowed to see the beginnings of the network).

It was in these tunnels that Diem and his brother hid before fleeing to the Chu Tam church in Cholon on 1 November 1963 (see p150) on discovering the US-organized coup against Diem. The contents of the museum are also worth seeing – displays of VC weapons fashioned out of US army throwaways, a boat with a false bottom for smuggling weapons and photographs of anti-colonial agitators. Many of the displays are in Vietnamese only so you may wish to use one of the self-appointed guides. The museum is at 65 Ly Tu Trong St, one block south-east of Reunification Palace and is open from Tuesday to Sunday 8-11.30am and 2-4.30pm.

Of the other museums, the **Art Museum** is the most interesting with good displays of Funan art, politically correct Soviet-style art and contemporary art works; it is housed at 97A Pho Duc Chinh St and is open Tuesday to Sunday 7.30am-4.30pm. Otherwise the **History museum**, at the main entrance to the zoo at Nguyen Binh Kiem St, has interesting ancient artifacts which you may wish to skip if you intend to see any Cham towers, while **Ho Chi Minh Museum**, 1 Nguyen Tat Tanh St, has one of Ho's personal effects but otherwise is nothing like as good, or weird, as the one in Hanoi. Likewise the **Military Museum** across from the History Museum is not as full or interesting as the Army Museum in Hanoi.

Temples and pagodas

Vietnamese pagodas in general are not as stunning as those of, for example, neighbouring Thailand, but there are some fine examples of the genre in the country and in Ho Chi Minh City. Certainly in HCMC's pagodas you can see some of the largest and most pungent incense coils you are ever likely to see. In addition the Cha Tam church in Cholon has a ghoulish history – some come to experience the feel of the last hiding place of President Diem and his brother after the coup of November 1963 which ended with the assassination of both.

Perhaps HCMC's finest pagoda is the **Jade Emperor pagoda**, in the north-east of the city at 73 Mai Thai Luu St, built at the beginning of the 20th century by the Cantonese congregation. It is their best exhibit, combining magnificently grotesque portrayals of dragons and heroes with possibly the most pungent incense around, such that all senses are assailed with representations of nirvana and hell; it's very fire and brimstone.

Inside, the generals to the great Taoist Jade Emperor lead the way to his luxuriously robed body and moustached face at the altar as they stand victorious over the defeated bodies of the White Tiger and Green Dragon. The Jade Emperor himself is flanked by his two keepers of heaven – one with a lamp to light the way for the virtuous and the other with an axe for the damned.

Do make sure you also find the little side room which holds miniature figures of women sat in two rows. Each represents a different human characteristic and in parallel represents a different year in the 12-year Chinese calendar. Note the wood carvings on the walls and doors; and you can't miss the incidental turtle pond in the courtyard.

Once at the Jade Emperor pagoda you could take the time to go 1km further north to the **Vinh Nghiem pagoda**, which is off Nguyen Van Troi St, though in contrast to the previous pagoda Vinh Nghiem is as the ridiculous to the sublime. Built in the 1970s its main feature is an eight-storey bright pink tower each floor of which houses a different Buddha. The most venerable is lit by a whole array of neon lights which the caretaker delights in switching on for you. Monks gather to pray and eat in the small building next door and are most welcoming if you wish to join them.

Yet another contrast is **Giac Lam pagoda**, 3km north of Cholon at 118 Lac Long Quan St. It is the city's oldest pagoda, built in 1744, and is an appealing place to think yourself back into earlier times amid the carved wooden pillars, antique tables, terracotta tiles and monks. The pagoda celebrates Quan Am, the goddess of mercy, who stands next to the bodhi tree in the courtyard but the many buddhas on the altar are the main focus. Giac Lam is an old ranging pagoda stretching over a large compound and it is well worth a trip to see.

Down into Cholon the temples and pagodas centred around Nguyen Trai St are worth seeing. Heading westwards along Nguyen Trai St from Pham Ngu Lao St you first come to the strangely incongruous Cholon mosque on the left side at No 641 – its clean white lines and aspiring minarets are a contrast to the dark and intricate pagodas of Cholon, the first two of which are shortly after (though these two are rather missable).

On the right at 678 Nguyen Trai St is **Nghia An Hoi Quan pagoda** most distinguished by its woodwork (and the large red representations of the honoured generals of Quan Cong and his horse) and opposite it on the left (though accessed by an entrance at 118 Trieu Quang Phuc St) is **Tam**

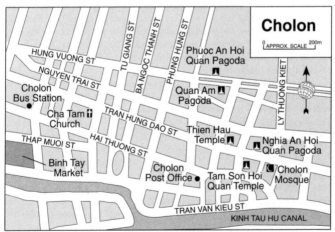

Son Hoi Quan temple which is a decorative 19th-century affair but which has seen better days. Again Quan Cong is celebrated here along with Thien Hau, the goddess of the sea – note the dragon dance costumes and photographs.

Next along is **Thien Hau temple** at 710 Nguyen Trai St. This has been much renovated recently (not entirely to its benefit) and has even been somewhat commercialized, but the saving graces are that the temple has a very active congregation of worshippers praying or thanking Thien Hau for safe water journeys, or worshipping at the figure of Me Sanh, goddess of fertility, and there are fantastic carvings on the roof.

Turning right up Chau Van Liem St and right again onto tiny Lao Tu St will bring you to **Quan Am pagoda** at No 12. This is also an active pagoda and in somewhat better condition. Through the entrance of stallholders you come into the courtyard with a wonderful view of the impressive colourful roof decorated with ceramics telling traditional Chinese tales with hundreds of figures, ships, dragons and the like. Inside the huge lacquered doors of the pagoda you will find more elaborate wood carvings on the walls which lead to the 150-year-old figure of A Pho, mother of heaven.

Retracing your steps onto Chau Van Liem St and heading north then turning right into Hung Vuong St and crossing to the northernmost side of the dual carriageway will bring you to **Phuc An Hoi Quan pagoda** at No 184. Again dedicated to the puce Quan Cong this temple is highly decorated with fine carvings and the chambers to either side of the sanctuary are stuffed with gorgeous antique furniture giving away that this was once a wealthy Chinese merchant's house.

Finally in Cholon, **Cha Tam church** at 25 Hoc Lac St remains to be visited. It was in this inauspicious pink and white building that President Ngo Dinh Diem and his brother Ngo Dinh Nhu sought refuge after the coup on 1 November 1963 which had them fleeing from Gia Long Palace. Early the following morning Diem telephoned the apparently Vietnamese organizers of the coup and agreed to give up power unconditionally, revealing their hiding place.

Diem and his brother sat in this church and waited for the car which was to arrive to take them into custody. But any dreams of life to come as ordinary citizens were soon shattered. Before the M-113 armoured vehicle arrived back with the powers that be in central Saigon, Diem and his brother were dead. They were shot in the head at point-blank range by ARVN soldiers.

Later, US sources did not deny they were behind the coup, but they protested vehemently that they had not ordered Diem's assassination and very much regretted it had occurred. Much of the rest of Saigon's population, sad to say, were only too pleased to hear the news of the repressive Diem's death. But perhaps the coup in itself would have been enough for them too.

PRACTICAL INFORMATION
Arrival and departure

By train HCMC's large and modern railway station – Ga Saigon – is 3km north of the city centre at 1 Nguyen Thong St. It houses a post office and a foreign exchange booth which will exchange dollar cash for a good rate. There is a large reasonably-comfortable waiting area in the air-conditioned hall. Outside the station there are several small eateries, large numbers of cyclos and some taxis.

The foreigners' booking office in the station is open 7.30am-7pm; there is also a booking office in the city centre (which also has give-away timetables) at 136 Ham Nghi St (across the roundabout from Ben Thanh market) which is open daily 8-11am and 1.30-3pm.

By bus HCMC has several bus stations with services operating in different directions. Buses to destinations in the Mekong go from Cholon bus station at the western end of Tran Hung Dao St in Cholon, or from the larger, but more inconveniently located Mien Tay bus station (also called the Western bus station), 10km west of HCMC; you can reach Mien Tay bus station by local bus from the bus station outside Ben Thanh market. Mien Tay station has ranks of shared taxis as well as express and non-express buses.

Mien Dong bus station serves long-distance routes north of HCMC, such as to Nha Trang, Danang, Hué, Buon Ma Thuot, Hanoi and Haiphong. The station is 5km north-east of the city centre at 78 Quoc Lo 13 St, which is the continuation of Xo Viet Nghe Tinh St.

Van Thanh bus station serves northern destinations closer to HCMC including Dalat and is 2.5km north-east of HCMC at 72 Dien Bien Phu St.

Tay Ninh bus station is 7km north-west of the centre on Le Dai Hanh St; it serves destinations north-east of HCMC including Cu Chi and Tay Ninh. Express buses depart around 5-5.30am, non-express buses depart when full throughout the day. Tickets for non-express buses can be bought just before departure, but those for express buses are best purchased the day before travel.

Shared taxis (minibuses) to different destinations congregate at the relevant bus station.

By air Ho Chi Minh City's modern Tan Son Nhat airport is 7km north of the city centre. There is a post office at the airport and a bank in the arrivals area which exchanges dollar cash at a good rate without commission.

There are also plenty of meter and non-meter taxis – a ride into the city centre should cost around $4. Slick-looking sunglass-wearing taxi drivers will approach you at the baggage reclaim area – you can negotiate a fee or wait to see if they have a meter taxi. Either way be ready for their insistent hotel recommendations. There is no bus into town. It is possible to take a cyclo for 15-20,000d but these are not allowed inside the airport perimeter so you have to walk to the gates and try your luck as there are not always cyclos waiting.

Numerous airlines fly in and out of HCMC, usually via Bangkok or Hong Kong. (Vietnam Airlines makes regular domestic flights from HCMC to other destinations in Vietnam – see p89.) If you want to book an international flight you can talk to a mini travel agent such as those along Pham Ngu Lao St or contact the airline directly, but for long-distance flights you are much more likely to get discount fares from travel agents in Bangkok, and one-way flights to Bangkok from HCMC cost only $150. To reconfirm a flight (very wise) you should speak to the airline directly. Vietnam Airlines acts as the booking office for Cambodian Airlines and Lao Aviation. See the box (p152) for details for all the airlines in HCMC; all are in District 1 unless stated otherwise.

Orientation
Ho Chi Minh City (Saigon/HCMC) is a big city, divided into 11 districts and with a hinterland that stretches much further. For most visitors there are three areas of key interest. One is the Dong Khoi St area (rue Catanat in Graham Greene's day) which has stylish sweeping streets and is home to the poshest hotels and shops as well as some of the city's nightlife and cafélife. One kilometre to the west is the Pham Ngu Lao St area which is the budget backpacker zone stuffed full of the cheapest hotels and guest-houses and travellers' cafés where you can refuel with a banana pancake or milkshake and get all your travel arrangements sorted out.

The third area is Cholon, the Chinese area. Literally meaning 'big market' there are hundreds of closely packed streets and several Chinese pagodas. HCMC's section of the Mekong runs right through the city and of course is a busy and active part of the city's life. Many of the streets close to it are not particularly picturesque unless you like walking through mud or rotten vegetables; you also have to like rotten vegetables to like much of the river.

Services
Post and telecommunications
As might be expected HCMC has a large **post office** with all the facilities, including fax (note that it costs $0.50 to pick up incoming faxes), telex and poste restante. The post office is at the head of Dong Khoi St, next to Notre Dame Cathedral and is open daily 6.30am-10.30pm. Several private mail carriers also have offices here including DHL and Fedex. Staff, of course, speak English.

The Pham Ngu Lao St area is now chock-a-block with **cyber cafés** and hotels with internet connections. Cyber cafés include Saigon Net (☎ 837 2573, ✉ tiendat@saigonnet.vn) Hoang Anh Interpia, (☎ 836 7815, ✉ detham.vn@yahoo.co.kr) at 266 De Tham St.

Many of the small hotels are now on the net, including two excellent establishments on the westernmost alleyway between Pham Ngu Lao St and

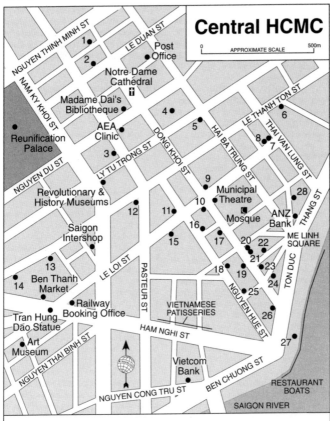

Central HCMC

0   APPROXIMATE SCALE   500m

Places to Stay
9 Continental Hotel
11 Rex Hotel
26 Majestic Hotel

Places to Eat
3 Vy Restaurant
4 Annie's Pizza
5 Monte Rosa Café
6 Ashoka Indian
  Restaurant
8 Camargue
  Restaurant

12 Baskin Robbins
14 Legros Restaurant
16 Lemongrass Restaurant,
  Augustin Restaurant &
  Globo Café
17 Tan Nam Restaurant
18 Ciao Café
19 Vietnam House
  Restaurant
22 Ice Cream Café 24
23 Paloma Café
28 Quan An Restaurant &
  Apocalypse Now

Other
1 Sawaddee
2 Press Club
7 Sama
10 Q Bar
13 Marine Club
15 Queen Bee Club
20 Ice Blue
21 Garbenstadt
24 La Fourchette
25 Santa Lucia
27 Hammock Bar

Bui Vien St – Thao Nhi (☎ 836 0020, 🖃 837 2282, 💻 huynhquangliem@hcm. fpt.vn), and Giang Hotel (☎ 836 9559, 💻 tunglam@hcm.vnn.vn or pqgiang @yahoo.com). This hotel throws 20 minutes of free internet time in with the cost of the room.

The usual price for internet usage is 400d per minute (which is easyeverything.com's standard European price of $1.30 per minute), although some charge as little as 300d per minute.

Money HCMC and Hanoi are the only cities which have ATM machines for Cirrus and Delta cardholders. In HCMC, ANZ's (☎ 829 9319) ATM (open 24 hours) is at 11 Me Linh Square, District 1, close to Caravelle Hotel. HSBC's ATM is at the western end of the New World building, near the Pham Ngu Lao St area.

There are several banks along Ben Chuong Doung St on the river-front: Vietkombank at No 17 (☎ 829 7045) gives the best terms for changing money; it charges 0.5 per cent commission to change dollar travellers' cheques into dong and 1 per cent to encash them into US dollars; cash advances on Visa or MasterCard credit or debit cards cost 4 per cent commission. The cash counter is open Monday to Friday 8-11.30am and 1-4pm. This bank will also exchange a large number of other foreign currencies charging no commission to change between currencies and 0.5 per cent commission to change into dong. A branch of Vietkombank (☎ 836 8018) which is closer to the budget area of town and open longer (Monday to Saturday 7am-9pm) is the one at 195 Pham Ngu Lao St on the corner with De Tham St. This charges 2 per cent commission to change dollar travellers' cheques into dong or US dollars.

A word about **exchange rates**: more people quote prices in US dollars in HCMC than elsewhere in the country and most will charge you a disadvanta-

geous rate for paying in dong – meaning that you end up paying more dong for a dollar then you can actually receive in the bank. The result is that you are often best off paying in US dollars in Ho Chi Minh City rather than dong.

Visa extensions In theory HCMC has a police station, at 254 Nguyen Tran St, which deals with visa extensions, but you are much better off going to one of the mini travel agents on Pham Ngu Lao St or to a travellers' café where you should be able to obtain one for $25 with minimum hassle.

Medical The best general medical facilities in HCMC are to be found at the Dien Bien Phu Hospital at 280 Dien Bien Phu St, District 3. For services outside of hospitals try the usually very good multilingual doctors who can provide treatment 24 hours a day at AEA International Clinic (☎ 829 8520), 65 Nguyen Du St, District 1, or at the Emergency Centre (☎ 829 2071), 125 Le Loi Boulevard, District 1. Consultations at either usually cost around $40.

Cho Ray Hospital in Cholon (210B Nguyen Chi Thanh Boulevard, District 3), is the largest hospital in the country with 1000 beds and has an out-patients facility and an in-patients ward for foreigners (a snip at $25 a night), but not all its equipment is of the best. HCMC's excellent pharmacies are on Nguyen Hué St or Dong Khoi St.

The best dental treatment in the country is at Unit 10, Ground floor, Grand Hotel, 8 Dong Khoi St, (☎ 824 5772).

Local transport
HCMC is a big city, by far Vietnam's largest. However, it is no Bangkok and most of the places you would wish to see can be reached on foot or by bicycle (there aren't any hills); longer distances are very easily covered by motorbike or

❏ **Consulates**
Vietnam's foreign embassies are all located in the capital, Hanoi, but HCMC is replete with foreign consulates: **Australia** (☎ 829 9387), 5B Ton Duc Thang St, District 1; **Belgium** (☎ 824 3571), 230G Pasteur St, District 3; **Cambodia** (☎ 829 2751), 41 Phung Khac Khoan, District 1; **Canada** (☎ 824 2000) 203 Dong Khoi St, Suite 102 District 1; **China** (☎ 829 2457), 39 Nguyen Thi Minh Khoi St, District 1; **France** (☎ 829 7321), 27 Nguyen Thi Minh Khai St, District 1; **Germany** (☎ 829 1967), 126 Nguyen Dinh Chieu St, District 3; **India** (☎ 823 1539), 49 Tran Quoc Thao St, District 3; **Indonesia** (☎ 822 3799), 18 Phung Khac St, District 1; **Italy** (☎ 829 8721), 3rd floor, 4 Dong Khoi St, District 1; **Japan** (☎ 822 5314), 13-17 Nguyen Hué St, District 1; **Laos** (☎ 829 7667), 98 Pasteur St, District 1; **Malaysia** (☎ 829 9023), 53 Nguyen Dinh Chieu St, District 3; **Netherlands** (☎ 823 5932), Saigon Tower, 29 Le Duan St, District 1; **New Zealand** (☎ 822 6907), 41 Nguyen Thi Minh Khai St, District 1; **Singapore** (☎ 822 5173), 5 Phung Khac Khoan St, District 1; **Thailand** (☎ 822 2637), 77 Tran Quoc Thao St, District 3; **UK** (☎ 829 8433), 261 Dien Bien Phu St, District 3.

taxi – there are always plenty of the latter roaming the streets and gathering outside the top hotels. Alternatively there are several phone-up taxi services – try Airport Taxis (☎ 844 6666), or to book a taxi for a day the best prices are from the travellers' cafés.

Cyclos are equally plentiful though HCMC has the small kind, common in the south, which can fit two Westerners only with difficulty. Most hotels rent out bicycles by the day for $1 and there are endless places along Pham Ngu Lao St and environs from where you can rent a motorbike for the day ($4-6).

Tours
HCMC's travellers' cafés offer excellent deals on tours to the Mekong Delta, the Cao Dai temple at Tay Ninh and the Cu Chi tunnels. They can also organize the cheapest taxi and tourist bus deals around (eg $7 for a tourist bus to Dalat). These cafés are found especially around the Pham Ngu Lao St area and offer pretty similar tours and prices. Many of the guides for Kim Café and Sinh Café are South Vietnamese army veterans so you can often get to hear some very interesting stories.

Some sample tours offered by Kim Café (☎/🖶 836 9859) at 270 De Tham St, are a one-day tour to Cao Dai temple at Tay Ninh and the tunnels of Cu Chi costs $4, plus $3 entrance for the tunnels and a stop for lunch. A one-day tour to Mytho in the Mekong Delta will cost only $7 including boat trips and a visit to a bee farm or the like. A two-day tour will cost around $20 (including accommodation) and take you further into the Mekong to Cantho and to some floating markets, while a three-day tour costs roughly $30 and will take you from Cantho to Sam mountain next to the Cambodian border. While these are terrific value for money, they do involve being herded about in a crammed minibus for hours on end.

However, Sinh Café and Kim Café have become such big businesses that their customer service seems to have dropped. Happily there are new players on the tour scene with a more personal service and smaller buses, such as the very friendly Tomateco Pro Tour (☎/🖶 837 3716, 🖂 pro_tours@yahoo.com) at 40 Bui Vien St.

At the other end of the spectrum the various branches of Saigon Tourist in the city's smartest hotels will arrange

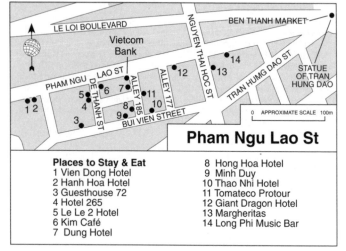

Pham Ngu Lao St

Places to Stay & Eat
1 Vien Dong Hotel
2 Hanh Hoa Hotel
3 Guesthouse 72
4 Hotel 265
5 Le Le 2 Hotel
6 Kim Café
7 Dung Hotel

8 Hong Hoa Hotel
9 Minh Duy
10 Thao Nhi Hotel
11 Tomateco Protour
12 Giant Dragon Hotel
13 Margheritas
14 Long Phi Music Bar

more luxurious trips, at several times the price.

Where to stay
The hotel market is huge and varied: somewhere amongst the hustle and the bustle there is accommodation for most tastes. There is such a wealth of accommodation in the city that it is possible to bargain down prices, often considerably, even in the most expensive hotels.

Most of the cheap to mid-range hotels are located around the Pham Ngu Lao St area; the finest hotels in town are to be found in the Dong Khoi St area. There is a small area in Cholon where a few hotels have congregated, but they are not particularly good or good value for money. There is no good value accommodation near the airport, but the centre of town is only $4 and a 20-minute ride away. Nor is there any very good accommodation near the railway station: *Saigon Station Hotel* (☎ 843 6189), 1A Nguyen Thong St, offers not very clean or pleasant doubles but it might be your best bet, unless you want to pay $15-20 for a smallish room and

sloppy service in *Huong Son Hotel* (☎ 843 5815), 69/10 Nguyen Thong St, 10-minutes' walk from the station.

Pham Ngu Lao St was traditionally the budget haven. These days this street mostly has hotels in the $20-40 category, while De Tham St around the corner mostly has hotels in the $10-20 category, and rounding another corner brings you to Bui Vien St where the main hub of budget accommodation activity has shifted to.

The stretch of Bui Vien St to the west of De Tham St is literally packed with tiny three- or four-room hotels. Most of these have small pleasant-enough rooms and many have very friendly and helpful staff. Their prices are permanently negotiable but should be no more than $6-8 for doubles with bathroom and fan and $10-12 for doubles with air-con. Two of the friendliest are *Guesthouse 72* (☎ 836 8421), 72 Bui Vien St, and *Minh Duy Hotel* (☎ 836 8956), at No 135. There are around 15 other such hotels along this stretch, some names include *Minh Phuc*, *Hoang Long*, *Van Chau*, *Haiha*, *Hong*

Loi and *Van Thi*. A large cheapie at 325 Pham Ngu Lao St which should be avoided is *Thanh Binh Hotel*: there have been many reports of thefts there, which appear to have been committed by the hotel staff.

For doubles at around $10-15 there are a few relatively quiet hotels along alleys 175 and 185 which run between Pham Ngu Lao St and Bui Vien St east of, and parallel to, De Tham St. Two such are *Hong Hoa Hotel* (☎ 836 1915), 185/28 Pham Ngu Lao St and *Dung Hotel* (☎ 836 7049), 185/6 Pham Ngu Lao St which despite its name is very nice.

Two hotels offering good doubles with air-con, fridge and telephone for around $15-20 along De Tham St are *Hotel 265* (☎ 836 7512, 🖹 836 1883), at No 265, and *Le Le 2 Hotel* (☎ 836 8585, 🖹 836 8787) at No 269.

The new *Hanh Hoa Hotel*, 237 Pham Ngu Lao St, is a pleasing hotel with friendly staff and good standard doubles with air-con, fridge, telephone and TV for $20-30. The imposing building of *Giant Dragon Hotel* (☎ 836 4759, 🖹 836 7279), at No 173 on the same street, has well decorated good doubles and suites it offers for $30-50. The staff are helpful and the upper floors have a good view of the city. *Vien Dong Hotel* (☎ 836 8941, 🖹 836 8812), at No 275A, has had a complete renovation and is now even better than before, though it no longer has any budget rooms. It offers rooms at $63 and suites for $100 – but these can often be bargained down to half the price.

If you can afford it, the city's finest hotels all offer beautiful accommodation and great service with a variety of historical attractions. *Majestic Hotel* (☎ 829 5514, 🖹 829 5510), 1 Dong Khoi St, is truly majestic and with its beautiful riverside location, gorgeously decorated rooms and inner courtyard with swimming pool it has to be the best of the best. It's not cheap though; expect to pay at least $100 unless you bargain.

Rex Hotel (☎ 829 6043, 🖹 829 6536), 141 Nguyen Hué St, has many rooms which are rather small (but commensurately cheaper) and it was the scene of the Five O' Clock Follies (see p142) and has a fantastic roof garden with the best cocktails in town (see p160). *Continental Hotel* (☎ 829 9201, 🖹 824 1772), 132 Dong Khoi St, still retains the old-world colonial charm and outdoor terraced bar, the *Continental Shelf*, so frequented by journalists during the American war. It has fine rooms and a wonderful breakfast.

Where to eat

HCMC serves up some of the best food in the classiest restaurants in the country. It also has a wealth of good food cooked up in an instant by street vendors. Whether you want to eat Vietnamese, Chinese, Japanese, French, Italian, Indian, Russian, Thai, seafood, snake, turtle, dove or fieldmouse – it's here.

For the best value Vietnamese food, head to Ben Thanh Market; the many competing food stalls in the back of the market serve up great food at good prices amid a lively household shopping scene. Outside the market there are a number of stalls distanced from the bouquet. There are many small touristy travellers' cafés selling Vietnamese and Western food along De Tham St in the Pham Ngu Lao St area – generally the Western food here is better than the Vietnamese; though there are many stalls down the side streets in this area which serve good food. In the Dong Khoi area, Thi Sach St is famous for seafood. Of the many good seafood restaurants on this street the most notable is *Quan An* at 2A, directly next

---

❏ **Area code**
The area code for Ho Chi Minh City (HCMC/Saigon) is ☎ 08

door to *Apocalypse Now*. Also in the Dong Khoi area, Hai Ba Trung St is home to some large busy restaurants popular with Vietnamese, such as *Ben Thanh Phuong Dong* (☎ 829 3804) at No 104.

A couple of blocks north on the same side of the street are several **wild-food restaurants** such as one which is a large open-air restaurant filled with tanks of live animals where you can choose from python, cobra, turtle, field-mouse or bat. A casserole of the cheapest snake (red-spotted) would set you back only around 90,000d. It is surprisingly tasty, although not if you act on the owner's insistence to eat the skin. The menu is in English and Vietnamese.

Good food can also be found on the boats tied up along the riverfront opposite Majestic Hotel, though the main advantage of these 'floaters' is the atmosphere; they are very popular in the evening with Vietnamese. Some actually do float off between 7 and 9pm (the times are printed on signs outside).

While you can often find delicious **Vietnamese food** on the streets or from tiny restaurants for next to nothing, some of the food served in HCMC's most expensive Vietnamese restaurants is truly sumptuous: Lemongrass, Vy, Tan Nam, Vietnam House and TIB, which are all around the Dong Khoi area, serve some exquisite dishes. In all of these it is possible to spend around $10 a head including a couple of beers, or to spend considerably more according to the dishes you choose. The big hotels in town all have good Vietnamese restaurants, and often have a good buffet deal, but they lack the charm of HCMC's great restaurants.

Lemongrass (☎ 822 0496), 4 Nguyen Thiep St off Dong Khoi St, is a beautifully elegant place; the vegetable dishes here are exceptional. There is usually one Vietnamese performer quietly playing the lyre until around 9pm. *Vy Restaurant* (☎ 829 6210), 164

Pasteur St, and *Tan Nam Restaurant*, 59-61 Dong Khoi St, both do very good food although most dishes are expensive. *Vietnam House* (☎ 829 1623), 93-95 Dong Khoi St, is a lovely restaurant in an old French villa. A group of Vietnamese play traditional instruments from around 7-9pm; the restaurant closes shortly after 9pm. *TIB* (☎ 829 7242), 187 Hai Ba Trung St, set back from the road, also does fabulous food which you can enjoy inside or outside under the umbrellas to the sound of the cicadas.

The two biggest cuisines in HCMC after Vietnamese are French and Chinese. Cholon is of course the area for **Chinese food** and many of its streets are packed with small restaurants. The most popular of the larger restaurants is *Ritz Taiwanese Restaurant* (☎ 822 4325) in Ritz Hotel at 333 Tran Hung Dao St; indeed it is so popular that reservations are often necessary.

The best **French restaurants** are the following, listed in ascending price order, all are in District 1 unless otherwise indicated. All these restaurants have a fairly extensive wine list though for pretty high prices. *La Fourchette* (☎ 829 8143), 9 Ngo Duc Ke St, has a friendly bistro atmosphere as does *Augustine* (☎ 829 2941) at 10 Nguyen Thiep St. *Madame Dai's Bibliotheque* (☎ 823 1438), 84A Nguyen Du St, has a great set menu of Vietnamese and French food and Madame Dai (leader of the opposition in the South Vietnamese parliament in the 1960s) is a fascinating character to talk to – in English, French or Vietnamese. *Globo Café* (☎ 822 8855), 6 Nguyen Thiep St, is a very trendy spot serving as a bar and restaurant. More traditional French restaurant styles are to be found at *Legros* (☎ 822 8273), 267-269 Le Thanh Ton St, and *Le Cigale* (☎ 844 3930), 158 Nguyen Dinh St, opposite Omni Hotel in Phu Nhuan district. A new French-Vietnamese restaurant, which many consider to be the best restaurant in the country, is *The Mandarin* (☎ 822 9783) at 11A Ngo Van Nam St; here you are guaranteed excellent service and fine food, for around $20 a head.

Le Bordeaux (☎ 899 9831) is miles away from anywhere at F7-F8, D2 Road, Commune 25, Binh Thanh District, but does beautiful food. *Le Caprice* (☎ 822 8337), Landmark Building, 5B Ton Duc Thang St, meanwhile offers a commanding view of the city and great food. Perhaps the two most expensive restaurants are *L'Etoile* (☎ 829 7939), 180 Hai Ba Trung St, which will probably set you back around $40 per head (although it is good it is perhaps not as excellent as it once was) and the renowned *Camargue*, 16 Cao Ba Quat St (☎ 824 3148), which offers a small menu, good food, good music and a lovely setting in exchange for around $50 a head which is about as expensive as it gets in Vietnam.

For food of other nationalities (all in District 1 unless otherwise stated): the two best cheap places for **Italian food** are *Margherita* (☎ 836 8435), 175/1 Pham Ngu Lao St, and *Ciao Café* (☎ 822 9796), 21-23 Nguyen Thi Minh Khai St. A good option for a much more up-market candlelit affair with a selection of Italian wines is *Santa Lucia* (☎ 822 6562), 14 Nguyen Hué St. *Marine Club* (☎ 829 2249), 174A Le Thanh Ton St, run by the city's noted expat Jeremy Hogue, also does excellent pizzas and has the only wood-fired pizza oven in HCMC. Look out for the new restaurant he is rumoured to be opening.

Two places serving good **German food** and excellent German beer are *Bavaria* (☎ 822 2673), 20 Le Anh Xuan St, opposite New World Hotel, and *Gartenstadt* (☎ 822 2673), 34 Dong Khoi St. *'A' Restaurant* (☎ 835 9190), 361/8 Nguyen Dinh Chieu St in District 3, does excellent **Russian food**.

Ashoka (☎ 8231372), 17/10 Le Thanh Ton St, and *Mosque restaurant*, 66 Dong Du St (no telephone), behind the mosque are very good **Indian** restaurants: the latter is a very popular place for lunch. *Sawaddee* (☎ 822 1402), 29B Thai Van Long St, has long served excellent **Thai food**. For good **Japanese food** at reasonable prices head to *Akatonbo* (☎ 824 4928), 38 Hai Ba Trung St.

There are a number of choices for **Western fast food, bakeries and ice cream**. The outlets of *Annie's Pizza* (☎ 822 3661, deliveries 839 2577), famous for its Australian menu, are at 57 Nguyen Du St and 21 Bui Thi Xuan St.

The best sandwiches in the city are to be found at *Sama* (☎ 822 4814) 35 Dong Du St. Near here along Dong Khoi St are several French-style fancy patisseries; more standard Vietnamese patisseries are to be found along the lower end of Ham Nghi Blvd. *Ice Cream Café 24* (☎ 829 2871), 24 Ho Huan Nghiep St, does good ice cream as does *Monte Rosa* (☎ 824 4425), 125A Hai Ba Trung St.

There are three branches of *Baskin Robbins* in HCMC: at 128A Pasteur St (☎ 829 5775), 148 Tran Hung Dao St District 5 (☎ 855 3517), and at the superbowl at A43 Truong Son, Tan Binh district (☎ 885 1865).

HCMC's **supermarkets** and **mini-markets** can sell you everything Western from corn flakes and camembert to Swiss chocolate and Gordon's gin. The biggest and best is the Minimart inside the Saigon Intershop at 101 Nam Ky Khoi Nghia St, just off Le Loi St; this is open from 7am to 7pm. There is also a large supermarket (☎ 845 8119) at the superbowl at 141, A43 Truong Son, Tan Binh district. In addition there are plenty of minimarkets around the city such as the one at 160 Hai Ba Trung St (☎ 829 9258). These tend to be open later, until around 9pm.

If you are searching out a more extensive range of alcohol than these shops provide you should look at Ton That Thiep St which is affectionately known as 'street of booze shops'. Saigon Duty Free Shoppers allows you to do your airport duty-free shopping in relaxed air-conditioned comfort. You need to show a ticket with a flight out of the country leaving soon in order to buy goods, which get transported to the airport where you pick them up.

Entertainment

Vietnamese culture If you don't catch the performances of traditional Vietnamese music outside the War Crimes museum there are more convivial places to be caroused – most of the good restaurants on Dong Khoi St have live traditional concerts in the evening.

For more adventurous entertainment it's worth checking out the Municipal Theatre, opposite the Continental Hotel, which often has plays or operas in Vietnamese, but also circus acts and other multi-cultural events.

Although water puppetry (see p77) was mostly a northern tradition, Saigon now has its own water puppet theatre troupe who perform daily for early risers at 9am and for others at 2pm at 28 Vo Van Tan St, District 3 (☎ 825 8496).

And finally for something really racy and very Vietnamese check out the racecourse with its legalized gambling, the love of so many Asians and Orientals. Races are run in the early afternoon every Saturday and Sunday and foreigners are also allowed to place bets, although the maximum bet is still only a few US dollars. In order to win for such huge stakes you have also to correctly place both the first and second horse. It's all great fun. Phu Tho racecourse is just north of Cholon at 2 Le Dai Hanh St.

Bars There are some great places in Ho Chi Minh City to enjoy an evening drink, many of them are located in the Dong Khoi area. For a good range of beer and delicious free popcorn try *Ice Blue* (☎ 822 2664), 54 Dong Khoi St, if you can bear the sight of Aussie expats chatting up some or all of the waitresses; if not try *Gartenstadt* (☎ 822 3623), 34 Dong Khoi St. Another venue with a pub feel to it is the expat haunt *Hammock Bar* (☎ 829 1468) in an old cargo boat which has floated along the river to its new address at 1A Ton Duc Thang St near the Floating Hotel. To catch up on the latest news you could try the *Press Club* (☎ 8291948), 39 Le Duan St, which is the hangout for HCMC's journalists.

Some trendy bars with good eats are *Paloma Café* (☎ 829 5813), 26 Dong Khoi St, *Café Latin* (☎ 822 6363), 25 Dong Du St, which does good tapas and the stylish *Globo Café* (☎ 822 8855), 6 Nguyen Thiep St. The highly trendy *Q Bar* (☎ 823 6424), 7 Cong Truong Lam Son St, in front of the old Caravelle Hotel on the side of the National Theatre, is still at the top of the list of HCMC's bars after five years. *Long Phi Music Bar* (☎ 836 9319), 163 Pham Ngu Lao St, has a great stock of music as well as atmosphere and drinks, as does *Marine Club* (☎ 829 2249), 174A Le Thanh Ton St, which has live music every Tuesday night. *Apocalypse Now* (☎ 824 1463), 2C Thi Sach St, is an old favourite with some music and drink lovers. It also serves standard Western food, though the Vietnamese seafood restaurant next door has much better fare.

Most of the best hotels, such as the Omni, Rex, Majestic, Amara and Saigon Prince (see p157), have a rooftop **cocktail bar**. The rooftop of the Rex with its

---

(Opposite) **Top**: Culinary influences from around the world: snails served with chillis, washed down with a bottle of Bailey's Irish cream! **Bottom**: Phung Hiep floating market near Cantho (see p172).

revolving lit crown, bizarre topiaried animals and open-air swimming pool cannot be beaten for atmosphere; a wonderful pina colada costs around 90,000đ. The more restrained rooftop of the Majestic is very attractive and its triple sec cocktail sensational.

Nightclubs When HCMC's nightclubs are not closed for being 'social evils' – which does happen – there are some excellent night-time venues which are very popular with young Vietnamese. Most have no cover charge but the drinks are very expensive; some serve rather unpleasant food. Perhaps the two best for good dance music, techno and lightshows are *Artist Discotheque* (☎ 886 1421), 25 Phan Phu Tien St (at the eastern end of Cholon), District 5 and *Gossip* (☎ 824 2525), in Mercury Hotel, 79 Tran Hung Dao St, which is popular despite a cover charge.

The biggest *Queen Bee Club* (☎ 829 8860) in Vietnam is at 104 Nguyen Hué St; it had a big disco, bar and karaoke but has recently been closed for being a social evil though it may re-open. *Apocalypse Now* (☎ 824 1463), 2C Thi Sach St, is generally busy and blasts out loud music until late, but is more popular with foreigners than with Vietnamese. The same cannot be said of the Superbowl complex, which also houses the very popular *Planet Europa* (☎ 885 0184) at A43 Truong Son St, Tan Binh district.

Many areas of HCMC have a selection of karaoke bars. The larger and tackier hotels have glitzy top floor karaoke rooms and these are just a fraction of the thousands of neon signs proclaiming karaoke that you will see all around the city. Take your pick – perhaps the best way to experience such an evening is to go with a group of Vietnamese (remember not to criticize anyone's singing as this is very rude!).

Be aware that if you enter a nightclub as a single male or in a male-only group you will be hard pushed to avoid the advances of prostitutes. Even just walking down the street as a single male will get you approached by pimps by day and prostitutes (complete with white ao dai and motorbike) by night.

Cinemas CLB Phim Tu Lieu Cinema (☎ 822 2324), at 212 Ly Chinh Thang St in District 3, shows English-language films nightly, subtitled in Vietnamese. Here you can see blockbusters for a lot less than in the West – around $1.

French-language films are shown nightly at the French Cultural Centre IDECAF (☎ 829 5451) at 31 Thai Van Lung St, District 1.

Things to buy
HCMC is stuffed full of great things to buy from the latest fake Christian Dior watches and Polo shirts (Ben Thanh market) to fabulous silk cloths and clothes (Dong Khoi St). The finest wine shop in the city is Thien Minh (☎ 823 6265) at 29 Le Duan St.

Ben Thanh market is a good place to begin any shopping exploits as you can find most functional things here amidst the tightly-packed stalls. This is also the place to buy the best-quality wool for men's suits if you are thinking of having one made up. For your tailoring requirements head to Le Thanh Ton St which is peppered with many good tailors as well as designer clothes shops and the finest cotton shops (patchwork furnishings for children are a particular speciality of several shops).

At the very bottom of Dong Khoi St next to Majestic Hotel are the finest

(Opposite) Top: Cao Dai temple in Tay Ninh (see p162), 100km north-west of HCMC. **Bottom**: Crossing the river in Cantho (see p172).

silk shops in town – the variety of silks is fantastic and the tailoring is good and inventive (though more expensive than in Hoi An). Some shops here can make you a whole matching silk outfit including bag and shoes. These shops also stock some outstanding combination fabrics – such as 50 per cent linen, 50 per cent silk. Further up Dong Khoi St are many shops selling touristy arts'n'crafts which are not especially good, and peddling great reproductions of endless numbers of classic and modern paintings. You can commission the artists to create one for you, or of you – either way having a photo which can be copied is the most reliable method. Beware, though – see p125!

There are many good opticians around 120 Le Thanh Ton St, who can make up excellent prescription glasses and sunglasses for a fraction of Western costs. But imported designer frames are much more expensive than the lenses, although still cheaper than Western prices.

AROUND HO CHI MINH CITY

As well as being Vietnam's largest city with its own host of attractions HCMC is also the springboard for several excellent excursions. Perhaps the single most popular excursion, and justifiably so, is to the **Mekong Delta**. All the travellers' cafés offer tours to the delta which are extremely good value for money (see p155) or you can easily travel independently. Either way the sights and sounds of the Mekong – from the bright colours of floating markets to the hordes of waving children from the riverbanks – are often an unforgettable part of any visitor's time in Vietnam. If you travel here independently or in a tour you will find it easy to explore the waterways and sample the delicious food of this huge garden that the Mekong waters; if you travel in a tour you will also be taken to see some interesting remnants of the war, such as VC hideouts and the inevitable bomb craters.

But there are also other great trips to do from HCMC – most notably visiting the fabulously colourful Cao Dai temple at Tay Ninh and exploring the tunnels of Cu Chi – a vast network of underground tunnels in which large numbers of VC troops hid and then emerged from hidden entrances in the middle of US positions to devastating effect. Travellers' cafés offer an excellent deal of seeing both sights within the day for $4 (plus $3 entry for the tunnels).

Finally the seaside resort of Vung Tao is much visited but often disappoints. It is not an attractive resort as it has been developed beyond any natural saturation point, but it is the closest beach to the big city. If you do visit the best way to get there is by hydrofoil (see box on p163 for details); the bus costs half as much as the hydrofoil but takes twice as long. Once in Vung Tao you can take your pick from a million similar places to stay.

Cao Dai temple at Tay Ninh

Tay Ninh's Cao Dai temple is possibly Vietnam's most amazing religious structure. It is a fantastic Disneyesque creation of brightly coloured drag-

❏ **Hydrofoil services**
Hydrofoil ferries leave from the quay in HCMC, and tickets can be bought
from the ticket office – Vina Express office (☎ 829 7892 or 821 5609) – on the
riverfront where Ham Nghi boulevard meets Ton Duc St. All services are daily
and prices quoted are for single journeys.

HCMC to Vung Tau: ferries leave every two hours between 06.30 and 16.30.
The journey takes 1¼hours and costs $10.

HCMC (dep)	Mytho (dep)	Cantho (arr)	
07.30	09.30 ($12)	11.30 ($24)	
Cantho (dep)	Mytho (dep)	HCMC (arr)	
13.30	15.30	17.30	
HCMC (dep)	Mytho (dep)	Vinh Long (dep)	Chau Doc (arr)
08.00	09.55	10.55 ($16)	13.00 ($28)
Chau Doc (dep)	Vinh Long (dep)	Mytho (dep)	HCMC (arr)
08.30	10.30	11.30	13.30

on-clad pillars reaching up to a blue sky ceiling dotted with perfect clouds
swooped over by swift nesting birds who fill the air with their chirping
cries. The extraordinary medley of symbols and icons was perfectly
described by Norman Lewis (see box on p164) as 'fun-fair architecture'.
In the midst of this merriment the local strong collection of followers file
in each day at dawn, noon, sunset and midnight, splendid in white or
coloured robes and solemnly pray and advance up the nape of the cathedral. It is a fantastic sight and one particularly worth seeing as the followers are clearly so welcoming to visitors; the sashed stewards are happy
to talk about their faith or their history, or even how they manage to retain
such bright painted colours in the humidity of the country which so notoriously crumbles paint. Tours to the Cao Dai temple take you to the noon
ceremony which makes the visitors' gallery very full at this time – but the
church is big enough to take the crowds and they lend the occasion something of a festival atmosphere.

Tay Ninh is around 100km north-west of HCMC off Highway 22.
Buses and shared taxis to and from the town congregate in Tay Ninh bus
station in HCMC, 7km north-west of the centre. Alternatively travellers'
cafés offer tours combined with the Cu Chi tunnels for an unbeatable $4.

The Cu Chi tunnels
The network of over 250km of underground tunnels accessed around the
village of Cu Chi stretching from the outskirts of Ho Chi Minh City to the
Cambodian border were dug in the 1960s by Viet Cong troops as a brilliantly effective way of both escaping enemy fire and enabling sudden
devastating raids into enemy areas at no warning. The tunnels are terrify-

> ❏ **From *A Dragon Apparent* by Norman Lewis**
>
> 'Cao Daism sounded extraordinary enough to merit investigation. There was a cathedral that looked like a fantasy from the brain of Disney, and all the faiths of the Orient had been ransacked to create the pompous ritual which had been grafted on an organization copied from the Catholic church.
>
> From a distance this structure could have been dismissed as the monstrous result of a marriage between a pagoda and a Southern baroque church, but at close range the vulgarity of the building was so impressive that mild antipathy gave way to fascinated horror. This cathedral must be the most outrageously vulgar building ever to have been erected with serious intent. It was a palace in candy from a coloured fantasy by Disney; an example of fun-fair architecture in extreme form.
>
> Over the doorway was a grotesquely undignified piece of statuary showing Jesus Christ borne upon the shoulders of Lao Tse and in turn carrying Confucius and Buddha. They were made to look like Japanese acrobats about to begin their act. Once inside one expected continually to hear bellowing laughter relayed from some nearby tunnel of love.'

ingly small (even the ones widened to fit Western, tourist, frames) and the entrances superbly hidden. The tunnels were hewn out of the red clay, which soft and pliant was perfect for the task, although disposing of the soil was more difficult (at least the VC had rivers to dump it in where the Colditz inmates did not). The snakes and scorpions which were regularly encountered in the digging process claimed their share of victims. But it was worth it because for several years local US troops simply didn't understand how it was that VC troops seemed to appear deep within their enclaves, and then just disappear again – seemingly melting into the undergrowth. The answer of course was the tunnels with their magnificently complex network, often running to four levels deep and complete with ventilator shafts and wells.

Once US intelligence had understood what must be going on special crack troops of 'tunnel rats' were formed – the smallest of US soldiers were picked for the unenviable and invariably deadly job of going down the tunnels to kill their inhabitants. But in this wargame the VCs clearly had the advantage and they did not hesitate to press it home. Tunnels were turned into blind alleys which ended in a drop onto deadly upturned sharpened bamboo stakes, home-made bombs using thrown-away American equipment were placed in wall recesses, snakes and scorpions were collected, concealed and unleashed. Meanwhile the VC tunnel moles lived in the tunnels, often not seeing daylight for weeks, and grew pale and thin on the supplies they had begged or harassed from villagers and breathed the foul hot air of the tunnels.

The Cu Chi tunnels played a significant part in the southern thrust of the VC Tet Offensive of 1968 although this also brought about the decimation of part of the tunnel network as US forces laid waste to the whole region. The area was carpet bombed, thus destroying many of the tunnels, and the region was subjected to huge doses of napalm to deforest it and deprive the tunnel entrances of cover. The tunnels were never quite as effective again, but they had played their part.

The tunnels of Cu Chi are well worth visiting both for their sense of history and to experience their extraordinarily tiny proportions. Do not attempt to enter them if you are physically big or claustrophobic. The section of the tunnels which has been renovated and prepared for inspection is near the village of Ben Dinh, 30km north-west of Ho Chi Minh City. To reach it head out of HCMC by Highway 22 and turn right off the highway when you reach the post office of Cu Chi village; the tunnels are signposted from there. Entrance costs $3. There is another section of tunnels open at Ben Duoc (15km north-west of Ben Dinh) with the added dubious attraction of a firing range from where you can fire an AK-47 or an M-16 for $1 a bullet – who says war doesn't pay?

The Mekong Delta

MYTHO

Mytho is the town on the Mekong nearest to Ho Chi Minh City (HCMC). It is not the most attractive in the area, with its legacy of the destructive effects of war, and the hotels are not the best – the legacy of a time when Mytho was subject to substantial police harassment of the tourist trade.

The lack of waving children along the riverbank so common around Cantho and elsewhere, and the presence still of cyclos, not the *xe honda loi* unique to the delta also make one feel as if Mytho is not quite the real Mekong Delta. However, it's well located for short boat trips on the river to visit the nearby plentiful orchards or see the huge areas of mangrove swamp.

Mytho can be reached as a day trip from HCMC, but many tourists who have a little more time go on to the livelier centre of Cantho, which is also better connected by bus services than Mytho.

PRACTICAL INFORMATION
Arrival and departure
By bus Mytho is served from HCMC by buses which take around two hours departing from Tien May bus station when full.

It is possible to get a shared taxi to Mytho from the same bus station, but may be difficult to find one back to HCMC from Mytho. The bus station in Mytho is 4km west of the centre. Cyclos usually gather here.

By boat Mytho's ferry port is 2km west of town. A passenger ferry leaves HCMC daily at around 11am from the

TO TIEN MAY
BUS STN. 4KM

Mytho

0   APPROXIMATE SCALE   400m

NAM KY KHOI NGHIA ST

HUNG VUONG BLVD

NGUYEN TRAI STREET

Hung Vuong
Hotel

LE LOI BOULEVARD

TRUNG TRAC ST

BEN DINH CHANNEL

Vietkom
Bank

Hospital
Entrance

MARKET

KHOA HUAN ST

Song
Hotel

Pharmacies

RACH GAM STREET

Rang Dong
Hotel

Hung Duong
Hotel

Post
Office

EATING
PLACES

30TH APRIL ST
TO FERRY
PORT 2KM

Tourist
Office

New
Hotel

Cong Doang
Hotel

COCONUT ISLAND
& BEN TRE

Cafés

TIEN GIANG RIVER (MEKONG)

dock at the end of Ham Nghi Blvd for
Mytho. The trip takes around six hours.

Ferries leave Mytho bound upriver
for Vinh Long and Chau Doc at
12.30pm. The trip takes six hours and a
mammoth 17 hours respectively; for
50,000d and 17 hours in a hammock you
can truly experience Vietnamese life on
a passenger ferry.

The hydrofoil service between
HCMC and the Mekong is fast, reliable
and enjoyable, and infinitely better than
the dusty, dreary, road connection. This
also means there is less reason to take an
organized tour of the Mekong which
would mean that you spend hours on
these roads.

For details of hydrofoil services to
Mytho from HCMC and Cantho see the
box on p163.

Orientation

Mytho is bounded to its north-east and
south by rivers. The Ben Dinh channel
to Mytho's east is a waterway busy with
fishing boats and lined with wooden stilt
houses. On the left bank of this channel
is Mytho's market. On the banks of the
broad sweep of the Tien Giang river to
the south of Mytho are cafés where you
can enjoy a beer and the view. Coconut
Island and Ben Tre province are across
the river as are many plentiful orchards.

Services

Post   The post office is on the riverfront at No 59, 30th April St.

Money   There is a branch of
Vietkombank at 15B Nam Ky Khoi
Nghia St. It is open Monday to Saturday

7.30-11am, 1.30-4pm. It will exchange travellers' cheques into US dollars for a $2 commission and claims not to charge any commission to change travellers' cheques into dong.

Medical The address of the hospital is 2 Hung Vuong St, but actually its entrance is on Khoa Huan St. Near here are several pharmacies.

Local transport
There are many cyclos in Mytho. There are always a number to be found cruising the riverfront and Trung Trac St. Hiring a motorbike or car and driver is not particularly easy here, but the best place to try is along Le Loi St.

Where to stay
There are several fairly unpleasant government-owned hotels open to foreigners and a few more which aren't. Moreover the prices here are not especially low and the hotels will not bargain. Two good privately-owned hotels have opened and one more is being built, but these are all more expensive, in the $20 range. This means there are no good cheap hotel options but this may change as more tourists come to Mytho since the private boat market is now open to foreigners.

Song Tien Hotel, 101 Trung Trac St (☎ 073-872009), offers the cheapest rooms at $6. These are fairly clean although the building is extremely dilapidated. The more expensive rooms here are not worth it. *Hung Duong Hotel*, 33 Trung Trac St, offers large clean rooms with air-con for $10; the building is very grotty, but the staff are friendly. *Cong Doang Hotel*, 61 30th April St (☎ 073-874324), is a trade-union guest-house and has good river views for its big clean rooms with fan at $8 but the $20 rooms are overpriced. The hotel, however, exudes a joyless atmosphere, is extremely noisy early in the morning because of the proximity of the river and a football pitch outside, and the staff are so paranoid of security that there have obviously been thefts here in the past.

Hung Vuong Hotel, 40 Hung Vuong St (☎ 073-876868), is a well-kept hotel inland with pleasing rooms for around $20. *Rang Dong Hotel*, 25 30th April St (☎ 073-874400), has the advantage of being nearer the centre of town, with river views and has good rooms with friendly English-speaking staff for $18-25. A new hotel likely to be of a similar standard is currently being built near the Rang Dong on the riverfront.

Where to eat
There are a number of eating places towards the south end of Trung Trac St. Some of these serve Mytho's speciality – vermicelli soup. None of these are outstanding and a better option for a delicious dinner if you visit an orchard from a boat trip (see below) is to take up the owner's likely offer to cook you a meal. The most likely dish is *tai tuong* fish – meaning 'elephant's ears' – grilled with nuts and then wrapped with green vegetables in rice paper. But do be sure to ask the total price before agreeing. Eating supper as the sun goes down means that you will experience the beauty of the dark Mekong river lit on the way back only by the moonlight and the boatman's torch.

AROUND MYTHO

Boat trips
The government tourist office used to monopolize the boat trips from Mytho such that the police would fine tourists who hired private boats. This practice has stopped and it is now extremely easy to hire a small

motor-driven boat for around one-fifth of the cost of the tourist office boats to visit some of the islands and waterways around Mytho.

Tan Long Island – Coconut Island

Across the Tien Giang river is the so-called Coconut Island. This island was named after its former colourful inhabitant, the Coconut Monk – so-called because it is said that he once ate nothing but coconuts for three years. He founded a religion which combined elements of Buddhism and Christianity and led a small community here on the island from the splendour of his wildly painted and decorated sanctuary. However, he was imprisoned for anti-communist activities and died in 1990. The sanctuary has fallen into great disrepair and the government's attempt to capitalize on the fame of the island has turned it into a tourist trap: 5000d is charged to look around the island. You may decide it is best to take a look at the ruins from the water.

Beyond Coconut Island there are countless small channels leading off the Tien Giang river in Ben Tre province. A small hired boat can glide down these waterways lined with huge water coconut trees and dotted with underwater fishing nets. Leading off the channels are small paths which connect with inland houses in the midst of bountiful orchards. The owners are happy to show you around, although they will charge you for sampling the fresh fruit. These orchard owners will often offer to cook for you and it can be the best-value food in Mytho.

Ben Tre

Around 20km south of Mytho is Ben Tre, the capital of Ben Tre province. This province consists of a series of islands in the middle of the Mekong river. It is famous for its endless numbers of coconut trees and is home to a floating market during the morning.

It is easy to get to Ben Tre from Mytho by hired boat or by ferry (the crossing takes around an hour), but continuing further south from Ben Tre is difficult unless you are prepared to try to hire one boat for the whole journey or make numerous transactions with different boats. Small boats can be hired from along the waterfront at Mytho near the Cuu Long café for around $1 per hour. If you wish to pay the vast extra cost of a government tourist boat you can book one at the tourist office at No 10, 30th April St (30 Thang 4 St) or through Song Tien Hotel.

CANTHO

Cantho is a bustling city on the Mekong. It has a large hinterland so you can avoid the main riverside thoroughfare and explore inland finding numerous small cafés and restaurants.

From this touristy drag you can also watch the neon lights light up on the other side of the river just after an often beautiful sunset. The city is

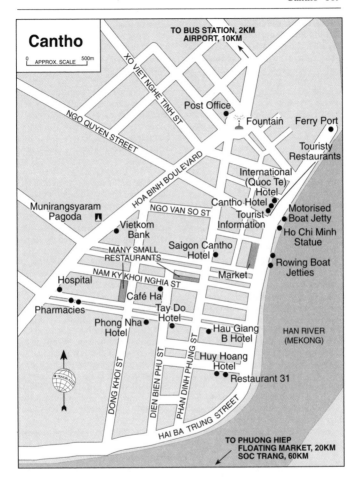

home to good food and is the perfect jumping-off point for seeing the delights of the Mekong.

Munirangsyaram Pagoda

The simple colourful elegance of the Khmer Munirangsyaram pagoda is worth a visit and is best seen early in the morning. At this time some of Cantho's 2000 Khmers come to make offerings amidst the heady scent of numerous joss sticks to the Historical Buddha sat beneath a boddhi tree. The pagoda is at 36 Hoa Binh Blvd.

PRACTICAL INFORMATION
Arrival and departure

By bus Cantho's bus station is around 2km north of town. Many xe Honda loi (see Local Transport below) gather here to transport you into the centre – this should cost around 5000d. Cantho's shared taxi stop is at the ferry port to Vinh Long. This is around 3km north-east of town; xe Honda loi and cyclos also gather here.

Buses leave at around 6am and again at around 7pm from Cantho (and from Soc Trang) for HCMC. The journey takes around five hours and eight hours respectively, including two ferry crossings. There is a regular shared taxi service from Cantho to HCMC departing from the ferry port to Vinh Long. The easiest time to catch these is around 2pm. The price could be as little as 50,000d if you bargain very well.

All buses and shared taxis use Mien Tay Bus Station (also called the Western bus station), inconveniently located 10km west of HCMC. This bus station is served by buses from Ben Thanh Bus Station in District 1 (near Ben Thanh Market at the end of Ham Nghi Blvd). Some motorized cyclos also gather here to charge extortionate rates to the centre of town – a taxi which the staff can call by telephone for you will cost little more at around 30,000d. Given the distance from the centre if you are travelling by shared taxi it's worth negotiating to pay a little extra so that you can be taken direct to your hotel.

By boat For details of the excellent hydrofoil services to Cantho from HCMC and Mytho see the box on p163.

By air Cantho's airport is 10km north-west of town and it is only a short flight to HCMC, assuming Vietnam Airlines has restarted flights to and from Cantho.

Orientation
Cantho is bounded by rivers to its north,

east and south. Cantho river is a tributary of the larger Hau river to its east which must be crossed by ferry to reach Cantho from Ho Chi Minh City. The eastern waterfront of Cantho is host to a great deal of river activity, Cantho's lively market and some hotels and tourist restaurants, all in the glow of a huge silver statue of Ho Chi Minh.

Services
Tourist information The tourist information office is at 20 Hai Ba Trung St (☎ 071-821852); travellers have found the staff extremely helpful in recommending modes of transport cheaper than the overpriced ones they offer.

Post At the northernmost end of Hai Ba Trung St, rising up behind the roundabout fountain, is Cantho's post office housed in an imposing five-storey building. This offers all the usual services and is open every day 8am-9pm.

Money Vietkombank, at 7 Hoa Binh Boulevard, is open Monday to Friday 7.30-10.45am and 1.00-4.45pm, and on Saturday 7.30-10.45am. It offers the standard Vietkombank commission rates on exchanging travellers' cheques (0.5 per cent into dong, and 1.5 per cent into US dollars). Surprisingly the bank charges only 3 per cent commission for cash advances on credit or debit cards.

Medical There are two large pharmacies at the western end of Chau Van Liem St, opposite the hospital which is at the corner of Chau Van Liem St and Hoa Binh Boulevard.

Local transport
There are some cyclos in Cantho but the main form of transport is the xe Honda loi. This is a great invention and unique to the Mekong Delta. It comprises a cyclo cart, pulled by a motorbike, thus retaining all the comfort of a cyclo, but all the speed and ease of a motorbike.

The cyclo cart is slightly larger than a standard cyclo and can easily seat three. Travelling by xe Honda loi costs around the same as a cyclo for a given distance – you should pay no more than 5000d for a trip right across town.

Where to stay

Accommodation in Cantho is mainly found in two areas: the riverfront, the most picturesque place to stay, and the centre of town. The cheapest accommodation in the centre is along Chau Van Liem St; some of the many places on this street are listed below.

The best of the cheap options is *Phong Nha Hotel* (☎ 071-821615), 75 Chau Van Liem St; the friendly service and the cleanliness of the rooms makes this a bargain at $6 for a double. The once-popular *Huy Hoang Hotel* (☎ 071-825833), 35 Ngo Duc Ke St, has become a less good deal, with small airless doubles offered for $9. *Hau Giang B Hotel* (☎ 071-821950), 27 Chau Van Liem St, offers a range of good doubles in pleasant surroundings from $8 to $15. At the time of writing *Tay Do Hotel*, at No 61, did not receive good reports.

On the riverfront *Cantho Hotel* (☎ 071-822218), 14-16 Hai Ba Trung St, offers simple but elegant doubles without air-con for $10. The staff are friendly and the hotel has balconies from which to enjoy the river view.

Next door is the more up-market *International* or *Quoc Te Hotel* (☎ 071-822079, 🖹 08-21039), 12 Hai Ba Trung St; this hotel has some doubles with fan for $12, but most doubles cost around $30 for good facilities. The hotel is a large complex with a fine restaurant and complete with souvenir shop and karaoke bar.

The best hotel is *Saigon Cantho Hotel* (☎ 071-825831, 🖹 08-23288), 55 Phan Dinh Phung St; it offers excellent doubles from $40 to 58.

Where to eat

As so often in the Mekong the food in Cantho is good, specialising in freshwater fish, and overflowing with fresh vegetables and tropical fruit. As in Mytho, the delicious fish tai tuong, or 'elephant's ear' is often available.

There are numerous small Vietnamese restaurants specialising in fish and frogs along Nam Ky Khoi St. Along the riverfront to the north of the market there are many small touristy restaurants with very persistent owners in which you can get reasonable Vietnamese food, or just drink a beer and enjoy the view.

In the market and along the back streets of Tho Huan and Tran Quoc Hoan several small streetside cafés serve a variety of fare, including exotic dishes such as snake and turtle.

Restaurant 31, 31 Ngo Duc Khe St, is an excellent and good value restaurant next door to Huy Hoang Hotel. A speciality which is not listed on the menu is *Lau Mam*, which is a delicious seafood steamboat to which you add, and thereby cook, noodles and green vegetables.

For a more up-market experience the upstairs restaurant in *Quoc Te Hotel* serves very good Vietnamese food. For a lively evening drink *Café Ha* on Dien Bien Phu St is popular with young Vietnamese.

AROUND CANTHO

By boat

There are many delightful boat excursions which can be made from Cantho and a wealth of sellers offering them. There are two types of boats, and trips.

Women with very small **wooden boats** will offer to row you along the Cantho river to take a look at the eastern side where you can explore the tiny waterways between wooden houses. This is an enjoyable way to pass an hour or so, especially to witness the typical Mekong standing up method of rowing. The virtues of an extended ride are limited by the slow progress the boats make meaning you are likely to spend a lot of time passing through Cantho's industrial river zone if you opt for a longer trip. The best place to hire one of these small boats is from one of the small jetties in the market. The boats can hold two or three passengers and cost under $1 to hire for an hour.

The other boat-trip option from Cantho is to **hire a boat** with a small motor to take you on an extended trip around the winding waterways of the delta. These boats are still small and ramshackle enough to keep you in tune with the setting of the delta, but they phut-phut through the water at a good pace. If you are on a tour up to 20 of you can be jammed into one of these boats, but they are idyllic for two or three, or a small group. Gliding through the many waterways surrounded by a mass of lush vegetation, small wooden houses and waving children is one of the enduring experiences of Vietnam.

There is a great network of rivers heading south from Cantho and a number of possible destinations. A common excursion is to **Phung Hiep floating market** 20km south of Cantho. The market takes place every day from 6 to 11am during which time small boats loaded with fruit, vegetables and bowls of *pho* paddle around dispensing their wares. This takes place underneath a road bridge which provides a perfect photo spot. The market is not especially large and the town of Phung Hiep on the banks is not particularly attractive; the main attraction is the journey to reach the market.

The town of Phung Hiep specializes in a particular kind of snake alcohol which can be sampled at any of the numerous sellers of this foul looking, smelling and tasting liquid – if you can stand the sight of the miserable snakes and mongooses kept in tiny cages. The journey to Phung Hiep from Cantho is around 20km which will take a boat with an average-sized motor around 2-2½ hours. Phung Hiep can also be reached more quickly but far less enjoyably by road. The best place to hire a boat assuming you do not want to pay the prices offered by Cantho's tourist office is from the area along the riverfront by the small touristy restaurants.

Further afield is the town of **Soc Trang** which houses some colourful Khmer Buddhist temples and which is host to an extraordinary festival, the Oc Bom Boc festival. Soc Trang is 60km from Cantho, 40km beyond Phung Hiep. The most notable Khmer sanctuary in the Mekong is the Kh'leng Pagoda (Chua Kh'leng). This must have been stunning in its original bamboo before it was replaced by concrete at the start of the 20th century. Nevertheless it is interesting to visit, especially because of the friendly and chatty monks. But it is only one of the many Khmer pagodas in the region, which is home to one of the delta's strongest Khmer communities. The Oc Bom Boc Festival is held on the 14th day of the 10th lunar month (roughly December, see lunar calendar for exact date p103). Khmers from miles around will gather here to enjoy the festival atmosphere including dances and songs. The height of the festivities consists of a longboat race where local boats paddled by 40-50 men race against the boat belonging to the Khmer temple; it is a fantastic sight. Accommodation in Soc Trang at this time is at a premium so it is best to make a reservation.

Another draw for visitors to Soc Trang is the Bat Pagoda 6km west of the town. This has all the usual features of the bat temples scattered across Asia – hundreds of bats which screech early in the morning and before sunset and pollute the air with the foulest of smells and the ground with their droppings. Soc Trang can be reached by boat from Cantho in a day if you make a very early start – the return trip should cost $30. Bus transport to Soc Trang is rather irregular; it is best to ask Cantho's helpful tourist office for information on the current situation. A car or motorbike could easily make the return journey in a day. Alternatively you could stay at Soc Trang in which case the best hotel is ***Khanh Hung Hotel*** (☎ 079-21027) at 15 Tran Hung Dao Blvd.

PART 5: THE CENTRE

The central region

The central region is home to the beautiful royal tombs of Hué, thunderous China Beach surrounded by the Marble Mountains, the gorgeous little town of Hoi An with its wealth of seamstresses, and the fascinating sights of the DMZ. In addition the central highlands can be visited – though many find them less rewarding than in the Sapa area and much more trying to get to.

Hué, Vietnam's 19th-century royal capital, is a must see. The azure Perfume River glides through the city and a boat trip on it, or a bicycle ride by it, to visit the royal tombs is very much the thing to do. In addition, the accommodation here is good, the food fantastic and a local specialist craft is embroidered silk. But be prepared for the sights you won't see in Hué: most of the opulent buildings of the Imperial City were destroyed in the Tet offensive of 1968.

Just north of Hué is the **DMZ** (demilitarized zone). This misleading term is the name given to some of the most fought-over territory during the American war. Ruined churches, pock-marked bunkers and abandoned tanks are just some of the sights of the DMZ evocative of war. If you do visit the DMZ always go with a guide – the area is still dangerous. Further and far more grisly reminders of the horrors of war can be experienced by visiting the site of the horrific My Lai massacre at Quang Ngai.

For normality again there is the big pleasant city of **Danang**, in which the Cham Museum at least is worth a look. From Danang a Honda om or taxi can take you to the pagodas of the **Marble Mountains** with their beautiful sea views, then on to the crashing foam and unspoilt palm-fringed sand of China Beach and finally land you in the lazy travellers' haven of **Hoi An**. If you want silk or cotton clothes tailor-made this is where to get them – and even if you don't, it's a wonderful place to spend a few days relaxing, taking in some culture, or just eating the fabulous local food.

Meanwhile up in the central highlands, to the west, there is the quaint and rather strange hill station of **Dalat**, the coffee-growing expanses around Buon Ma Thuot and the small centres of Kontom and Pleiku. Visiting these areas gives you a chance to see some of Vietnam's *montagnards*, or hill tribes, but many visitors find the journey to Sapa a more rewarding one.

CLIMATE

The beautiful Hai Van pass north of Danang marks Vietnam's geological break between north and south. South of here experiences warm weather year-round while the north has a real winter. In the winter it is cold enough to need jumpers for comfort (beware that almost nowhere has heaters). Additionally Hué is subject to severe monsoonal rains in the months of October and November; visiting the royal capital at this time is likely to be a wash-out. Meanwhile the central highlands are cool year-round, with temperatures between 15 and 25°C (60-75°F).

Central Highlands

DALAT

Dalat, the cool hill station home to the Lat hill tribe and peppered with various kitsch haunts, 1500m above sea level, 300km and a day's drive away from Ho Chi Minh City is a popular tourist destination – especially with Vietnamese. Some Westerners find the allure of the 'city of love' or 'city of eternal spring' palls a little after discovering that the Valley of Love has little to recommend it other than the unusual sight of Vietnamese dressed up as cowboys and that the weather in eternal spring is always a bit on the chilly side. But although Dalat may not live up to all the stories told about it by the Vietnamese it is a quaint town which still has cobbled streets because it escaped bombing by both the French and the Americans. It also houses the extraordinary Hang Nga guest-house and art gallery, and is surrounded by pleasant-enough countryside peopled by the Lat tribe and peppered with curios, such as the huge statue of a chicken at the eponymous Chicken village. There are plenty of good cheap places to stay in Dalat and an abundance of locals willing to show you the sights around the town.

The site of Dalat was discovered by Alexandre Yersin, a protégé of Louis Pasteur, and the French turned it into a gentle cool haven, an escape from the pressures of running the colony in Saigon. They built a funicular railway connecting Dalat with Thap Cham and although the line has long since stopped normal service, it was discontinued in the 1960s due to repeated VC attacks, you can visit the old-fashioned railway station in Dalat and can even pay ($3) to have yourself transported 8km down the line and back again.

Sights

Dalat has its share of buildings of historical interest which are worth seeing, from Emperor Bao Dai's Summer Palace to Hang Nga's Crazy

House. The town also has the luscious flower gardens and a number of temples and pagodas to visit, of which perhaps the most interesting is a convent inhabited by charming elderly French-speaking nuns.

Bao Dai's Summer Palace is a grand old villa built for Vietnam's last emperor and was a haven for him to which he increasingly retreated when he found the pressures of reluctant rule rather too much for him. During his sojourns here his main occupation was elephant hunting, for which he had special roads and huts built which could be used only by him; such attitudes contributed to his downfall. Today the building is much as he left it (except of course for the bust of Ho Chi Minh), complete with Bao Dai's hunting trophies and a bust of the man himself in his office. The palace is open daily from 8 to 11am and 1 to 4pm and costs $1 and the removal of your shoes to enter. The palace can be found at the end of a pine grove, 500m south-east of the Pasteur Institute.

Another site of historical rule is the French **Governor-General's residence**, but there is much less to see inside or out in this modernist building, for although the decor is genuine it's far less original. The residence is open daily from 8 to 11am and 1.30 to 4pm and is to be found off Tran Hung Dao St, 2km east of the town centre. Entrance also costs $1 and your shoes. Infinitely more exotic and definitely worth a look if you decide not to stay there is the Crazy House – or Hang Nga Guesthouse – at 3 Huyen Thuc Khanh St (see p178). The quaint Dalat **Flower Gardens** are also worthy of mention for their displays of highly fragrant flowers from orchids to cool-weather hydrangeas, although the monkeys in cages do rather detract from the experience. The flower gardens are off Ho Xuang Huong St at the north-eastern tip of Xuan Hoang lake and are open daily from 8am to 4pm. Dalat also has a number of buildings of different religious persuasions, from the **Lam Ty Ni Pagoda** 500m north of the Pasteur Institute at 2 Thien My St with its notoriously talkative monk, to the conventional Catholic **Dalat Cathedral** on Tran Phu St next to Dalat Hotel and the picturesque **Thien Vuong Pagoda** topping a pine-clad hill 5km south-east of the town centre on Khe Sanh St which is particularly popular with ethnic Chinese Vietnamese.

Perhaps the most noteworthy of all Dalat sights is the **Domaine de Marie Convent** where the French-speaking nuns are delighted to show visitors around their pink-roofed convent on a pretty hill top and talk about their life of good works in the community and of their gruelling daily schedule.

PRACTICAL INFORMATION
Arrival and departure
By bus The tourist bus from Ho Chi Minh City is the most common way to get to and from Dalat; buses generally drop you at the market, a short walk from the hub of the town. The fare to HCMC is usually around $7 and to Nha Trang around $8. Both are full-day journeys (with stops for lunch) and both are easily booked just the night before from almost any of the town's mini-hotels.

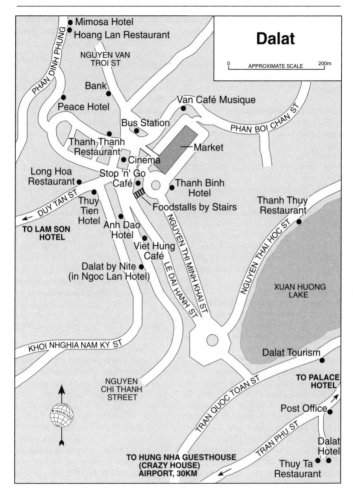

If you wish to travel in one of the crowded non-tourist buses you can attempt to do so by going to the main bus station on Highway 20, 2km south of town, but beware that the police authorities in Dalat go through phases of flexing their muscles and one of their common practices is to prohibit foreign-ers travelling on non-tourist buses. If this happens you can at least comfort yourself with the thought that you are not missing much.

By air Although Vietnam Airlines can book you on a short-hop flight several days a week from Ho Chi Minh City to

Dalat or vice versa this is not as great a way of getting to Dalat as it might seem because the nearest airport is 30km south of the town and the only taxis allowed within the airport compound are government-owned ones who charge around $20.

Orientation and services

Dalat's sights are very spread out. Many find themselves dotted around the hilly streets to the north of large limpid Xuan Huong lake. The streets are rather too hilly for cyclos – although there are a few they are rather sorry specimens. Instead Honda oms are the main source of transport or, of course, you can walk. The town's **post office**, offering the usual services, is at 14 Tran Phu St. You can change travellers' cheques or dollar cash at the **Agriculture Bank of Vietnam** on Nguyen Van Troi St, dollar cash can also be changed at most hotels.

Where to stay

Dalat has a large range of accommodation for most budgets and many tastes, though hotels tend to get booked up on Saturday nights during the summer as the cool climate draws many weekenders from HCMC.

At the lower end of the market, and slap bang next to Dalat's market, is *Thanh Binh Hotel* (☎ 063-822909), 40 Nguyen Thi Minh Kahi St, with singles from $8 and doubles from $12 to 20. At around the same price and with very friendly staff is *Peace Hotel* (☎ 063-822787), at 64 Truong Cong Dinh St. *Mimosa Hotel* (☎ 063-822656), 170 Phan Dinh Phung St, and *Lam Son Hotel* (☎ 063-822362), 5 Hai Thuong St, an old French villa, are both good budget places a little out of town which have been running for years. They have rooms from $8 to $22 and are worth a look if you don't mind the 10-minute walk into the centre.

The next rung up has the very pleasant *Thuy Tien Hotel* (☎ 063-822482), in the agreeable French area at the corner of Duy Tan and Khoi Nghia Nam Ky streets, with singles from $25 and doubles from $30. But if you are thinking of spending this kind of money then you should certainly consider the fantastic *Hang Nga Guesthouse* (☎ 063-822070), 3 Huynh Thuc Khanh St, which is also called the Crazy House by locals, or the House of A Thousand Roofs. It's a marvellous fantasy creation combining hotel and art gallery. Each room has been designed to create a different all-encompassing scene – one has you walking up stairs and into a lion's mouth. The rooms also have a mirror above the bed.

The hotel is the creation of Hang Nga who still lives here and is a fascinating character to talk to. She trained in architecture in Vietnam and Moscow and has been granted unheard of indulgence by Party officials to express her creativity because of her connection to one of Ho Chi Minh's key advisers; he was her father. Rooms here cost $20-60 and are worth every cent. (If you can't afford to pay this, you can still visit the place.)

There are three other hotels in the top price range which are certainly worth the cost; all are old colonial buildings. Up on the hill above the market is the beautifully-decorated *Anh Dao Hotel* (☎ 063-822384), 50 Hoa Binh Square, with rooms for around $30-40, while down by the lake *Dalat Hotel* (☎ 063-822363), 7 Tran Phu St, has rooms for around $100; opposite it is Dalat's premier hotel – the grand and elegant *Palace Hotel* (☎ 063-822203), 2 Tran Phu St, with rooms starting from over $100 a night.

Where to eat

Dalat is a real market garden town as the countryside surrounding it is very fertile. This means that you can eat well here and differently from the rest of the country. The cuisine is Vietnamese, of course, but with different vegetables to provide the characteristic medley of textures. The range of fruit and vegetables is different from that found in the rest of the country – strawberry, mulberry, blackberry and plums can be eaten raw, in jams or drunk in pleasant, sweet wine.

For rough and ready eating the stairway on Nguyen Thi Minh Khai St leading down to Dalat's market becomes alive with a hundred food stalls as the afternoon wears on into evening. For still very cheap food *Long Hoa restaurant* on Duy Tan St does a fine range of standard Vietnamese food with yoghurt and the commonly-found strawberry wine. Likewise *Hoang Lan Restaurant,* 118 Phan Dinh Phung St, has good Vietnamese and Chinese fare.

The town's three top restaurants where a meal costs between $5 and $10 are *Thanh Thanh Restaurant,* 4 Tang Bat Ho St, which has a delicious range of varied Vietnamese dishes and the two restaurants by the lake – the well-situated *Thuy Ta restaurant,* 2 Yersin St, and *Thanh Thuy* on Nguyen Thai Hoc St which offers unusual-sounding dishes which actually taste very pleasant.

Dalat also has a few choice cafés or bars in which to sample the coffee from the surrounding hills and the home-made cakes and patisseries. There are two next to the market: *Stop'n' Go Café* on Hoa Binh Square can serve evening drinks to go with your supposed breakfast fare, while *Van Café Musique* on the northern side mixes drinks with modern and not so modern music.

Meanwhile if Dalat's temperate climate is not cool enough for you Nguyen Chi Thanh St has the great ice cream of *Viet Hung Café* at No 7, then you can live it up until late at *Dalat by Nite* at No 42.

AROUND DALAT

First there is the weirdness – Vietnamese guides and tourists queuing up to dress as cowboys and have their photographs taken in the 'Valley of Love' and the regimented pine trees around the Quang Trung Reservoir. Then there are the waterfalls – pleasant enough, but not exactly the Niagara Falls. Then there is the countryside which again is agreeable, but not as beautiful as the mountains of the Sapa region or the hills of the DMZ. Finally, perhaps the main interest in the area around Dalat is the hill-tribe people – the Lat – and that gets you back to the weirdness with Chicken village. Note that the tribal people are very poor and fatal diseases are rife; interest can become ghoulish if you are not careful.

Dalat is surrounded by lakes and waterfalls and also has a lake at its centre but the countryside is rather too forested for beautiful walks, instead the carnival atmosphere of the prettier places has to be seen to be believed. Primary candidate is the **Valley of Love** 5km north of central Dalat, home to the infamous Dalat Cowboys – they pose, you photograph, you pay. If you do visit here you might as well take a look at the pretty **Lake of Sighs**, which is 3km to the south-east as the crow flies, so-named after a tragic love story; boy meets girl, boy and girl's families hate each other, boy leaves, girl stays, girl leaves, boy returns, tragedy ensues.

Close runner-up is the **Quang Trung reservoir** 5km south-east of Dalat which is being turned into a huge tourist resort and already has the

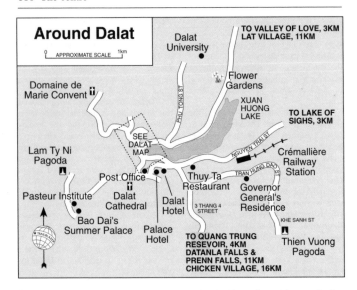

Around Dalat

APPROXIMATE SCALE 0 — 1km

Dalat University

TO VALLEY OF LOVE, 3KM
LAT VILLAGE, 11KM

Flower Gardens

Domaine de Marie Convent

PHU TONG ST

XUAN HUONG LAKE

TO LAKE OF SIGHS, 3KM

SEE DALAT MAP

Lam Ty Ni Pagoda

NGUYEN TRAI ST

Crémallière Railway Station

Post Office

Thuy Ta Restaurant

TRAN HUNG DAO ST

Pasteur Institute

Dalat Cathedral

Dalat Hotel

3 THANG 4 STREET

Governor General's Residence

KHE SANH ST

Bao Dai's Summer Palace

Palace Hotel

TO QUANG TRUNG RESEVOIR, 4KM
DATANLA FALLS &
PRENN FALLS, 11KM
CHICKEN VILLAGE, 16KM

Thien Vuong Pagoda

brightly-coloured paddle boats contrasting against the regimented pine trees. Just 250m beyond the turning for the Quang Trung reservoir is the ¼km pleasant path leading to perhaps Dalat's most agreeable waterfall experience, the **Datanla Falls**. Free of the commercialization threatening the Prenn Falls, 7km further south-east of Dalat, (and free of the free-fall monsoonal mud slides) Datanla Falls present a reasonable cascade in an area of natural beauty.

The **Prenn Falls**, however, present a much finer cascade and give you the opportunity of walking behind the gushing water and looking into the pool below if you don't mind the tourist atmosphere around them.

Visiting the **settlements of the Lat people** used to have to be negotiated with the Dalat police. These days you rarely encounter problems – arranging a Honda om trip with a Vietnamese through your hotel or one of the cafés for $5-8 a day is an easy matter and they should be able to tell you what the current situation is. Often the police demand permits ($5) to visit Lat village, but guides often have ways round this. Permits are never needed for Chicken village, increasing its popularity even more.

The Lat people live in primitive wooden and thatch huts; the roofs of which hiss and crackle if you stand still – the sounds of hundreds of thousands of tiny insects moving around amongst the wood and corn. They are often friendly people but desperately poor. Their tradition is of matriarchy. Thus when a daughter of a family marries she does not become the lowliest member of the groom's family, as in standard Vietnamese tradition, rather the son becomes a member of the bride's family. He leaves his family home to live in hers, bringing a dowry of animals with him. If he wishes to leave her and the marriage he has to depart with nothing more than the shirt on his back.

Rising above the Lat villages is volcanic **Lang Bian mountain**, 2160m high, which can be climbed in a four-hour hike up a gash of a path and then through forests in the upper reaches. The view from the top is said to be good – if you can see through the trees that is. You will certainly need a permit to climb Lang Bian mountain and an official guide, so it can be an expensive excursion depending on the current police mood. First stop for sorting this out is Dalat Tourism at 4 Tran Quoc Toan St. Lat village is 12km north of Dalat.

Last but not least is **Chicken village**. This is an unremarkable settlement of thatched Lat houses and friendly people with a remarkable monument – a huge concrete statue of a chicken. It really has to be seen. Everyone has their different versions of how and why the chicken got there, some more unlikely than others – ask around and take your pick. Chicken village is 17km south-east of Dalat.

Central coast

THAP CHAM/PHAN RANG

Thap Cham is visited mainly because of the meaning of its name – Cham Towers. The towers, on a hill overlooking the town and surrounding area, are fine examples of the beautiful Cham art. A major attraction for railway enthusiasts is the large railway repair yard lying below the Cham towers.

Another benefit of visiting Thap Cham is that if you explore the surrounding area you are likely to come upon traditional Cham villages and see the few surviving Chams in their brightly-coloured headcloths – Tuan Tu village is one such centre. Alternatively you can visit the nearby beach.

These attractions do not, however, make Thap Cham a pleasant place to visit and the nearest hotels (mostly dirty or overpriced) are in the grimy town of Phan Rang. So, given that the towers and rail yard are very near the train station and are only about 6km from Phan Rang, it is recommended that a visit here is no more than a short excursion between trains (provided that you are prepared to climb the Cham tower hill with luggage or that you can fit it on a Honda om) unless you can splash out on a beach hotel.

Thap Cham has its own railway station even though it forms the westward extent of the nearby larger town of Phan Rang.

Phan Rang

0 _____ APPROXIMATE SCALE _____ 300m

TO
THAP CHAM,
PO KLONG GARAI
CHAM TOWERS,
THAP CHAM
RAILWAY STATION
& REPAIR YARDS, 7KM

LE HONG PHONG ST

Bus Station

HUNG VUONG ST

THONG NHAT ST (HIGHWAY 1)

●Thong
Nhat
Hotel

FOOD
STALLS

MARKET &
FOOD STALLS

THONG NHAT ST

Huu Nghi
Hotel ●

VO THI SAN ST

Agri ●
Bank

● Local Bus
Station

CAI
RIVER

TO NINH CHU HOTEL

Sights and excursions

The **Po Klong Garai Cham towers** are well-preserved beautifully-carved strong red sandstone buildings which have occupied a commanding position and panoramic views over the region since the early 14th century.

These Hindu temples were built during the reign of the Cham monarch Jaya Simhavarman III. The fabulously-carved towers of the first building you come to, which is also the largest, warrant the greatest attention, and indeed the carvings are the finest here because this is the heart of the towers – the sanctuary. Above the doorway a six-armed Shiva dances around Cham inscriptions and stony flames.

Inside the vestibule a statue of Shiva's bull, Nandin, used to be the recipient of offerings from local farmers wishing for a good harvest; during festivals the image of King Poi Klong Garai, which nestles in one of the niches, is worshipped. These rituals are also observed during the Kate festival in October which is still celebrated by local Cham people. The Klong Garai Cham towers are around 7km north-west of Phan Rang town, high above the train station of Thap Cham.

Lying below the Cham towers across the tracks from the railway station are **Thap Cham's railway repair yards** where all manner of methods of repairing old rolling stock go on. If you can persuade the guards that you are a railway enthusiast you may well find the yards worth a look. They were founded by the French during the building of the section of the Trans-Indochinois railway (the French name for the Saigon–Hanoi line) due to run between Saigon and Nha Trang, and were intended to serve the entire metre-gauge network. Work goes on every day in the yards – metal presses grind and pound, while mechanical cutters churn out standard nuts and bolts for repair in cramped sheds. Mechanics in standard blue shirts are everywhere, male and female, looking more or less skilled, carrying out the work which needs to be tailored to the stock which has come in for repair. The fizzing bright blue light of blowtorches contrasts with the black of the old engines and trains.

Thap Cham was also the starting point of an 86km **funicular railway** which ground its way up the steep hillside to Dalat, dragged upwards by huge chains. The line has been closed since the early 1960s due to continued VC attacks, and there are no plans to re-open it. The tracks can be seen from Highway 20 which runs to Dalat. Alternatively, you can make the journey to Dalat in order to travel a few disappointing kilometres downhill then twiddle your thumbs for half an hour before returning uphill again. Mind you, the trip is almost worth it to see Dalat's lovely Art Deco station, built in the 1930s.

Less-frequented Cham towers than those near the station are the **Po Ro Me Cham towers**. These towers are less ancient, built at the end of the 16th century, and less finished but they do still exult in fine sculptures as well as some wall paintings and there is an attraction in their remoteness. Inside the largest building which is again the sanctuary there is a bas-relief of a dancing Shiva surrounded by depictions of Cham royalty of the time and Shiva's bull, Nandin. The towers were built during the reign of the last independent ruler of the Champa kingdom, Po Ro Me, who actually died a prisoner of the Vietnamese. The towers are to be found 12km south of Phan Rang, 7km to the west of Highway 1 along a dirt track. This track is hard to find, so it is wise to go by Honda om.

Chams still live in this region, though because of their history with the Vietnamese they keep a very low profile. They can sometimes be recognized by their headcloths in the market of Phan Rang, or you can take a trip out of Thap Cham to a Cham village, such as **Tuan Tu village**. Here you will find houses built in rows; often a family owns a whole row. This is a Muslim community, and its members keep their religion alive, worshipping at a very plain mosque against which the bright red scarf and tasselled hat of the priests stands out in sharp relief, which is presumably the idea. To reach Tuan Tu village head south out of Phan Rang along Highway 1 turning to the south-east just after a petrol station and continue along this beautiful track for around 3km.

PRACTICAL INFORMATION
Arrival and departure
By train Thap Cham's small station is 7km north-west of Phan Rang, lying almost at the foot of the hill topped by the Po Klong Garai Cham towers. Plenty of Honda om gather here willing to make the dusty ascent to the Cham towers.

By bus The bus station is centrally located just north of Thong Nhat Hotel. The bus station is filled with a desultory selection of rickety buses, except in the early morning when there is a throng of buses running south to Ho Chi Minh City, north to major cities, and if you are lucky west inland along the rough mountain road to Dalat.

Orientation and services

Thap Cham, 6km north-west of Phan Rang, is strung along Highway 20, which is the road leading towards Dalat. The **Agribank**, at 334 Thong Nhat St, will change dollar cash, but not travellers' cheques. There is no pharmacy of any significant size here nor a hospital.

Phan Rang is a dirty little town in which all the services are spread along its section of Highway 1, called Thong Nhat St, which runs north-south.

Where to stay

If you must stay in Phan Rang, *Thong Nhat Hotel*, 99 Thong Nhat St (☎ 068-827201, ▤ 068-822943), is certainly the cleanest hotel but still its rooms are not particularly great and are certainly not worth the vast $35 charged. Clearly the huge hotel of 33 rooms, restaurant, massage etc was built in the optimistic hope of a tourist boom.

The cockroach-ridden rooms of *Huu Nghi Hotel* to the very south of Phan Rang town at 354 Thong Nhat St (068-822606) are certainly not worth the $10-15 charged.

If you can afford it, you could head to Ninh Chu beach, 7km south-east of Phan Rang, and enjoy the reasonable comfort of *Ninh Chu Hotel* (☎ 068-873900) for $20-40. If you do stay here be sure to make the excursion to the more scenic Vinh Hy bay.

Where to eat

The hotel restaurants offer reasonable fare, or alternatively there are food stalls near the market or good eateries on Le Hong Phong St near the junction with Thong Nhat St.

NHA TRANG

Nha Trang is Vietnam's primary seaside holiday resort, both for Vietnamese and foreign visitors, and justifiably so. The town looks out on to an attractive bay filled with the blue waters of the South China Sea and dotted with pleasant islands.

The fine sand of the beach, patrolled by just the right number of sellers of seafood, fruit, doughnuts and boat trips, combined with good weather year-round make this an excellent place for a little relaxation and an easy tourist life. But Nha Trang is also a sizable town full of good seafood restaurants or stalls and great coffee houses. Plus, even if you find the much-vaunted snorkelling somewhat unimpressive and don't fancy a dive, you may well enjoy the excursions you can make from the town.

During Vietnam's winter Nha Trang is still warm enough for beach life, though night-time rain and possible strong winds between November and January rule out diving. Be aware that much of the year Nha Trang has notoriously, and evidently, big waves – so body surfing can be fun but only if you're strong enough to be crashed, inevitable at some point, from the top of a wave to the seabed.

History

During the American war Nha Trang's central position in south Vietnam meant that it was considered pretty safe from Communist attack. So when the central highlands fell so dramatically in March 1975 (see p67) the Southern Vietnamese General Phu moved his headquarters to Nha Trang and expected to govern operations from there. But events moved much more quickly than he had anticipated and he was there for only three weeks before some dramatic events, as related by Frank Snepp, unfolded:

'On Friday, the twenty-eighth, General Phu met with his airborned commander and told him unequivocally to give up Nha Trang – without telling the Americans. In the event of a full-scale NVA assault, Phu declared, the defense line of the city need be held only long enough for him and his staff to escape. After that, he couldn't care less what happened. [On the morning of 1 April] the local province chief called Phu...to inform him that the municipal bureaucracy, including the police, had literally disintegrated overnight. Phu, already in the throes of an emotional breakdown, was in no condition to absorb this latest piece of bad news, and even before the province chief had finished his sad tale the harassed commander slammed down the phone and leaped up from his desk in a frenzy. "Get out!" he screamed at the top of his voice to the secretaries and orderlies around him as he dashed out of his office, down the steps of the headquarters building and out into the courtyard, where his own private helicopter was idling. "Get out!" he yelled to the pilot who promptly began revving the motors.'

General Phu left behind him hundreds and thousands of Vietnamese who had worked with and for him, and all the Americans and third country nationals in the city. Once the Americans realized Nha Trang had been abandoned by South Vietnamese forces they did their best to airlift out Vietnamese CIA agents, as well as all the Americans in the city. The Americans made it; not all the Vietnamese did.

Sights and excursions

The most impressive sight in Nha Trang is the **Long Son Pagoda** (also known as the Hai Duc Pagoda). Located around 500m west of the railway station up on Trai Thuy mountain this is most notable for the huge 24m-high white Buddha statue up 152 steps behind the pagoda sitting atop the hill. The pagoda is a 1930s creation (built on the site of a pagoda that had been destroyed by fire) and is highly decorated with brightly-coloured tiles and glass shapes of huge dragons adorning the walls and pillars which draw the eye's attention towards the large bronze Buddha on the altar. Behind the pagoda the many steps rise towards the huge Buddha, known as the Kim Thanh Buddha. It was built in 1963 as a symbol of Buddhist resistance to the Catholic Diem regime, as the depiction around the base of the Buddha, of monks in flames who opposed the regime shows. These days it is as much a symbol of Nha Trang as anything else, and the good views of the nearby mountains from the top are as good a reason as any to make the excursion. The pagoda is to be found at the end of a narrow lane leading north off the continuation of Thai Nguyen St, a further 500m out of town from the railway station.

For a taste of the beneficial legacy of French colonialism you can visit the **Pasteur Institute** at the top end of Tran Phu St founded by Pasteur's protégé, Dr Alexandre Yersin, whose library and office have also been turned into a museum. Dr Yersin was a scientist who came to South-east Asia at the end of the 19th century after studying under Louis Pasteur in Paris. He travelled to Vietnam where he undertook much fieldwork in the central highlands, including discovering the site of Dalat and recommending that a hill station be built there. But he settled in Nha Trang where he became famed and loved for his work on sanitation and basic health programmes which led to a substantial improvement in health standards in the region. He also gained considerable respect from fishermen for his ability to predict typhoons by the use of the barometer.

The Pasteur Institute was founded by Yersin to promote scientific and health research and although the equipment and budget has not improved much with the times, it is still an active institute producing much-needed vaccines and undertaking further research. Meanwhile in the **Yersin Museum**, walking round his office and library, you can get an idea of the broad nature of his knowledge from the vast number of textbooks on subjects from botany to zoology and astrology to sanitation, and see the fruits of this knowledge in the gifts given him as tokens of appreciation from Nha Trang's grateful citizens. The Pasteur Institute and Yersin Museum are next door to each other at the northern end of Tran Phu St and are open Monday to Saturday from 8 to 11am and 2 to 4.30pm. The combined entrance cost is 10,000d.

Boat tours and diving

There are numerous mini travel agents along the beach off Tran Phu St offering daily boat trips out into the bay stopping to snorkel and visit islands. The most notorious of these by far is **Mama Hanh's Green Hat boat tour** (beware the many imitations which you will be hustled to buy almost everywhere; if you want to be sure you are getting the real thing, book at the Rainbow Bar on the beach behind the Ferris wheel).

Standard fare on all of these boat tours is a good Vietnamese lunch made and served on board, snorkelling in sea a little too deep to give perfect vision of the nonetheless brightly coloured fish and coral, and visits to two of the (rather indifferent) islands in the bay. The difference of the Green Hat boat tour is Mama Hanh herself; she is an extraordinary bon viveur, fond of loud music on the roof of the boat and of doling out far too much local sweet wine from a floating cool box buoyed up by rubber rings

– all for $7 per person. The only problem with the Mama Hanh boat tour, and most of those priced at $7, is that the islands they visit, Mun and Tam islands are not the most impressive: Mun island at least has the snorkelling around it as an attraction, and has the advantage over Tam island of not costing 5000d to go onshore.

There are other boating options: **Mieu Island** is a living island housing a bright fishing village, corresponding eateries, and even a fish breeding ground just offshore, home to hundreds of fish, crabs, sea turtles and reef sharks. You don't need to hire a boat to reach the island as there is a regular ferry service costing 14,000d to the island's village, Tri Nguyen, from Cau Da dock at the foot of Nha Trang's bay. You may find a boat tour offering trips to **Tre Island**, 'bamboo' island, where you can delight in the bright white sand of vast Bai Tru beach which nestles under dark sheer cliffs before they build a resort here. You will probably need to charter a boat for the three-hour journey to reach the rich shores of **Salangenes**, or 'sea-swallow' island – rich, that is, in the nests of sea-swallows whose saliva-spun creations are harvested to make the delicacy of birds-nest soup. A good company which has daily boat trips to some of these islands is Papa Lang's (which ironically advertises it runs the second-best island tour) – book at the bar complex on the beach opposite Grand Hotel.

Monkey Island, 10km north of Nha Trang, can also be reached by boat, but is easier to get to by road plus ferry (see p193) which also has the advantage of going past the charming promontory and temple en route. There is usually a large range of boats, many of which can be hired, from the Cau Da harbour at the southern end of the Nha Trang bay – but you need to arrive before 9-10am to get a boat.

Alternatively, there is **scuba-diving** (though note that the diving centres are closed from November to January). There are a few places offering diving; the three most recommended are the PADI-recognized Blue Diving Club (☎ 058-825390, 🖹 058-824214) in the Coconut Cove Resort (on the beach opposite Hai Yen Hotel), founded and run by a Frenchman Jean-Pierre Prina, the PADI-recognized Rainbow Bar (☎ 058-829946, 🖹 058-811223), and the PADI-recognized Sailing Club (☎ 058-813788). Check out what they have to say at 💻 www.divevietnam.com or contact them at 💻 rainbowdivers@hotmail.com.

Given that diving is a potentially dangerous business it is wise to dive with a highly-reputable organization; in addition to the three listed above, there are other companies offering dives and claiming PADI status, but beware, it is cheaper to buy a PADI sign than hire a trained diver.

Diving around Nha Trang makes sense because the sea is just a little too deep for snorkelling to be ideal, whereas diving captures the full glory of the sea world, but of course it is not cheap. A one-day boat trip with lunch and two dives costs $60 per person; the four-day PADI course costs

$340 per person, although the price falls a little if you are a group of four. If you are already a qualified diver the prices are refreshingly reasonable, at $40 for one dive, $60 for two, or $80 for three (make sure you bring your diving certificate).

PRACTICAL INFORMATION
Arrival and departure
By train The train station in Nha Trang is small, friendly and central. It is around 1km west of the main beach area – a short cyclo ride away.

Since Nha Trang is a tourist attraction the station throngs with cyclos who will usually try to impress their choice of expensive, or not very central, hotel on you. The popularity of the place can also mean that it is difficult to get a train ticket out, but many of the beach-side mini travel agents or the bigger hotels can often arrange a ticket for you at shorter notice than you might achieve through the usual channels and for a reasonable commission. Alternatively the foreigner's booking office at the station is open 7.30am-6pm.

By bus Nha Trang's long-distance bus station is on the same road as the train station, around 1km further out of town.

Nha Trang is served by long-distance buses to most destinations. The bus station for local buses and shared taxis is next to the railway station, opposite Royal Hotel.

By air Nha Trang's airport is around 3km south of the town's centre. Many cyclos gather here to take you the short hop into town which should cost around 6000d (there is no bus).

There are two daily flights between Nha Trang and Ho Chi Minh City, and Hanoi, and four flights a week between Nha Trang and Danang. Vietnam Airlines' office is at 91 Nguyen Thien That St (☎ 058-826768, 🖹 058-825956).

Orientation
Tran Phu St runs the length of Nha Trang beach and is dotted with many of the town's hotels and bars. The town centre is a few blocks inland at the northern end of the bay, focusing around the hub of activity of the Dam market, and stretching back inland.

Services
Post and telecommunications The post office is at 2 Tran Phu St; it is open daily from 6.30am to 9.30pm and offers all the usual services. Next door, at No 4, is an express post office.

The cheapest place to get online is at the bureau opposite the post office, on the corner of Pasteur St.

Money Nha Trang's Vietkombank is at 17 Quang Trung St and is open Monday to Friday 7-11am and 1.30-4pm. Here you can change foreign cash or travellers' cheques into US dollars for a 1.5 per cent commission charge and into dong at 0.5 per cent commission, and withdraw money on credit or debit cards at 3 per cent commission.

Visa extensions Most of the mini travel agents along the waterfront can arrange visa extensions for $25.

Medical Nha Trang has a number of pharmacies on roads parallel to the beach which lead to the hospital, which is below the stadium, on Yersin St.

Book exchanges Mr Lang's exchange between the bars on the beach opposite Grand Hotel has an increasingly good selection.

Local transport
As you would expect, Nha Trang is flush with cyclos, and just about every hotel can supply you with bicycles or scooters to hire for a day, though Nha

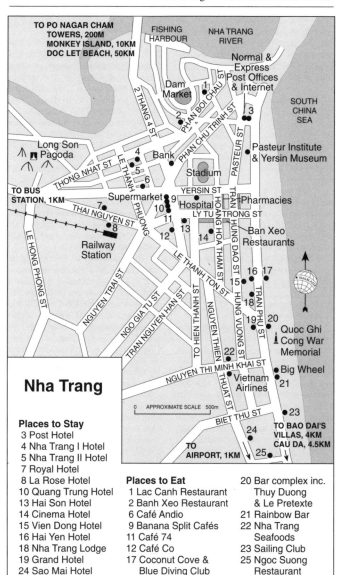

TO PO NAGAR CHAM TOWERS, 200M MONKEY ISLAND, 10KM DOC LET BEACH, 50KM

FISHING HARBOUR

NHA TRANG RIVER

Normal & Express Post Offices & Internet

Dam Market

2 THANG 4 ST

PHAN BOI CHAU ST

PHAN CHU TRINH ST

PASTEUR ST

SOUTH CHINA SEA

Pasteur Institute & Yersin Museum

Long Son Pagoda

Bank

THONG NHAT ST

LE THANH

Stadium

TO BUS STATION, 1KM

Supermarket

YERSIN ST

Hospital

LY TU TRONG ST

Pharmacies

THAI NGUYEN ST

PHUONG

HOANG HOA THAM ST

TRAN

Ban Xeo Restaurants

Railway Station

LE THANH TON ST

HUNG DAO ST

NGUYEN TRAI ST

NGO GIA TU ST

TRAN NGUYEN HAN ST

TO HIEN THANH ST

NGUYEN THIEN THUAT ST

HUNG VUONG ST

TRAN PHU ST

Quoc Ghi Cong War Memorial

Big Wheel

Vietnam Airlines

NGUYEN THI MINH KHAI ST

BIET THU ST

TO BAO DAI'S VILLAS, 4KM CAU DA, 4.5KM

TO AIRPORT, 1KM

0   APPROXIMATE SCALE   500m

Nha Trang

Places to Stay
3 Post Hotel
4 Nha Trang I Hotel
5 Nha Trang II Hotel
7 Royal Hotel
8 La Rose Hotel
10 Quang Trung Hotel
13 Hai Son Hotel
14 Cinema Hotel
15 Vien Dong Hotel
16 Hai Yen Hotel
18 Nha Trang Lodge
19 Grand Hotel
24 Sao Mai Hotel

Places to Eat
1 Lac Canh Restaurant
2 Banh Xeo Restaurant
6 Café Andio
9 Banana Split Cafés
11 Café 74
12 Café Co
17 Coconut Cove & Blue Diving Club

20 Bar complex inc. Thuy Duong & Le Pretexte
21 Rainbow Bar
22 Nha Trang Seafoods
23 Sailing Club
25 Ngoc Suong Restaurant

Trang is also a pleasant place to walk around. Nonetheless its burgeoning tourist trade has led to the appearance of several taxi companies – the best are Emasco (☎ 058-814444) and Nha Trang Taxi (☎ 058-818181).

Where to stay

Nha Trang is well furnished with hotels. For a reasonable price you can choose between the history of Bao Dai's Villas, the pleasant weirdness of Grand Hotel or Cinema Hotel, or pay rather less at around $5-7 a night at a vast number of small hotels.

Very near the railway station are two hotels roughly equivalent in terms of reasonable service and price, and distance from the beach: *Royal Hotel*, 40 Thai Nguyen St (☎ 058-822298), has rooms with fan for $6-$14 and doubles with air-con for $18-20; *La Rose Hotel*, 11 Thai Nguyen St (☎ 058-823090), has similar prices though fewer rooms. Moving away from the station you can find accommodation which is much nearer the beach, or in the town centre.

A good area for cheap accommodation on or near the beach is at the southern end of the bay. On beachside Tran Phu St, south of Nguyen Thi Minh Khai St, there are a number of guest-houses and hotels offering doubles with fan from $6 to $9 and with air-con from $10 to $20. In the same area there are also a few mini hotels one or two blocks inland, such as the small and friendly *Sao Mai Hotel* (meaning morning star) which is at Nguyen Thien Thuat St (☎ 058-827412) which has air-con doubles at the bottom of the range, for $10.

An alternative hotel-rich area is around the stadium. This is much nearer the town centre and still only a few blocks from the beach. Here *Quang Trung Hotel*, No 68 on busy Quang Trung St (☎ 058-823072), offers small basic rooms for $5, while *Hai Son Hotel,* 3 Ly Tu Trong St (☎ 058-821641), is worth the extra expense for its pleasant rooms at $8.

There are a number of good-value small hotels just to the south of the stadium on Hoang Hoa Tham St, of which the most appealing is the groovy *Cinema Hotel*, which is literally in the cinema building, at 10 Hoang Hoa Tham St (☎ 058-821072), and has congenial doubles, rather reminiscent of a cinema auditorium, with fan at $8 and with air-con at $12. *Nha Trang I* and *II Hotels* are often recommended for foreigners but, in contrast to the other options available, are dives.

In the middle-range there are a number of hotels on the beach; one of the most delightful is *Post Hotel*, next door to the post office at 2 Le Loi St (☎ 058-821252), which has rooms for $25 or $28 with a sea view.

Hai Yen Hotel, 40 Tran Phu St (☎ 058-822974), is a reasonable government hotel with rooms at $17, but a much finer government hotel, combining colonial grandness but friendly service with strangely laid-out large rooms and quiet corridors is *Grand Hotel* (☎ 058-822445), 44 Tran Phu St. In theory it has changed its name to Guesthouse No 44 but nobody seems to have taken any notice. The hotel has huge shuttered rooms gazing out to sea for around $18 and its smallest rooms are only 70,000d.

The large all-inclusive complex of *Vien Dong Hotel* including swimming pool, steam rooms and tennis courts at 1 Tran Hung Dao St (☎ 058-821606, 🖹 058-821912) has long been a favourite with travellers, but the hotel has got rid of its very cheap rooms and most are now between $23 and $32, rising to $70 and the place is a rather stifling tourist cocoon. The vast shining building of *Nha Trang Lodge Hotel*, 42 Tran Phu St (☎ 058-810500, 🖹 058-828800), dominates the skyline on the waterfront but it is not top of its field as a hotel, despite official prices from $75 to $145.

At the opposite end of the spectrum from this functional modern comfort are **Bao Dai's Villas** (☎ 058-8281471), 4km south of Nha Trang at Biet Thu Cau Da. The buildings of the former holiday home of Emperor Bao Dai are set in lush gardens on hills overlooking the bay of Nha Trang to beautiful effect. Since reunification the well-kept rooms have been patronized by Vietnamese Communist party officials, with the suite of Bao Dai himself being reserved for the highest ranking. You can install yourself in these glamourous rooms for around $70.

Where to eat and drink

There is good food, especially seafood, to be had in Nha Trang and no shortage of places at which to indulge, whether it be at a beachside café, bought direct from a beach hawker and cooked in front of you, or at one of the many restaurants in the town itself.

Apart from seafood some of the town's restaurants specialize in a partic-ular chicken dish – *cock testes*! Counter-intuitively, however, (given that you would expect the birds to fly away if they knew this was going to happen to them) 24 hours' notice is generally required.

There is also a good range of bars, from classy watering holes on the beach to the usual collection of bia hoi stalls, plus lively trendy coffee bars at which Nha Trang's old and young mingle to take in the pleasant surroundings and the coffee, served numerous ways.

The number of pleasant **beachside cafés** in Nha Trang has been on the increase; you can now enjoy a drink at most points along the bay. But the two most popular spots are at the south of the bay, where you can find the noisy expat atmosphere but good food of **Nha Trang Sailing Club** (actually a bar and restaurant and not a sailing club), 74 Tran Phu St (☎ 058-826528), and **Rainbow Bar** (☎ 058-829946) at No 52,

on the beach behind the ferris wheel, or in the very middle of the bay where you can enjoy average Vietnamese food and great cocktails while luxuriating in the swish palm-treed and sandy environs of **Coconut Cove Resort**, located opposite Hai Yen Hotel. The best of the beach-side restaurants for Vietnamese food is probably **Thuy Duong Restaurant**, next to Le Pretexte, opposite Grand Hotel.

But you don't have to move even that far from your beach lounger if you don't want to, as the **beach-hawkers** will come to you selling their wares of delicious doughnuts, ice-cold coconut and all manner of raw seafood.

Having king prawns or crab cooked for you on the beach is a real treat, but do ensure if you eat prawns that you remove the small black 'nerve' (actually the prawn's intestines) which runs the length of the spine if you want to avoid a few days' stomach upset. Beware also that your supine position doesn't lead to you getting ripped off – a doughnut should cost 500-1000d, coconut 5000d, and a king prawn around 4000-5000d.

In the town, but just a few blocks away from the beach, restaurants are clustered along certain streets. Phan Chu Trinh St holds many small touristy Vietnamese restaurants, offering good food and good cheery atmospheres.

Yet more appealing is the long-established and still superb **Lac Canh Restaurant** (☎ 058-821391) at 11 Hang Ca St – the steamboats and grilled meats on small charcoal burners are fantastic. To get away a little from the tourist crowd try Ly Tu Trong St which is home to several small Vietnamese restaurants, many specialising in Nha Trang's seafood *banh xeo* – literally meaning noise pancakes these are quick fried pancakes which you roll in crisp rice paper with assorted salad leaves, then dip into *nuoc mam*.

An excellent very Vietnamese street-side place, at 50 Phan Boi Chau St, produces what many think is the best banh xeo in town – though if you arrive at a very busy time you may have to be both patient and polite to have any chance of being served. Inviting a cyclo driver to eat with you is a good way of getting served and of helping you out, if you're unsure how it all works.

Quang Trung St also has a number of splendid little joints, such as *Café 74*, at No 74, and *Café Co*, at No 80, and the rival *Banana Split cafés* on the corner of Yersin St at Nos 58 and 60 Quang Trung St offers good tourist fare and Sinh café tours as their respective pint-sized hustlers are keen to point out.

By going further away from the beach you can escape the tourist crowd altogether and take your pick of the stalls selling pho in the morning and banh xeo by day. The town's best restaurants can be found on Tran Quang Khai St – the restaurant at No 16, *Ngoc Suong* (☎ 058-827030) is where you can delight in a variety of Vietnamese food, including the famed testicules grillés. Another excellent restaurant is *Nha Trang Seafoods*, 46 Nguyen Thi Minh Khai St (☎ 058-822664). Alternatively, cheap food can always be had at Dam Market, and now you can get hold of some Western foodstuffs from the supermarket complex next to the Banana Split cafés at the junction of Quang Trung and Yersin streets.

The **bars** on the beach are choice locations for a sophisticated evening drink or merely for a few beers. Again, the *Sailing Club*, 74 Tran Phu St, is popular while the burgeoning complex on the beach opposite Grand Hotel already has the excellent *Le Pretexte bar* with its comfy chairs and free games, plus the atmosphere of *Log Bar* in Coconut Cove Resort opposite Hai Yen Hotel is good; its cocktails can't be beaten and the bar, made of an entire carved log, is amazing.

For a more Vietnamese experience Hai Ba Trung St has many beer cafés serving up bia hoi and more. Even better are the lively coffee houses inland (Hung Vuong St is packed with them); these can be spotted by their music, often accompanied by bright lights advertising them and a sign announcing Ca Phe. Different varieties of hot or cold coffee served with sweet condensed milk are the house favourites. One such venue is *Café Audio* at 50 Yersin St (☎ 058-829966).

Entertainment

Vietnamese culture Vien Dong Hotel, at 1 Tran Hung Dao St (☎ 058-821606), has delightful nightly classical music and theatre performances which are free to diners from 7.30 to 9pm.

Cinemas Below Cinema Hotel is, of course, the cinema at 10 Hoang Hoa Tham St, if you crave a dose of Vietnamese film.

AROUND NHA TRANG

There is a superb day excursion which can be covered from Nha Trang by road taking in Cham towers just north of the town, the Hon Chong Promontory, Monkey Island, and finally the glorious Doc Let beach. Bear in mind that a car will not easily cover the tracks which lead to Doc Let beach – a motorbike or bicycle is much more suitable.

(**Opposite**) Dragon fruit, custard apple, rambutan, papaya, orange, banana, coconut? Fruit seller on the beach at Nha Trang, Vietnam's main seaside holiday resort.

Head north out of town along Quang Trung St which becomes 2 Thang 4 St (2 April St) just before the road crosses the Cai River giving you the delightful scene of a million fishing boats, bright blue and cherry red darting like exotic fish through the water, or depositing their treasure on the shore. Just beyond the bridge are the **Po Nagar Cham towers**, meaning Lady of the Kingdom, dominating the verdant hill on the left of the road.

The towers are important religiously and historically, and comprise some of the finest examples of impressive Cham architecture, but, sadly, they have been afflicted by weathering, graffiti and by attempts at reconstruction such that they resemble Cham towers under construction more than anything else. As such their great baked red towers warrant a look from the road, but you may not think them worth the 10,000d entry to get a little closer, unless you happen to be in Nha Trang around the time of the Merian festival, on March 22.

On the day before the festival the statue of Po Ino Nagar is cleaned to perfection, revealing her exemplary six arms, and then she is dressed with a number of luxurious cloths and jewellery. On the day of the festival ritual celebrations take place involving gift-giving and praying. This modern-day practice means that the Cham towers have acted as a religious centre with little interruption for a millennium. Still visible in the stonework are crafted four-armed shivas dancing above the doorways and Cham inscriptions as well as dancing maidens are sculpted into the walls rising up to the gables.

Less than 1km from the Cham towers is the pleasant viewpoint of the **Hon Chong Promontory** reaching out into the spraying sea, famously so in Vietnamese folklore. You can clamber down to the large rocks which stick out into the sea and get a lovely view of the mountain coastline as well as of Nha Trang bay – this is also a good way of avoiding the touristy kiosks which have started to overrun the place. In the largest of the rocks with the eye of faith you can see the shape of a huge handprint. This was said to have been left by a giant male fairy who slipped into the sea after gawking at a bathing female fairy. To reach the promontory, continue north from the Cham towers for 400m where there is a roundabout and a sign for Hon Chong Promontory.

A further 10km north is the beautiful promontory with a temple from where you can take a ferry to **Monkey Island**. Highway 1 runs close to the shore and there are lovely views across the waterway between the mainland and Monkey Island. A pretty, small temple clings to the edge of the land and from below here ferries run over to the island. As the name suggests, the island is inhabited by hundreds of our small furry friends. The monkeys love to be fed but are also not indifferent to grabbing food

(**Opposite**) **Top**: Doc Let beach, 40km north of Nha Trang. **Bottom**: This Nha Trang hawker even carries her own mini barbecue and will cook king prawns or crab for you right on the beach.

out of your hand, or even from your bag if the food is bananas. Of course beware, as wild monkeys can carry diseases. To reach the temple turn off the road along a cobbled track which forks off to the right as you become level with Monkey Island.

Next stop is beautiful **Doc Let beach**, 40km further north. To relax away from it all in unsullied calm beauty this is the place to go. The wide sweep of the bay is fringed by palm trees and a sandy very gently sloping beach. This gentle slope continues in the water thus making the sea extraordinarily calm. Wading out and then swimming in the limpid blue waters is a wonderfully tranquil experience, which may be disturbed only by the joyous splashing of Vietnamese in the shallow waters. On the beach you may be able to find someone to sell you a coconut or cook some fish for you, if you are reasonably patient, or the tiny restaurant may even be open. There are bungalows here if you wish to stay offering basic cabins for $10, and ones which are a little more plush for $15.

To get to Doc Let beach by public transport is difficult as there is no direct bus – by self-propelled transport (motorbike is recommended) the only problems are of simple navigation and of somewhat rough tracks which become a little like junior kick-start championships if it is rainy. Head north along Highway 1 until you are 30km beyond Nha Trang when you will reach a group of several petrol stations after which the road forks in two (ignoring small turns). Take the right hand fork and continue straight on for 8km, then take a left turn continuing for 3km, before turning right for another 2km after which you will come upon the beach. There are now signposts to the beach at these last two turns, simplifying the task considerably. There is a charge of 2000d to leave a motorbike at the beach.

Many recommend visiting **Ba Ho Falls**, 11km south of Doc Let beach. However, if you have ever seen any waterfalls in your life you may find the 100m clamber up rocks to see a few small pools and desultory unimpressive falls and paying 10,000d for the privilege, not exactly worth it. If you do wish to see them, though, Ba Ho falls are easy to find – 19km north of Nha Trang there is a sign to the falls pointing down a track heading west through impressive-looking gates which suggest that the track will not be as small and rough as it in fact is; finally you have to get off and walk even to reach the ticket kiosk.

QUANG NGAI

Quang Ngai is a small dusty backwater of a town with little to offer except the compelling experience of visiting the horrifically grisly but intensely moving site of the most notorious episode, during the American war, of brutality by American soldiers – the My Lai massacre. The horrible fate which met Son My village – the target of the massacre – was just the latest instance of retribution by invading powers against the Quang Ngai area which was an important centre of resistance against the French during the French colonial war. Quang Ngai as an important Viet Minh stronghold was heavily attacked by French troops whose cause was later picked up by American bombers in the ensuing American war, and the area was particularly heavily bombed. These scars of war can still be seen in the area in the many remains of demolished bridges and most devastatingly at the My Lai massacre site.

The My Lai massacre site

The My Lai massacre site 14km north-east of Quang Ngai preserves a shocking yet still understated vision of the horrors of war which, like the preservation of Dachau, has but one aim – to cry out 'never again'. It should succeed. The well-kept grass and the tidy signs indicating where whole families died provide a sickening contrast to the vile photographs and narratives kept in the small museum telling the story of what happened that day on 16 March 1968 (see the box on pp196-7).

Today there are five survivors of the massacre from the My Lai hamlet still living. The My Lai memorial site was established just after the end of the war in 1986 and the husband of one survivor who died in 1996 by the name of Vo Thi Lien built the statues at the site in 1982. Since then the excellent little museum has opened and collects donations which the museum claims are given to the survivors and their families, although this has been questioned. The site charges 2000d for the parking of a car, 1000d for a motorbike and 500d for a bike.

The My Lai site is to be found by heading out of town north along Quang Trung turning right just after the northern end of the bridge over the Tra Khuc river and continue along this road in between the rice paddies for 12km until you reach the site, signalled by a sign. A return Honda om ride should cost around $4.

Beaches

There are some pleasant entirely-undeveloped beaches along the coast to the east of Quang Ngai. You can reach the closest one continuing east from My Lai for around 3km until you hit the sea; following the coast north or south from here reveals more.

PRACTICAL INFORMATION
Arrival and departure

By train Quang Ngai's station is around 2.5km west of the town centre at the end of a small side street which runs off Phan Boi Chau St at the point where the continuation of this street curves around to the left. The station is too small to have a separate foreigner's ticket booth, but tickets can be bought from the main booth at any time during the day prior to a train's departure.

Quang Ngai has few foreign visitors so it is not difficult to obtain a train ticket out (hard or soft seat only, if you want to upgrade you will have to do it on the train). A few cyclos gather here.

❏ The My Lai massacre

The Son My area (covering the hamlets of My Lai and others) had long been thought to have substantial pockets of Viet Cong (VC). Recent encounters between US infantry divisions including Charlie Company platoon, and the Viet Cong had led to a number of US casualties from booby traps or snipers hidden in the jungle, but no open fighting. Frustration was setting in among these trained career soldiers who had recently arrived in Vietnam but whose expertise, and expectation, was not of guerrilla warfare. Then a rumour was spread that the 48th North Vietnamese Army Division had set up base in the villages of the Son My area, so there was now a definable target. It was also thought by US army intelligence that local villagers in the Son My area were sheltering and feeding VC fighters; thus they themselves were somehow made legitimate targets. In fact you only need read any Vietnamese account of the war, such as Le Ly Hayslip's *When heaven and earth changed places* to know that such sheltering of VC troops happened everywhere, because the villagers were made to realize that they had no choice.

It is still not clear whose idea it was to make an example of My Lai and the other villages, but at a briefing on the night before the attack, the 'search and destroy' mission was set out to three infantry divisions. They were told by their officers that the raid would begin in the early morning when all the villagers would be at market and that literally all Vietnamese left were genuine VC targets. It seems hard to believe that any of the GIs could have really believed this – it certainly was not true.

At 7am nine helicopters flew over the villages, scattering artillery and machine-gun fire on villagers and their houses, and bombarding chosen landing sights in the fields with more artillery and rocket fire. They encountered no resistance, no returning fire. The helicopters landed and disgorged the three platoons of Charlie Company who then unleashed one of the most vicious and violent attacks on undefended fleeing civilian villagers in recent recorded history. The soldiers and officers rampaged through the hamlets bayonetting or shooting men, women, children, the elderly, even babies. They rounded up families out of their houses, assembled and executed them. Or they threw grenades into families' shelters, then dumped any stray bodies into the wells to poison the water. Some GIs raped or sodomized young girls, then shot them. Around 100 villagers were rounded up, pushed and shoved one on top of each other into a single muddy ditch – then rounds and rounds of machine gun fire were rained down onto the bloody mess. This ditch can still be seen, at the far end of the walk through the My Lai massacre site.

It is thought in all that 500 Vietnamese were killed in this raid, of which over 300 came from the hamlet of My Lai. The US army met with no VC resistance – there was only one US casualty: the American soldier Herbert Carter shot himself in the foot, to avoid taking any part in the slaughter.

After the attack the soldiers were told to keep their mouths shut about the incident and at first the American media was told of an alleged military victory that morning in Son My. But a year and a half later the truth came out of the traumatized mouths of some GIs and confirmed by the photographs of the military photographer Ron Haeberle. Haeberle had taken 40 black and white photos of the morning's proceedings which were handed in to the army afterwards.

The My Lai massacre (cont'd)

These photos were kept under wraps but he had also taken 16 colour photographs which he released in November 1969, to public horror, in *Life* magazine. (The museum at My Lai paid $11,000 to buy these photos which it now displays.) After the shocking revelations enquiries were begun to find the key culprits. In the end only Lt William Calley, head of one of the platoons of Charlie Company, was convicted of murder. He was sentenced to prison, but served only two days before Nixon commuted the sentence to house arrest.

Although there was a lack of formal judicial actions against the perpetrators of these atrocities the army as a whole was not let off the hook by the public of America, or indeed the world. Rather, the result was that all who served in Vietnam then became tainted by the butchery of My Lai. More than anything else it was this incident that gave the anti-war crusaders the moral high ground. Thus My Lai came to be seen as typifying and thereby condemning the 'search and destroy' strategy which was indeed dropped as the war became more 'Vietnamized'. Also the consequence for individual soldiers who fought in Vietnam was that increasingly they returned home not to be greeted as war heroes, but reviled as murderers. Most crucially, in trying to understand why the My Lai killings came about some have seen a lesson for democracy.

All the soldiers in Son My that morning were professional soldiers or men who had volunteered to fight in Vietnam; they were not there because of the draft. Not only does this mean that self-selection principles will make it likely that these soldiers were more, rather than less, bloodthirsty, but it also shows that they are fighting a war which their government would like to keep sealed away from their society – and if you volunteer to do somebody's dirty work for them you feel entitled to choose your own methods. The My Lai massacre should not be forgiven, but it needs to be understood. Armed soldiers who are frustrated with the methods of guerrilla war their opponents use are always dangerous, especially when their own army had officially sanctioned the permanent use of napalm and scatter rocket attacks which inherently implied that Vietnamese life was to be considered very cheap. It is not merely that these policies are at root to blame, the issue is more deeply that a democratic power should involve its societies in its wars if it wishes to avoid the excesses that inevitably come with unaccountability.

By bus Quang Ngai's large dusty and chaotic bus station is in the centre of town just off the town's section of Highway 1 – from going along Quang Trung in a southerly direction turn left where the road widens and curves right towards HCMC. Quang Ngai is not a stop for express buses. The only decent buses to any destination leave the station early in the morning, bound principally for Danang, HCMC or the central highlands. At any other time of the day the bus station is populated by the most remarkable primary-coloured comedy buses which get packed to the gunnels with all manner of people and animals and go very very slowly. Alternatively, because Quang Ngai is on Highway 1 (called Quang Trung St in the town) it is generally very easy to pick up shared taxis to go either north or south.

Orientation and services

Highway 1 runs through Quang Ngai which is bounded to the north by the Tra Khuc river.

The small **post office** is 300m west of Highway 1 at the corner of Phan Boi

Chau (also called Hung Vuong St) and Phan Dinh Phung Streets. It is open Monday to Saturday 7am-7pm and offers the usual services.

Currently there is no bank in town at which you can change foreign cash or travellers' cheques, nor is there a hospital. The biggest **pharmacy** is on the corner of Quang Trung and Le Trung Dinh Streets.

Local transport
There are a few rather down-at-heel cyclos hobbling around town grateful for custom. None of the hotels readily rents out bicycles or mopeds and there are no other hire places. If you intend to make the trip out to My Lai your best

bet is to talk to hotel staff to see if they can organize Honda oms – the best motorbikes the town has to offer are old Russian models with manual gear changes which even the owners regularly stall.

Where to stay
Of the few hotels in Quang Ngai the best by far is *Kim Thanh Hotel* at 19 Phan Boi Chau St (☎ 055-823471, 🖹 055-826134). This pleasant private hotel has air-con doubles for $16 and a few rooms for only $8.

Situated on the highway passing through the town (Highway 1) *Dong Hung Hotel*, at 497 Quang Trung (☎ 055-821704), offers helpful service

Quang Ngai

0   APPROXIMATE SCALE   200m

TO MAY LAI, 13KM

TRA KHUC RIVER

Song Tra Hotel

1KM

Kim Thanh Hotel

Pharmacy

TO RAILWAY STATION, 2.5KM

PHAN BOI CHAU ST

QUANG TRUNG ST

LE TRUNG DINH ST

Post Office

PHAN CHU TRINH ST

PHAN DINH PHUNG ST

QUANG TRUNG ST (HIGHWAY 1)

Market

Bus Station

Dong Hung Hotel

but not such nice accommodation for $10.

The dismal grimy vast structure of *Song Tra Hotel* at 1A Quang Trung St (☎ 055-822665) is to be avoided if at all possible – the rooms at $30 are barely better than the dingy triples at $15.

Where to eat
Due to the scant choice of places to enjoy a good meal the restaurant in *Song Tra Hotel* is probably unduly popular – particularly as there is a good beef banh xeo (quick fried 'noise' pancakes) stall just outside.

For a fuller meal there are some reasonable restaurants along Phan Boi Chau St near Kim Thanh Hotel and near the post office, especially along Phan Chu Trinh St, and some good roadside cafés along Quang Trung St.

DANANG

Danang is a bustling city which is Vietnam's fourth largest (Haiphong being the third). It offers a rare opportunity to be a part of life in a growing modern Vietnamese city, but one which is little touched by tourism, although the effects on the city of housing the largest US airbase in Vietnam between 1965 and 1975 can still be seen. The vices and virtues associated with this led to Danang being termed the Saigon of the north, and led to a current population of 20,000 Amerasians.

The reason for the lack of tourists today is of course that there are few actual sights to see, other than the excellent Cham museum. But it is worth taking in the feel of this city where the main activity of the evenings is to cruise round on a motorbike, eat, drink and talk in an atmosphere reminiscent of film renderings of nightlife in 1950s America or Britain.

Few tourists stop here for longer than it takes to see round the Cham museum, before taking the trip out to nearby China Beach and the Marble Mountains or to Hoi An, but this is a shame. Although it does mean it's easy to get a train ticket out.

History
Danang is essentially a city of south Vietnam: it was ruled by Hué during the 18th century (when it was known as Tourane) while the country was split in two, and defended the southern regime and the French when the country was again split in the 20th century.

During the American war there was a strong American presence here, showing how the forces of the south had their grip on the city. Danang was a southern and American stronghold – until March 1975, when chaos took over.

As South Vietnamese troops abandoned Hué to the north, and Quang Ngai was taken by the Communists to the south there was a rush of desperate troops, their families, and hundreds of thousands of other refugees to Danang. But the Communists were closing in on Danang too. The result was desperate attempts by civilians to flee the city before the Communists arrived, which they surely would, and did.

❑ The human tragedy

'During the afternoon [of 28th March 1975] the loading of the Pioneer Contender [a US naval ship dispatched to evacuate US Consulate and CIA staff and Vietnamese refugees] had accelerated as more and more smaller vessels pulled alongside. Each time one appeared, gangplanks or ladders would be lowered; then the passengers would begin their perilous climb to the main deck. Many of them, often the youngest and oldest, lost their footing and fell overboard, to be crushed to death as their own vessels slammed into the side of the Contender with the pitch of the waves. By nightfall Ron Howard [the CIA chief in Danang] had stopped counting the casualties. He had already seen nearly 1,000 people go over the side.' Scenes at the airfield were, if it's possible, even more gruesome.

'During the morning [of 29th March 1975] World Airways President Edward Daly decided to attempt a last rescue mission of his own into Danang. Embassy representatives had argued with him through the night, trying to persuade him not to go. But he did so anyway, insisting that his planes were now the only hope for the thousands still trapped in the city. Shortly after daybreak two of his 727s took off from Tan Son Nhat airport [in Saigon] and flew north toward Danang. Daly himself was in the lead aircraft.'

'When the first plane touched down at the city's main airstrip thousands of armed soldiers and civilians swarmed toward it. Daly tried to slow them down by firing warning shots over their heads, but to no effect, and in less than ten minutes over 270 people – all soldiers except for two women and a child – jammed themselves inside his plane. As the big jet lumbered down the runway, someone who had not been able to get aboard threw a hand grenade at the wing, the explosion rippling the landing flaps into the open position. At that moment North Vietnamese rockets began dropping in at the far end of the runway. The second 727 did not come in.'

'Scores of people clung to the wings and the landing gear as the plane took off. Many were crushed under the wheels. Others fell off after it was airborne, and several bodies were later found mashed in the wheel wells. The aisle in the cabin glistened with blood. It was the last American plane out of Danang.' *Decent Interval* Frank Snepp

The mission to flee the city by civilians and south Vietnamese troops now reached massive proportions, for which no-one was sufficiently prepared. The human tragedy, as President Ford rightly called the loss of Danang, was so great it needs a first-hand account to give it the gravity it deserves. Frank Snepp in his excellent book *Decent Interval* (see p28) describes what happened (see the box above).

Danang today is lively and busy. Much of its economic potential derives from being a city with a deep port and it has long been one of Vietnam's important trading port cities. Port cities historically tend to be prone to prostitution, and Danang is no exception – many, although not all, of the signs offering massage in the city bear witness to this. However, the central government is attempting to foster other routes to economic prosperity. In November 1996 Danang City was made a separate province in its own right in an attempt to widen the gate to foreign investment in Danang, which had been held up by the particularly hidebound attitude of the local bureaucracy.

Sights and excursions

Cham Museum is certainly worth visiting. It is open every day from 6am to 7pm and costs 10,000d. It contains three rooms displaying magnificent sandstone sculptures from different regions and periods of Cham civilization. The pieces in the museum enable you to trace the development of Cham culture from strong Hindu influences – as the parables of Shiva are beautifully told in frieze works – then Buddhist influences and finally Indonesian and Japanese influences. The pieces also enable you to trace the rise and decline of the Champa culture: in the early period of prosperity and growth the most detailed and beautifully designed sculptures are of people, and particularly show wonderful friezes of daily life in Champa, whereas in the latter period of decline the most ornate sculptures are of animals – the animal God 'protectors'. It was during this period that Champa civilization was comprehensively flattened by the Vietnamese.

The My Son room is the first (on the left on entry to the museum), covering the period of the 8th-9th centuries with statues depicting ritual Hindu singing and dancing ceremonies extracted from the My Son ruins for preservation. Other statues in the room such as of Ganesh, the elephant God, show influences of nearby civilizations – Indian, Khmer and Thai. Other sculptures show the different ways in which ordinary Chams interact with nature.

The major piece in the Tra Kieu room is the delicately-decorated altar from the Tra Kieu capital adorned with epic images from the Ramayana of the preparations for, and celebrations of, the wedding of Princess Sita and Prince Rama. A finely-carved altar from the 9th-century capital of Dong Duong is the main item in the connecting building of the Dong Duong room.

The final Thap Mam room is of the latest period of Cham civilization from around the 12th-14th centuries when the kingdom was increasingly retreating south as the Viets pushed down from the north. Most of the items displayed here are large bold sculptures of animal Gods, such as Makura the sea-monster, and a large Garuda statue.

The ticket booth sells a moderately interesting guide to the museum for 10,000d, but more worthwhile, assuming you are not with a tour, is the amusing, although quirky tour of the museum offered by Nguyen Phu Luy Louis for around the same price; he walks around outside the museum waiting to give you his tour in English or French.

Rising out of the land near the coast by Danang are five large rocky hillocks giving beautiful views from the top and studded with caves,

Buddhist shrines and Cham relics known as the **Marble Mountains** or Ngu Hanh Son. The outcrops are grouped close together around 11km south of Danang about a third of the way to Hoi An.

The largest of the five has a large cave filled with statues, a pagoda and many small caves which have been turned into Buddhist shrines (bring a torch). This outcrop, named Thuy Son, can also be climbed and its summit, named the Path to Heaven, gives stunning views. Unfortunately this mountain has become very touristy, but despite the hassle it is worth seeing, provided you are prepared to pay the 40,000d admission charge.

The five mountains are said to represent the five elements of the universe, and have been named accordingly – Thuy Son is the largest, representing water, Moc Son embodies wood, Hoa Son symbolizes fire, Kim So metal and Tho Son earth. The Marble Mountains are said to have been formed from the five cracked pieces of a giant turtle egg shell from which emerged a beautiful maiden who married the young man to whom the egg had been given (by a giant turtle who rescued the man from drowning). This story intertwines the mountains with the sea reflecting the geological history of the mountains which suggests that they were once islands.

The Marble Mountains have long been a focus for religious activity: the Chams turned their grottos into Hindu shrines, which the Vietnamese modified into Buddhist sanctuaries where the Nguyen emperors came to worship, and still today the shrines on the Thuy Son Mountain ring with the sound of religious ritual during Tet. Moreover, Ho Chi Minh himself is immortalized in marble from the mountains which were quarried to make his mausoleum in Hanoi. The smaller mountain symbolising earth – Tho Son – still has some Cham relics on it, most notably sculptures hewn out of the rock.

The most notable sight on all the Marble Mountains is **Huyen Khong cave** on Thuy Son mountain at around midday. For it is at this time that rays of light shine through the five holes in the high roof of the cave illuminating the central Buddha statues and lending an even more ethereal atmosphere to the eerily darkened incense-filled cavern.

The cave can be hard to find if you have not picked up one of the many child 'guides' on the mountain as its entrance is behind that of another cave. There are two sets of stairs flanking the mountain and the circular route of choice is to take the seaward stairs to ascend, giving increasingly fine views as you climb, and to continue round the mountain in an anti-clockwise direction. Turn off the main paved path where there are small rocky paths for here you will find panoramic view spots and occasional small grottoes. To reach the Huyen Khong cave climb just over 100 steps where you will come upon the colourful Ling Ung pagoda. Behind this are the first of Thuy Son's darkened cave pagodas. Continue uphill and you pass through a bullet-holed brick gate on the left of which is Tam Thai pagoda, but it is the nearby naturally-formed rock arch which you need to note, for it is behind this that the antechamber to the Huyen Khong cave is found. The main occupant of this is a large sandstone Buddha and to the left of that is a passageway leading to a sudden opening to the sky which heralds the entrance to the mystical Huyen Khong cave. The entrance is flanked by statues of mandarins who act as guardians to the cave, which is further filled with altars and statues to Buddhist and Confucianist deities. There is also a wall plaque here commemorating the Hoa Vang female guerrilla fighters who hid out here in the cave and who shot down 19 American planes from the outcrop of the mountain on 15 April 1972 with only 22 rockets.

You can get a bus to the Marble Mountains from the bus station opposite 350 Hung Vuong St in Danang. Get off at the sight of the first one, on your left, and then walk the remaining distance; a one-way motorbike ride will cost around $3.

China Beach is a wonderful stretch of white sand backed by groves of trees and lapped by breaking surf. It begins around 11km south of Danang, just after the first Marble Mountain, heading south and continues for several kilometres. It is important to know that the section of China Beach which has been developed for tourism costs money to enter (4000d), and to rent a deck chair (5000d), and even to park a bike (negotiable!). This stretch of the beach is also overrun by hawkers, but it does offer the only luxury accommodation on the beach at *China Beach Hotel* (☎ 0511-836216) which has doubles from $20, or $35 with air-con, and *Furama Resort* (☎ 0511-847333, 🗎 0511-847220) next door which is much more expensive at $60 upwards for a room. Alternatively, there is a long stretch of beach which is free, closer to Danang and served by three unassuming guest-houses which have a total of 12 simple double rooms.

For privacy and the chance for real relaxation this is the place to come, and *Tan Toan Guesthouse* (☎ 0511-836188), just 20m from the beach, is ready with friendly hospitality and basic clean doubles for $6. To get here by road from Danang cross to the east side of the Han river by Nguyen Van Troi bridge and then turn right heading south towards Hoi An. After around 10km and directly after the first Marble Mountain turn right towards Non Nuoc hamlet, a marble masonry village, following the sound of chisel meeting stone. Continue straight on, turning left to the beach after around 1km when the road curves round to the right. Tan Toan guest-house is just before the beach on the right hand side of the road.

To reach the fee-paying section of the beach don't turn left at the first sight of a beach but instead follow the road round to the right and continue on until you reach the resort complex. You can get a bus from the bus station opposite 350 Hung Vuong St in Danang to the Marble Mountain and then walk the last 1km to the beach. A one-way motorbike will cost around $3.

Danang houses the largest **Cao Dai temple** outside the sect's headquarters in Tay Ninh. It is worth a visit if only for the sight of the huge globe at the altar on which a depiction of the 'Divine Eye' – the official symbol of the religion – stands out in relief. However, the ornate building and the bright yellow-washed exterior conceals a spartan interior. The two main items of interest are the globe and a picture of the founders of the five great world religions of which Cao Daoism is a bizarre form of fusion. From left to right these are Mohammed, Laotse, Jesus, Buddha and Confucius. There are several other pagodas and cathedrals scattered around Danang but most have been seriously damaged by the ravages of war and time.

The stretch of sand along the peninsula to the east of Danang is **My Khe beach**, a popular venue for beach picnics for American GIs during the war. Although it is the closest beach to Danang and you may visit it for its history, today the beach has few visitors because it lacks cafés and other amenities and because it backs onto a military complex. The result is not conducive to a beach party, despite the best attempts by locals to exploit the beach's surfing potential.

PRACTICAL INFORMATION
Arrival and departure
By train   The train station is about 1.5km from the city centre, on Haiphong St. A cyclo ride through the busy markets around the station to most hotels will cost around 6000d. The booking office for express trains is open 6am-5pm where the staff are very helpful and there is a decent waiting room and good small eating area.

It is generally easy to buy express tickets from Danang – you can normally obtain them just before departure. But before you press on to Hué an excursion to Hoi An is highly recommended if you are in the mood for R&R travellers' style, want to visit the large Cham ruins of My Son or to kit out your wardrobe in tailor-made silk.

By bus   The bus station is around 3km west of town, opposite 350 Hung Vuong St. The booking office is open 7-11am and 1-5pm. Danang is served by express buses to all the main cities in Vietnam and by many stopping services.

By air   Danang's airport is 4km south of the city. The distance is so short that there is no airport bus: a taxi to or from the airport will cost you around 15,000d, a cyclo 6000d.

Danang is Vietnam's third busiest airport; there are two flights per day to Hanoi, and HCMC (1,000,000d) and several flights a week to other centres such as Nha Trang, as well as international flights to and from Bangkok and Singapore. Vietnam Airlines' booking office (☎ 0511-822094) is at 35 Tran Phu St and is open every day 7am- 6pm.

Orientation
Danang is situated on the west bank of the Han river, separated from the South China sea by a long peninsula on the east bank of the river.

On the eastern edge of the peninsula, 6km from Danang is My Khe beach where the Americans were airlifted during the war to enjoy a day at the seaside, sometimes their last, as immortalized in the American TV show 'China Beach'. Since opening the door to foreigners the

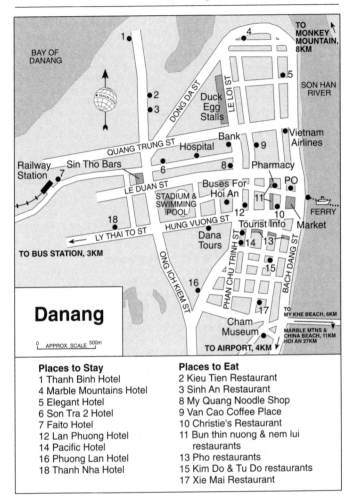

Danang

0 APPROX. SCALE 500m

BAY OF DANANG

TO MONKEY MOUNTAIN, 8KM

SON HAN RIVER

Railway Station

TO BUS STATION, 3KM

TO AIRPORT, 4KM

TO MY KHE BEACH, 6KM

MARBLE MTNS & CHINA BEACH, 11KM HOI AN 27KM

Places to Stay
1 Thanh Binh Hotel
4 Marble Mountains Hotel
5 Elegant Hotel
6 Son Tra 2 Hotel
7 Faito Hotel
12 Lan Phuong Hotel
14 Pacific Hotel
16 Phuong Lan Hotel
18 Thanh Nha Hotel

Places to Eat
2 Kieu Tien Restaurant
3 Sinh An Restaurant
8 My Quang Noodle Shop
9 Van Cao Coffee Place
10 Christie's Restaurant
11 Bun thin nuong & nem lui restaurants
13 Pho restaurants
15 Kim Do & Tu Do restaurants
17 Xie Mai Restaurant

Vietnamese government has built a tourist resort 5km to the south and named it China Beach, trying to capitalize on the name. Their optimism continues: part of the programme for economic prosperity for Danang is a new multi-million dollar resort which is being built on 'China Beach'. At the northernmost tip of the peninsula is the mountain Americans called Monkey Mountain. Eleven kilometres south of Danang on the coast springing up out of China Beach are the five jagged outcrops called the Marble Mountains.

Danang is a relatively easy city to find your way around because most streets run either north-south or east-west. The main north-south road in the centre is Phan Chu Trinh St (also called Le Loi St in north Danang), and the principal east-west road is Hung Vuong St (also called Ly Thai To St and Dien Bien Phu St travelling westwards out of the city).

Services
Post and telecommunications
Danang's main post office is at 62 Bach Dang St (☎ 0511-821327) and is open every day 6am-10pm. It offers post, phone, fax and Fedex services.

Money Vietkombank is at 104 Le Loi St (☎ 0511-822110) and is open Monday to Saturday 7.30-11am and 1.30-4pm. It charges 1.5 per cent to change travellers' cheques into US dollars but surprisingly does not charge to change travellers' cheques into dong.

Newspapers and book exchange
Foreign-language newspapers can be bought from a stand just outside the post office. Danang being a big city means papers can usually be bought in the afternoon as well as in the morning. Christie's Restaurant at 112 Tran Phu St runs a good one for one book exchange of foreign-language books.

Medical The largest pharmacy in Danang is on the corner of Phan Dinh Phuong St and Tran Phu St. The hospital is at 35 Haiphong St.

Local transport
Danang is well supplied with cyclo drivers and Honda om. Alternatively most hotels rent bicycles for the good price of 10,000d a day. Any of these options is preferable to walking in Danang as it is a fairly large city with deceptively long distances between road intersections, and the streets are particularly dusty and very hot in summer.

Tours
Wildly overpriced tours running from Danang to My Son (Cham towers) or China Beach and the Marble Mountains are offered by the government tourist service (☎ 0511-823660) next to Pacific Hotel at 92A Phan Chu Trinh St, or much more reasonable deals can be obtained from Dana Tours (☎ 0511-822516) at 95 Hung Vuong St. There is little competition because Hoi An has cornered the market in such tours.

However, it is easy enough to arrange a motorbike or car to any of the nearby sights from most of Danang's hotels or from outside the railway or bus station. A day trip to China Beach and Hoi An should cost no more than $6 by motorbike, $10 by car; while trips to My Son cost a little more.

Where to stay
Danang is packed with hotels, many built in the last two to three years in the so far unforthcoming expectation of a tourist boom here. This means that there are a few cheap hotels here; the majority are moderately expensive, but because there are many more hotel rooms than tourists, the higher priced hotels can often be bargained with.

The three best cheap options which all have reasonable doubles with fan for around $8 are *Thanh Nha Hotel* (☎ 0511-821721) which is the closest to the station at 68-70 Ly Thai To St, *Thanh Binh Hotel* (☎ 0511-829139), 2 Ong Ich Kiem St, which is good despite being a trade union hotel, and *Marble Mountains Hotel* (☎ 0511-23258) at 5 Dong Da St. These last two have the dubious advantage of being close to the rather unimpressive Thanh Binh beach.

There are several good mid-range options. The new *Son Tra 2 Hotel* (☎ 0511-823834, 🖹 0511-823856) is 500m from the station at 82 Haiphong St and has 14 beautifully furnished identical rooms for $15 single, $18 double all with air-con, TV, bath and IDD phone.

Lan Phuong Hotel (☎ 0511-835001) is more central at 25 Phan Chu Trinh St and offers equally well-equipped doubles for $18, or $15 for a four-flight climb. *Phuong Lan Hotel* (or Bamboo Hotel) is just south of the centre, 500m from the Cham Museum and offers pleasant clean doubles in a friendly atmosphere for $12. *Pacific Hotel* (☎ 0511-822137), 92 Phan Chu Trinh St, is an extremely good government hotel; a basic double costs from $12 but for one with the essential phone in the bathroom and a fax in the bedroom you should expect to pay $30-40.

You can reside in luxury adjacent to the railway station at *Faifo Hotel* (☎ 0511-827901, 🖷 0511-827929), 120 Haiphong St (go outside the station and look left), for $47-$125 per night – though it is only really the suites that are truly luxurious. Or you can have classier luxury for around the same price at a number of hotels on the riverside. Of these *Elegant Hotel* (☎ 0511-892893, 🖷 0511-855179), 22A Bach Dang St, is probably the best and has a rooftop bar.

Where to eat and drink

Danang has a lot to offer in terms of local specialities. A meal of turmeric-flavoured *my quang* (pronounced me quang) noodles and beef is exclusively a Danang dish and should be tried. There are many venues offering this fare – one of the best is at 1A Haiphong St.

Other specialities from the surrounding region include *khanh* for breakfast, which is beef and eggs fried on a hotplate. This can be found at *Xie Mai*, 31B Hoang Van Thu St. There are many small restaurants on Yen Bai St specialising in *bun thin nuong* (grilled beef over noodles with peanut sauce) and *nem lui* (grilled beef and salad in spring rolls). For the excellent local variant of stuffed quick-fried pancakes, *ban canh*, try a small unnamed street off Nguyen Chi Tranh St, turning off where there is a sign on the street saying Ban canh. The small street one block south of Hung Vong St running across Phan Chu Trinh St and Nguyen Chi Phuong St has many small *pho* restaurants.

Restaurant Kieu Tien, 47 Ong Ich Kiem St, is a good all-round Vietnamese food restaurant; a few doors south of it at No 83 is *Sinh An*, a good restaurant offering vegetarian Buddhist food. The northerly section of Le Loi St is alive at night with the dim glow of many oil lamps which thankfully don't quite illuminate the food served under them – cooked eggs with small ducks inside, to be eaten whole. Also around this district there are many small touristy cafés, but really the only place in Danang for Western food is *Christie's Restaurant* (☎ 0511-824040). Sadly it had to move from its river spot after the typhoon of 1999. It is now at 112 Tran Phu St, and here you can occasionally catch up with its Australian proprietor, Mark, when he is not in Saigon, but you can always savour the imported Australian wines and tender beef. It has a relaxing atmosphere and you can while away the hours perusing the books in the book exchange. Christie's also does good Vietnamese food – the manager's wife is Vietnamese. Other more expensive options for Vietnamese food include *Kim Do* and *Tu Do* restaurants at 124 and 172 Tran Phu St, and the town's good hotels.

A cocktail bar range of drinks is available at Christie's, or in many of Danang's more expensive hotels. Danang's local beer is a good light one called Songhan which can be seen advertised at many small street cafés. Alternatively many street stalls emerge at night especially on Ong Ich Kiem St offering delicious *sinh tho* – freshly squeezed fruit juice. Or if it's coffee you need, try *van cao* on a small street off Nguyen Chi Thien St just south of Quang Trung St – to find it turn down the small road opposite a company sign announcing itself to be 'Vietranschart'.

HOI AN

Hoi An is an attractive, busy place with a lovely lazy feel where ancient buildings with elaborate wood or stone carvings nestle between welcoming cafés, restaurants and hotels. And that's to say nothing of the countless shops offering to make you fabulous tailor-made silk clothes, nor the busy market which gives onto a tiny quai from where, early every morning, hundreds of small fishing boats appear through dream-like mist and disgorge their catch.

In short, Hoi An is well worth the 27km trip from Danang. It's true that Hoi An gets rather full of tourists in summer, but there are good reasons for its popularity – and anyhow it still seems to win through. Plus when you do make the effort to meet the local people they seem to be less affected by the traumas of Vietnam's past than many in the country. And if you need to get away from your fellow travellers there is the alternative of cycling out towards the sea through the pretty, quiet peninsula, or taking a day trip out to see the Cham ruins at My Son.

The only drawback is the cost of entry to the assembly halls and merchants' houses – the much-touted ticket enabling you to see five attractions for 50,000d is tough for those on a budget – but just as pleasurable is viewing the delicate wooden carvings on the outsides of the houses of the once-wealthy Chinese merchants who first settled here four centuries ago when the river was unsilted and Hoi An was a fantastically busy port.

Hoi An is a Unesco-heritage site. This honour brings with it millions of dollars of protection money to be disbursed over the next 15 years and expert advice on how to conserve ancient buildings. The long-term aim of the Unesco plan is to move all commercial activity out of the town centre which would be restored to residential quiet. If this plan were implemented it would involve the closure of the shops, bars, restaurants and hotels in the centre; these would be moved to an out-of-town development. This sounds an unappealing, and frankly unlikely, prospect, but even so make sure you catch the delights of Hoi An, before the regulators step in.

History

Hoi An's importance as a port grew during the Champa kingdoms from the 2nd century AD reaching a peak of activity in the 16th century. At this time it became the most important trading post between China and Japan, and Japanese, Chinese and European merchants jostled for place on the busy Thu Bon river. The town, then known as Faifo, became shaped in architecture and culture by these prosperous visitors. Increasingly, Japanese and Chinese merchants took to settling here to take care of off-season business even after their compatriots took to their boats to let the seasonal south-east winds blow them home.

They used the money earned from trading oriental silk, medicines and spices with Europeans (whose metal, lead, they sold on to markets in the east) to build large elaborately-carved houses in dark wood. The Chinese also built meeting houses fabulously decorated with coloured tiles and carved dragons. These played an important part in the administrative rule of the town, and still today are culturally important to Chinese living in Vietnam who travel here from elsewhere in the country to attend congregations and seasonal rites. The Japanese's most significant contribution is the pink-washed stone-covered bridge which was designed to withstand earthquakes and to link the Japanese quarter (whose population dwindled to almost nothing after the Japanese Shogun prohibited foreign travel) with the Chinese quarter on the other side of the stream.

Hoi An continued living its life of Riley until the late 19th century, when the Thu Bon river connecting it with the sea began silting up, and it became too shallow to carry seagoing ships. Danang started taking over as the primary port in Indochina, but many of the resident Chinese had been here for generations and so remained – so too did their buildings. Remarkably, the town and its ancient buildings suffered hardly any damage from the wars of the 20th century. Its current attraction to tourists is

❑ **Cultural events**
The best time of the year to visit Hoi An is during its 'week of cultural tourism' which first took place in 2000 to commemorate the 25th anniversary of Hoi An's liberation (ie when the Viet Cong took control) and which the local government looks set to decree a yearly event. Assuming it takes place it will begin each year on the date of Hoi An's liberation – 28 March – and last for four days. During this time traditional Vietnamese games are held around the town (including one of pictoral bingo), concerts are held from boats on the river surrounded by hundreds of floating candles, there are shows of traditional and modern Vietnamese fashions, slapstick theatre and a parade of floats. An enjoyable experience for all present.

During this time ancient merchant houses open up as intimate guest-houses charging from only $3 per dorm bed to $15 for a double room of beautiful old mahogany furniture. These charming and cheap places to stay are found at 60 Nhuyen Thai Hoc St, and just across the Japanese bridge at 6 and 7 Nguyen Thai Minh Khai St. Contact Hoi An Hotel to enquire about booking.

But if you don't happen to be in Hoi An during this time you may still be able to hit the 15th of each lunar month when Hoi An is closed off to traffic, as during its cultural tourism festival, and all fluorescent lights have to be extinguished; the town is lit only by coloured silk lanterns. A beautiful sight.

And if you miss this, you can still catch the nightly cultural events held in Hoi An. When the troupes are not on tour in the country or abroad there are excellent one-hour concerts at 7.30pm on traditional Vietnamese instruments in the cultural music boat moored on the river off Bach Dang St, and at 9pm of traditional Vietnamese theatre upstairs in Champa Bar at 75 Nguyen Thai Hoc St. The concert costs 20,000d and the theatre 40,000d. Both can be booked from the travel agent at 78 Le Loi St, or the theatre can be booked at Champa Bar.

both a testimony to its colourful past, and to the openness of the people so often found in port towns.

Sights and excursions

When seeing the sights of Hoi An you should be aware that some places are not covered by the five sights for 50,000d scheme and are free, some are covered by the ticket (or you can pay the individual entrance fee of 10,000d-15,000d directly), and some can only be visited with the ticket.

Perhaps the finest of the buildings which can be seen for free is the **Chinese All Assembly Hall** at 64 Tran Phu St. This was founded in the 18th century to be an umbrella organization for all the ethnic Chinese of the region. The pavilions on each side show 19th-century French influences.

A few doors east at 46 Tran Phu St is the much larger and fuller **Phuc Kien Assembly Hall** which can be visited only with the 50,000d ticket (for five sights). This hall, which began life as a pagoda until the Chinese rejuvenated it and turned it into a meeting hall two centuries ago, is dedicated to Thien Hau – the goddess of the sea and protector of fishermen and sailors, who was in theory born in the Phuc Kien area of China. Friezes depict her rescuing ships in storms and the main chamber has an ancient statue of Thien Hau at the altar flanked by two assistants who can spy ailing ships from hundreds of miles.

The nearby **Hainan Assembly Hall** (representing the Chinese from Hainan province) at the eastern end of Tran Phu St near Hoang Dieu St has the most interesting history, having been built as a tribute to over a hundred merchants who were killed on the orders of a Vietnamese general who claimed to mistake their ships for pirate ships. It is worth continuing a little further east along Tran Phu St because after it turns into Nguyen Duy Hieu St at No 157 you will come upon the **Trieu Chau Assembly Hall** built at the end of the 18th century and still preserving wonderful wood carvings. On the altar, surrounding the painted figure of the Chinese general Bon who was believed to have mastery over the wind and waves, is a frieze teeming with animal and bird life and depicting life on land and beneath the waves.

If you head down to the river from here you will come upon the kernel of a would-be **French quarter** – Phan Boi Chau St is lined with the louvred shutters and classic design of French colonial buildings.

Walking back into town feel free to admire the gorgeously cool and shady **merchants' houses** built with finely-carved dark wood and adorned with Yin Yan symbols and eyes watching out for evil spirits all along Nguyen Thai Hoc St and Tran Phu St; there are three particularly notable buildings. The house of Tam Ky at 101 Nguyen Thai Hoc St is a beautifully preserved shop-house two centuries old, with store rooms still stuffed with goods hauled in directly from the river through access at the back of the house. On the other side of the road at 80 Nguyen Thai Hoc St for only a small donation ($1-2 is fine) you can see the house of Diep Dong Nguyen, most notable for its charming collection of antiques on display upstairs. Tracking north to 77 Tran Phu St, again for only a small donation you can see the old merchant's house of Quan Thang which has some fine carving and colourful ceramic tiles and is three centuries old.

Continuing north off the unprepossessing Phan Chu Trinh St you surprisingly find two interesting old **Chinese family chapels**, visitable for a donation, founded by Chinese merchant families as centres for their spirituality and ancestor worship. The Tran family chapel is at 21 Le Loi St, on the north-east corner of the junction with Phan Chu Trinh St, and the Truong family chapel is down an alley next to 69 Phan Chu Trinh St.

Finally if you head west along Phan Chu Trinh St and south down Nhi Trung St you will come to the **Cantonese Assembly Hall** at 176 Tran Phu St. You can enter this for 10,000d (or with the ticket) but the courtyard of colourful showy dragon and carp carvings and its pleasant planted surroundings is the main attraction. Then once you've explored the delights of the Japanese bridge just a few doors west you can feel justified in returning to the delights of café life.

Cam Nam Island
It is well worth hiring a bicycle to ride around the pretty shady groves of Cam Nam Island if Hoi An is too bustly for you. People wave you into their homes and you can sit out back sipping cool drinks overlooking wide tranquil Thu Bon river; you can even take a jaunt on the river if a rowing boat passes. You may even happen on some of the factories where the trinkets on sale in Hoi An are made.

Boat trips
All of the small boats along the river by Bach Dang St are keen to offer boat trips from around $1 an hour. The Thu Bon river is a pleasant one to be rowed along and local highlights include the woodcarving village, where the annoying animal whistles sold all over town are made, and the pottery village. A much longer trip is to Cham Island, around 10km out to sea, but if you wish to take a boat here beware that you will need to enjoy the boating itself, because there is not much to see on the island.

Cua Dai beach
Hoi An has a beach, only 5km from the town, lined with beach loungers and drink stalls. It's not a patch on the grandeur of China beach, but it has a nice-enough aspect to lie and splash away an afternoon or two. To reach it go east along Tran Hung Dao St through lovely countryside for 5km.

Excursion to Cham towers of My Son
The Cham ruins of My Son (meaning good mountain in Vietnamese) are the most important Cham remains in the country, being a collection of

❏ **Warning**

Don't wander too far from the ruins of My Son as the area around here still throws up the occasional unexploded mine. So don't, for example, climb up the Cat's Tooth mountain nearest to group B which would clearly give a panoramic view of the remains as there is no guarantee that all the explosives have already claimed their victims.

religious buildings which served the ancient capital of Tra Kieu from the 4th century AD. However, many who visit My Son are disappointed by what they find – after the Viet Cong used the towers as a base during the war the ancient bricks received a pounding from B-52s and now only a few towers stand amidst a mass of fallen bricks increasingly reclaimed by the lush vegetation all around. But provided you are prepared to see ruins rather than temples you can enjoy the glorious faded majesty of the place; this is best done by wandering around the red brick structures catching occasional glimpses of many-armed Shivas and an impressive Garuda statue in between the bullet holes.

All the buildings and monuments at My Son were meticulously categorized and labelled by French archaeologists at the end of the last century when the site was discovered, extremely well preserved, under a mass of verdant vegetation.

The ruins of today are still grouped under this system but the damage done by American bombers is such that what was once the most important group – group A – is now mostly ruins, but there is much to see in groups B and C. Group B was considered by archaeologists to be the spiritual epicentre of the collection. Group C was known as the court of stelae, although today only the inscribed plinths remain, littered around the ground.

My Son is around 40km south-west of Hoi An. To drive there by motorbike head out west from Hoi An until you reach Highway 1 where you should turn south, until you cross the Thu Bon river. One kilometre after crossing the bridge take the road/track to the right, heading up into the mountains and to the town of Tra Kieu. Continue west out of Tra Kieu across an increasingly rough track for around 18km until you reach the tranquil valley of the My Son ruins. The route is not easy to find and there have been reports of visitors' motorbikes being tampered with by locals who then charge as many dollars as they can get away with to mend it, so you might be better off going by Honda om.

Alternatively, Hoi An's hotels and restaurants offer half-day bus tours to My Son for the very good price of $3 – although appropriately enough the cheapest offer in town is for only 40,000d from Champa Bar. Entrance to My Son costs 50,000d.

PRACTICAL INFORMATION
Arrival and departure
By train If you plan to leave Danang by train you should have no problem going to the station and getting a ticket for the next train. However, you can buy a ticket from many of the mini travel agents in Hoi An if you prefer.

By Honda om If you arrive in Hoi An by Honda om you should have no problem being dropped wherever you wish. It's less than an hour from Danang by motorbike (the ride should cost around $5) and you can choose to stop off at the Marble Mountains and/or China Beach on the way.

By bus Virtually every hotel in Hoi An can sell you a **tourist minibus** ticket to every major city to the south as well as a ride to Danang ($3), but it is hard to find a minibus going the other way, ie starting in Danang.

Although there are always plenty of vehicles hanging around Danang station ready to do the Hoi An trail you could consider getting one of the fairly frequent **public buses** from the bus station opposite 350 Hung Vuong St in Danang to Hoi An's bus station which is 500m west of the centre of town on Huong Thuc Khang St.

Orientation
Hoi An lies along the northern side of the Thu Bon river, separated from the coast by a few kilometres of peninsula. Many of Hoi An's notable buildings and eateries are along Tran Phu St.

Services
Post and telecommunications The efficient post office which is open daily 6am-9.30pm is on the north side of Tran Hung Dao St where it junctions with Ngo Gia Tu St.

Hoi An has many internet cafés, mostly on Le Loi St, such as Ho Van Dan (☎ 0510-861071, 🖳 ho.v.dan@ bvdn.rnd.net) at 35 Le Loi, and Khnah Hoi (🖳 khanhhoi@dng.vnn.vn) at 46 Le Loi. All charge 500d per minute.

Money A new branch of Vietincombank has opened at 78 Le Loi St; it is open 8am-6pm Monday to Friday. There is no commission charge to convert travellers' cheques into dong, but 1.35 per cent is charged to convert into dollars and 3 per cent to take money out on credit or debit cards.

The bank is closed at the weekends, but the travel agents next door will change cash and travellers' cheques, although the latter with a punitive 2 per cent commission.

Visa extensions It takes only a day to extend your visa in Hoi An, but you may only extend for one month at a time. The first extension costs $28, second and subsequent extensions cost $38.

Visas to Laos (via Lao Bao) can also be arranged here. It takes two days and all visas are for one month. For most nationalities the cost is $65, although it is $70 for US, Japanese and Israeli citizens, and for some reasons Canadians have to pay $75.

Medical Hoi An's hospital is directly opposite the post office on the east side of Ngo Gia Tu St.

Book exchanges There are a number of good book exchanges – mostly along Le Loi St, such as the good selection at No 52. Tam Tam Café's exchange is free and one for one, but the selection is small.

Local transport
Hoi An is small enough for all of it to be accessible on foot and the town is easy to find your way about as the streets are almost in a grid pattern. For exploring further afield you can hire a bicycle from almost every hotel for $1 a day, or a scooter motorbike from $3 a day.

Tours

Virtually every hotel, restaurant and café in Hoi An advertises its services for organising tours to My Son or railway or airline tickets to everywhere else. You can take your pick, although one business which never disappoints is Ho Van Dan (see Post and communications above) run by the delightful Ty and her husband. A branch of Sinh Café (☎ 0510-863948) is at 37 Phan Dinh Phung St.

Where to stay

Hoi An has a mini-hotel (a small private hotel) springing up on almost every street corner so you should be able to take your pick, except perhaps during the summer; at this time it can be wise to stroll a little away from the centre of town to find a room for the night. But if they have room the following central hotels are extremely pleasant:

At the low end of the market *Hoai Thanh Hotel* (☎ 0510 861171) at 23 Le Hong Phong St, 10 minutes' walk from the centre of town, has spacious clean doubles for $7 – good value for the sound of croaking frogs by night, if you can stand the noise of the road by day. It also has the cheapest bicycle rental in town at only 5000d per day.

In town the cheapest hotel is the forbidding-looking but friendly *Thuy Duong Hotel* (☎ 0510-861394) at 11 Le Loi St; it has clean dorms for $3 and rooms from $8. It also has comprehensive-looking train timetable information on display in reception; but beware, it is wildly inaccurate.

Huy Hoang Mini Hotel (☎ 0510-861453), 73 Phan Boi Chau St, has rooms from $10 although the ones which look out over the river and on to a pretty patio are more. Even more central is *Phu Thinh Mini Hotel* (☎ 0510-861297), 144 Tran Phu St, which has good rooms in a very pleasant hotel from $7 with fan or $15 with air-con; what the hotel lacks in river it makes up

for with its garden. Nearly opposite, at 143 Tran Phu St, is *Vinh Hung Hotel* (☎ 0510 861621) with lovely rooms set in an old Chinese merchant house. Rooms with fan start from $10, with air-con from $15. The beautiful large rooms with two canopied four-poster beds upstairs go for $45. Or, for around the same price *Thanh Binh Hotel* (☎ 0510-861740), 1 Le Loi St, offers really lovely rooms with beautifully white sheets.

New impressive hotels are opening up at quite a pace. *Thanh Binh II Hotel* (☎ 0510 863715, ▤ 864192) on Nhi Trung St is built to look a little like an old merchant's house and has good doubles from $15. *Vinh Hung 2 Hotel* (☎ 0510 863717, ▤ 864094, ▱ quang huy.ha@dng.vnn.vn) also on Nhi Trung St, is opposite Thanh Binh II Hotel and is similar to it, but with an added swimming pool. It has very good-value elegant doubles from $15, some with balcony. Meanwhile *Hoi An Hotel* (☎ 0510 861373, ▤ 861636, ▱ hoianhotel@ dng.vnn.vn) at 6 Tran Hung Dao St is constantly upgrading and now has dorm beds for $10 each and rooms from $20 to $100, as well as a fountain in the courtyard, a tennis court and swimming pool.

More preparations for the tourist explosion in Hoi An have been made, and from summer 2000 you can stay at *Hoi An Hotel Resort* on Cua Dai beach in a plush villa from $60 a night (bookings should be made through Hoi An Hotel).

Where to eat and drink

Hoi An is well known for its food; the town has a number of delicious local specialities and many restaurants produce great Western fare, plus in Hoi An's market you can find what one traveller has called 'the best spicy ham rolls in Vietnam'; the way to order one of these is to say how much you want to pay and the sandwich will get filled accordingly, ranging from 1500d for lit-

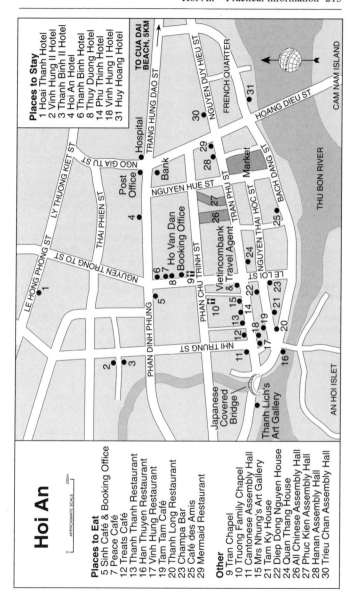

Hoi An

0 ── 250m
APPROXIMATE SCALE

Places to Eat
5 Sinh Café & Booking Office
7 Peace Café
12 Treats Café
13 Thanh Thanh Restaurant
16 Han Thuyen Restaurant
17 Vinh Hung Restaurant
19 Tam Tam Café
20 Thanh Long Restaurant
23 Champa Bar
25 Café des Amis
29 Mermaid Restaurant

Other
9 Tran Chapel
10 Truong Family Chapel
11 Cantonese Assembly Hall
15 Mrs Nhung's Art Gallery
21 Tam Ky House
22 Diep Dong Nguyen House
24 Quan Thang House
26 All Chinese Assembly Hall
27 Phuc Kien Assembly Hall
28 Hanan Assembly Hall
30 Trieu Chan Assembly Hall

Places to Stay
1 Hoai Thanh Hotel
2 Vinh Hung II Hotel
3 Thanh Binh II Hotel
4 Hoi An Hotel
6 Thanh Binh Hotel
8 Thuy Duong Hotel
14 Phu Thinh Hotel
18 Vinh Hung I Hotel
31 Huy Hoang Hotel

tle filling in a small baguette to 4000d to a substantial amount in a large baguette.

Hoi An's speciality *cao lau* is signposted as being available from every restaurant in town – it's a wonderful bowlful of mint-flavoured soup stuffed full of flat white noodles mixed with vegetables and croutons and topped with pork slices, then sprinkled with crumbled crispy rice paper.

While if you really look for it you can get something similar to *cao lau* outside Hoi An, in theory it is only here that produces the genuine article because the soup has to be made with water drawn from the town's Ba Le well and anyway nowhere else in Vietnam produces food as fresh, fast and fantastic as in Hoi An.

The town is also very strong on seafood and most restaurants advertise particular Hoi An methods of producing delicately-flavoured seafood dishes, such as White Rose (prawn wrapped in a shaped noodle casing).

Freshly-baked bread or ham rolls from the market are a great way to start the day; for lunchtime fruit shakes and cau lau try any of the million places along Tran Phu St, such as the friendly *Vinh Hung Restaurant* at No 147.

It is in the evening that Hoi An's food scene really comes alive; this is when the many restaurants which line Tran Phu St and Bach Dang St set up neatly tableclothed tables al fresco; at a place like *Mermaid Restaurant* (☎ 0510-861527) at 2 Tran Phu St you can drink a great pina colada cocktail and dine in luxury on lemongrass flavoured melt-in-the-mouth beef, for but a few US dollars.

Of the restaurants by the river *Han Huyen 'restaurant flottant'* (☎ 0510-861462) is the most charming looking, though it is actually built on stilts rather than floating; bear in mind that the name Han should give you a clue that it serves Chinese not Vietnamese food. The restaurant opposite, *Thang Long* (☎

0510-861944), at 136 Nguyen Thai Hoc St, serves superb Vietnamese food from a substantial menu. The fish dishes in particular are excellent.

Café des Amis (☎ 0510-861360), 52 Bach Dang St, is legendary amongst French visitors for its Francophone proprietor and his great Vietnamese cuisine, though the atmosphere lacks something in comparison with the other restaurants by the river or along Tran Phu St or Le Loi St. Don't expect to peruse a menu because in the French tradition each day has a different set menu – beware that the more courses you eat the higher the total price, but you'd have to be pretty determined to eat your way through more than $5.

There are lots of backpacker restaurants along Le Loi St, but superb cao lau is to be had at *Thanh Thanh Restaurant* (☎ 0510-861308) at 162 Tran Phu St.

For real gin and tonics, and certainly for Hoi An's most impressive sound system, you need *Peace Café* (☎ 0510-861951) at 7 Le Loi St. But in the high season this small bar, complete with pool table, tends to fill up and the noise level rises. This is the time to de-camp to *Tam Tam Café* (☎ 0510-862212, ✉ tamtam.ha@dng.vnn.vn), 110 Nguyen Thai Hoc St, run by an expat Frenchman, Christophe, who mixes a wonderful variety of alcoholic and non-alcoholic drinks and even offers a range of good French wine and fantastic profiteroles.

For the best happy hours in town, a good atmosphere and sound systems, check out *Champa Bar*, at 75 Nguyen Thai Hoc St, and *Treats Café* at 158 Tran Phu St.

Things to buy

There is one thought in the mind of many visitors to Hoi An – buying tailor-made silk clothes. Certainly the town is stuffed with shops and market stalls selling many different kinds of very

> **❑ Tips for having clothes tailor-made**
> 1. The first rule is choose your design carefully: it is wisest to ask for something that follows the designs already made in the shop. Alternatively, bring along something you would like copied – but don't expect the copy to be exact. If you design something yourself try to amalgamate other designs already in the shop, or be prepared for disappointment.
> 2. Always allow time for fittings and alterations – needing up to three alterations is not unusual.
> 3. It is often best to follow the tailor's advice in terms of what fabric suits what design: a floaty dressing gown will not work in thick Japanese silk, however pretty the pattern, but beware that the Vietnamese are unlikely to insist so it is wise to listen very carefully and if no advice is offered, ask the question.
> 4. Remember that you may be thinner in unexpected places when travelling!

good-quality silk and offering to make up a vast range of styles. Hoi An is in many ways the best place to have clothes made because a hang-over from its port history means that it generally has the widest selection of imported silks – both brocade from China and very high-quality non-crease washable patterns from Japan; see p126 for a guideline of prices. But before you buy do bear in mind that Vietnamese ways are not Western ways and a lack of caution could wind you up with a wardrobe full of unwearable clothes.

Amongst the many cod art shops in Hoi An there are some real artists. Mr Thanh Lich's art gallery just across the Japanese bridge at 1 Nguyen Thai Minh Khai St, has paintings combining art and poetry for $20-200. While a famous Vietnamese artist who specializes in paintings in lacquer, Mrs Huynh Thi Nhung, has a gallery at 120 Tran Phu St. (When the gallery is closed you need to take a cyclo or motorbike to her home outside Hoi An at Ben Tre Thon 2B, in the Cam Ha commune, to see her dark lacquer works.)

HUE

Hué is an historic city situated on the banks of the beautiful azure-blue Perfume river. It is geographically nearer to Hanoi than Ho Chi Minh City, but politically it is a southern city. The founder of the Nguyen Dynasty, Emperor Gia Long, proclaimed Hué the new capital of Vietnam after conquering Hanoi with French help.

Hué remained the capital during the rule of the Nguyen Dynasty from 1802 to 1945. During this time Hué was transformed from a small regional centre to a city boasting a remarkable collection of palaces, pagodas, tombs and precious objects. Sadly, most of what was not sacked by the French in 1883 and 1945 was destroyed by the bloody fighting of the Tet offensive in 1968. Nevertheless there remains much of interest in Hué (though, at $5, entry to sights is expensive).

The city is a pleasant place to visit: there is a market, many opportunities to experience speciality Hué food, and, if you believe it, Hué women are famed for being the most beautiful in Vietnam.

History

Hué became a part of Vietnam in the 14th century when it was given to the northern territories as a wedding present from a Champa king who married a Vietnamese princess. After shaking off Chinese rule in AD939 the country was ruled from Hanoi, but Hué was the capital of the south when the country was again split in half in 1620. For the next 150 years Vietnam was ruled by the Trinh Dynasty in the north, and the Nguyen Dynasty in the south; both houses proclaimed allegiance to the Later Le Dynasty in Hanoi.

The Tay Son rebellion of the 1770s and 1780s changed all that. The Tay Son brothers overthrew the Trinh and the Nguyen lords, who ruled over both the northern capital of Hanoi and the southern capital of Hué, and looked set to establish a new dynasty. However, this did not happen, as the rebels succumbed to the French-supported lone survivor of the family that had ruled the south, Nguyen Anh. His forces conquered the north and regained the south. He styled himself Emperor Gia Long, proclaimed Hué the capital of Vietnam and immediately set about the construction of the Citadel, Imperial City and Forbidden Purple City.

These monuments of Hué were certainly the greatest achievements of this, the last dynasty of Vietnam, but they also helped precipitate its downfall. They were constructed at extraordinary expense and also represent another reason why the dynasty lost power: Emperor Gia Long and his successors brought about a sudden shift to Confucianism and shut the doors on the West. Isolation from the West and the development of strict hierarchies encouraged by Confucianism stagnated the country, leading to ineffective resistance to the French.

Independence from the French was finally lost in 1883 after a vicious attack by French forces during which the city of Hué was looted for every valuable object that could be found. Much of Hué's former glory can now be seen in the Guimmet museum in Paris, France.

Hué's political fortunes reversed sharply at the end of WWII. Emperor Bao Dai abdicated in favour of Ho Chi Minh's provisional government and suddenly power was refocused on Hanoi in the north, and Saigon in the French-controlled south. From this time on, Hué suffered the unfortunate consequences of being in the centre of Vietnam, sandwiched between the powerful forces of the north and south. Its position became increasingly difficult whenever the north was ascendant because Hué, having been the royal home, was everything the Communists hated, especially as it had deprived Hanoi of being the capital city for the previous 150 years. In 1968 the north had its chance for revenge against Hué and took it. The Americans' part in the destruction of Hué which followed the VC takeover was not personally motivated, but was just as deadly.

During the Tet offensive of 1968 North Vietnamese and VC troops occupied Hué for 25 days. It was the only city in the south to be occupied by the VC during the war for more than a few days. The north gained control by diverting the Americans' attention by a battle at the Khe Sanh combat base only to walk into Hué and raise the Communist flag. The Communists were armed not only with flags and propaganda to gain converts, but also with a death list for around 3000 of Hué's civilian population. During the 25 days of Communist rule Buddhist monks, professionals and merchants were shot to death, or less quickly killed. The lucky few hid in a small network of tunnels around Hué.

The VC grip on the city was strong enough to resist the advances of South Vietnamese troops, but could not hold out against the combined military force of the Southern troops and American bombs. A deadly combination of VC rockets, South Vietnamese artillery, B52 bombs and house to house fighting decimated the Citadel and Imperial City and the population of Hué with it. It is estimated that 10,000 people died in Hué during the Tet offensive; most of them were civilians.

Today, Hué is a poor city: a ghost of its former glory. It was never a major industrial or commercial centre and when stripped of its political power it lost many of its skilled people – traitors to the northern regime. Many of those who survived and did not move away became victims to the post-war 're-education camps'. The resentment against the north is almost palpable.

Recently, tourism has sprung up as a new profitable business; Hué now boasts two very grand hotels. However, the steep entrance fees for the sights here do not enrich Hué: they go into the government's coffers. It is ironic that the name of this city with such a tumultuous history should be a bastardization of Hoa, of the province of Thuan Hoa, which means peace, or harmony.

Sights and excursions

Many visitors are drawn to Hué because of its historical sights, but the extent of devastation inflicted in the 19th century and during the American war leaves many tourists disappointed. To prevent this, be prepared: there is very little left to see in the Citadel, containing the Imperial City and Forbidden Purple City. The flag tower, main gate (Ngo Mon) and the Palace of Supreme Harmony (Dien Thai Hoa) are intact as structures and worth seeing, though the palace was comprehensively looted in 1883 by the French. Several other buildings are undergoing restoration. Other than this, the area of the Citadel comprises small quiet roads, modest private dwellings and vegetation. The temples and pagodas in Hué and its environs are well-preserved structures although there may be little left inside. Likewise the museums.

The magnificent tombs along the river to the south of Hué, however, have been fairly untouched by war: the damage they have incurred is mostly simply that of the passage of time. It is well worth taking a good look at several. Most are easily accessible by a delightful and leisurely day-long bicycle ride; bear in mind that ferries patrol the Perfume River during the day, so if you find a stopping point you and your bicycle can easily hitch a ride back to the city for less than $1. The tomb of Gia Long is the furthest away, 18km from Hué (as the crow flies), so you may wish to hire a boat for the day to see the quiet grassy site. You can arrange to hire a boat from most little eateries frequented by tourists – it should cost around $10 a day, or a little more including lunch.

According to official Vietnamese history **The Citadel** is a 'colossal fortification complex, largest and most strongly built in Vietnam's monarchy. Constructed during the first three decades of the 19th century, it called for a lot of mind, materials, and toil of the whole country.' Which, all in all, makes it rather a shame that so many of the precious artefacts were sacked by the French and so many of the buildings were destroyed by the Americans. Today most of the citadel walls are still intact and the Noon Gate and Palace of Supreme Harmony have been restored to their full glory, but most of the buildings of the Imperial City and the Forbidden Purple City are in a state of ruin. But the citadel is still worth seeing and it is lovely and quiet walking in the north of the enclosed citadel.

The citadel is nearly square (one side follows the curve of the river) is 10km in circumference, the wall is 6.6m high and 21m thick. It was originally made of earth in 1805, under the guidance of the first Nguyen emperor, Gia Long. Thirteen years later work was begun to replace the earth with brick. The walls of the citadel were built to protect the royal houses and offices within.

Within the citadel is the second wall of the Imperial City. This is around 2.4km in circumference and encloses the offices where the monarch and mandarins came daily to work. Within this is the wall, 1.2km in circumference, of the Forbidden Purple City. The dozens of buildings and temples here were reserved solely for the emperor and his family.

Despite its name the walls of the Forbidden Purple City were painted yellow (purple, however, was the royal colour because it was considered to be the colour of the pole star). Between these yellow walls men other than the emperor and eunuchs were not admitted, while within the walls girls chosen to be 'maidservants' (ie the emperor's harem) could not go out. Virtually all the buildings of the Forbidden Purple City were destroyed during the American war.

It costs $5 to enter the citadel, for this you also get a map of the Imperial City and Forbidden Purple City.

Hué's **flagtower** opposite the noon gate into the citadel was the most potent symbol of the Communist Tet offensive in 1968 when the VC flag flew defiantly from its top for 25 days. It was built in October 1807 during Emperor Gia Long's reign; it was 17.4m high with three terraces and housed eight little buildings on the topmost terrace with one canon in each and two sentry boxes at opposite ends. The tower was covered in new wood in 1846; this lasted until it was smashed to bits in a violent typhoon. It was replaced with a cast-iron structure in 1914; this tower lasted only three and a half decades until clashes with the French left it in ruin. In 1948 the current 21m concrete structure was erected.

The **noon gate** is often seen as the symbol of Hué – principally because it is one of the few structures which was left standing after the century's ravages. The noon gate was constructed in 1833 and was intended for use by the emperor only, except during regular court functions and occasional festivals when it was used to welcome guests. To fulfill both these functions the doors of the central passageway were painted yellow, signifying they were for the emperor's use only, while the two levels of the gate are both U-shaped, symbolising arms being open for guests. The upper level, the Five Phoenix Pavilion, is covered with nine roofs (the middle one being yellow for the emperor) and is supported by 100 columns – to the Vietnamese 100 is considered an infinite and countless number. It was from here that Vietnam's last emperor, Bao Dai, abdicated to a delegation from Ho Chi Minh on 30 August 1945. The gate is open every day from 7am to 5.30pm and costs $5 for foreigners.

Through the noon gate is the **Palace of Supreme Harmony**. This houses the throne which seated the 13 emperors of the Nguyen Dynasty, from Gia Long to Bao Dai. It was built in 1805 and has been restored to its brightly painted dragon-adorned glory. Eighty ironwood columns in the palace are lacquered and decorated with dragon and cloud designs symbolising the rendezvous between the monarch and his subjects. According to Chinese Classics, both the dragon and the number nine symbolize the monarch. This explains the presence of the nine-dragon motif all around the palace.

Can Canh Palace, **Palace of Audiences**, which unfortunately was almost totally destroyed by war in 1947, had been the working home of the emperor, despite being furnished with a huge carved bed, complete with elbow rests. It was also where many of the most valuable antiquities were sacked by the French. As General de Courcy wrote on July 24 1885 'Golden and silver objects are of some 9 millions of francs worth. Many seals and golden books of more millions of francs worth have been recently found'. He went on to say, with characteristic understatement that, 'collecting met with difficulties.' A better display of these treasures is in the Guimmet Museum in Paris, France.

Mieu Temple was built by Emperor Minh Mang to honour the past (and future) Nguyen emperors and their queens. Surprisingly the temple survived the wars of the century intact and the royal yellow roof tiles and the altars for the emperors and their queens are as fresh as they ever were. The temple is also worth locating for the nine huge dynastic urns outside it in the courtyard. These were cast by order of Emperor Minh Mang and each is dedicated to a particular emperor. They are very alike in size and weight (although not identical), but each is decorated with very different bas relief designs, which as a whole aim to describe the varied landscape of Vietnam and its culture. Look out in particular for the distinctive scenery of Halong Bay – showing that the beautiful vista of sharp cliffs rising out of a sea peppered with small boats was as celebrated a symbol of Vietnam for the Vietnamese 150 years ago as it is today.

Temples and pagodas

Hué has many small pagodas and temples, many of which have been partially or completely destroyed. Of those which remain the Thien Mu Pagoda and Hon Chen Temple are the most interesting.

The seven-storeyed **Thien Mu Pagoda** (Pagoda of the Heavenly Lady) dominates the skyline of a section of the Perfume River from a bluff above the river 4km south-west of the Citadel. The pagoda is not much to see close up and it is not possible to go inside to see the gold Buddha statues, but the temple at the back is ornate and in a shed near it is a horribly special Austin car.

The pagoda was built in 1601 by a southern Nguyen lord on hearing of the legend that long ago an old woman appeared every night on the hill and told people that a Lord would come and built a Buddhist pagoda there for the prosperity of the country. The pagoda was partially restored in the 18th and 19th centuries. However, several buildings have completely disappeared.

To the left of the main temple housing statues of the Buddha of the past, the historical Buddha, and the Buddha of the future is a shed out of which pokes the nose of a blue Austin Sedan car, number plate DBA599. It was in this car that on August 15 1963 the monk of the pagoda, Thich Quang Duc, drove to Saigon and then calmly set fire to himself to protest against the repressive policies of the Diem regime. Photographs taken of the burning monk caught the world's imagination and this negative publicity for Diem's regime was an important factor in the US organising a coup against him. Not that much changed under the next puppet leader. Thien Mu Pagoda is easily reached by boat (see p220), or by road by taking Tran Hung Dao St westwards and continuing on the same road for 4km.

Terraced on a mountainside beside the Perfume River around 8km south-west of Hué on the site of an old Cham temple sit the three small temples which make up the **Hon Chen Temple** (Temple of the Jade Cup). The temples are well kept and the principal one has a small but beautiful collection of Imperial possessions to rival that of the Antiquities Museum. The main temple, Hué Nam Temple, has always been dedicated to women: first to the Goddess Ponagar of Champa, and subsequently to Goddess Thien Ya Na of Vietnam. Emperor Dong Khanh, who ruled in the

❏ **Nam Giao Esplanade**
Built in 1896 4km south of Hué, Nam Giao Esplanade was the site where
Nguyen emperors came to preside over ceremonies where sacrifices were
offered to God for the country's welfare and the stability of the dynasty. It was
therefore at one time the most important religious site in the country. The
Esplanade consists of three terraces symbolising the Oriental theory of Three
Agents: Heaven, Earth and Man. The lowest terrace represents Man, the second Earth, and the circular top terrace represents Heaven. The first ceremony
here took place in 1807 under Gia Long's rule, and the last took place in 1945
during Bao Dai's rule. Nam Giao is to be found at the end of Dien Bien Phu
St, 4km from the city centre, en route to the royal tombs.

1880s, was very fond of this temple and had it restored. He honoured
Goddess Thien Ya Na worshipped in the temple, calling her his older sister. He decreed that the two most important ritual ceremonies in the temple would become national festivals. One of these is still celebrated at the
temple; it falls on the 8th day of the lunar month, mid-August in our calendar, and commences at 6am.

To see the best of the temple you must endeavour to climb the steep
stairs behind the altar. Upstairs is the dusty and dark but exquisite collection
of dusty Imperial ornaments and clothes – look particularly at the phoenix-
shaped shoes made from gold. You need a torch (flashlight) in order to see
much. The first temple to the left is a sparse temple dedicated to the old
ladies. The furthest temple is dedicated to Konan Kong, a 4th-century
Chinese general. Outside it are statues complete with bristling beards.

Hon Chen Temple is most easily reached by boat (see p220) or by a
cycle or motorbike ride hugging the west bank of the Perfume River
southwards from Thien Mu Pagoda, or northwards from Minh Mang. It
may be possible to cadge a ferry across the river 2km south of Hon Chen
where the road is close to the river on the east side.

Tombs of the Nguyen emperors

These tombs, scattered around the outskirts of Hué, are expensive but well
worth visiting as many of the buildings and enclosures have been finely
restored and several are set in lovely watery surroundings. Most can be
easily reached in a day trip by bicycle, though the tomb of Gia Long is
several kilometres further from Hué than any other so a day's boat trip is
recommended for this. The entrance fee for each tomb is $5, payable in
US dollars or dong, except for Gia Long which is free on grounds of being
rarely visited because it is in such a poor state of repair, so rarely manned.

The largest and most impressive of all the tomb enclosures is that of
Emperor Tu Duc who ruled the longest of all Nguyen emperors, 35
years, from 1848 until his death in 1883. The tomb enclosure was built for
Tu Duc to enjoy during his life – from the serene lakes and frangipani

trees, to the deer raised for Tu Duc to hunt here, and to the theatre (Minh Khiem) and the harems. Each of the royal tombs contains a stele house where the accomplishments and exploits of the emperor are engraved onto stone tablets. Tu Duc's stele is the largest in the whole of Vietnam – weighing a massive 20 tonnes – and the description of his life on it he wrote himself. Inevitably, the very impressiveness of his tomb is a monument to his lack of success as a political ruler – he reigned over the country during its annexation by the French. Tu Duc's tomb is 7km south of Hué. The way to the tomb is well-signposted and the entrance is surrounded by numerous small eateries mostly serving extremely indifferent food. Bicycles can be parked and guarded for free at the entrance booth, whatever the food sellers say.

Emperor Thieu Tri was Minh Mang's son and Tu Duc's father. Unlike the other tombs, Thieu Tri's was designed and constructed after his death under his son's orders. This was because Thieu Tri died suddenly at the age of 40. As official Vietnamese history romantically puts it 'In his dying breath, he had just enough time to advise his successor on his tomb construction.' Some consider Thieu Tri's mausoleum not worth the trip because it is similar to Minh Mang's but in worse repair and not enclosed attractively by walls. But Thieu Tri's tomb does have an atmosphere of serenity and, as Vietnamese history would have it 'Emperor Tu Duc made use of the surrounding mountains as a natural wall'. The monuments are divided into two parts, 100m from one another. On one side is the temple area and on the other the tomb area, such that 'figuratively, constructors had made Thieu Tri's tomb by cutting off the middle part of Minh Mang's tomb and then joining the two ends together' – obviously. This royal tomb is 7km south of Hué, close to the banks of the Perfume River, and is signposted 'Lang Thieu Tri'.

Khai Dinh's tomb is a gaudy, brash collection of brightly-painted tiles and fantastically-Gothic turrets and stone dragons with glass eyes. It's the kind of site which you either love or hate. The official leaflet has decided to hate it, declaring the uncomfortable mixture of Vietnamese and European styles symptomatic of the decline of Vietnamese culture during colonialism. But it's well worth a look, if only for the majesty of the setting on a steep hill, requiring 36 steps from the courtyard to the palace and for the well-preserved glistening interior. The stone mandarins in the stele courtyard are also very well preserved. These mandarins are a feature of all the tombs; their function was much the same as China's famous terracotta army – to act as guards to the emperor in his death. Khai Dinh's tomb is 10km south of Hué, around 2km from the Perfume River.

(**Opposite**) Carved stone dragon at the entranceway to Khai Dinh's tomb.

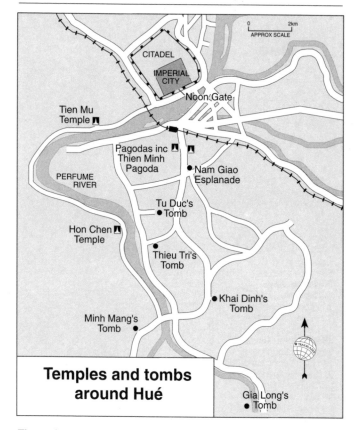

0   2km
APPROX SCALE

CITADEL

IMPERIAL
CITY

Noon Gate

Tien Mu
Temple

Pagodas inc
Thien Minh
Pagoda

Nam Giao
Esplanade

PERFUME
RIVER

Tu Duc's
Tomb

Hon Chen
Temple

Thieu Tri's
Tomb

Khai Dinh's
Tomb

Minh Mang's
Tomb

**Temples and tombs
around Hué**

Gia Long's
Tomb

The tomb enclosure of **Minh Mang** is the second largest (after Tu Duc's) and its setting amid small lakes in which most of the monuments mirror themselves is beautiful. Minh Mang ruled for 20 years, from 1820 to 1840 during what is thought of as the peak of the Nguyen Dynasty. His tomb took four years to build. It is thought that the insistent symmetry of the construction reflected the pre-eminence of Confucian ideals of order and subjugation to hierarchy – the emperor being at its head. The tomb is reached after 700m of walkways through buildings and across bridges

(**Opposite**) **Top**: One of the gates to Hué Citadel (see p220). **Bottom**: Seven kilometres south of Hué, the impressive tomb enclosure of Emperor Tu Duc (see p223) is built around a peaceful lake.

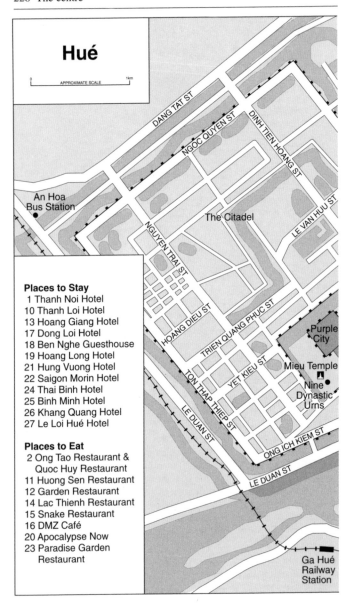

Hué

0   APPROXIMATE SCALE   1km

DANG TAT ST

NGOC QUYEN ST

DINH TIEN HOANG ST

An Hoa Bus Station

The Citadel

LE VAN HUU ST

NGUYEN TRAI ST

HOANG DIEU ST

TRIEN QUANG PHUC ST

Purple City

Mieu Temple

TON THAP THIEP ST

YET KIEU ST

Nine Dynastic Urns

LE DUAN ST

ONG ICH KIEM ST

LE DUAN ST

Ga Hué Railway Station

Places to Stay
1 Thanh Noi Hotel
10 Thanh Loi Hotel
13 Hoang Giang Hotel
17 Dong Loi Hotel
18 Ben Nghe Guesthouse
19 Hoang Long Hotel
21 Hung Vuong Hotel
22 Saigon Morin Hotel
24 Thai Binh Hotel
25 Binh Minh Hotel
26 Khang Quang Hotel
27 Le Loi Hué Hotel

Places to Eat
2 Ong Tao Restaurant & Quoc Huy Restaurant
11 Huong Sen Restaurant
12 Garden Restaurant
14 Lac Thienh Restaurant
15 Snake Restaurant
16 DMZ Café
20 Apocalypse Now
23 Paradise Garden Restaurant

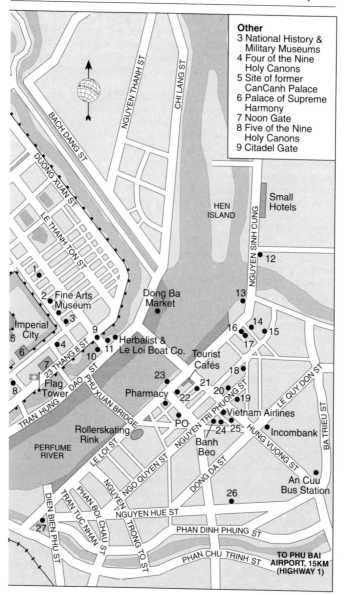

Other
3 National History &
  Military Museums
4 Four of the Nine
  Holy Canons
5 Site of former
  CanCanh Palace
6 Palace of Supreme
  Harmony
7 Noon Gate
8 Five of the Nine
  Holy Canons
9 Citadel Gate

NGUYEN THANH ST

CHI LANG ST

BACH DANG ST

DUONG XUAN ST

LE THANH TON ST

HEN
ISLAND

Small
Hotels

NGUYEN SINH CUNG

12

1

2 Fine Arts
  Museum

3

Imperial
City

Dong Ba
Market

13

14

16   15
17

9

Herbalist &
Le Loi Boat Co.

Tourist
Cafés

4

THANG 8 ST

10   11

23

18

21

Pharmacy

22

20

19

LE QUY DON ST

7

23

Flag
Tower

8

DAO ST

PHU XUAN BRIDGE

PO

NGUYEN TRI PHUONG ST

24   25

Vietnam Airlines

Incombank

BA TRIEU ST

TRAN HUNG

Rollerskating
Rink

Banh
Beo

HUNG VUONG ST

PERFUME
RIVER

LE LOI ST

NGUYEN

NGO QUYEN ST

DONG DA ST

An Cuu
Bus Station

26

DIEN BIEN PHU ST

TRAN TUC NHAN ST

PHAN BOI CHAU ST

TRONG TO ST

NGUYEN HUE ST

PHAN DINH PHUNG ST

27

PHAN CHU TRINH ST

**TO PHU BAI
AIRPORT, 15KM
(HIGHWAY 1)**

over the surrounding lakes. Minh Mang's tomb is 12km south of Hué, only 4km from Khai Dinh's tomb, but on the left bank of the Perfume River. Ferries ply their trade opposite the lane leading to the tomb, but often overcharge; if you are asked more than $0.50 it is worth tacking along the river in search of other boats – it doesn't usually take long to find a better deal.

Gia Long was the first Nguyen emperor, coming to power in 1802 as the final, regressive, event of the Tay Son revolution. He ruled for 17 years until his death in 1819, and the building of his tomb took six years and was only completed after his death, in 1820. The tomb was begun on the death of his first queen, Thua Thien, in 1814 when he ordered the construction of a double grave tomb. He chose a site of pine-clad hills, close to the Perfume River some 20km from Hué because several of his ancestors were already buried here. Gia Long's tomb has suffered significantly from the ravages of war and its long distance from Hué did not help the reconstruction cause, but still it is worth seeing for the charm of the stone constructions arising out of the vegetation. The massive tomb is impressive and virtually unscathed – although if you look carefully you will see a chip on the Queen's sarcophagus, apparently made by a B-52 bomb. Gia Long's tomb is 20km from Hué, 0.5km from the left bank of the Perfume River and is free. It is best seen by boat trip from Hué.

Museums

The **Fine Arts Museum**, also called the Antiquities Museum and the Imperial Museum, is at 3 Le Truc St, inside the Citadel. It is open every day from 7am to 6pm; the entrance fee is 22,000d. It houses antiquities which the French did not loot from Hué, or destroy, including many pieces of imperial wooden furniture with technically outstanding mother-of-pearl inlay, and a great, if small, collection of boots and shoes. However, the most interesting aspect of the museum is the building itself. It was built in 1845 and was originally Long An Palace. Decorating the walls are hundreds of landscape motifs setting off hundreds of verses by the emperor. The roof is decorated with designs of Vietnam's four sacred mythical creatures – the dragon, kylin (unicorn), phoenix and tortoise – and by a representation of two dragons fighting for a gem.

On the other side of Le Truc St from the Antiquities museum are the **Natural History Museum** and the **Military Museum**. These are open every day from 7.30 to 11am and 1.30 to 4.30pm, and cost $1.50 for both. The Natural History Museum has some interesting ancient exhibits. The best bit about the Military Museum is exploring the rusting tanks outside on the grass. Otherwise, the museum is small and boasts little more than the usual display of photos of the war and occasional AK47 guns.

PRACTICAL INFORMATION
Arrival and departure
By train The train station is around 2km south-east of Hué. There are always a large number of cyclos meeting trains and several hotel touts. The journey into town costs about 3000d.

The ticket office for express trains is in the main station building. It is open 8am-4pm and the staff speak good English. The nearest station where you can buy an express ticket for trains heading north is Ninh Binh, heading south is Nha Trang. To buy a ticket for Dong Ha you must travel by local train which generally leaves around 2pm but the times change often. The ticket office for local trains is outside the station on the right in a small ramshackle booth. It is in theory open from 8 to 11am and 1.30 to 4pm but in practice it is always possible to buy a ticket for a local train within the hour before departure whatever time of the day or night that is.

By bus Hué has two long-distance bus stations: An Cuu bus station, 1km south-east of the centre, serves destinations to the south, while An Hoa, 4km north of Hué on Highway 1, is where buses travelling to and from the north arrive.

By air Hué's Phu Bai airport (once an important American airbase) is around 15km south-east of the city centre. A taxi costs around $8, or there is an air-port bus for only $1 or $2 to or from your hotel. The Vietnam Airlines office is in the Thuan Hoa Hotel at 7 Nguyen Tri Phuong St.

Orientation
Hué lies on Highway 1, 15km inland from the South China Sea. The wide Perfume river bisects the city. The west bank is the site of the Citadel which houses the Imperial City and the Forbidden Purple City. The east bank has most of the accommodation and services. The Imperial tombs are scattered over a large area close to the banks of the Perfume river south of the city.

The Perfume river is crossed in the city centre by two bridges. The northern one was built by the French in 1885, after their successful sacking of the city. It survived the 20th centuries' wars well, losing only a little of its framework. Being French it is picturesque and being old it is reserved for light traffic, such as cyclos and bicycles, only. The other bridge was built by the Americans during the eponymous war. It is therefore far newer, but it takes the heavy traffic so shakes rather alarmingly when you cross it.

Services
Post and telecommunications The main post office is at 8 Hoang Hoa Tham St and is open 6.30am-9pm. International telephone calls at the standard rate can be made from the post office, or from the telephone booths bizarrely located inside the Imperial City and Minh Mang's tomb.

Email facilities have arrived at Dong Loi hotel at 11A Pham Ngu Lao St (☎ 054-822296). English-language newspapers and magazines can be bought outside the post office; Monday is the best day to buy the weeklies.

Money Hué's palatial and bureaucratic Incombank (☎ 054-822281) is at 2A Le Quy Don St and is open Monday to Saturday from 7 to 11.30am and 1.30 to 4.30pm.

The bank charges 0.5 per cent commission to change travellers' cheques into dong, 1 per cent for changing into dollars, and 3 per cent to take money out on a credit or debit card.

Medical There are many pharmacies with a fairly extensive range of medicines. Two are on Dinh Tien Hoang St, next to and opposite Thanh Loi Hotel. On the east side of the river there is one at 28 Le Loi St. There is a very well-stocked herbalist at 15b Tran Hung Dao St. The hospital is at 16 Le Loi St.

Local transport

Hué is replete with cyclos and Honda om, but in many ways the city and environs are best seen by bicycle; many hotels hire them out for $1 a day, although Lac Thien restaurant at 6 Dinh Tien Hoang St may charge less.

Tours

Several of Hué's hotels and restaurants offer fairly identical tours of the DMZ, although all are gruelling full-day minibus experiences. Lac Thien restaurant is one place to book such tours and to book the tourist bus to Hanoi or HCMC (Saigon).

Many of the restaurants and hotels on Le Loi St offer tours, such as DMZ Café at 44 Le Loi St. However, there have been bad reports of the open tour to Hoi An organized by the An Phu Tourist Company at 38D Le Loi St.

Where to stay

Happily, one of Hué's best (and newest) hotels is 100m from the railway station; *Le Loi Hué Hotel*, 2 Le Loi St (☎ 054-824668, 🖷 054-824527), has doubles with shower from $6 to $44. The hotel has 170 rooms, and is classy with a glossy restaurant but is still friendly. It is not easy to miss being fronted by extraordinary topiaried dragons.

Also on the east side of the river there are a number of hotels and villas around 1.5km from the railway station. *Ben Nghe Guesthouse* at 4 Ben Nghe St (☎ 054-889106) has 21 rooms for $6-$12; some are triples and quads. The rooms are fairly small and warm due to the erratic power supply for fans but are clean enough. The good prices mean that the guest-house is often full. Another low budget option are the tourist villas on Ly Thuong Kiet St which have rooms from $7. There are a number of good hotels on nearby Nguyen Tri Phuong St, such as *Hoang Long Hotel*, 20 Nguyen Tri Phuong St (☎ 054-828235), and *Thai Binh Hotel* (☎ 054-828058) which is listed as 10/9 Nguyen Tri Phuong St but actually is just off the street down a small alleyway running southwards. These two hotels offer rooms from $10 to $20 with air-con.

The delightful *Binh Minh Hotel*, at 12 Nguyen Tri Phuong St (☎ 054-825526, 🖷 054-828362), offers spacious clean triples from $12 to $20 all with air-con, TV and telephone, and lovely doubles complete with a bathtub and panoramic views from the private balcony for $22-$35. (The best room in the hotel is 402.) Nearer the river the government-run *Hung Vuong Hotel* at 2 Hung Vuong St (☎ 054-823866) is currently being expanded and improved. It offers doubles with air-con, bath and TV for $10-$45. However, it does still retain something of a government atmosphere. The palatial style of the nearby *Dong Loi Hotel*, 11A Pham Ngu Lao St (☎ 054-822296, 🖷 054-826234, 🖳 interser@dng.vnn.vn), by contrast, exudes customer service. It offers beautifully equipped and maintained doubles and quads for $15-$40. The hotel offers email services when its computer is working.

On the west side of the river *Thanh Loi Hotel*, 7 Dinh Tien Hoang St (☎ 054-524803), has clean doubles from $6 to $12. The rooms facing the road are very noisy. In contrast *Thanh Noi Hotel*, at 3 Dang Dung St (☎ 054-522478), is quiet and now has a swimming pool – though beware that the hotel sometimes charges per swim! Its clean, well-equipped doubles are $15-$30; much less nice doubles are $12.

Two options which are best avoided are *Phu Hoa Guest House* at 47 Le Duan St; the only thing to recommend this venue is its proximity to the bus station. It offers grotty doubles for $11. Likewise the government-run *Hung*

Dao Hotel, 81 Tran Hung Dao St, has $10 doubles which are very poor value for money, although you cannot find a cheaper double in Hué than their $5 formica-walled affairs. The manager will ruefully confess that they are constrained by it being a government hotel and with disarming honesty admits that it is the worst hotel in town.

Hué also has many small hotels which are further from the centre and are generally occupied by Vietnamese guests. These are not necessarily cheaper, but are less touristy. For example, **Khang Quang Hotel** is at 29 Nguyen Hué St (☎ 824424) and there are many such hotels on Thuan An St (also called Duong Nguyen Sinh Cung St).

The two grandest hotels are **Saigon Morin Hotel** (☎ 054-823526, 🖳 054-825155, 🖳 sgmorin@dng.vnn.vn) at 30 Le Loi St and **Huong Giang Hotel** on the Perfume river at 51 Le Loi St (☎ 054-82122, 🖳 054-823102). Saigon Morin is large, impressive and has rooms from $50 to suites for $300, but sometimes they get full up. Huong Giang, meanwhile, is large and exquisite. Charming doubles here are $50; the two absolutely fantastic royal suite rooms are $220 a night.

Where to eat and drink

Hué is famous for its excellent food. Its access to the river and the sea means it produces very good fish and seafood dishes. Hué has many speciality dishes such as *Banh nam* and *Banh loc*, which are shredded and whole shrimp respectively encased in pork fat and cooked wrapped in banana leaves. These may not sound it but are truly delicious. There are many small restaurants off the tourist track which specialize in these Hué foods and can easily be found by asking a Vietnamese; the cost should be around 6000d for two people. The most central are **Banh Beo** at 2 Nguyen Tri Phuong St, and **Codo** at 4 Ben Nghe St.

Another local speciality is *com hen* – hot mussel soup poured over cold rice. The best way to try this delicious food is before 9am from one of several small cafés on Truong Dinh St, or from women carrying baskets over a shoulder pole at Dong Ba market. Frog is commonly found in Hué; snake and gecko less so. One place that specializes in all three is **Phi Long Restaurant** at 60/3 Thuan An St.

Still the most popular eating spots for travellers are the **Lac Thien** and **Lac Thanh** restaurants at 6 Dinh Tien Hoang St. These places have proved so popular, and so Lonely Planetized, that they have spawned a series of copies the length of the street. One of the copies even went to the length of hiring a deaf-dumb person to mimic the remarkable family of the original who are all deaf and dumb but can lipread in several languages! The food in the original is still excellent – speciality seafood salad pancakes you roll yourself are a highlight; having the cooker at the front of the original Lac Thanh restaurant on the streetside is its distinguishing mark. The food in the others is variable.

There are several tourist cafés serving Vietnamese and European food and drinks along Le Loi St and just off it on Hung Vuong St. For good cheap Vietnamese food, there are many stalls at the northern end of Dong Ba market which run from early in the morning to late at night.

For more up-market food **Huong Sen restaurant** at 42 Nguyen Trai (☎ 054-828755) is under new management and its food is now very good. It is also charmingly situated on stilts above a lotus pond and has very good service. However, it cannot be recommended in the evening as there are rumours of frequent night-time brawls in this area. **Ong Tao** (meaning Mr Tao) **Restaurant** inside the citadel next to Hien Nhon gate (☎ 054-823031) does wonderful food and has tables outside beneath lychee trees with nothing but the buzz of cicadas to disturb the quiet. A large meal for two will cost around $7. For roughly double that, **Garden club Restaurant** at 12 Vo Thi Sau St (☎ 054-828074) serves good food in Western-style luxury; its clientele is mostly foreign. Two other restaurants worth trying are the excellent **Quoc Huy Restaurant** (☎ 054-525310) at 43 Dinh Cong Trang St and **Paradise Garden Restaurant** (☎ 054-832221) with its lovely riverside location opposite Saigon Morin Hotel at 17 Le Loi St.

For the ultimate in luxury at $80 **Huong Giang Hotel** will treat its guests to a full-scale banquet in the royal dining suite complete with a traditional Vietnamese music concert and outlandish costumes for the band and diners.

For a daytime drink a wander or cycle through the northern byways of the citadel will take you past small shady drinking spots on the banks of lotus ponds. As dusk slips into evening the cafés along the banks of the Perfume river become a charming place to sink a few drinks, largely freed from the hundreds of sellers that can make these places almost uninhabitable for foreigners by day. Or for Western revelry you can try **Apocalypse Now** at 7 Nguyen Tri Phuong St, or the **DMZ Café** at 44 Le Loi St.

Entertainment

Traditional Vietnamese music is played every night on boats up and down the Perfume river. The trip is enjoyable, if touristy. Tickets can be bought from the Tourist Boat Company (☎ 054-826532) at 11 Le Loi St for $5. Boats leave nightly from the booking office at 7pm and 8.30pm. Food and drink can be bought on board.

For more modern Vietnamese culture you could try the cinema at 11 Tran Hung Dao St which shows films in Vietnamese at 8pm every night except Sunday. If you go with a Vietnamese you will have a chance of paying only the Vietnamese price, of 2000d. Hué also has a rollerskating rink on Le Loi St which attracts crowds of young Vietnamese each night. If you crave (relatively) modern music to dance to, then Ngoc Anh on Nguyen Tri Phuong St is the best option or the ubiquitous Apocalypse Now.

Things to buy

Shopping in Hué almost starts and ends with Dong Ba market. You will find a huge variety of hats including exclusively Huéan conical hats which are embroidered with poems or designs on the inside or outside. Tailored clothes can also be made upstairs in the market, or there are many such shops all around town. Silk enthusiasts should note that Hué is *the* place to buy silk embroidered with hand-made designs which you can commission yourself. Tourist-frequented shops are on Le Loi St, otherwise look upstairs in Dong Ba market.

DONG HA

Dong Ha, gateway to the DMZ (the demilitarized zone), is an unattractive little town with a latent highly-charged political atmosphere. It is the nearest town to the Ben Hai river which cut Vietnam in half from the time of the Geneva Accords in 1954 until the North Vietnamese army finally pushed through the defences here reunifying the country in 1975.

Five kilometres on either side of the artificial boundary of the river, almost on the 17th parallel, is the so-called 'demilitarized zone', which, contrary to its name, was the most militarized area of the country as the southern and northern edges of it comprised the American and North

> ❏ **Warning**
> The sights and scenes of a day or two spent around Dong Ha help to bring
> home the realities of modern warfare, but the ugly tools of war still draw
> blood. Since the end of the American war it is estimated that at least 6000 peo-
> ple have been wounded or killed in this area. For this reason it is extremely
> unwise to see the DMZ without the help of a guide – easy enough to find in
> Dong Ha. Whatever you do, don't touch anything metallic that you find lying
> around – the people here live on the miserly proceeds of the scrap metal, so if
> they haven't picked something up there is probably a very good reason (see
> p122 dangers and annoyances for more on this).

Vietnamese front lines. The region was once home to American and South
Vietnamese bases to the south of the partition and, to the north, the start
of the Ho Chi Minh trail. Exploring this area gives you the chance to visit
the sites of some of the most hotly fought-over terrain of the war, such as
the Khe Sanh American firebase which was under siege for 75 days – time
which proved crucial in distracting the Americans from protecting the
cities prior to the turning point of the Tet offensive.

The DMZ is also home to such moving sights as the massive Truong
Son cemetery and the remarkable Vinh Moc tunnels. For anyone interested in the American war the DMZ is very much worth visiting, though be
aware that despite the devastation the area suffered from inordinate vol-
umes of firepower and defoliants such as Napalm, foliage has finally
returned to the area so the bases are largely overgrown. But providing you
don't expect to see large numbers of tanks lying around you are unlikely
to be disappointed. But above all do remember that the area is still the
scene of extremely dangerous detritus, including unexploded bombs.

Dong Ha is also the gateway to Laos. The crossing point is 80km west
of Dong Ha along Highway 9, 3km from the little village of Lao Bao.

PRACTICAL INFORMATION
Arrival and departure
By train The station is just off
Highway 1 and around 1.5km south of
the centre of town.

There do not tend to be any cyclos
or other taxis waiting outside this station
so, if you don't want to walk to the hotel
area, it is often worth making a telephone reservation with a hotel before
arriving in Dong Ha so you can be met
at the station

It can be difficult to get hold of tickets for express trains from Dong Ha
because its daily allocation of foreigners'

tickets is small, so try to buy a ticket out
as much in advance as possible.

By bus Dong Ha's bus station is at the
junction of Highways 1 and 9. Regular
buses depart early in the morning to Khe
Sanh where you must change bus to
reach Lao Bao and the Lao border.
Alternatively, express buses depart once
every two or three days from Danang
and pass through Dong Ha around
10am, bound straight for Savannakhet
in Laos. This is certainly the most hassle-free way to make the trip, though at
$15 it is not the cheapest.

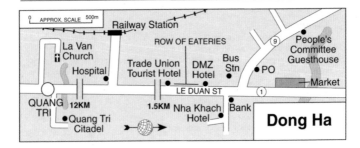

Orientation and services

Highway 1 is known as Le Duan St when it passes through Dong Ha forming its main artery. Highway 9, which leads to the Lao border, forks left in the middle of town forming the other principal road. The **post office** and **bank** (cash only) are located just off Highway 1, near the junction with Highway 9.

The government **tourism office** is in Dong Truong Son Hotel (☎ 053-52415), 2.5km out of town on Tran Phu St, but it is not a useful source of information and it is not recommended that you book DMZ tours here – see below.

Tours

Booking a government tour of the DMZ area will cost around $120 for two days. Part of this is a fee for a 'travel permit' which the agent will tell you the police require. This is, in fact not necessary, and is no more than a device by the tourist officials to raise money to fill their pockets.

In addition to this the strong government grip over the hotel market here, illustrates that the government is not keen on tourists seeing the DMZ from Dong Ha, because its proximity to the area encourages independent travel. This attitude is, in itself, a symptom of the political divisions in Dong Ha where the forces from North Vietnam now call the tune, while many in the population were militantly in favour of the other side. This difficulty does not mean that you should consider touring the DMZ without a guide: a guide is essential, not only to understand what you are looking at, but also to avoid stumbling across live bombs. The danger is real.

The upshot of this is that there are several local guides who speak good English and can be hired for a day for $10-$20 for a motorbike trip, and for $30-$40 by car; try Mr Le Van Quang (☎ 053-850178) or Mr Tinh Tran Van (☎ 053-851838).

To see all the sights of the DMZ requires at least two days: one to cover the places of interest north and east of Dong Ha, one to visit those south and west.

Where to stay

Another advantage of reserving a room in advance (see By train) is that you can avoid *Trade Union Hotel* (☎ 053 851345), 4 Le Loi St, even though it is the closest to the railway station. However, the difficulty is that the competition is not great.

The two best places are *Provincial People's Committee Guesthouse* (☎ 053-852361), 68 Tran Hung Dao St, which is surprisingly good for a government property and has basic rooms for 50,000d and pleasant doubles with air con, TV, telephone and shower for 100,000d.

The other option is the smaller *Nha Khach Hotel* at 105 Nguyen Trai St (☎

053-851277). This has basic doubles and triples at $5, and adequate doubles with air con and shower for $12.

At the time of writing *DMZ Hotel* on Highway 1 was dirty and shabby so it is not recommended. It is also linked to the government tourist office so you will be hustled to buy an expensive DMZ tour.

Where to eat
There are a number of small eateries along Highways 1 and 9, and a particularly good row of streetside cafés around 1km before the railway station.

If you are taking a tour of the DMZ the guide will be likely to take you to an excellent if basic roadside restaurant at lunchtime. Expect to be expected to pick up the bill.

SIGHTS OF THE DMZ AND ITS ENVIRONS

The following sights can be covered in two full days by motorbike or jeep provided you have a guide. Without a guide you not only risk losing your way several times as the tracks are often small and labyrinthine, but if you stray from the safe areas you risk losing your life. (Sorry to labour the point but it's a vital one).

North and east DMZ

Con Thien Firebase was the largest firebase along America's front line with North Vietnam and was set up as part of a plan to prevent infiltrations from the north. Originally the base was a key link in the extraordinary scheme of US Defence Secretary Robert McNamara to prevent North Vietnamese troops crossing the border into South Vietnam by rigging up a vast electronic fence to stretch across the country. When the electronic barrier was abandoned, due to frequent malfunctions and the ease with which it could be disabled, the firebases remained and their purpose became more directly to fight over the surrounding territory and to hit targets at long range well into North Vietnam.

In late 1967 North Vietnamese forces crossed the DMZ, shelled and then besieged the Con Thien Firebase. The Americans responded with the might of US firepower. Hundreds of B-52 sorties dropped thousands of tonnes of ammunition on surrounding North Vietnamese troops transforming the gently sloping lush hills into a lunar landscape of craters, ashes, twisted metal and bodies. But even though the bombing lifted the siege and drove back the North Vietnamese they were the real victors from this battle which was actually a diversionary attack which enabled Viet Cong forces to strike hard and effectively elsewhere during the Tet offensive of 1968.

Today there is still a pock-marked US bunker to mark the scene of the former base and from the highest point on the hill there are views across into Laos, Cambodia and northwards to the positions then held by the North Vietnamese. The vegetation has grown back and it is only the occasional (deadly) white phosphorous bomb or US supply card littering the foliage which can persuade you to believe that these peaceful hills were the scene of so much carnage.

Con Thien Firebase can be found by heading west out of Dong Ha along Highway 9, turning north at Cam Lo along Highway 15 and following this road for around 10km. The firebase is off the road to the right.

The vast, peaceful and well-tended **Truong Son National Cemetery** commemorates the sacrifices made by over 20,000 North Vietnamese men, women and children who lost their lives on the trail along the Truong Son mountain range, better known as the Ho Chi Minh Trail.

The bodies of around half this number were never recovered – just some of Vietnam's Missing in Actions – but are commemorated here as if they were, while the remainder are buried in great lines of graves, set out according to province of birth, and beneath white headstones adorned with incense. Each headstone is engraved with the name, place and date of birth, date of enrolment into the army, rank and date of death of the *liet si* – martyr. Reading the headstones reveals that many were as young as 12 or 13. Truong Son cemetery is signposted to the east off Highway 15, a few kilometres beyond Con Thien Firebase.

The **Ben Hai river** at the centre of the DMZ and marking the division of Vietnam into north and south from 1954 to 1975 flows serenely through the countryside a few kilometres north of Truong Son cemetery. Hien Luong Bridge which takes Highway 1 over the river was the point from which the country was divided, and therefore the point from which the **Ho Chi Minh Trail** began; it remains an important symbol of the division of Vietnam. Until the bridge was destroyed by American bombs in 1967 the northern side was painted red and the southern side yellow – an expressive illustration of the divide.

The bridge was rebuilt following the Paris ceasefire agreements in 1973 and flag towers on both sides were built. But the northern side got its come-uppance when it tried to outdo the southern side with a higher flag tower – the northern flag tower was felled by a typhoon in 1985. Looking to the west of the bridge you can see the wooded and jungle country of central Vietnam and Laos through which thousands of North Vietnamese and local ethnic minorities drove, carried and dragged hundreds of thousands of tonnes of equipment from the North to the South on what became immortalized as the Ho Chi Minh Trail (see box on p237).

A testimony to the courage and tenacity of locals determined not to be driven from their land by the pounding American bombing are the large network of **Vinh Moc tunnels** which were hacked out of the red soil in just two years and protected the villagers for many more. The tunnels are really worth seeing especially because they are wider and taller than the Cu Chi tunnels in the south, and yet have not been altered or touristed. Also, unlike Cu Chi, the Vinh Moc tunnels were primarily for housing locals; any military use they were put to was secondary.

❏ **The Ho Chi Minh Trail**
The story of the Ho Chi Minh Trail symbolizes for the North Vietnamese still today both their victory over the superior forces of America, and their sacrifice to achieve that victory. But at the heart of the story is something not so much heroic as extremely clever. For while the North Vietnamese did struggle and strain to bring supplies and military hardware to the south over mountainous, malarial and difficult terrain in Vietnam, Laos and Cambodia circumventing American forces and suffering great losses amidst massive aerial bombardment, despite what many Vietnamese think, the effort was not vital to the war – except that it massively distracted American forces from the real route the supplies from the North took.

It was only in 1970 when Prince Lon Nol took power in Cambodia and allowed American action in Cambodia to break the Ho Chi Minh Trail that it was discovered that American intelligence had been completely wrong about its importance – in fact 80 per cent of military hardware from North Vietnam which reached the south were transported by sea and unloaded at the Cambodian port of Sihanoukville. That doesn't stop the history and anecdotes of the heroism of those who walked these miles back and forth carrying heavy loads by cover of darkness being a fascinating story. And of course as a diversionary tactic keeping thousands of American troops locked up along the DMZ it was vital.

The tunnels were built on three levels, with the lowest at 20m deep and everywhere through the 2km network there are ventilation shafts, freshwater wells, eventually a generator providing lighting as well as clinics, family caverns and even a school for the children.

In the underground maze you can still see the maternity room where 17 children were born. Safe from the bombs the villagers still had to contend with a lack of fresh air and sunlight as well as bombs strafing their rice paddies and vegetable plots which they could only tend at night. These days the tunnels are still sometimes used as shelter from the typhoons which regularly buffet Vietnam's northern coasts.

The small museum has a graphic display of the tunnel network from which you will see that an exit from the tunnels leads directly onto a nice sandy beach, Cua Tung beach. The tunnels are around 15km east of Highway 1 at the end of a small twisting unsignposted track and are open every day from dawn to dusk; entrance costs $2. Bring a torch (flashlight).

Cua Tung beach's long stretch of sand around the Vinh Moc tunnels used to be frequented by Emperor Bao Dai; it is now much populated by locals at weekends and is a pleasant place at any time whether it's for splashing in the sea, or relaxing in the small basic cafés behind the beach. When Vietnamese are present this seems like one of the few areas in the region where life has truly returned to normality.

The American **Doc Mieu Base** just off Highway 1 was also once part of McNamara's electronic fence plan (as was Con Thien Firebase). When the attempted barrier was abandoned Doc Mieu Base saw heavy fighting as the cratered and pock-marked landscape bears witness. The area has been extensively picked over by scrap-metal merchants, but also recently by American veteran groups searching for American MIAs (missing in actions). Most of the remains unearthed in recent years have been those of Vietnamese. Doc Mieu Base is just east of Highway 1 on a low rise 8km south of the Ben Hai river.

West and south DMZ

Standing proudly over verdant vegetation 24km from Dong Ha is a 230m-high pile of rocks, known as **The Rockpile**. During the war it was used as a lookout and sniper post and later became a highly important firebase. From its commanding position US Marines were on constant surveillance for any North Vietnamese infiltration of the DMZ. To keep control of the area it was crucial to keep the two opposing hills, known as Hill 400 and Hill 484, free of Viet Cong. So the knolls were heavily bombarded with artillery fire, but despite this they did fall to the enemy. Captain Carroll and his company were assigned with the unenviable task of retaking the hills and the ridge. Amid the maelstrom of battle in the air and on the ground the Marines succeeded in taking Hill 400, but over 20 men died taking Hill 484, including Captain Carroll.

The Rockpile can be seen from Highway 9 to the west of it around 8km after the junction with the Cua Valley. Hills 400 and 484 and the ridge are to the north-west of the Rockpile.

Camp Carroll was named after Captain Carroll because of his courageous leadership in retaking Hills 400 and 484 during which he lost his life. The camp is also famous for the actions of the South Vietnamese commander of the camp, Lieutenant Pham Van Dinh, who in 1972 changed sides and joined the North Vietnamese army. Some guidebooks claim that he is now a high-ranking official in Hué; in fact he works as a driver for Sinh Café! Camp Carroll is 3km south of Highway 9, 12km beyond the small settlement of Cam Lo.

In 1962 US Special Forces established a small base in **Khe Sanh** town in order to recruit and train people from the Bru tribe. However, in the late 1960s Khe Sanh was turned into a major firebase and then became the scene of a world-famous siege which turned around North Vietnam's war effort both because it distracted the Americans from the upcoming Tet offensive, and because the media attention that attracted suddenly shocked the American public into a realization that they had been lied to when the politicians had told them that the war was fully under control. The anti-war movement in the US was given a big boost. Even though the Americans eventually broke the siege, after inflicting massive casualties on the North Vietnamese troops, and so avoided the tag that America had met its Dien Bien Phu, the long-term damage was substantial.

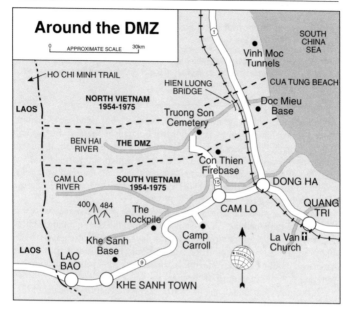

Around the DMZ

0 APPROXIMATE SCALE 30km

HO CHI MINH TRAIL

LAOS

NORTH VIETNAM
1954-1975

BEN HAI
RIVER   **THE DMZ**

CAM LO
RIVER   SOUTH VIETNAM
1954-1975

400 ↑ ↑ 484

LAOS   LAO
BAO

Khe Sanh
Base

The
Rockpile

Camp
Carroll

KHE SANH TOWN

SOUTH
CHINA
SEA

Vinh Moc
Tunnels

HIEN LUONG
BRIDGE   CUA TUNG BEACH

Truong Son
Cemetery   Doc Mieu
Base

Con Thien
Firebase

CAM LO

DONG HA

QUANG
TRI

La Van
Church

The siege of Khe Sanh

Serious skirmishes began in early 1967 and towards the end of the year American intelligence detected a massive build-up of North Vietnamese troops around Khe Sanh base, and responded by matching the increase. By the start of 1968 America had amassed 6000 US Marines and were supported by some South Vietnamese troops and the recently-trained Bru. The build-up of equipment was also huge: over 500 planes were brought to Khe Sanh. It wasn't long before they began raining down high explosives – but on 21 January 1968 the North Vietnamese launched a massive artillery attack and held the base under siege.

As headlines around the world began talking of another Dien Bien Phu so Lyndon Johnson and General Westmoreland became obsessed with the idea and decided the siege was to be broken at all costs to prevent the base being overrun. In the next nine weeks 100,000 tonnes of explosives were dropped on the surrounding area and vegetation was stripped away by vicious defoliants, including napalm.

The North Vietnamese in their dug-in positions managed to withstand the onslaught and never ceased to return fire, despite around 10,000 casualties; American forces lost at least 500 men. But there was never an attempt by the North Vietnamese to over-run the base and after the

❑ **Crossing the border into Laos**

To reach Laos from Lao Bao you can hire a Honda om to take you the last 3km to the border as there are no buses which go directly to the border, or take a Honda om all the way there from Khe Sanh. There are buses in Laos on the other side of the border to Savannakhet and then to Vientiane, but you need to walk around 1km between the border posts.

Americans broke through the siege on 7 April the surrounding VC troops melted away. Three months later, following a tour of Vietnam by General Westmoreland, American forces at Khe Sanh were redeployed. It was no longer deemed necessary to hold the base for which so many Americans had died. Indeed, the entire camp was abandoned – all the men were relocated and the base was totally bulldozed to deprive the North Vietnamese of any rich pickings.

Meanwhile, ten days after the siege of Khe Sanh began, the North Vietnamese launched the Tet offensive plunging into over a hundred cities and towns and taking control for several days. The Tet offensive was in many ways a turning point of the war particularly because it showed the American public that despite the assurance of the military leadership America was not in control of the war.

It became clear that the siege of Khe Sanh was merely a means of distracting American forces away from the cities and populated areas so that the North Vietnamese could break through in the Tet offensive. In defending the base so resolutely the Americans had fallen right into the Communists' trap; they did so because they were haunted by the spectre of Dien Bien Phu. But, in wishing to avoid a Dien Bien Phu the Americans turned the Khe Sanh siege into exactly that – because the lesson of Dien Bien Phu is that a place which is in the middle of nowhere, holding no vital supply routes, nor any populated centre can only ever become a real issue if one side insists on making it one.

Today the area around Khe Sanh base is one of the few where vegetation still won't grow; the scars of war meld with the perilous holes dug by scrap-metalhunters. The red gash of the airstrip stands out from the dismal scene.

Khe Sanh base is 2.5km north-west of Khe Sanh town; take the road towards Dong Ha for 500m then turn off to the north-west at the intersection with a small monument; the base is off the road on the right.

Khe Sanh town and around

There is not much to see in Khe Sanh but there are a couple of basic hotels if you are intending to cross the border into Laos; Khe San is around 19km from the Laotian border.

There are a number of Bru minority villages around the area, especially in the last 10km before the border. These tribespeople tend to be friendly and welcoming to foreigners, making a trip to see their hamlets of stilt houses and pipe-smoking women a rewarding experience. You can take a local bus to the village of Lao Bao near the border (the most reliable service is at 6am from Khe Sanh town) and find a Honda om from there, or hire a bicycle or Honda om directly from Khe Sanh town.

Quang Tri and around

Quang Tri, 12km south of Dong Ha, used to be the provincial capital of this region and was a bustling centre founded on the site of an ancient citadel the remains of which can now just about be seen. It is a fascinating place, ironically due to what you cannot see. In the 1940s and 1950s the area was a hotbed of Viet Minh activity and attacks against French units were common, but it was during the American war that the town was virtually razed to the ground. In 1972 North Vietnamese forces pushed southwards and held Quang Tri for several hard months before South Vietnamese troops regained the town through intense house-to-house fighting backed up by the constant battering of B-52 bombing raids; it is the destructive result of these events that are to be seen in Quang Tri.

The remains of the **citadel** are preserved within an area that has been pleasantly landscaped. To get there take Highway 1 south from Dong Ha for around 11km turning right off the road around ½km after a bridge over the Quang Tri river. Continue along this road for around 2km turning right on reaching Quang Trung St. Further along this road you will see the ivy-covered stone gate which leads to almost all that is left of the citadel.

Back on Highway 1 heading south you come to the two most pressing reasons to make the trip to Quang Tri: the empty shell of a bullet-ridden building and the bombed-out remains of **La Van Church** just off the main road. The huge skeleton of the church is preserved in all its ruined glory. Standing beneath the decimated towers and arches of the church you can really get a sense of what house-to-house fighting actually means. Next to the ruins there is an extraordinary Catholic monument showing a colourful Mary perched among vast mushrooming trees; this is meant to represent the a vision of Mary appearing before believers on this spot two centuries ago.

La Van Church is signposted from Highway 1 by a small blue sign which indicates right about 12km from Dong Ha. After around 2km you will see the church off the track to the right at the end of a grass plain.

Hanoi and the north

Hanoi, Vietnam's victorious political capital, has not seen nearly as much change as economically much more prosperous Ho Chi Minh City (Saigon). This means the city retains much of its old-world charm, with French colonial buildings and boulevards complemented by the tranquillity of the lakes on the one hand and the bustle of the streets on the other.

The heart of the city, the 36 streets (also known as the old quarter), rarely fails to delight, but if it makes you want to get away from it all take a day trip to the beautiful Perfume Pagoda or an afternoon trip to the charming pottery village of Bat Trang.

Further afield the north holds the delights of the 'inland Halong Bay', at Hoa Lu near Ninh Binh, and the glorious majesty of Halong Bay – truly one of the wonders of the world. From here you can take the lovely train journey through beautiful Kep and ethnic minority hilltribe areas up to the border near Lang Son. From there you can continue on into China.

Branching west from Hanoi is the railway line running up the Red River valley to Lao Cai, an hour's bus or motorbike ride from the hilltribe centre of Sapa. Here you can relax in comfort at the Auberge, walk through the montagnard settlements in the Sapa valley, explore the fairly untouched region in the north-west, or even climb Vietnam's highest mountain, Fansipan. Alternatively get back on the railway tracks and follow the line which leads into China's Yunnan province clinging to mountain sides through such fantastic scenery that it is known as the 'ligne acrobatique'.

CLIMATE

The north experiences a real winter from November to February, so be prepared. If you intend to visit during this time you will need more than a fleece to keep warm as hardly anywhere, even in Hanoi, has heaters. Temperatures during these months range between 12 and 20°C (55-65°F).

The rest of the year is warm with temperatures rising to over 30°C (90°F) during June, July and August. This is also when one of the monsoons hits the north so expect some days of downpour. Meanwhile in the late summer and autumn typhoons regularly batter northern coastal regions.

NINH BINH

History

Ninh Binh is an unremarkable little town in the midst of truly remarkable scenery which is peppered with impressive places of worship.

The capital of Ninh Binh province sits on a plain of rice paddies out of which rise hundreds of huge jagged limestone crags. The landscape is referred to as 'Halong Bay on land'. Most notable of the historic sights are the temples of the ancient citadel of Hoa Lu. This was the capital of Vietnam under the Dinh Dynasty, in the 10th century, and the early Le Dynasty. Sadly, the temples are all that remain of the citadel.

Sights

All the hotels are happy to tell you about the sights around Ninh Binh and many will furnish you with maps to help you get around. The caves and temples at **Hoa Lu** can easily be reached by bicycle – the return ride (about 25km) along the flat plain is enjoyable. The road to Hoa Lu winds through small habitations at the feet of the huge outcrops of limestone.

Once you have arrived it costs only a few dollars to be rowed a delightful ride of several hours in a small boat through a watery cave to a small temple; depending on the season the waters can be choked up with pretty purple water lilies. Banana and tablecloth-selling locals and young kids congregate around the temples of the Hoa Lu citadel which are accessed by a short walk.

The temples date from the 10th century and house painted statues of the Dinh and Le emperors and their advisers, as well as carved stone tortoises. Note also the wood carvings on the rafters of the roofs. Climbing the limestone crags affords glorious views of the surrounding country, if you can make it up the 265 steps.

To reach Hoa Lu turn north along Highway 1 for around 6km, then turn left along the rough road when you see a blue sign for Hoa Lu on the left, continue for another 6km.

If, instead of turning off for Hoa Lu, you continue north along Highway 1 for a further 6km you will find a less official **boat trip** leading to a temple in the river. This can be found by taking the small rough road on the left immediately before the road crosses the wide Nam Dinh river. The boats here are tiny wooden ones and the price is around $0.30 for a ride around the sights. However, the temple-keepers often decide on your arrival that the temple is closed.

Cuc Phuong National Park, around 65km north of Ninh Binh, can be visited in a day; going by car is likely to cost around $30-40, on the back of a motorbike will be $8-10 but this would be a long and tiring day.

There is a ticket office at the entrance to the park; entry costs $5 and you can hire a guide for around $10. A guide is highly recommended so that you can make the most of the jungly vegetation and the chance to see

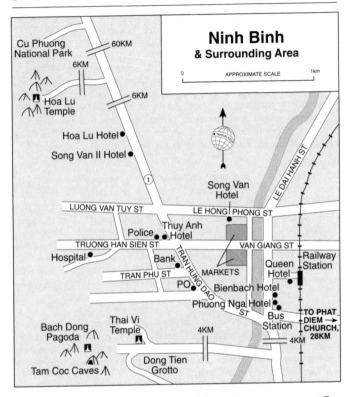

some of Vietnam's rarer flora and fauna. Mammals are very scarce at Cuc Phuong; the recently-discovered Tonkin Leaf-monkey is found here but is extremely rare. But the giant forest trees are a sight to behold as is the fabulous birdlife, including the blue-rumped pitta and fork-tailed sunbird. The best times to visit the park are in April, May and June; there is little point visiting when it has been raining hard during the monsoon season.

South and west of the city are the **Tam Coc caves** and the pagoda of Bich Dong. To cycle there head out on Highway 1 towards Ho Chi Minh City for 4km and turn right crossing a bridge over the Nam Dinh river. After another 4km you will reach the caves, and a further 3km will take you to the pagoda atop a limestone mountain. The caves are similar to those at Hoa Lu, though the boat trip costs a little more.

Bich Dong pagoda is well worth a visit, both for the enjoyable walk and views and because the several hundred of steps to ascend provide distance between you and all but the hardiest of tourists. Another way to achieve the same effect is to strike out into the countryside along the paths on a bicycle or on foot; there is much to see everywhere.

There is a bus service operating to the remarkable Vietnamese-style **Catholic church** at Phat Diem 28km south of Ninh Binh. Buses depart from the station at 7, 8, and 9am and cost 5000d.

PRACTICAL INFORMATION
Arrival and departure
Ninh Binh has only eight foreigner tickets for trains in each direction to allocate per day. Since this is below the usual number of foreigners in the town in peak season it is often impossible to get a ticket out on the same day, so try to book a day or two in advance.

Orientation and services
Ninh Binh's **railway station** is on the east of the town, very close to all the services including the bus station. Regular buses to Hanoi leave throughout the day, taking around 2 /2 hours. The **post office** is on the town's main road, Tran Hung Dao, which is also Highway 1. Close by on Tran Phu Road is a branch of **Vietcombank** which can change travellers' cheques and cash. It is open 7-11am, 1.30-5pm Monday to Saturday.

There is a police station on Truong Han Sieu St where it is possible to obtain **visa extensions**, though it is easier to obtain an extension by asking the staff at Queen Mini Hotel. A further 1.5km past the police station on Thuong Lan Ong St is the local **hospital**.

Where to stay
Ninh Binh has many good hotel options, including three friendly places very close to the bus and railway stations: *Queen Mini Hotel* (☎ 030-871874), half a minute's walk from the railway station at 21 Hoang Hoa Tham St, offers homely doubles with attached shower and air con for $8 and $10. The helpful hotel staff will arrange bikes etc and often invite guests to share a delicious family meal with them. Only a little further away is the delightful *Bienbach Hotel* (☎ 030-871449) at 195 Le Dai Hanh St. Clean, acceptable double rooms with attached shower are $8, or spacious doubles are $10. Slightly further away is *Phuong Nga Hotel* (☎ 030-871921), 197 Le Dai Hanh St, which offers an exceptionally cheap deal of two rooms, each at $8, with two, and three, double beds.

Other hotels include *Song Van* (☎ 030-71943), Le Hong Phong St, and *Song Van II* (☎ 030-860168), 1A National Road, with doubles at $15-20, and the clinical *Thuy Anh Hotel* (☎ 030-871602), 55a Truong Hon Sieu St, which is linked to Sinh Café and offers minibus tours of the area as do most hotels. For an up-market, but Soviet-style hotel, your one port of call is *Hoa Lu Hotel* which has 120 rooms ranging from $35 to $45. It also has some small charming rooms at $8 but cannot let these to foreigners.

Where to eat
Most of the hotels offer good fare; otherwise there are innumerable small rice and noodle outfits and bia hoi ventures on Le Dai Hanh St and all along Highway 1.

Hanoi

Hanoi is a city of lakes, a busy old quarter of crowded trading streets, home of the pith helmet and seat of government. It is also the capital because the North won the war, even though its economic capacity does not begin to approach that of Ho Chi Minh City (HCMC). This is made evident in the reams of Ho Chi Minh memorabilia in the city (such as his stilt house and embalmed corpse) and the power wielded from government offices along the tree-lined avenues is a less visible but more potent fact of victory.

Compared to HCMC, Hanoi is far less Westernized and modern and it is partly this that makes it such an engaging city, whether strolling along charming streets, visiting historical sites and museums or just taking your ease along the lakeshore. You can also buy luxury here, from the huge Daewoo Hotel or from the newly-opened Hanoi Hilton Hotel – a sign of the times is that this hotel opened just as the building of the old Hanoi Hilton (a vicious POW camp) was demolished. Hanoi is also the gateway to the superb train journeys to the north, west and east as well as the springboard to some excellent excursions.

HISTORY

The site on which Hanoi is built has been populated for many centuries. A few kilometres north of today's city centre are the still discernible remains of the Co Loa citadel from the 3rd century BC, Vietnam's earliest fortified citadel. Emperors made this the capital for the following millennium but for almost all this time Vietnam was ruled by the conquering Chinese invaders.

Emperor Ngo Quyen was the first Vietnamese emperor to rule from the citadel in the 10th century after he led a defeat of the Chinese armada in the Bach Dang river delta (see p40). Emperor Ly Thai To followed on, founding the Le Dynasty and establishing Hanoi as a centre of government after seeing off the final Chinese invaders with a golden sword given him by the spirit of Hoan Kiem lake according to legend (see p247).

Hanoi continued to hold the reins of power until rivalries resulted in the country being split in 1620. Different houses ruled Vietnam from Hanoi in the north, and from Hué in the south but both claimed allegiance to the later Le Dynasty based in Hanoi. This schizophrenic situation lasted until the Tay Son rebellion of the 1770s overthrew both houses, only to give in to a French-supported lone survivor of the family which had ruled the south. His forces captured the south and marched into Hanoi claiming it.

In 1802 Hanoi fell to this self-styled Emperor Gia Long, and Hué, not Hanoi, was now the capital of the country, which later that century also became a colony.

Hanoi didn't become the capital of the whole of Vietnam again until 1975 – a 173-year gap. Between times it was the capital of what the French called Tonkin, the north of the country, while Hué remained the capital of the central part, Annam, and Saigon the capital of Cochinchina. During the early period of colonial rule Hanoi was enriched by the building of fine sweeping boulevards, an elegant opera house, and countless ochre villas graced with dark green shutters which today complement the ubiquitous dark green pith helmets as charmingly as anything else in the city. Later, towards the end of the 19th century, Hanoi formed the centre-piece of Governor Doumer's great railway projects of the north with spurs shooting west, north and east.

During WWII anti-colonial Viet Minh activity grew especially in the North, with Hanoi as its capital. And when the Japanese occupation was summarily ended after the dropping of the second H-bomb on Japan, Ho Chi Minh, who had returned from his time raising revolutionaries in China and the mountains of Vietnam, was quick to exploit the power vacuum. Backed by Viet Minh demonstrations rocking Hanoi, on 2 September 1945 from Hanoi's Ba Dinh square he declared the independence of the Democratic Republic of Vietnam. And so began 30 years of struggle with French and American forces operating from the south.

But the years of privations and strafing by B-52 bombers ended with victory for the North, for Hanoi, for Communism, and for ten years until the North launched market reforms. Still today Hanoi hasn't got near Saigon's economic prosperity but its very isolation from the West is what makes it such a delightful place to spend time in.

SIGHTS

Hoan Kiem lake

This is a lovely circle of water to find in the centre of a city, and it has a typically charming Vietnamese legend explaining the origin of its name and importance to the city. According to the myth Emperor Ly Thai To fought and won against the Chinese invaders with a gleaming sword he had retrieved from the lake while out fishing.

Once victorious the emperor returned to thank the lake's spirit with the trusty sword in hand but no sooner was he on the lake than a golden turtle suddenly appeared, sent from the Gods, and clutched the sword, returning it to the deep. Hence the emperor christened the water 'Lake of the restored sword'. As a latter-day monument the pretty Turtle tower was built on an islet on the lake – and today it is often used as an emblem of Hanoi.

Meanwhile, on the northern shore of the lake Ngoc Son temple (Jade mountain) was built two centuries after the emperor's heavenly experience to commemorate the prosaic military victories by General Tran Hung Dao. It is remarkable as a temple not so much for its interior as for the path leading to it – after the red bridge called 'a flood of morning sunlight' you come upon the 'brush tower' (proclaiming in Chinese characters 'a pen to write on the blue sky') – and the quiet shady vantage point over the lake you find at the end.

Old quarter (or the 36 streets)

The hustle, bustle and craftsmanship of the old quarter (or the 36 streets) is what many people think of as the essence of Hanoi. And certainly it is an area full of local colour which is great to explore. It too owes much of its history to Emperor Ly Thai To, for it was during his reign of independence from China in the 11th century that the old quarter gained its reputation as a crafts area, as the tiny workshop villages which clustered around the palace walls evolved into craft guilds. The streets each became named after the craft made and sold there.

The names have survived as has the practice of having a different craft/product on each street; sometimes the craft is still the same as the street's name. So, Hang Bac means 'silver street' and today jewellery and funeral tablets are made here; Hang Chieu, mat street, still produces mats; Hang Gai means 'silk street' and silk clothes are still sold here; Hang Ma means 'street of religious paper flags' and paper goods are still made here; and Hang Thiec, meaning 'tin street', still produces masses of tin goods.

The houses which make up the old quarter are also very distinctively Hanoian. They were built as 'tube houses' – 3m wide but sometimes reaching back as much as 60m. This was because shopkeepers were taxed according to the width of their shopfront. Many of these houses still stand, which is a testimony to the level of craftsmanship in their construction, for in the absence of cement the bricks were held together by a recipe of sugar, cane juice and lime.

One Pillar Pagoda

Another popular symbol of Hanoi, the One Pillar Pagoda is a charmingly designed tiny place of worship only a little overshadowed by the vast Ho Chi Minh museum nearby. Supported by a single pillar it was built in the 11th century during the reign of Emperor Ly Thai Trong to represent a lotus flower – and in the summer it is surrounded by many flowering lotus plants as if to emphasize the resemblance. It's thought the heirless emperor had the pagoda built and dedicated to the goddess Quan Am because he saw her in a dream holding a lotus plant and a baby boy. The story then runs that, once mollified in this way, the goddess granted him a son. Sadly, this is not the pagoda's only history – the French blew it up as one of their last acts in leaving Hanoi in 1954. This reconstruction apparently retains

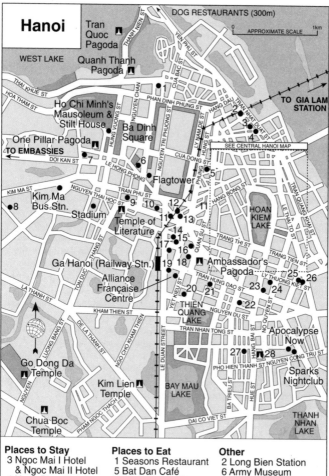

Places to Stay
3 Ngoc Mai I Hotel
  & Ngoc Mai II Hotel
4 Hang Phuc Hotel
8 Hanoi Daewoo Hotel
11 Hoang Cuong Hotel
12 Cuu Long Hotel
15 Saigon Hotel
19 Hotel 30/4

Places to Eat
1 Seasons Restaurant
5 Bat Dan Café
13 Kinh Do, Café 252
14 Indochine
21 Com Chay Veg
  Restaurant
22 Soho Café/Deli
23 Le Bistrot
24 Le Splendide
25 Nam Phuong
26 Hue Quan
  Restaurant

Other
2 Long Bien Station
6 Army Museum
7 Ho Chi Minh Museum
9 Fine Arts Museum
10 Sunset Pub
16 Bia Hoi
17 Fansland Cinema
18 Site of former
  'Hanoi Hilton'
20 Bia Hoi
27 QT
28 Hai Ba Trung Temple

the design well enough, but the concrete pillar, instead of wood, is an unwelcome giveaway. The One Pillar pagoda is in the Ba Dinh area in the shadow of the Ho Chi Minh Museum.

Other pagodas and temples

Ambassador pagoda (Quan Su), 73 Quan Su St, is probably Hanoi's most impressive pagoda, appropriate given it is the centre of Buddhism in the city. It is called the Ambassador's pagoda because it was originally built, in the 15th century, to accommodate Buddhists from Cambodia, Laos and Champa.

Also worth seeing is **Hai Ba Trung temple** on Tho Lao St, 2km south of Hoan Kiem lake. This temple commemorates the rebellion against the Chinese in the 1st century AD led by the Trung sisters (see p39) and holds a statue depicting them.

Hanoi's **Temple of Literature** houses what was once the National Academy of Learning, an institute in the Confucian tradition. Strolling along pleasant paths between elegant gates you walk through courtyards dedicated to different elements of learning and come across sanctuaries to Confucius and his disciples, as well as stele recording the names and dates of those successful candidates in the triennial exams for doctors of literature during the Le Dynasty (15th-18th centuries). It is worth visiting the temple at lunchtime, for at 1pm daily there is a concert using traditional instruments.

At the end of the first courtyard in the temple you pass through a gate symbolising the attainment of talent and accomplished virtue. The second courtyard symbolizes success, and at its end the two gates lead you to the third symbolising the crystallization of letters and the magnificence of letters. The fourth is aptly named the Sage courtyard as its role is to honour Confucius and his 72 disciples. The fifth holds the remains of the academy – unfortunately this was destroyed by bombing in 1947, and still 50 years later there are no plans to restore it.

If you take a ride (by bicycle is delightful once you have got a bit out of town) along the road to the east of West Lake you will come across some other pagodas and temples.

Ho Chi Minh's mausoleum and stilt house

Despite his express instructions to be cremated and his ashes scattered over his beloved country, in the great Soviet tradition Ho Chi Minh's colleagues embalmed his body for future generations to honour and built this cold, impressive mausoleum to house it.

If you can take the rather grisly nature of it, seeing Ho's impassive face and small still body is quite an experience, particularly as you are likely to file around the sarcophagus in the midst of perhaps a hundred Vietnamese pilgrims. But be aware that between September and December Ho is taken to Russia for embalming maintenance.

The mausoleum is open daily except Monday and Friday from 8 to 11am and is free, but there are very strict entry requirements in terms of dress (no shorts, short sleeves etc) and the appropriate behaviour required (nothing indecorous!). It is worth hanging around outside to see the changing of the white-suited guard on the hour.

In the parkland near the mausoleum is Ho's stilt house where he lived, when not hiding from B-52s in the jungle, from 1958 to 1969. The simple unassuming house with the desk and telephone he used to carry out the business of government and of war, are apparently just as he left them. There is also a well-tended garden.

Museums

Ho Chi Minh Museum behind the One Pillar pagoda is possibly the most visited museum in Hanoi – presumably by people who don't know that it's one of the most surreal experiences you can legally have inside a public building. For 20,000d you get to walk round the symbolic visual representation of the 'past' and 'future' of Ho's life which ranges from a vast plastic table and chairs (the table replete with huge plastic food) fixed diagonally to the wall, to a massive mock-up of a Ford (car) which was a commercial failure – to symbolize America's military failure. It's great fun and highly bemusing; don't expect to learn much about Ho Chi Minh. The museum is open Tuesday to Sunday 8-11.30am and 1.30-4pm and is unmissable being the huge concrete building between the One Pillar pagoda and Ho's mausoleum.

The **Army Museum** is probably the next most visited museum and deserves at least this ranking. Outside you can wander freely among French, American and Soviet fighter jets while inside the star exhibits are the meticulously laid out display of the battle of Dien Bien Phu and the actual T-54 tank, No 843 of the 203rd Armoured Brigade, which first blasted into the compound of the Presidential Palace when Saigon was declared captured; beside the tank there also lies a fragment of the gate it drove into. The museum is on Dien Bien Phu St, next to the flag tower which is a popular symbol of Hanoi. Entry costs 15,000d and the museum is open Tuesday to Sunday 8-11.30am and 1.30-4pm.

If the army museum hasn't satiated your appetite for the machines of war you can head to the **Air Force Museum**. This has a variety of, mostly Soviet, fighter planes, helicopters etc as well as a range of smaller, mostly US, artillery such as machine guns, hand grenades etc. The museum is on Truong Ching St in the Dong Da district of Hanoi, around 6km south-west of the city centre.

Hanoi has a few other museums of which by far the most worthwhile for non-Vietnamese speakers are: the **History Museum**, 1 Pham Ngu Lao St, notable for its artefacts from Vietnam's ancient history illustrating the successive struggles against invaders and including what the museum claims are some of the bamboo stakes planted by General Tran Hung Dao in the Bach Dang river (see p42); the **Women's Museum**, 36 Ly Thuong Kiet St, which is large and well kept and worth seeing especially for its visual representations of Ao Co, the legendary queen who gave birth to all of Vietnam's first sons, and for its display of the costumes of the ethnic minorities of Vietnam; and the **Fine Arts Museum**, 66 Nguyen Thai Hoc St, which has an impressive collection of traditional Vietnamese paintings, sculptures and lacquer work.

PRACTICAL INFORMATION
Arrival and departure
By train Hanoi has three railway stations – Ga Hanoi, Long Bien and Gia Lam.

All express trains go from Ga Hanoi which is at 120 Le Duan St, at the western end of Tran Hung Dao St, 1km west of Hoan Kiem lake (although trains to the Chinese border and Haiphong leave from platforms at the back of the station and deposit you here, requiring a walk or cyclo drive through small winding streets to the front). The station is housed in a fine building with a booking office (open daily 7.30am-12 and 1-4.30pm) from where you can book tickets for trains from all of Hanoi's stations, and with taxis which drive along the platforms themselves.

Long Bien station is on the western bank of the Red River at the foot of Long Bien Bridge, while Gia Lam station is 5km east across Long Bien bridge (note that cyclos cannot cross Long Bien bridge so they have to take a circuitous route to Ga Gia Lam.) Both stations are considerably less plush than Ga Hanoi. Non-express trains go east to Haiphong from Long Bien, while non-express trains to Kep and Dong Dang at the Chinese border go from Gia Lam.

There are trains from Hanoi to China passing through Beijing via Kep and Lang Son twice a week, see p312 for times; the journey takes 54 hours. There is a change of trains to the rather more luxurious Chinese variety and a three-hour wait at Dong Dang. Trains leave Beijing at 8.30am on Mondays and Fridays.

By bus Hanoi has three main bus terminals, none of which are central.

Kim Ma bus station, serving the north-west including Lao Cai and Dien Bien Phu, is 1km west of Ga Hanoi opposite 166 Nguyen Thai Hoc St.

Gia Lam bus station is across the Red River near the train station of the same name about 5km from central Hanoi; buses from here serve places north and east of Hanoi including Haiphong, Halong Bay and Lang Son.

Giap Bat bus station is 7km south of central Hanoi and serves areas south of the city.

By shared taxi If you arrive by shared taxi the journey will end at the bus station which serves the area you have come from, unless you arrange otherwise with the driver. This also means that the relevant bus stations are good places to pick up shared taxis from Hanoi – before 10-11am is best. But there is also a shared taxi rank near the top of Hoan Kiem lake along the north-west side.

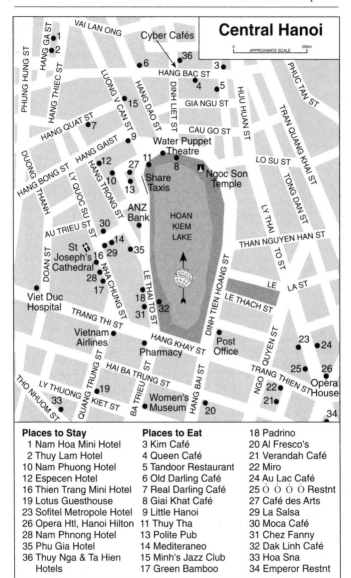

Central Hanoi

0   APPROXIMATE SCALE   250m

Cyber Cafés

HANG BAC ST

GIA NGU ST

CAU GO ST

Water Puppet Theatre

Ngoc Son Temple

Share Taxis

ANZ Bank

HOAN KIEM LAKE

St Joseph's Cathedral

Viet Duc Hospital

TRANG THI ST

Vietnam Airlines

Pharmacy

Post Office

Women's Museum

Opera House

Places to Stay
1 Nam Hoa Mini Hotel
2 Thuy Lam Hotel
10 Nam Phuong Hotel
12 Especen Hotel
16 Thien Trang Mini Hotel
19 Lotus Guesthouse
23 Sofitel Metropole Hotel
26 Opera Htl, Hanoi Hilton
28 Nam Phnong Hotel
35 Phu Gia Hotel
36 Thuy Nga & Ta Hien
   Hotels

Places to Eat
3 Kim Café
4 Queen Café
5 Tandoor Restaurant
6 Old Darling Café
7 Real Darling Café
8 Giai Khat Café
9 Little Hanoi
11 Thuy Tha
13 Polite Pub
14 Mediteraneo
15 Minh's Jazz Club
17 Green Bamboo

18 Padrino
20 Al Fresco's
21 Verandah Café
22 Miro
24 Au Lac Café
25 Ö Ö Ö Ö Restnt
27 Café des Arts
29 La Salsa
30 Moca Café
31 Chez Fanny
32 Dak Linh Café
33 Hoa Sna
34 Emperor Restnt

❏ **Embassies in Hanoi**

Algeria (☎ 825 3865), 13 Phan Chu Trinh St; **Argentina** (☎ 831 5578), Daeha Business Centre, 360 Kim Ma; **Australia** (☎ 831 7755), Van Phuc Compound; **Bangladesh** (☎ 823 1625), Van Phuc Compound; **Belgium** (☎ 845 2263), 48 Nguyen Thai Hoc St; **Brazil** (☎ 843 0817) 14 Thuy Khue St; **Bulgaria** (☎ 845 2908), 358 Van Phuc Compound; **Cambodia** (☎ 825 3788), 71 Tran Hung Dao St; **Canada** (☎ 823 5500), 31 Hung Vuong St; **China** (☎ 845 3736), 46 Hoang Dieu; **Cuba** (☎ 825 2426), 65 Ly Thuong Kiet St; **Czech Republic** (☎ 845 4131), 13 Chu Van An St; **Denmark** (☎ 823 1888), 19 Dien Bien Phu St; **Egypt** (☎ 846 0219), Villa 6, Van Phuc Compound; **European Union** (☎ 934 1300), 7F, 56 Ly Thai To St, Metropole Centre; **Finland** (☎ 826 6788), 31 Hai Ba Trung St; **France** (☎ 825 2719), 57 Tran Hung Dao St; **Germany** (☎ 843 0245), 29 Tran Phu St; **Hungary** (☎ 845 2858), 43-47 Dien Bien Phu St; **India** (☎ 824 9489), 58-60 Tran Hung Dao St; **Indonesia** (☎ 825 7969), 50 Ngo Quyen St; **Israel** (☎ 843 3140), 68 Nguyen Thai Hoc St; **Italy** (☎ 825 6246), 9 Le Phung Hieu St; **Japan** (☎ 846 3000), 27 Lieu Giai St; **Laos** (☎ 825 4576), 22 Tran Binh Trong St; **Malaysia** (☎ 845 3009) Block A3, Van Phuc Compound; **Myanmar** (☎ 845 3369), Block A3, Van Phuc Compound; **Netherlands** (☎ 843 0605), D1 Van Phuc Compound; **New Zealand** (☎ 824 1481), 32 Hang Bai St; **Norway** (☎ 826 2111), 56 Ly Thai To St; **Philippines** (☎ 825 7948), 27B Tran Hung Dao St; **Poland** (☎ 845 2027), 3 Chua Mot Cot St; **Romania** (☎ 845 2014), 5 Le Hong Phong St; **Russia** (☎ 8454632), 58 Tran Phu St; **Singapore** (☎ 823 3966), 41-43 Tran Phu St; **South Korea** (☎ 831 5111), Daeha Business Centre; **Slovakia** (☎ 845 4334), 6 Le Hong Phong St; **Sweden** (☎ 845 4825), 2 Road 358, Van Phuc Compound; **Switzerland** (☎ 823 2019), 77B Kim Ma St; **Thailand** (☎ 823 5092), 63-65 Hoang Dieu St; **Turkey** (☎ 822 2460), 4 Do Tuong St; **UK** (☎ 825 2510), 31 Hai Ba Trung St; **United States** (☎ 843 1500), 7 Lang Ha St; **Yugoslavia** (☎ 845 2343), 47 Tran Phu St.

By air   Hanoi's Noi Bai airport is around 35km north of Hanoi. The journey to the city centre takes slightly under an hour and you have the choice of taking a government-run taxi (drivers will approach you at the baggage reclaim area, expect to pay $20), or go outside and bargain for a cheaper fare, but if you do this you may find yourself being asked to pay the toll over the bridge just outside the airport (though this should only be $1 each).

The cheapest way to the airport is to take the Vietnam Airlines bus ($4) from the booking office at 1 Quang Trung St, but in the summer you may have to book a day in advance. Alternatively book a shared taxi from

the travellers' cafés, such as Darling Café, which also offer the cheapest way to book an individual taxi to the airport – $13.

It is possible to fly direct to Hanoi from Bangkok, Hong Kong, Seoul, Taipei, Vientiane, Moscow, and Nanning and Guangzhou in China. Changing in Bangkok, Hong Kong or HCMC enables you to get to most destinations in the rest of the world. (Vietnam Airlines makes regular domestic flights from Hanoi to many destinations – see p89).

To book an international flight you can talk to a mini travel agent, such as the travellers' cafés, or contact the airline directly, but for long-distance

❏ **Airline offices**
Aeroflot (☎ 825 2376), 4 Trang Thi St; **Air France** (☎ 825 3484), 1 Ba Trieu St; **Cathay Pacific** (☎ 826 7298), 49 Hai Ba Trung St; **China Southern Airlines** (☎ 826 9233), Binh Minh Hotel, 27 Ly Thai Tho St; **Japan Airlines** (☎ 826 6693), 1 Ba Trieu St; **Lao Aviation** (☎ 826 6538), 41 Quang Trung St; **Malaysia Airlines** (☎ 826 8820), 15 Ngo Quyen St; **Pacific Airlines** (☎ 825 2684), 31B Trang Thi St; **Singapore Airlines** (☎ 826 8803) 17 Ngo Quyen St; **Thai Airways International** (☎ 826 6893), 44 Ly thuong Kiet St; **Vietnam Airlines** (☎ 8250888, or 826 8913), 1 Quang Trung St.

flights be aware that you are much more likely to get discounted seats from travel agents in Bangkok, and a one-way flight to Bangkok costs only $175. To reconfirm a flight (extremely wise) you should speak to the airline directly – there is almost always someone who speaks good English. See the box above for details of the airline offices in Hanoi.

British Airways has opened a handling office in Hanoi (☎ 974 0041) at 330 Ba Trieu St through Trans Viet Promotions Co Ltd, with a view to flying directly to Vietnam in the future.

Orientation

Hanoi's lakes are its most enduring symbol and they are also the key to working out where you are in the city. Hoan Kiem lake is in many ways the spiritual heart of the city and much of interest is found near its shores. Around the west and north is the main tourist area, complete with the hectic picturesque old quarter.

Off the eastern shores the smart Sofitel Metropole Hotel and the Opera House are located in the midst of grand avenues around the old state bank and post office. South of the lake are several wide French-inspired streets the most northerly of which, Trang Thi St, has many useful services such as bookshops and pharmacies while on the parallel streets south of this are several smart eateries as well as good bia hoi joints. If you venture further south, to the area east of Bay Mau lake, you will find streets full of life and mostly tourist free.

There are lakes dotted all around Hanoi, which is bounded to the east by the Red River, but the other most noticeable lake is West Lake, which is indeed to the north-west. This area is spawning urbanization and has seen the development of some very expensive business hotels, which sadly even before the Asian crisis were encountering financial difficulty.

The lake is very beautiful, especially at dawn and along its eastern shores are many out of the way temples. South of the lake there is substantial greenery and landmarks such as the One Pillar Pagoda and Ho Chi Minh's mausoleum as well as many of the city's embassies.

Services
Post and telecommunications The post office at 75 Dinh Tien Hoang St is open daily 7am-8pm and offers postal, telephone, fax, telex and a telegram service that is available 24 hours a day. Note that, unlike in smaller cities, you can just post letters in a red box and don't need to supervise them being stamped.

Poste restante services are also available here, the office is open every day except Monday 7.30am-12 and 1-4.30pm. You need to bring your passport to collect any items. Next door to the post office are several international parcel service companies, including DHL and Federal Express.

Hang Bac St has the greatest collection of cyber cafés and thus the cheapest connection rate at 300d per minute.

Money There are branches of several international banks in Hanoi, but Vietkombank gives the best deal on changing money, except that you can use a Cirrus or Delta card at the ATM at ANZ Grindlays Bank at 14 Ly Thai To St (☎ 825 8190) (on the western shore of Hoan Kiem lake).

Hanoi's modern Vietkombank is at 23 Phan Chu Trinh St. Here you are charged 0.5 per cent commission to change travellers' cheques into dong, and 1 per cent to change them into dollars (there is a minimum $1 commission). You have to pay 3 per cent to withdraw money on a credit or debit card.

If you need to change travellers' cheques or US dollars out of bank hours several jewellers in the city run official exchanges such as the one at 3 Hang Bong St, but of course they charge a higher commission. Whatever you do avoid the moneychangers around the post office unless you actually want to be scammed.

Visa extensions The police station dealing with visa extensions doesn't welcome direct approaches from tourists, however well dressed. You are much better off going through one of Hanoi's mini travel agents such as Green Bamboo (☎ 826 8752) at 42 Nha Chung St.

Embassies There are many foreign embassies in Hanoi and, with the final razing of the old POW camp for American GIs known as the Hanoi Hilton, America is even establishing its first-ever embassy in Hanoi and the first in the country since the ignominious departure of Ambassador Martin on 30 April 1975 (see p70).

See the box on p254 for details of the embassies in Hanoi.

Medical Viet Duc Hospital (☎ 825 3531), 40 Tranh Thi St, has English-speaking doctors and can carry out emergency surgery. A consultation here, or with the English-speaking doctors at the intensive care unit at Bach Mai Hospital (☎ 869 3525) on Giai Phong St, 2km south of Hoan Kiem lake, will cost around $10-20.

The Swedish Clinic (☎ 825 2464), opposite the Swedish embassy at 358 Van Phuc St in the embassy quarter, is a very good place to turn for medical or dental problems if you can afford the $80 consultation, or if you are covered by insurance. A doctor is on call 24 hours a day.

Asia Emergency Assistance (☎ 821 3555), 4 Tran Hung Dao St, can offer routine medical care for a $60 consultation fee and offer advice for emergency evacuation plans.

There are several good pharmacies in the city; the largest is at 3 Trang Thi St (☎ 825 5998) at the bottom of Hoan Kiem lake.

Local transport

Hanoi is packed with spacious cyclos (larger than those in HCMC) but the influx of young men from the countryside anxious to earn a few dong as a cyclo driver is just one reason why Hanoi's government has decided to restrict cyclos' freedom of movement by banning them from a large, and increasing, number of streets. So, while you may have a crowd of cyclos gathering

---

(**Opposite**) **Top**: Temple on the shores of West Lake, Hanoi. **Bottom**: Hoan Kiem Lake in the centre of Hanoi is popular with local people as a place to relax.

outside your hotel and while they are still a great way to get about be aware that they may have to take a circuitous route.

Cyclo drivers do have the advantage of knowing how to navigate Hanoi's twisting streets which are a challenge if you try your own pedal power – bicycles are available for hire from many hotels for $1 a day.

Riding pillion on a Honda om is also a common method of getting about, you can pick them up on street corners, or watch out for the words xe om scrawled on trees. If you are in real need and are willing to pay, almost any car or motorbike is potentially a taxi. Otherwise, meter taxis roam the streets at reasonably regular intervals showing a red light on the dashboard if they are empty.

Tours Hanoi's travellers' cafés offer good deals on tours to Halong Bay, Sapa, the Perfume Pagoda and the north-west. They can also organize the cheapest taxi and tourist bus deals in the city as well as organize a trip of several days by jeep.

The cafés are mostly found in the old quarter, such as **Real Darling Café** (☎/🖨 825 6562) at 33 Hang Quat St, or **Kim Café** (☎ 928 1378, 🖳 kimcafe@hn.vnn.vn) at 135 Hang Bac St, although **Green Bamboo café** (☎ 828 6504, 🖨 826 4949, 🖳 bamboo-tours@fpt.vn) at 2B Trang Thi St at the bottom of Hoan Kiem lake is an exception. (Beware that bad reports have been received from travellers about the tours organized by **Queen Café**, 65 Hang Bac St.) The tours are good value for money if you can bear being herded around in a tourist minibus. They can usually be booked only a day in advance.

☐ **Area code**
The area code for Hanoi is ☎ 04

A two-day tour to Halong Bay including a standard hotel costs around $24 per person, or a three-day tour taking in Cat Ba Island as well increases the cost to around $35. Trips further afield to the north-west can be costly as jeeps are the only suitable vehicles – prices are somewhat negotiable with Kim Café usually having the best deal.

Travellers' cafés can also organize more luxurious trips and you still don't have to pay the excessive prices of government-run Vietnam Tourism.

Where to stay
Budget There is a reasonable amount of cheap accommodation in Hanoi and it is at least all central – near Hoan Kiem lake and mostly around the old quarter. Probably the best is **Real Darling Café** (☎ 826 9386), 33 Hang Quat St, which has dorm beds for $3, singles for $8 and pleasant doubles from $10. The rooms highest up tend to be the best and even those which don't have private balconies are near the roof garden. Close by, if you can stand the rather musty atmosphere, is **Queen Café** (☎ 882 6086), 65 Hang Bac St, which has small, hot and dingy singles for $4.

Scattered around the central area are nine **Especen** hotels which offer average rooms from $6; the main hotel (☎ 825 8845), 79E Hang Trong St, will phone around for a room and show you to the hotel. A better option if one of their few rooms is free is either **Lotus Guesthouse** (☎ 826 8642), 42V Ly Thuong Kiet St, which has some dorm beds for $4 and five other rooms from

---

(**Opposite**) Ho Chi Minh's mausoleum, Hanoi (see p250), was built in 1974 and modelled on Lenin's mausoleum in Moscow. Top Soviet embalmers were also involved in preserving the body, which is visited by pilgrims and tourists.

$6 or *Nam Hoa Mini-Hotel* (☎ 825 7603), 49 Hang Ga St, which has well-equipped rooms for $11.

Mid-range There is a substantial choice in the middle-price range. *Thien Trang Mini Hotel* (☎ 826 9823), 24 Nha Chung St, south of Hoan Kiem lake, is a friendly place, overrun with well-fed cats and dogs, and with a French-speaking proprietor, offering rooms from $15 to 25, all with IDD phone, TV, and air-con and some with fine views. Be certain, however, to confirm exactly the price you have agreed as we have heard of several incidences of the owners getting shirty over the bill. Meanwhile, next door at No 26 is *Nam Phuong Hotel* (☎ 8246894), which has rooms with balcony for $12 and the softest sheets in Vietnam. *Green Bamboo Café* (☎ 826 8752, ▨ 8264949, ▭ bamboo@netnam.org.vn), 42 Nha Chung St, has four rooms only but they are well kept and cost $15.

Up at the north of the lake *Thuy Lam Hotel* (☎ 828 1788), 17B Hang Ga St, is a quirky hotel perfect for bird lovers – provided you don't mind them being kept in cages – as the in-house aviary sends the twittering sound of tiny birds through the house. The rooms are more prosaic but are nice enough with doubles from $17.

Back in the heart of the old quarter two good-value hotels that are next door to each other are: *Thuy Nga Hotel* (☎ 826 6053), 24C Ta Hien St, which is a cosy hotel with very clean rooms housing big beds and stuffed with ornate wooden furniture for $15, and *Ta Hien Hotel* (☎ 825 5888), 22 Ta Hien St, which has very friendly staff who can show you their windowless rooms ($6) or their larger rooms with fan ($12-15). A little further from the lake *Hang Phuc Hotel* (meaning happy family) (☎ 825 3290), 3 Thanh Ha St, has good large clean doubles, some with balconies, from $12. Despite its name the hotel is a

little impersonal but the area is full of bustle. Back near the lake *Nam Phuong Hotel* (☎ 8258030), 16 Bao Khanh St, is a small friendly hotel whose rooms ($20) have fine balcony views.

The good *Phu Gia Hotel* (☎ 825 5493, ▨ 825 9207) at 136 Hang Trong St has some rooms high up near the roof garden with lovely views overlooking Hoan Kiem lake. Small viewless rooms start at around $15, while spacious lake-view ones go for $20-35 depending on your bargaining powers and who is on duty.

If you're happy to pay a bit more try small Cua Dong St where there is both *Ngoc Mai I Hotel* (☎ 828 6236) at No 7 which has good rooms with nice furniture and a fairly cosy atmosphere for $30, and *Ngoc Mai II Hotel* (☎ 828 2083, ▨ 828 2131), at No 27, which has more impressive but less cosy rooms from $25 to 30 with dining tables and fine views from the balcony. You can also satisfy any desire to make a phone call whilst sitting in a bath since the phone is in the bathroom.

There are a few decent hotels near the railway station. Of these, the cheapest and closest is *Hotel 30/4* (meaning 30th April, the date North Vietnamese troops took Saigon) (☎ 825 2611), 115 Tran Hung Dao St. Given its name it's not surprising it's a government-run hotel – what is surprising is how friendly the staff are and how good the rooms are for the cost, $8-10 gets you large echo chambers with good shared bathrooms, or you can pay $30 for your own bath.

A short walk north from the station there is an area around the intersection of Trang Thi and Dien Bien Phu streets where there are many hotels mostly patronized by Vietnamese people rather than foreign tourists. Two such are the friendly *Hoang Cuong Hotel* (☎ 826 9927), 15 Nguyen Thai Hoc St, which has rooms with wooden furniture for $20-30, and the very pleasant *Cuu Long Hotel* (☎ 823 3541), 6 Dinh Ngang St (just off Nguyen Thai Hoc St), which has good rooms, some with large balconies, from $20 to 35.

Up-market You can certainly pay as much as in HCMC for an up-market hotel, but you don't get the charm of the historical hotels there. In Hanoi most hotels, with the exception of *Sofitel Metropole* (☎ 826 6919, 🖹 826 6920) at 15 Ngo Quyen St, are orientated to business. Sofitel Metropole is a luxurious hotel with a wonderful Parisian feel which charges a mere $200 a night for a room. But if modern-day flash is more your style for this kind of money you need to be at *Daewoo Hotel* (☎ 831 5000, 🖹 831 5010) in west Hanoi at the Daeha Centre. Or try the ultra-new *Hanoi Hilton Opera* – next to the Opera House. Close to the station, at 80 Ly Thuong Kiet St, is the clinical *Saigon Hotel* (☎ 826 8505); rooms are upwards of $100.

It is hard to find the other expensive hotels in the city (around $100 a night) such as the Alpo, Galaxy, or Huu Nghi worth the money.

Where to eat
By far the greatest of Hanoi's speciality dishes is one by the name of *bun cha*. Bun cha is much like any really good bowl of noodle soup, except for two added ingredients – heaps of cold fresh greens which you add progressively to give flavour and texture, and succulent sweet-smelling grilled pork. Sitting down at a streetside café gorging yourself on bun cha is an opportunity not to be missed (unless you're vegetarian I suppose). Look out for signs advertising bun cha as you can't get it everywhere; note that the price basically depends on how much pork you want.

As ever, the cheapest places to eat are in the markets, but for the next step up, or for evening eating there are several little streets in the city teeming with competing pho stalls. Try the street which links Hang Bong St and Dien Bien Phu St, or the small road connecting Hang Quat St with Hong Gai St, or the collection of stalls at the top of Hoan Kiem lake just around the corner from the puppet theatre. There is also a good crab stall outside 45 Cau Go St. Sometimes you will find that bia hoi stalls also do good cheap food. *Little Hanoi* (☎ 926 0168) at 51 Luong Van Can St is a new good Vietnamese restaurant in the old quarter which has become immediately popular.

If you feel like something more exotic, there are a host of restaurants characterized by thatched roofs on Duong Nghi Tam St between West Lake and the Red River which can fill you up with a whole snake (first the blood then the meat – which is a bit like turkey, but more chewy) or even with dog – a bit like roast beef but more scary. Dog is reasonably cheap, but expect to pay upwards of $10 for a snake – the price will depend on whether you opt for a bog-standard grass snake, or a much more pricey Boa constrictor (do make sure it's dead first).

❏ **North v south – attitudes to food**
People from Hanoi, whether or not they have ever been to South Vietnam, will tell you how much they detest the food there. And vice versa of course.

The key difference is that southerners sprinkle sugar into almost every dish and northerners don't. Certainly northern food is in general far less aromatic but of course, there are certain northern specialities, such as *bun cha* which are truly delicious, and there are many restaurants in Hanoi which offer fabulous food and you can even go wild on snake or dog.

❏ When to eat dog
Bear in mind that the first half of the lunar month is an inauspicious time to eat dog, so dog-meat only restaurants will be closed, while the second half of the lunar month is an increasingly auspicious time to eat dog so the restaurants get fuller and fuller until the last day of the lunar month when they are packed.

For up-market Vietnamese food Hanoi has a fine selection of restaurants. *Indochine* (☎ 824 6097), 16 Nam Ngu St, has long been a favourite with the expat community for its food and good service. *Nam Phuong* (☎ 824 0926), 19 Phan Chu Trinh St, is another excellent choice and *The Seasons* (☎ 843 5444), 95B Quan Thanh St, is a beautifully presented old colonial home with great food. But the best restaurant surely has to be the sumptuous *Emperor* (☎ 08-8268801, 🖳 emperor@fpt.vn) at 18B Le Thanh Tong St, which serves up exquisite Vietnamese food in truly imperial surroundings.

Another restaurant in a French villa is *Com Duc Vien* (☎ 943 0081) at 13 Pho Ngo Thi Nham St. There are several places serving Huéan food, of which the best still seems to be *Quan Hue* (☎ 826 4062), 6 Ly Thuong Kiet St, where the rather sparse decor is made up for by the gorgeously aromatic food – the steamboats are particularly good. Hanoi has two fine vegetarian restaurants – *Com Chay* (☎ 826 6140), 79A Tran Hung Dao St, and *Bodhi Tree restaurant* (☎ 839 4645) at 265 Vo Van Tan St.

But if you want to opt out of Vietnamese food, there is a wealth of choice for Western foods. Hanoi's travellers' cafés whip up the usual fare of delicious little eats like banana pancakes – particularly worth trying are *Old Darling Café* (☎ 853 4545), 142 Hang Bac St, and *Green Bamboo* (☎ 826 8752) at 42 Nha Chung St. For pizza, pasta or burgers it's worth frequenting Bao Khanh St near Hoan Kiem lake and the vicinity around it as there are a number of popular Western-style eateries.

A bit further from the lake is *Al Fresco*, 231 Hai Ba Trung St, where the Australian owner ensures you get enough beefburgers and pizza to keep you from hunger. For snacks, a popular eat-in or take-aways is *Cock-a-doodle-doo* which in Vietnamese translates as 'O O O O!' (☎ 828 8520), 38 Le Thai To St; it serves great fried chicken. Or check out the good atmosphere of *La Salsa* (☎ 828 9052) at 25 Nha Tho St, which has a small but good Mediterranean menu. La Salsa is run by a Canadian but it attracts Vietnamese as well as foreigners. Next door, at No 23, is *Mediteraneo* (☎ 826 6288) where you can find pizzas baked in a wood-fired oven.

One of the most relaxed atmospheres for Italian food is *Bat Dan Café* (☎ 828 6411), 10 Bat Dan St, which not only does great food but also has a vast stock of Western board games which expats gather to play until the place closes at midnight. At *Club Opera* (☎ 826 8802), 59 Ly Thai To St, you can choose between a Western and a Vietnamese restaurant in the same lovely villa. Another restaurant in an old French villa serving very good food in a fine ambience is *Le Bistro*, 34 Tran Hung Dao.

There are several good cafés, often selling delicate pastries, on the shores of Hoan Kiem lake; the smartest is *Thuy Ta Café* on the north-west shore. *Café Au Lac* (☎ 825 7807), 57 Ly Thai To St, used to have premises on the lakeshore but the local government made life so difficult for the Viet Kieu owner he had to close down. It's wonderful to see it open again and business is deservedly booming – try the great coffee and the bacon sandwiches. Alternatively drop in to the superb *Moca Café* (☎ 825 6334) at 14-16 Nha Tho St for delicious Vietnamese, Indian and Western food, and fantastic iced chocolate. Beware the coffee, though, it's American style, thanks to its American owner, not true Vietnamese. *Hoa Sua* ('The boulangerie') (☎ 824 0448), at 81 Tho Nuam St, set up and run by Madame Bideaux, a French-naturalized Vietnamese woman, is rightly famous for the superb French breads and patisseries the young Vietnamese chefs make. Many were orphans or street children until Mme Bideaux took them under her wing. The Vietnamese food is also very good – the stewed pork in caramel sauce is tremendous.

Kinh Do Café (☎ 825 0216), 252 Hang Bong St, is deservedly the most popular expat breakfast spot, although the owner seems more proud of a compliment Catherine Deneuve once made about the pastries. The best ice cream in town is to be found at *Chez Fanny's* (☎ 828 5656) at 48 Le Thai To St by Hoan Kiem Lake. Or for real Vietnamese café fare look no further than the tiny 50-year-old *Café Giai Khat* upstairs at 13 Dinh Tien Hoang St overlooking Hoan Kiem lake; it serves up coffee topped by a raw egg for 6000d.

Entertainment
Vietnamese culture Hanoi has several locations to enjoy the unique Vietnamese art of **water puppetry** – great fun for kids and adults. The Thang Long Water Puppet Theatre (☎ 825 5450), 57b Dienh Tien Hoang St, is on the northern shores of Hoam Kien Lake. The performances of live music accompanying wonderfully choreographed water puppetry are given nightly from 8 to 9pm (except Mondays). Entrance costs 20,000d plus 10,000 if you admit to taking your camera in, and 50,000d for taking a video camera in. The theatre is large, attractive and air-conditioned, but can be very popular with tourists and Vietnamese, so to avoid having your ticket stamped with a back row seat it can be worth buying tickets a few hours in advance. A new water puppet theatre has opened in Lenin Park. Performances are at 8pm each night and cost 10,000d. The best way to see other puppet shows is to book a tour through one of the travellers' cafés.

Vietnam's **National Circus** performs in Hanoi, and is based, appropriately enough given its Russian origins, in Lenin Park (near the northern entrance). Performances take place several nights a week when the troupe is not on tour.

Buy a copy of the daily *Vietnam News* or the monthly *Vietnam Economic Times* to find out about the cultural events which take place fairly regularly in Hanoi.

Bars Hanoi is replete with places to enjoy a quiet or noisy drink. There are several good *bia hoi venues* which serve fresh tasty beer in the early evening – try in particular the stand outside 60 Ly Thuong Kiet and the stall at 14 Tran Binh Trong St which serves food too, and also the stalls in the streets around Seasons restaurant on Quan Thanh St.

There are several good drinking locations around Hanoi's various lakes, from the smart *Dak Linh café* opposite Chez Fanny's on the shore of Hoan Kiem lake to the expensive *Floating Hotel* on the northernmost section of

Thanh Nien St which runs between West Lake and Truc Bach lake.

Hanoi also has a number of smart bars, many of which are particularly expat joints: the pick of the lot are probably the *Library Bar* and the *Terrace Bar* at the Press Club, 59A Ly Thai To St. Yet more up-market (and air-conditioned to be very cold) is *Met Pub* in the Sofitel Metropole at 15 Nguyen Ngo St. Be sure to check out Bao Khanh St which is chock full of happening joints and home to the good French cuisine and lovely atmosphere of *Café des Arts* (☎ 828 7207) at 11B Bao Khanh St and run by a Parisian, Gerard. Also on offer are the equally long-established expat haunts of *Polite Pub,* 5 Bao Khanh St, with a real pub feel to it, and the noisier atmospheres of *Sunset Bar,* 31 Cao Ba Quat St, or the cacophonous *Apocalypse Now* at 5C Hoa Ma St, 1km south of the centre. Or for drinks, Italian food and games *Bat Dan Café*, 10 Bat Dan St, will keep you needing to change more travellers' cheques.

Cinemas As well as the usual fare of Vietnamese cinema you can see English- and French-language films.

Fansland cinema (☎ 825 7484), 84 Ly Thuong Kiet St, shows blockbuster Western films, whereas the small Dan Chu ('democracy') cinema (☎ 851 6702), 211 Kham Thien St, not far from the railway station shows slightly less mainstream English-language films. The Alliance Francaise (☎ 826 6970), 42 Yet Kieu, hosts frequent cultural events and regularly shows French films.

Nightlife Hanoi has a reasonable choice of music and dancing places for the evenings, and Quyen Van Minh's new jazz club in the heart of the old quarter is a great addition. Two nightclubs which still pump out an interesting mixture of music to dance and swing to are *Sparks* (☎ 825 7207), 88 Lo Duc St,

and *Roxy* in Ta Hien St. An old rival for the affections of Hanoi's clubbers, *Apocalypse Now*, has opened up new premises at 5C Hoa Ma St (☎ 921 2783) where the theme and the music live on late into the night.

For live music *Minh's Jazz Club* (☎ 828 7890) at 31 Luong Van Can St has great jam sessions and performances by local musicians and occasionally expats.

Karaoke is of course the preferred night-time occupation of young Hanoians with an evening free from work or family chores, and there are literally hundreds of places around the city, varying from the up-market lounges advertised by the big hotels to front rooms of people's houses decked-out with all the equipment. If it's the latter you're after any young Vietnamese you meet will almost certainly be delighted to suggest where to go and come with you to give you the full experience.

Things to buy
Hang Gai St is the main thoroughfare for all manner of gifts and souvenirs. Stroll between the junction of Hang Gai and Hang Manh streets and the lake and you will find a variety of shops selling traditional Vietnamese instruments and brightly-painted water puppets; there are several good art galleries and the spacious government shop at No 13 sells fine lacquer ware at good fixed prices amid hundreds of tailoring silk shops and street hawkers. Take your pick, spotting the silk fabrics unavailable in Hoi An, but beware of bad lacquer work (where you can see the circles of the rafia through the polish). If you don't make it to Bat Trang there are several stalls stocking stacks of pottery at Hang Da market where you can also find street stalls selling fantastic bean drinks and all manner of local and imported booze.

AROUND HANOI

The two finest excursions from Hanoi are to the pottery village of Bat Trang and to the fabulous river and mountain surroundings of the sacred cave pagoda that is Perfume Pagoda. Travellers' cafés offer tours to both, and to other less exciting but still interesting pagodas, but both are also easy enough to reach under your own steam – motorbike to the Perfume Pagoda and motorbike or bicycle to Bat Trang.

Bear in mind if visiting the Perfume Pagoda that the third lunar month (usually March and April, see p100) is the most sacred time to visit the pagoda, meaning that there is more chanting and religious celebration, but also that the waterways and paths are almost overrun with people and stalls.

Bat Trang

This pottery village, is around 11km south-east of Hanoi. It's a small pretty village stuffed with little workshops whose kilns burst with classic heavy Bat Trang blue and white dragon and fish decorated plates, bowls, tureens that fill many small showrooms. It's a popular excursion for Hanoian day-trippers and tourists alike but still has much charm. The village often gets so flooded in summer that small boats become by far the best way to get around.

Bat Trang has been producing ceramics for several hundred years and the high walled parts of the village near the river have been standing since medieval times. The pottery is wonderfully cheap (a full dinner set costs around $25) though not much less than in Hanoi. Remember it is extremely heavy.

Bat Trang can be reached by heading out of Hanoi over Chuong Duong bridge then turning right along the first track. If you return in the late afternoon the best route back is to cut to the river where there is a ferry crossing point over the fast-flowing Red River which burns a deep vermilion red as the sun heads towards the horizon.

The Perfume Pagoda

The Perfume Pagoda rivals Huyen Khong cave in the Marble Mountains for Vietnam's finest cave pagoda, but this one has the extra ingredients of a beautiful boat ride and then a taxing climb of around two hours to the cave. Perfume Pagoda is around 60km south-west of Hanoi amidst jagged rugged limestone cliffs encircled by quiet, tranquil, flooded valleys.

The sampan ride to the pagoda in between the farmers and the fishermen is one of the highlights of the trip (it should be included in the hefty $7 foreigners' fee to see the pagoda). From where the boat drops you off at the bottom of the mountain the wide track is lined with stalls (crushingly so during the festive season) selling most things from bottled water and coconuts to spiritual necklaces and ritual offerings. The hard climb is worth it for the dramatic scene at the top as the steep steps of the path suddenly give way to a gaping hole in the ground. From here stone steps reach down through eerie shadows to the cavern below, amidst trees and vines searching for the light. The air is filled with incense smoke and Buddhist chants which emanate from the cold darkness. Descend the cool dripping steps; despite the endless visitors, the lingering incense and echoing chants make it almost impossible not to find it a tranquil spiritual place.

The road to the Perfume Pagoda is not especially easy to find, but it is a delightful one once you have left Hanoi, especially during the harvest season in early autumn. The expedition is of perfect day-trip length whether you reach the area by car or by motorbike – this is more tiring at around five hours on the bike, but of course cheaper. To find the way head west out of Hanoi past the huge Daewoo centre and the television centre (marked by the tall television mast) and get onto Highway 6 towards Ha Dong. Just after passing through Ha Dong turn left heading due south and head for the villages of Kim Bai, Van Dinh, and finally Que. In Vietnamese the Perfume Pagoda cave is called Chua Huong, or it is known by the festival name Huong Tich.

The north

HAIPHONG

Haiphong is Vietnam's third largest city and it looks set to grow even bigger because Belgium has pledged to invest $60 million to make the port into a deep sea port. This would mean that imports and exports would no longer have to go via Singapore where the ships are changed, and the price is doubled.

Haiphong is not visited by many tourists but is home to an increasing number of expats working on Foreign Direct Investment projects. They see Haiphong as a growing city which should soon reap the economic benefit of being one of Vietnam's four designated 'first-class urban centres'. If you spend more time in Haiphong than the average traveller you should find that the legacy of trading is evident in the range of food from different countries on offer in the city. There are also a number of interesting pagodas and temples to be explored and, of course, Haiphong is en route from Hanoi by train to Halong Bay and Cat Ba National Park.

History

As well as being Vietnam's third largest city Haiphong is also the country's third largest port. It was because of this that it figured significantly in both the Franco-Vietminh war and the American war. Firstly in 1946 an obscure customs dispute here escalated until France bombed the city and the port, and full-scale war began.

In the American war, it was crucial that Haiphong was the only one of Vietnam's three major ports that is in the north (Danang and Ho Chi Minh City being the other two ports). American intelligence was probably correct in thinking that much of the military hardware handed to North Vietnamese forces from Russia and China arrived on ships which docked in Haiphong harbour.

It was vital to America's interests to stem this flow which they could do by, for example, mining the harbour, but successive American presidents were afraid that by doing so they could inadvertently sink a Russian ship and suddenly bring about a direct Soviet-American conflict. So they took no action until late in the war, after Russia had agreed it was sending no more military hardware the way of the Viet Congs. So the harbour was mined after it could have little effect, and then after the Paris Peace agreements were signed, America agreed it would undertake the expensive operation to have the mines removed. Overall, not a stunning success.

Temples and pagodas

Du Hang Pagoda is an extremely ornate and very Vietnamese pagoda in attractive quiet gardens. It is 2.5km south-west of the centre at 121 Chua Hang St. The pagoda was built in the 17th century but has been renovated so is in good condition. It is possible to climb part of the way up the attractive three-tiered pagoda and look down on the lily pond flanked by white statues of monks illustrating various aspects of the wheel of life. The temple at the back of the complex houses a very ornate altar.

Le Chan Pagoda was built to honour Le Chan, the female military leader who fought with the Trung sisters. The pagoda is rather plain except for a highly ornate sedan chair and hammock. It is in the centre of town at the corner of Le Chan St and Me Linh 2 St.

The **Hang Kenh Communal House**, which once served as a communal centre and temple for the area, is notable for its beautiful wooden relief sculptures on the roof and beams. It is around 1km south of the station, off Hang Kenh St, set back from the road with grass around.

Dang Hai Flower Village

The village of Dang Hai is the central point for the fields of flowers which are grown in the surrounding area for sale internationally. In the spring and summer months the colours can be stunning. The village is around 7km south of Haiphong. To reach it follow Lach Tray St, then turn into An Da St and continue for several kilometres until you reach the village. Return motorbike taxis can be arranged for $2-4.

PRACTICAL INFORMATION
Arrival and departure
By train Haiphong's main train station, Ga Haiphong, where trains from Hanoi terminate, is near the market district and around 2km from the main hotel area. (Avoid getting off at Haiphong's subsidiary station which is far from the centre).

There are always plenty of cyclos in front of the station, and a ride to Dien Bien Phu St where most accommodation is located should cost no more than 3000d. Return train tickets to Hanoi are easy to get hold of as the foreigners' quota is high and the demand is low.

By bus The bus station is several kilometres south-west of town. A cyclo ride into town should cost you around 15,000d.

By ferry The ferry port is around 1km to the north of the town at the end of a street which is very dark by night. Some cyclos gather here when the ferries dock.

Three ferries daily leave the port at Haiphong for Halong, at 9am, 9.15am and 1.30pm. The ferries at 9.15am and 1.30pm take around three hours and cost 46,000d. The boats are often hot and crowded in summer. The 9.15am ferry is an express boat which takes only one hour and is generally not crowded, but costs 80,000d. There are also ferries daily to Cat Ba Island at 6am, 11am and 1.30pm. These take three hours and cost 60,000d. The ferry docks near Cat Ba village.

There are also ferries from Haiphong to other destinations, such as Cam Pha Island.

By air Haiphong's airport is an inconvenient 7km south of the city and remarkably there are no direct flights to or from Hanoi. Vietnam Airlines sometimes runs free minibus rides to its office in the city centre, otherwise look to pay $2 for a cyclo or $4 for a taxi. There are flights from Haiphong once or twice daily to Ho Chi Minh City for nearly 2,000,000d, and flights to Danang on Monday, Wednesday or Friday for 1,000,000d.

Flights can be booked at the Vietnam Airlines booking office from 7am to 6pm at 127 Dien Bien Phu St (☎ 031-823322).

Orientation
Haiphong is truly a port city, facing the sea to its east and with several rivers coursing through its environs. It lies on a piece of land jutting out into the Gulf of Tonkin and the city is bounded to its north and west by the Cua Cam and Tam Bac rivers.

All the city's services are fairly centrally located; the temples are scattered around the city's outskirts, and are often hard to find. Cyclo drivers are unlikely to know where they are so you need to be specific with the address.

Services
Post Haiphong's post office is at 3 Nguyen Tri Phuong St. It is open every day from 7am to 10pm and offers all standard services.

Money The VID Public Bank is at 56 Dien Bien Phu St (☎ 031-823999). It will change travellers' cheques for one per cent commission and is open Monday to Friday 8.30am-3.30pm, Saturday 8.30am-noon. The Asia Commercial Bank at 69 Dien Bien Phu St will change foreign currency, cash only, with no commission charge. It is open Monday to Friday 7.30-11.45am and 1.30-5pm.

Medical The largest of the many pharmacies is at the corner of Cau Dat and Hai Ba Trung streets. Haiphong has a Vietnam-Czech Friendship Hospital on Nha Tuong St. There is also an eye hospital on Nguyen Duc Canh St.

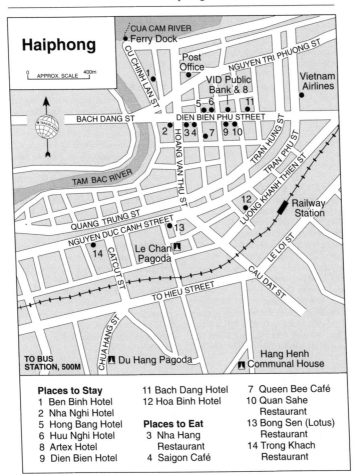

Haiphong

0 |___APPROX. SCALE___| 400m

CUA CAM RIVER
Ferry Dock

Post Office

VID Public Bank & 8

Vietnam Airlines

CU CHINH LAN ST

NGUYEN TRI PHUONG ST

BACH DANG ST

DIEN BIEN PHU STREET

HOANG VAN THU ST

TRAN HUNG ST

TRAN PHU ST

TAM BAC RIVER

LUONG KHANH THIEN ST

Railway Station

QUANG TRUNG ST

NGUYEN DUC CANH STREET

Le Chan Pagoda

CATCUT ST

LE LOI ST

CAU DAT ST

TO HIEU STREET

CHUA HANG ST

TO BUS STATION, 500M

Du Hang Pagoda

Hang Henh Communal House

Places to Stay
1 Ben Binh Hotel
2 Nha Nghi Hotel
5 Hong Bang Hotel
6 Huu Nghi Hotel
8 Artex Hotel
9 Dien Bien Hotel

11 Bach Dang Hotel
12 Hoa Binh Hotel

Places to Eat
3 Nha Hang Restaurant
4 Saigon Café

7 Queen Bee Café
10 Quan Sahe Restaurant
13 Bong Sen (Lotus) Restaurant
14 Trong Khach Restaurant

Where to stay

If you make it past the cyclo drivers in front of the train station, at the end of the street and a little to the right is the acceptable **Hoa Binh Hotel** at 104 Luong Khanh Thien St (☎ 031-859029). It is really set up to be a business hotel, with hairdressing, massage and karaoke services, but is fine for tourists too. The doubles at $10 are rather overpriced, although have huge bathrooms, but the doubles at $15 are good enough. However, the pick of the cheapest, and the best, accommodation is in the centre of town along Dien Bien Phu St.

There are so many hotels here it is needless to list them all. The cheapest is the bizarre **Nha Nghi** whose address is

135 Dien Bien Phu St, but in fact it is off the road behind a bike shed. Its near-hostile staff will, if you insist, show you basic rooms for as little as $4. Alternatively, *Hong Bang Hotel* (☎ 031-842229, ▤ 031-841044), 64 Dien Bien Phu St, is a wonderful colonial building offering a range of rooms from $5 to $45.

Towards the upper end of the price range the rooms have balconies looking onto the street. *Artex Hotel* (☎ 031-842945), 56 Dien Bien Phu St, has friendly staff and good rooms at $9. The nearby *Bach Danh Hotel* (☎ 031-842444), 42 Dien Bien Phu St, offers OK rooms for $10-45 – it would be a good place to stay near Christmas as the $45 rooms are permanently stocked with a huge Christmas tree. A very good mid-range hotel is *Dien Bien Hotel* (☎ 031-842264), 67 Dien Bien Phu St, where all rooms are $30; this is a charming rambling hotel with lovely rooms and friendly service.

Ben Binh Hotel (☎ 031-842260), 6 Ben Binh St, is conveniently located right next to the ferry port. It is set back from the road with a laid back feel to it and offers good rooms for $15. The best hotel in Haiphong is *Huu Nghi* (friendship) hotel (☎ 031-823310, ▤ 823245), 60 Dien Bien Phu St, which offers rooms from $50 to the super suite at $300, which is indeed super.

Where to eat
There are several good restaurants on Dien Bien Phu St, such as *Nha Hang* at No 103 which serves good Chinese food and *Quan Sake* at No 55 which serves very good Japanese fare.

For Vietnamese food, Nguyen Duc Canh St bordering the canal has many small street cafés serving good food and bia hoi, and two notable restaurants – *Lotus (Bong Sen)* at No 17 and *Trong Khach* at No 83. A branch of Café de Paris is expected to open here soon.

Entertainment
Until the Café de Paris opens the trendiest places for an evening drink are *Saigon Café* on Dien Bien Phu St, which has in-house singers and serves good draught and bottled beer and terrible cocktails, and *Queen Bee nightclub* at 121 Dinh Tien Hoang St. Like other branches of Queen Bee it offers a disco, karaoke and Chinese food.

HALONG BAY

Halong Bay is an exquisitely beautiful area of the northern coast, comprising over 2000 rocky limestone islands many of which have delightful tiny beaches.

Boating in Halong Bay can be one of life's great experiences. Gliding between the endless arrays of tall jagged cliffs which rise out of the clear blue of the sea and stopping at the occasional remarkable cave is a won-

---

❏ **Haiphong to Halong Bay**
The ferry to Halong first travels along the broad Cua Cam river which opens out into the sea. Then the route of the ferry takes you past the west coast of Cat Ba Island and introduces you to the remarkable scenery of Halong Bay.

Until near Bai Chay or Hon Gai the views from the ferry are close-ups of the forested cliffs of Cat Ba but when you dock the layers of stony cliffs of Halong Bay's islands come into sight.

derful way to pass the time for a few hours, or a few days. You understand why the French termed Halong Bay 'the eighth wonder of the world'.

Many Europeans have come to know the scenery of Halong Bay through the film *Indochine*. For the Vietnamese the scenery has long been famous, and indeed has for centuries been used as an emblem to symbolize Vietnam. The myth of its creation is also famous in Vietnam: the name means descending dragon bay. Legend has it that the tiny islands of the bay were made by a great dragon who ran to the sea from its home in the mountains above Halong City. Its huge feet and flailing tail gouged out valleys and crevasses inland, and when it reached the sea the areas dug up by the swishes of its tail were filled with water and only the higher land was left exposed, forming the islands in the bay. As one traveller said 'When you see the remarkable scenery here, you realize how incredibly right the legend sounds'.

The beach at Bai Chay is where most Vietnamese and foreign tourists stay to visit Halong Bay. The beach is not particularly stunning but Bai Chay is a perfect jumping-off point to explore Halong Bay. The incline of the beach is gentle so it's good for taking children swimming, as many Vietnamese do, but the long shallows become so hot in summer that it can feel more like a bath than a swim. There is currently a lot of development at the beach which may significantly change its character. There are beautiful small beaches on many of the islands in the bay, hardly any of which are inhabited. If you make your own way up the coast towards the Chinese border you can come across delightful beaches with views of the islands, in territory where there are almost no hotels.

Halong Bay is also home to Cat Ba Island and Cat Ba National Park. Cat Ba Island is inhabited and has an extremely varied landscape and diverse ecosystems. However, do not expect to find the rich jungle forests ringing with birdsong or buzzing with animal life; almost everything worth eating or selling has been; of course if you are given the chance to contribute to this situation by buying birds' eggs, don't.

Caves

Wind and water (or a dragon's tail if you prefer) have worn numerous caves and grottoes into the islands. Around 30 of these have been officially designated as tourist sites meaning that the paths through them are safe; they cost 10,000d each for foreigners. It is advisable to bring good shoes and a torch (flashlight) if you want to visit any of the caves. Bring walking boots if you want to really explore the caves. There are many other caves which have not been developed but you are only likely to find these if you take an extended tour of the bay region; always take great care when exploring them.

The Grotto of the Wooden Stakes, Hang Dau Go, is Halong Bay's most famous cave and is also the most accessible from Bai Chay. It is a huge cave consisting of three dramatic chambers of which the second has walls which sparkle when light is shone on them; it is known in French as *the Grotte des merveilles* – the cave of marvels. But its fame derives from the capacious third chamber which was used to store and preserve the vicious bamboo stakes which General Trang Hung Dao planted in the bed of the nearby Bach Dang River's estuary to impale and defeat the invading vessels of Kublai Khan in 1287.

Visiting Hang Luon cave is a remarkable experience as it is a hollow island, the dramatic cliff-lined centre of which can only be reached by a 30m long half-underwater passage.

PRACTICAL INFORMATION
Arrival and departure
From Haiphong The best way to get here is by ferry from Haiphong ferry port. Three ferries depart daily to the Bai Chay area (beach resort) of Halong City at 9am, 9.15am and 1.30pm. The 9am and 1.30pm boats take around three hours, cost 46,000d, and are often very hot in summer and crowded.

The 9.15am service is an express ferry which takes one hour, costs 80,000d, and is generally not crowded. These ferries arrive at a small harbour 1km east of the beach.

Motorbikes gather here to transport you to hotels at the beach area. A ride to the motorbike owner's hotel will be free, otherwise a ride should cost 3000d. It is rare to find cyclos here, and seems impossible to get a taxi. If you know you will need transport other than a motorbike, contact one of Bai Chay's good hotels and pre-arrange for a cyclo or hotel car to meet you.

Additionally there are ferries from Haiphong at 6am, 11am, 1.30pm and 4pm to the port of Hon Gai in Halong City east. As with the non-express service to Bai Chay this journey takes three hours on a boat which is hot and crowded in summer and costs 46,000d. From Hon Gai you need to take a short boat ride or a long motorbike ride to reach Bai Chay.

Ferries leave every 15 minutes or so to Bai Chay and cost 500d, or you could take up one of the many offers of a small extremely basic boat to take you there which should cost around $3 for the boat.

Haiphong is a major city and can be easily reached from Hanoi by train or bus (see p266).

From Hanoi (direct) A minibus to Bai Chay can be arranged from any of the travellers' cafés in Hanoi, and a ride back to Hanoi can be arranged through most of the small hotels in Bai Chay.

The journey can take between two and four hours and should cost around $10. Tours of two days ($20) or three days ($35) to Halong Bay (including boat tours of the bay) by bus from Hanoi can also be booked at Hanoi's travellers' cafés. The local bus stations in Halong are in the ferry port at Hon Gai and the harbour in Bai Chay.

From Kep (Dong Dang, Hanoi) There is one train a day from Kep to Halong Bay; the train leaves at 9.30am, arriving in Ga Halong at 2.15pm. The train from Halong Bay to Kep leaves from Ga Halong at 2.30pm and arrives in Kep at 7.15pm. A foreigner price ticket costs 47,000d.

Halong Bay's railway 'station' is little known to many in Bai Chay, though saying its other name, Gieng Day, sometimes helps. It is 5km east of Bai Chay off the main Halong Road. A sign on the road to the station points up a dirt track, along which after 50m is the small collection of huts and shacks

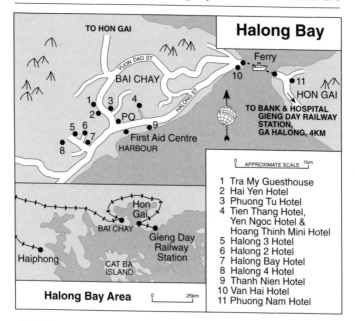

Halong Bay

TO HON GAI
VUON DAO ST
BAI CHAY
HALONG ST
Ferry
10
11
HON GAI
TO BANK & HOSPITAL
GIENG DAY RAILWAY
STATION,
GA HALONG, 4KM
PO
First Aid Centre
HARBOUR

0 — APPROXIMATE SCALE — 1km

1 Tra My Guesthouse
2 Hai Yen Hotel
3 Phuong Tu Hotel
4 Tien Thang Hotel,
  Yen Ngoc Hotel &
  Hoang Thinh Mini Hotel
5 Halong 3 Hotel
6 Halong 2 Hotel
7 Halong Bay Hotel
8 Halong 4 Hotel
9 Thanh Nien Hotel
10 Van Hai Hotel
11 Phuong Nam Hotel

Hon Gai
BAI CHAY
Gieng Day
Railway
Station
Haiphong
CAT BA
ISLAND

Halong Bay Area 0 — 25km

which is Halong station. You have to be incredibly persistent to get anyone to take you there because locals insist is doesn't exist; it should cost around 10,000d by Honda om.

The line to Kep is wide gauge, slow and has hard seat only; this trip is therefore definitely not for the fainthearted, but is recommended.

Orientation

The biggest habitation in the Halong Bay area is Halong City, which is divided into Halong City east (Hon Gai), and Halong City west (Bai Chay). These are separated by the mouth of a river which can be crossed by ferry for 500d, private boat for a little more, or traversed by road.

Halong City east is a large urban centre with a sizable trading port and no beach. It is to Bai Chay that Vietnamese and foreign tourists go for rest, recre-

ation and touring the bay since it is much less of an urban centre than Hon Gai.

Services

Post Bay Chai has a large post office next to the beach which is open daily from 7am to 9pm and offers postal, telephone, fax and telex services.

Money There is a branch of Vietkombank on Le Thanh Ton St in Halong City east which can change cash and travellers' cheques.

It is easy to change large dollar bills for dong at good rates in the large hotels in Bai Chay (often this is possible even if you are not a guest if you just take a drink or a meal there) or, for a reasonable rate, at one of the small hotels offering foreign exchange on Vuon Dao St.

Medical The best place in Bai Chay for medical supplies is a small first-aid centre on the beach near the post office. There is a hospital in Halong City east on Le Thanh Ton St.

Where to stay

The main road in Bai Chay, Vuon Dao Rd, is packed with over 30 hotels, mostly small, pleasant budget places and certainly the cheapest in town. In the busy summer season the prices for doubles with air-con range from $8 to 15. In general the prices get more reasonable the further up the road you go. Here is a brief selection: *Tra My Guest House* (☎ 033-845465), at No 115, which is at the top of the hill, *Phuong Tu Hotel* (☎ 033-845179), at No 52, and *Hai Yen Hotel* (☎ 033-846126) at No 57. The hotels on this street are not near the beach and only the very tall ones have a good view of the bay.

For a little more effort and money you could instead look at three friendly charming hotels perched above the town up a steep track with wonderful views of the bay from the balconies; you can drive up the track on motorbikes. Doubles here cost around $10 with aircon. *Tien Thang Hotel* (☎ 033-846914) and *Yen Ngoc Hotel* (☎ 033-846945) offer similar rooms, as does *Hoang Thinh Mini Hotel* (☎ 033-846944) but it distinguishes itself by the delicious meals the owner will serve on request.

There is also an array of luxury accommodation at Bai Chay with *Halong Hotels 1*, *2*, *3*, *4* and *5* and *Halong Bay hotel*. These hotels are next to each other off Halong Road but by far the best is the first – *Halong Hotel (1)* (☎ 033-845209, 845210, ▤ 846856). This is a glorious colonial building with good food, drink and service to match. The hotel was built in 1935 and generally houses the VIPs who visit Halong Bay, including Catherine Deneuve who stayed there during the filming of *Indochine* (room 208). Because there is

so much luxury accommodation in Bai Chay rooms in these hotels can often be had for a song after bargaining: so the asking price of $70 for a double at the Halong Hotel can often be reduced to just $35 even in the summer season.

Van Hai Hotel (☎ 033-846403) offers decent rooms for $25 at the small harbour in Bai Chay where the ferry docks from Hon Gai. Near the ferry port in Hon Gai, *Phuong Nam Hotel* (☎ 033-827242) offers rather shabby rooms for $17. There is only one hotel directly on the beach at Bai Chay. This is the truly grim *Thanh Nien Hotel* which, with rooms for $20, is best avoided.

Where to eat and drink

The seafront at Bai Chay is packed with a host of small restaurants offering Vietnamese food of extremely variable quality but the seafood can be very good.

There are a couple of very good small street cafés at the top of Vuon Dao Rd. If you can spend a little more a delicious meal can be savoured in colonial luxury for around $5 a head in *Halong Hotel I*. For a cool refreshing daytime drink you need look no further than the beach which is lined with an array of small cafés selling coconuts, sugar cane, good draught imitation foreign beer and even better bia hoi.

Local transport

There are almost no cyclos in Bai Chay. The town is small and very easy to get around on foot. To reach the harbour at Bai Chay or the harbour for ferries to Hon Gai the usual form of transport is xe om. Prices are very reasonable – the 2km ride to the harbour should cost no more than 3000d. The 5km ride to the railway station east of Bai Chay (for trains to Kep) should cost no more than 10,000d. Currently there are no taxis in Bai Chay; not even the best hotels can arrange for one unless you are a guest at the hotel.

Renting a boat The harbour in Bai Chay is normally packed with near identical luxurious tourist boats for hire. These would comfortably hold 20 or so but are affordable enough that accumulating a group of four or so is all that is needed to enjoy a tour of the bay. One of these boats can be rented for around $3 an hour after bargaining. Trips can be as long or as short as you choose, but at least half a day is recommended. These boats can also be hired for longer trips, staying overnight on the boat. A good price for this is around $65 for a day and a night, excluding food.

Sadly these boats are almost the only option for hire as there are no sampans which dock at Bai Chay's harbours or the harbour at Hon Gai.

There is in fact only one option for a smaller boat in the whole area – a gaudily painted small wooden piece of junk owned by the indomitable Captain Lap, who will take you out on the bay for almost as much as the large boats. To find Captain Lap head for the group of huts selling Coca Cola behind Bai Chay's main harbour and look for the sign proclaiming 'Captian Lap' (sic).

CAT BA NATIONAL PARK

An excursion which many who visit Halong Bay make is to Cat Ba Island, which contains a national park. There was a time when the island had no electricity, offered only basic accommodation and there was little distraction from the beach or the forests. Times have changed and these days Cat Ba is very tourist-friendly with a number of cheap hotels and restaurants in the only centre, Cat Ba Town, and an established tourist trail across the island or via the bay to the national park on the west of the island. Any of the island's hotels can organize transport to the national park and a guide. Hiring a guide is recommended if you want to see more than just trees, but you are still not guaranteed to see any representatives of the vast numbers of animal species which allegedly live among the tropical vegetation, though you can get bitten by snakes. Entrance to the park costs $1.

It is possible to reach Cat Ba from Hon Gai by taking a ferry to Haiphong but alighting at Cat Ba's neighbour island Cat Hai then waiting for a connecting ferry to Cat Ba. However, it may be a long wait; taking the new fast three-hour $5 hydrofoil service directly from Haiphong to Cat Ba may therefore be a better bet. Hydrofoils leave Haiphong at 6.30am and 12.30pm, and leave Cat Ba at 6am and 1pm. The route between Haiphong and Cat Ba crosses the Bach Dang River estuary where the Vietnamese twice repelled invaders by impaling their boats on upturned bamboo stakes revealed by the turning of the tide.

KEP

Kep (pronounced Kéap) appears to be a major rail and road junction, but is in fact a small town. There are two railway stations in Kep; in order to connect with Hanoi or Lang Son/China trains from the Ha Long branch you need to continue on the train to the second, more northerly, station.

This station is several kilometres outside the town of Kep. There is a lively atmosphere here because the waiting room has a table tennis table in it; there are several good food stalls outside the station and a small hamlet in the midst of rice fields.

Arriving by train and being directly in the midst of this delightful environment makes Kep one of the easiest ways to experience a little of Vietnamese countryside so it's a great place to stay the night if you can bear the very basic accommodation. Also bear in mind that virtually no-one speaks any English here or in other tiny settlements.

There is one ***resthouse*** in Kep which is round the back of the station around swampy fields full with the croaking of frogs by night. If you arrive after dark the station guard is likely to see you as you get off the train and will escort you to one of the basic rooms with hard wooden beds and mosquito nets which cost 4000d(!) for a night, and then will ask whether you have eaten. The beds are relatively comfortable considering, but the proximity of the station means that the occasional noise of trains and loudspeakers will wake light sleepers.

LANG SON

Lang Son (pronounced Lang Ssun) is a fairly scruffy provincial capital mainly visited en route to or from China, though it does have some interesting caves on its outskirts. While much of the population of Lang Son is from hill tribes by origin it is the proximity to the Chinese border which is the major influence on the town and which has dominated its history.

Chinese invaders have conquered Lang Son and progressed southwards too many times in Vietnamese history for Vietnam's liking. But the district struck back in China's most recent attempt, in 1979, when it invaded Vietnam – in theory as a reprisal for Vietnam's invasion of Cambodia to free it from Pol Pot's barbarous rule. When the Chinese army confidently marched southwards down the road which crosses the border and leads between Dong Dang and Lang Son they little expected to lose several thousand men in covering the 18km to Lang Son. They held Dong Dang for 20 days, but Lang Son for only four before retreating back to China.

Sadly, the Lang Son you see today is the result of that ignominious defeat, for Lang Son was deliberately demolished by the retreating soldiers who dynamited houses, hospitals, roads; the town was not fully rebuilt until 1986. Lang Son's experiences with Chinese fire power give it the pyrrhic honour of being fought over by more of the 20th-century's world powers than the rest of Vietnam: the sizeable road bridge between Dong Dang and Lang Son has been destroyed three times since WWII – by French colonials retreating south, by American bombing, and finally by Chinese invaders retreating north.

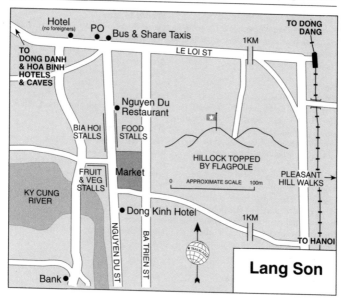

In those days relations with China were in the form of profitable (smuggled) trade but in 1991-2 official foreign relations were normalized. The result is that many Chinese goods are on sale here for reasonable prices. The other notable feature of the town's market is the prevalence of extraordinary carved creations made from animal horn – bizarre but fragile souvenirs.

PRACTICAL INFORMATION
Arrival and departure
By train The railway station is at the end of Le Loi St, around 2km from the main hub of town at the market area near Dong Kinh Hotel. Many motorbike taxis gather here, but the town is bereft of cyclos. A xe om ride to a hotel should cost around 3000d.

The train bound for China leaves Lang Son at 7.27pm on Tuesdays and Fridays. Three hours are spent at Dong Dang from 8 to 11pm going through customs and changing trains. It is possible to save time by making your own way to Dong Dang and buying a ticket there but you may find it takes longer

due to the difficulty of getting a reservation there. A taxi to Dong Dang should cost no more than $3; a motorbike taxi less.

By bus The bus station is next to the Post Office on Le Loi St. Here you can find some long-distance buses and many long-distance shared taxis. Many of these regularly leave at around 7-8am for Hanoi (usually to Gia Lam station), in considerably more comfort than the bus.

Orientation
Most of Lang Son's commercial activity lies between the prominent flag-topped

crag and the river. This is where Lang Son's large Dong Kinh market is located, around which are the town's best eating places. The caves are around 3km west of town across the river.

Services

Post The town's post office is on Le Loi St opposite Nguyen Du St. It offers the usual services and is open 7am-8pm. It is a prominent building in Lang Son, not least because it features an extraordinary Big Ben mimicking clock.

Money There is currently nowhere in Lang Son which can change travellers' cheques. The only bank which can change dollar cash is VBA Bank which is across the river at 1 Tran Hung Dao St, but the exchange rate it offers is rather poorer than the official one.

Where to stay

Currently there is only one hotel in Lang Son which is open to foreigners. This is the acceptable and prominent *Dong Kinh Hotel* at 25 Nguyen Du St (☎ 025 870166). The hotel offers decent doubles at $22 on the first floor and almost identical triples on the fourth floor for $12! The staff speak almost no English.

Where to eat

There are several good places to eat around the Dong Kinh market. The best of these is a two-storeyed restaurant whose manageress will invite you into the kitchen to choose your food. It is around 50m from Dong Kinh Hotel along Nguyen Du St.

There are also several street cafés along this road doing good food and bia hoi places.

AROUND LANG SON

There are three notable caves (called dong, in Vietnamese) to visit around Lang Son. **Thanh Canh cave** has a walkway and lights set into the wall. The entrance houses a sculpture of a lotus flower collecting drips of pure clear water from the roof leading to a walkway which has been constructed traversing the interior of the first cave. Deeper into the cave there is no development and if you have a torch (flashlight) and good shoes it is good to explore; this cave costs 5000d.

Nhi Thanh Cave is not for the claustrophobic: it is a long tunnel running alongside a stream under and through a crag. A good torch is essential in order to progress very far. A temple is built at the entrance of and housed by **Moi cave**. This is a delightful place to visit, especially because of the elderly nun who will show you round and point out stalactite formations more or less resembling creatures or objects. The bust of Ho Chi Minh, 'Bac Ho', on the roof of the cave is very good. Here there are also great musical stalactites; they make different notes when you tap them.

The caves are all within $1/2$km of each other and can be found by heading west out of Lang Son along Le Loi St. Motorbike taxis will take you there for around 5000d; a lift for the journey back is easy to pick up from the main road near the caves.

The countryside immediately around Lang Son has low vegetation-covered hills which are cut with red paths leading from one village to the next. This is pleasant walking territory, providing you stick to a path. The hills are easily approached by crossing the railway lines south of the station.

The north-west

LAO CAI

Lao Cai was, like Lang Son, another Vietnamese town near the Chinese border that suffered deliberate destruction by retreating Chinese following their unsuccessful invasion in March 1979. As a result, today there is little of interest here and few stop longer than it takes to journey on to Sapa, or to China. Accommodation here is decent, reasonably priced and closely grouped together but there is nowhere remarkable to eat, and Lao Cai's bia hoi is noted for being exceedingly flat.

Lao Cai

0 APPROX SCALE 500m

CHINA

VIETNAM

RED RIVER

Customs
Bank

Post Office

Hotel

Hanoi Hotel
Ngoc Chung Hotel & Restaurant

Vat Tu Guesthouse

Market
Pharmacies

NGUYEN HUE ST

TO SAPA, 37KM

Ga Lao Cai Railway Station

PRACTICAL INFORMATION
Arrival and departure
If you are journeying on to Sapa (or are in an express train bound for China) there is no need to explore Lao Cai because the town is around 2km from the station and a tourist bus bound for Sapa meets the train from Hanoi; a ticket costs 50,000d.

The bus station is in the centre of town next to the main market. Sapa can also be reached by local bus from the bus station for a pittance, although you need to be there in the early morning. Otherwise the town is full of Honda om, particularly at the train station. The ride to Sapa is most pleasantly achieved by Honda om, for around $7. The bus sta-

tion in the early morning is also the best time to try for a shared taxi ride to Hanoi.

Orientation and services
Lao Cai is dissected by the Red River and its domain is clearly bounded to the north by the border with China, 3km from the railway station.

The main body of the town is focused around the bridge over the Red River which forms the border with China and is 2km from the railway station. It is here that you will find the **post office**, open daily 7.30am-7pm, offering all the usual services and the town's hotels. There is a **bank** next to the border which changes dollar cash only, at a rather poor rate. The town's **pharmacies** are to be found around the market.

Where to stay and eat

The first place to stay that you come to along the road from the train station is also the cheapest – *Vat Tu Guesthouse* (☎ 020-831540), 67 Nguyen Hué St, has good triples at $11.

The best value hotel for one or two people, however, is the smart *Ngoc Chung Resthouse* (☎ 020-832199), 27 Nguyen Hué St, which has nice rooms with TV and air-con for $10. The place just across the way at 26 Nguyen Hué St, advertising itself only as '*Hotel*' (☎ 020-883007), is fairly grim and its doubles cost $11.

The only hotel in town which could beat Ngoc Chung is *Hanoi Hotel* (☎ 020-832486), 19 Nguyen Hué St, which has agreeable rooms for $15.

For places to eat, the only real option if you want something smarter than street stalls along Nguyen Hué St or in the market is the restaurant in Hanoi Hotel which is reasonable enough.

SAPA

Sapa, which mysteriously means town of sand, is a small pretty town which has opened itself up to tourism but is still very pleasant, with its commanding mountain views and easy access to valley or ridge walks to take in the scenery and see the colourful hill tribes.

The town is quite busy at weekends because tour groups arrive in time for the local speciality – the 'love market' on Saturday nights in which girls and boys of ethnic minorities meet to make a match outside family groupings, an ancient custom to avoid incest. The number of groups coming from Hanoi means this has become somewhat touristy; so on Saturday nights nowadays local people just gather socially while the real love market has moved out of prying eyes. Saturdays are still lively, but could be something to avoid if you want to see a more peaceful town and take advantage of cheaper midweek accommodation prices.

Sapa is at 1650m above sea level meaning that it is pleasant and cool by day and colder at night during the summer, while in winter the temperature can drop below freezing. All the hotels provide blankets or duvets for guests, but The Auberge is by far the most comfortable in winter when the real log fires in each room make for a romantic as well as comfortable stay. Sapa valley also has its own microclimate such that much of the weather is local, and volatile meaning that cloud and rain can descend at unpredictable times.

Vietnam's highest mountain, Fansipan, is visible from Sapa although its top is regularly shrouded in cloud, often only appearing in the early morning or late evening. It can be climbed, although you need a guide to do so, as well as a very tough disposition (see p286).

History

Sapa was discovered by Europeans in 1918 when a Jesuit missionary visited the area. French colonials were attracted by the cool climate, beautiful scenery and hunting possibilities and in 1932 they began developing the town as a hill station retreat. Existing minority settlements on the site of the town were moved and the standard colonial structures were put in place – a church, some hotels, an aerodrome (before that the stretch from Lao Cai to Sapa was covered by sedan chair), tennis courts, the hydro-electric power station and over 200 villas.

Hardly any of the original buildings remain, for those villas that were not abandoned as the French were driven out of Indochina were destroyed by the Chinese invasion of 1979. But the rebuilding of the town has resulted in a friendly hotch-potch of styles which nicely offsets the different colours of the hill tribes who come to the market here.

PRACTICAL INFORMATION
Arrival and departure
If you arrive by Honda om from Lao Cai ($7 one way) make sure you are happy with the hotel you ask to be taken to before finally alighting.

If you arrive by tourist bus from Lao Cai (25,000d) or local bus you will be dropped at the top of town and will have to make your own way to find a place to stay. Sapa is small enough to get around easily enough which is fortunate as there are no cyclos – indeed the roads are far too hilly and rough to support any.

Orientation and services
The main focus of the town is along the street running south-east from the football pitch to the Auberge. It is primarily along this street and the market street which junctions with it that dozens of Hmong and Red Dao hill tribespeople are to be found selling their colourful wares in pidgin Vietnamese or English.

There is a small **post office** at a junction on the way out of town towards Lao Cai. There is no pharmacy though there is a **hospital** of sorts out of town north off the road which leads to Lao Cai.

Most of the large hotels change dollar cash, at poor rates, and The Auberge converts dollar travellers' cheques, at a very poor rate so try to bring sufficient dong cash.

Where to stay and eat
There are a number of hotels and guest-houses around the market along the street heading south-east to the Auberge, but there are also many others spread out through the town which are often quieter and have better views.

The Auberge (☎ 020-871243, 020-871282) at the very bottom of town is well known amongst Hanoi's expat community as the finest place to stay and eat, for the quality of its rooms, food, panoramic views and notably for the French-speaking patron and his English-speaking son. A good double room here will set you back around $10, but beware the place fills up at weekends. It's a must during the winter as each room has its own real log fire.

Heading up into town from the Auberge you come across a number of small hotels, of which *Fansipan Hotel* is notable for its extremely charming owner who makes up for the noisiness of his cheap rooms – $5 for a double.

However, to really escape from the noise of town head for an oasis like *Darling Hotel* (☎ 020-871349) whose French-speaking owner offers pleasant doubles for $8-13 which look out directly onto the mountains opposite so you can see Fansipan from your bed.

For places to eat you need look no further than *The Auberge* where excellent Vietnamese fare, combined with such specialities as banana/papaya yoghurt shakes, is served on the terrace.

Alternatively, try the market or, in a throw back to French days, *Friendly Café*, which is on the way out of town towards Lao Cai and does the most fantastic crepes.

A super local speciality is **Sapa wine**; although this tastes like sherry it is in fact made from apples. It can be bought by the glass or bottle at most hotels' restaurants.

Another local product often preferred by tourists are the small bundles peddled by the Hmong which look just like grass and indeed are drugs, thus you should be careful as possession and smoking are illegal.

AROUND SAPA

Hill tribes

The French called them montagnards, mountain people, the Vietnamese called them moi, meaning savages. While the first description seems fairer and certainly more accurate it still leaves out a key ingredient – that the hill tribespeople are ethnic minorities, not of the same ethnicity as the Viets, or Kinh. Each tribe has its own very different language, traditions and heritage. Many of the minorities are thought to have occupied land in Vietnam since before the Viets arrived. Such old inhabitants include the Tay, Thai and Khmer minorities who moved onto the land from the west and south. These tribes are all part of the Australasian grouping.

The arrival of other tribes has been much more recent – those from the Sino-Tibetan grouping, which include people of Tibetan and Burman origin, probably arrived between the 17th and 19th centuries. Meanwhile the Chams are just one ethnic minority from the other main grouping, the Malay-Polynesian group, whose continued shadowy presence in Vietnam is testimony both to the existence of their former kingdom and to its overthrow by the Viets.

Not all Vietnam's 54 ethnic minorities live in the mountains, but the most colourful do, inhabiting much of the north-west. There is also another reason why they are called hill tribes – through the centuries in general the most recent arrivals take the highest elevations, working their way up, or rather down, to lower levels.

The French as colonialists had a mixed relationship with the montagnards. There were many who tried to 'civilize' them, including converting them to Christianity, while those who were in Indochina to make money grabbed their labour for forced work on the plantations. Since the French were kicked out the montagnards have in theory been able to remain independent provided they agree not to threaten the supremacy of Vietnamese sovereignty. In practice there have been attempts to curtail their way of life – for example opium smoking has been banned, despite it being a common habit with many hill tribes – although no-one has attempted to ban the extremely strong rice alcohol which nearly all hill tribes make. But while the French and then Americans pressed hill tribes into service in their wars (for example around the Khe Sanh base in the DMZ) not

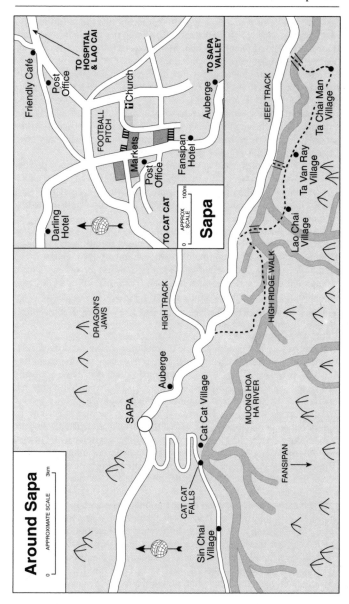

Around Sapa

0 APPROXIMATE SCALE 3km

Friendly Café
Post Office
TO HOSPITAL & LAO CAI
Church
Auberge
TO SAPA VALLEY
FOOTBALL PITCH
Markets
Post Office
Fansipan Hotel
Darling Hotel
TO CAT CAT
APPROX SCALE
0 100m
Sapa

JEEP TRACK
Ta Chai Man Village
Ta Van Ray Village
Lao Chai Village
HIGH RIDGE WALK

DRAGON'S JAWS
HIGH TRACK
Auberge
SAPA
Cat Cat Village
CAT CAT FALLS
Sin Chai Village
MUONG HOA HA RIVER
FANSIPAN

least the matter of a similar colour of skin meant that the hill tribes also lent support to the North Vietnamese side during the wars – most notably during the siege of Dien Bien Phu. Many today clearly identify with the Vietnamese cause against the Americans.

These days, voluntary population movement to the cities is probably the greatest threat to the hill tribespeople's way of life, but such a change is only likely to come about if the area is hit by a natural disaster or if the mountainous areas become much less isolated, which looks unlikely. For example although schooling in Vietnamese is offered to tribespeople, the schools' distance from their dwellings is but one reason why only three per cent of all ethnic children in the area attend.

Ethnic minorities make up around 13 per cent of Vietnam's population, but while some tribes are thriving, such as the Hmong or Tay which number about a million people each, some minorities, such as the O du, and Ro mam number only around 100 people and are dying out due to disease and population decline.

A sight you can't miss in Sapa is the ranks of very pretty children from the **Hmong** tribe – strictly speaking these are all from the Black Hmong subgroup, distinguishable by their indigo-dyed clothes. The Hmong are part of the Australasian grouping and first arrived in Vietnam around 300 years ago from southern China. The initial influx of 80 families who had objected to the Ming emperor's policy of replacing village chiefs with Han mandarins was followed by an immigration wave of around 10,000 Hmong after the failure of an insurrection against the Ching Dynasty in 1868.

The Hmong are a good example of minorities settling at different elevations through the passage of time, as they began by practising shifting cultivation on the slopes of rocky mountains but they have gradually descended and life has become correspondingly easier. Although not matriarchal as many ethnic minorities in Vietnam are (mostly around Dalat), Hmong society is only weakly patriarchal: the man is head of the family but property passes to the wife if the husband dies. The Hmong are also modern in their views on love – arranged marriages have all but died out and these days the Hmong eschew polygamy in favour of monogamy. The Hmong language was converted into written form with a Romanized script in 1961 – before this all history and culture were handed down in spoken form.

The second most common ethnic minority to be seen in Sapa are the wonderfully colourful **Red Dao** (pronounced Zao). Apart from their red head coverings the most striking and remarkably beautiful aspect about the Red Dao is that the girls have their hair and eyebrows shaved off in a ceremony at age 13 and the practice is kept up for the rest of their lives. Traditionally it has been the Dao that have been the traders in Sapa's 'love market' formalising an old tradition that couples would be brought

❏ **Spiritual beliefs**

Most ethnic minorities in Vietnam share with the Kinh the practice of ancestor worship, but customs, taboos and festivals vary widely. Many, such as the Hmong, worship the spirits of the house, cattle and the living and even more minorities believe in the soul of rice, and spirits of earth, wind, fire, rivers and mountains. Yet some beliefs are individual to different tribes – so the Dao hold celebrations in January to the tiger, in February to birds and the wind, in March to thunder and water, and above all they worship a legendary canine ancestor called Ban Ho, while the Giay honour the goddess of childbirth and their direct belief in intergenerational movements of the soul is so strong that they mark the ears of a stillborn child to prevent its reincarnation. Sacrifices are common elements of spiritual worship for the montagnards, so if you happen on a village during a festival season don't be surprised if you see parts of sacrificed animals such as buffalo or pigs' ears, chicken's feet or tufts of animal hair hung on poles at the entrances to villages.

together by the singing of songs to each other. If the singers each approve of the other (and the parents agree) the deal is done and a provisional wedding ceremony is held. Weddings being an expensive business, a full ceremony may not take place for many years by which time the couple may have fully grown children. The Dao bury most of their dead, but those who die from unusual deaths have an air burial. This means that the dead body is placed in a bamboo cage which is raised up into trees and left until only the bones remain. The bleached skeleton is then put in a pottery urn and buried.

There are many **Giay** (pronounced Zai) villages in the Sapa valley where the brightly-coloured chequered woollen headcloths of Giay women contrast against the natural greens and blues of the scenery. Some Giay women still wear full-length black or green hemp dresses ringed with thick bands of embroidery, but most wear simpler clothes these days. Giay people immigrated from southern China from the end of the 18th century until early this century. They are part of the Australasian grouping. The Giays have been favoured by Vietnamese Communists because most Giay fields are communal property rather than divided into private land. Perhaps the most interesting Giay custom is that each village has an area of trees which it considers forbidden and where the biggest tree is considered sacred. Each year the genie of the village is worshipped at the foot of this tree.

There are over a million **Tays** in Vietnam, mostly to the south and east of Lao Cai. They populate the villages encountered by road between Hanoi and Lao Cai, and are frequent if brief users of the railway between Kep and Dong Dang (see p301) where they adorn the countryside with indigo-dyed clothes cut to make elegant dresses, tied at the waist by a silk belt, bedecked with silver jewellery and topped by turbans of wound indigo cloth. As the Tay people are the largest ethnic minority in Vietnam and one of the oldest, arriving around the time of the birth of Christ. (roughly coinciding with the arrival of the Kinh), it is appropriate that many of their number are well integrated into Vietnamese society. However, there are still many who live traditional lives worshipping the earth genie at the foot of the banyan tree and cultivating rice, aniseed and cinnamon. The Tays are one of the few ethnic minorities who developed their own script (using the Chinese characters which used to be used in all Vietnam) so they have a written literature, and much more is known about their folklore than many other montagnards. Their language has also been converted into a Romanized script.

There have been **Black Thai** people living in stilt houses to the north and west of Sapa for at least a millennium practising traditional agriculture and creating a vast heritage of literature and music. Black Thai women and girls have some of the most elegant dress in the whole of Vietnam. Long black skirts are offset by short white or black blouses fastened at the front with a row of finely-worked silver buttons, topped by delicately-embroidered black and pink turbans. All Thai dress is very similar, despite the fact that their society is highly class-segregated. The Thais developed a written language based on Sanskrit by at least the 5th century and its beautiful form was put to great use creating histories, epics, poems.

Walks
● **Sapa Valley** Sapa valley is a beautiful dale sandwiched between watershed mountains to its back and facing the range of mountains opposite topped by Fansipan and surrounded by the Nui Hoang Lien nature reserve. In between there is a deep valley dropping away sharply below Sapa as plunging streams meet to form the Cat Cat falls in the midst of exquisite rice-terraced hills. The valley extends westwards traversed by a rough jeep track. Small paths descend from this to the Muong Hoa Ho river and to villages each housing a different ethnic minority. There are three notable walks from Sapa. You can also undertake guided treks around the area heading further afield – the best places to organize these are at the Auberge or at Friendly Café.

The beautiful Sapa valley is easy to access from the jeep track which heads south-west out of town from below the Auberge. This wide track peopled with Hmong children and adults and the occasional troop of ponies descends into the valley for around 5km until a path branches off to the right over the river to Lao Chai village. The round trip to Lao Chai takes around four hours, but it's really worth going on, especially as most visitors to Sapa have given up on the track by the time you reach this point so the rest of the valley is generally yours to explore. The best way to do this is abandon the track and follow the small paths which weave along beside the river. Lao Chai is a Hmong village and the next villages are even more interesting – Ta Van Ray is a Giay village and if you make it on to the next one you are in Dao territory.

Do bear in mind on such a trek that mountain people are unlikely to speak any English or French and only pidgin Vietnamese, if any at all. Nonetheless a great way to do this trip is to take an overnight bag with you and at the point when you still could turn back see if anyone in the dwellings you pass encourages you to take tea with them. The general rule is that if you are all still imbibing by the time night falls they are likely to convey the message that you are welcome to stay for the night. In theory this could land you in trouble with the police, but this has not been known to happen.

If you are invited to stay be prepared to rise when the sun does and try to pay particular attention to which water supply is for washing and which is for cooking. A small useful gift such as soap is often sufficient to show appreciation for the hospitality, although Vietnamese dong left discreetly will be much appreciated. You can take the same route back to Sapa, but there is an alternative. If you stay on the northern side of the river the path will lead steeply up a hill, a hill which turns out to be the beginning of a marvellous ridge walk bisecting the valley. If you do take this route, however, do be careful as at the top the ridge narrows to only around 20cm; do not attempt it in a strong wind. Also be aware that there will be points on this alternative route where route-finding will be difficult. It is not for the timid or novice walker. The path back to Sapa when you have descended is clear.

● **Cat Cat waterfalls** An alternative, and less ambitious, walk is to descend from Sapa to the head of the valley and visit the village of Cat Cat and its waterfalls, with the chance of walking around the beautiful valley floor and making an excursion to the Hmong village of Sin Chai. Just north of the market in Sapa a track junctions off to the left (east) then down for 2km into the valley floor; on the way down there are wonderful views of the whole valley and some stalls offering coffee and soft drinks; these are useful to remember for the way up. Incongruously there is also a fabulous tiny jewellery shop along this route. Once you have descended you have the choice of branching off to the left and taking your ease in green meadows occasionally trekked across by passing Hmong, or continuing along the main track another 2km to the south-east until you reach Sin Chai village, or descending down a smaller track to the meeting of three streams that is the Cat Cat waterfalls (beware: this path can become unbelievably muddy). Return to Sapa the way you came; either way this walk shouldn't take you more than four to five hours.

● **The Dragon's Teeth** In the midst of all this glorious scenery Sapa also has its own tame mountain tourist attraction for which you pay

5000d. This is to climb up endless stone steps to reach the rocky top of the mountain behind Sapa which, because of the pointiness of the rocks and the narrow gaps between them is called the 'Dragon's Teeth'. Actually this is quite a diverting 20-minute climb despite graffiti on the rocks which you are obliged to squeeze between, but even more rewarding is to continue on up beyond the rocks along small paths (beware mud in the summer) to the start of the ridge that looks like the dragon's jaws. But it's hard going to find a different and decent route down.

An alternative route to the views which the mountain top affords but avoiding the charge of the dragon's teeth (and the teeth themselves) is to locate the super path which traverses the mountain high above the jeep track passing above corn fields and near to small Hmong dwellings. The start of the path is a bit tricky to find – head out of Sapa for around 50m along the jeep track below the Auberge until you come to a small path heading sharply up on the left.

● **Climbing Fansipan** This is no small feat. To ascend its 3143m-high thickly forested slopes takes a fit good walker/climber at least five days' hard trek from Sapa. A guide is essential and porters are advisable as there are no dwellings to stay in on the mountain. No equipment is available to buy or hire from Sapa or Lao Cai, so you need to bring everything with you from Hanoi – and you can't even get the best equipment here.

An attempt is certainly best made in the summer rather than winter and even then many attempts are rained off. If you survive the weather you then have to tramp through bamboo jungles which become so thick near the top that to make any progress means hacking away at the vegetation with a machete while each of you wears a bell so as you can keep track of where the others are.

If you are serious about wanting to try, speak to the Auberge about hiring a guide ($20 a day) and porters – and good luck. Even if you don't make it the experience of trekking through the nature reserve and keeping an eagle-eye out for such delights as the red giant flying squirrel, a trident-nosed bat or even an Asian black bear is quite something.

PART 7: ROUTE GUIDES

Using these guides

These route guides have been designed to draw your attention to points of interest on train journeys. The maps for the Reunification Express route between Ho Chi Minh City and Hanoi have all been drawn south to north, but of course could equally well be used the other way round. For the northern branches of the railway the sections have been covered to take you firstly east to Haiphong, then north-west to Kep from Halong Bay, then north-east from Hanoi through Kep to Lang Son (Dong Dang), and finally north-west from Hanoi to Lao Cai. The northern branch to Lang Son continues on into China, leading to Beijing. The north-western branch of the railway also continues into China, to Kunming.

Station stops
The route maps show all the stops along the route of the Reunification Express, and the text covers briefly the stops which have not been covered elsewhere in the book because stopping in these places is not anticipated. The guide is divided into sections covering the route between one suggested stop and the next. The sections vary in length so the scale on each map is not the same. Kilometre distances between stations are marked on each map.

For some of the length of Vietnam's railways kilometre posts have been placed near to the railway track, usually to the east of the tracks. The posts, when they are visible within knee-high paddy fields, show the distance to the centre of Vietnam's capital, Hanoi.

Stops at stations vary in length according to the route taken and the size of the place. In general trains stop the longest at Nha Trang, Danang and Hué. The details are listed in the latest timetable at the time of writing (see p311). All trains terminate at HCMC and Hanoi. There are no through trains to China either from Hanoi, where it is necessary to change, or at the Vietnamese-Chinese border, where you must also change trains.

Ticketing
A reminder of how ticketing works: there is no through-ticketing system for Vietnamese trains, which means that you must purchase a separate ticket for each part of your journey. It is also useful to bring your passport when buying a ticket because it is often checked.

| **Rail Map Key** | ■ - City/Important Town | ▲ - War site |
| | ● - Town/Village | 🏖 - Beach |

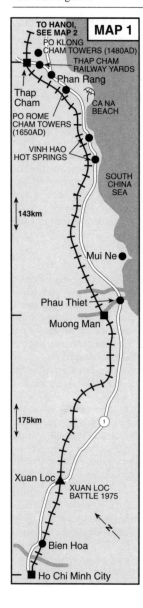

If you are taking a short journey you will not be allowed to travel on an express trains even if it stops at your designated station; you may have to take a local train, for which the timetables are highly changeable.

Bear in mind also that stations in small towns are allocated only a few foreigners' tickets, so you should purchase them in advance whenever possible. Small towns usually have no allocation for tickets above soft-seat category, but this is rarely a problem because you can upgrade on the train, and it is usually cheaper to do so. Finally, you must remember that it is essential that you keep your ticket because you have to hand it in when leaving the station. If you lose your ticket, you will literally have to buy a new one in order to be allowed out of the station and the clutches of the station police.

When getting around the country by train, remember that even-numbered trains, S2, S4, etc, go north, and odd-numbered trains, S1, S3 etc, go south.

HO CHI MINH CITY TO THAP CHAM [MAP 1]

The 319km between Ho Chi Minh City (HCMC) and Thap Cham take 5½-7½ hours. Once the train has pulled out of the extensive suburbs of HCMC, the scenery is generally characterized by Vietnam's ubiquitous luminous green paddy fields.

Sixty kilometres out of HCMC the line departs from the route of Highway 1 and passes through **Xuan Loc**, site of an important battle in the last days of the American war.

One hundred and seventy five kilometres east of HCMC at **Muong Man** the railway approaches the coast of the South China Sea which it will then track for most of the remaining 1551km to Hanoi. The tiny station of Muong Man is half an hour's drive from the fishing centre of **Phan Thiet**, which is a further hour's drive away from the swanky but soulless resorts of **Mui Ne**. Here you can luxuriate in air-conditioned bungalows seconds away from a well-kept sandy beach, and from the fine French food and wine of the dining area of *Coco Resort* (☎ 062-848401). But be prepared for the price – around $80 a night, excluding all meals. Since the resort is isolated you're stuck with the price of food there.

A hundred kilometres further on, the railway track runs very close to the coast to skirt around the edge of the Dalat mountain massif. Several kilometres to the east is the pleasant **Ca Na** beach. Fifteen kilometres before Thap Cham, when Highway 1 leaves the path of the railway and tracks closer to the coast passing near to the unimpressive **Po Ro Me Cham Towers**, built around 1650.

As the train pulls into Thap Cham station there is a fine view of the imposing terracotta-red **Po Klong Garai Cham Towers** just to the east of the track atop a vegetated, scrub and cactus hill. Meanwhile, at the bottom of the hill lie the **Thap Cham railway repair yards** (see p182), fascinating for rail buffs. Alighting at Thap Cham is recommended for a visit to the Cham Towers, but certainly not for the scruffy town, **Phan Rang**.

THAP CHAM TO NHA TRANG
[MAP 2]

The 93km between Thap Cham and Nha Trang takes 1½-2 hours. The route passes through several Vietnamese villages and the scenery comprises paddy fields, with

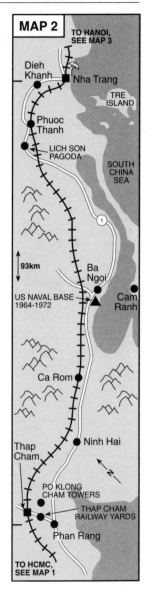

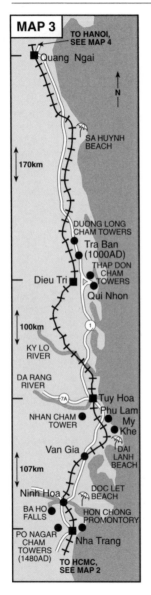

MAP 3

TO HANOI, SEE MAP 4

Quang Ngai

N

SA HUYNH BEACH

170km

DUONG LONG CHAM TOWERS

Tra Ban (1000AD)

THAP DON CHAM TOWERS

Dieu Tri

Qui Nhon

1

100km

KY LO RIVER

DA RANG RIVER

7A

Tuy Hoa

Phu Lam

NHAN CHAM TOWER

My Khe

Van Gia

DAI LANH BEACH

107km

Ninh Hoa

DOC LET BEACH

BA HO FALLS

HON CHONG PROMONTORY

PO NAGAR CHAM TOWERS (1480AD)

Nha Trang

TO HCMC, SEE MAP 2

Dalat's mountains visible to the west. Thap Cham used to be connected to Dalat by a rack railway on which carriages climbed the 1500m to the cool hill station reaching the end of their journey in Dalat's charming Art Deco railway station, opened in 1933. But sadly, various wars from WWII to the American war ravaged the line which has not been in use for decades. There is now a road to Dalat from Thap Cham which gets increasingly rough as it nears the hill station.

Halfway to Nha Trang are the sheltered waters of **Cam Ranh Bay**. This was the site of a major **US naval base** between 1964 and 1972. During the abandonment of the central highlands in March 1975, US naval vessels shuttled to and from Cam Ranh Bay trying to help with the emergency evacuation of Hué, then Danang, then Nha Trang.

Nha Trang (see p184) has a well-equipped railway station, replete with waiting cyclo drivers. Nha Trang is a great place to visit, not only for its lovely beach and boating possibilities, but also because it is a thriving and lively town. And the food is great too.

NHA TRANG TO QUANG NGAI
[MAP 3]

It takes around 8½ hours to cover the 387km between Nha Trang and Quang Ngai. The railway line tracks near the coast, skirting around the spurs of the mountain range stretching east from Buon Ma Thuot and, Pleiku and Kon Tum.

As the train pulls out of Nha Trang, crossing the Cho river above the busy fishing harbour, it passes the **Po Nagar Cham towers** to the west and then **Hon**

Chong promontory to the east. The railway line then runs close by attractive Ben Goi Bay with Highway 1 alternately to its right and left. This section of the railway was extremely difficult to construct because of the encroaching spurs from the Truong Sen mountain range. The result is several tunnels which had to be blasted through the rock; the longest is 1.2km.

After the train passes through the small town of Phu Lam and crosses over Da Rang river 100km from Nha Trang, the **Nhan Cham towers** lie to the west of nearby Highway 1. Seven kilometres further on is **Tuy Hoa,** a small unremarkable town. This is where route 7B, the disastrous road taken by army units and civilians fleeing the central highlands suddenly seized by Communists in 1975, finally hits Highway 1 – salvation for the few who made it (see p67).

The section of the railway between Tuy Hoa and Dieu Tri departs from the road and instead follows internal valleys. This route was chosen to avoid the difficult, hilly, terrain near the coast. Approximately 102km beyond Tuy Hoa is the small station of Dieu Tri, several kilometres from the small port town of **Qui Nhon** which has never made it as a beach resort despite half-hearted attempts. It was in this area that the Tay Son brothers launched their 18th-century rebellion (see p45).

Ten kilometres beyond Dieu Tri lie the remains of the Chams' 11th-century capital, **Tra Ban**. Tra Ban was the centre of the Chams' southern empire from 1000 to 1471 until they were defeated by the Vietnamese who were steadily moving south. The Tay Son brothers did not see this as a bad precedent and made this the capital of the central region of Vietnam, which they had split into three in 1771. They looked set to establish a new empire, but instead fell in with Nguyen Anh who became the first emperor to rule from Hué, Emperor Gia Long.

Ten kilometres further on, the large **Duong Long Cham towers**, towers of ivory, are visible from the train. These are good examples of the Cham architecture whose granite stone is decorated with elephants, lions, fanciful monsters and beautiful female dancers.

Where the train and Highway 1 track very close to the sea 65km before Quang Ngai the popular **Sa Huynh beach** lies just to the east of the village of Sa Huynh.

Quang Ngai's small railway station lies 2.5km to the west of the small, scruffy town's centre. The main reason to visit Quang Ngai (see p194) is to make an excursion to the well-kept and deeply-moving site of the **My Lai massacre** which took place on 16 March, 1968.

QUANG NGAI TO DANANG [MAP 4, p292]

It takes around three hours to cover the 136km between Quang Ngai and Danang. The journey takes you through endless paddy fields dissolving

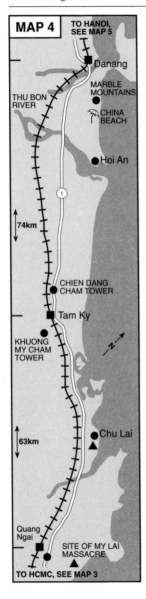

MAP 4

TO HANOI, SEE MAP 5

Danang

MARBLE MOUNTAINS

CHINA BEACH

THU BON RIVER

Hoi An

74km

CHIEN DANG CHAM TOWER

Tam Ky

KHUONG MY CHAM TOWER

63km

Chu Lai

Quang Ngai

SITE OF MY LAI MASSACRE

TO HCMC, SEE MAP 3

into distant mountains in the west. Note that the rice fields increase in size as the train heads towards Danang, showing that the wealth of rural families falls the further they are from a big urban centre.

Around Quang Ngai you can see some of the crops indigenous to the area, including maize, sweet potato and sugar cane. Thirty seven kilometres out of Quang Ngai to the east of the railway track lies the small village of **Chu Lai**. This area was the site of a major US military base during the American war.

Ten kilometres after the railway returns inland, having skirted a lagoon look out for the two reasonable examples of Cham towers on either side of the railway track, and south and north of the tiny station of Tam Ky. Look out for **Khnong My Cham Tower** on your left before you reach Tam Ky and then **Chien Dang Cham Tower** on your right after it. Beyond **Tam Ky** the rice paddies are interspersed with more tropical vegetation with green palm trees encroaching towards the railway. This then gives way to the sand, scrub and cacti that characterize much of central Vietnam.

Rice fields then take over once again around the several tributaries of the great Thu Bon river. The river connected **Hoi An** (see p208) a delightful little town, with the sea and thus with all the great trading nations of the world – until the river silted up during the 19th century. Hoi An is only an hour's drive from Danang; hundreds of Honda oms and taxis gather at Danang's railway station to take you there.

Between Hoi An and Danang is the wonderful white sand and crashing waves of **China Beach** (see p203), and the five rocky hillocks of the **Marble Mountains** (see p202) dotted with bright temples and giving fine views out to sea. These lie out of sight of the railway and road but are easily accessible on a day trip from Danang or Hoi An.

The railway then crosses over a couple of tributaries of the Cai river and approaches the suburbs of Danang. These suburbs become ever busier and noisier, and finally the train draws into the agreeable centre of **Danang**.

DANANG TO HUE   [MAP 5]

The rail journey between Danang and Hué takes around 3¼ hours, covers 103km, and takes you over the beautiful **Hai Van pass**, the Pass of the Clouds, affording some of the most stunning mountain and seascapes train travel can offer. The route is a famously beautiful one in Vietnam, and justifiably so. Ensure that you sit on the right side of the train going north and on the left going south to get the best views.

Hai Van pass is also notable for marking a geological split in the country: all areas north of the pass experience a real winter – the climate is no longer equatorial.

Departing from Danang the train cuts quickly through the city, temporarily bisecting streets and revealing front gardens patched with sand, with cacti and rice growing cheek by jowl. Once across the estuary, as signs of industry recede, the train starts to climb and the tunnels which mark the ascent and descent begin. The tracks then pass over fast bubbling streams, populated with large grey/brown rocks, which do somewhat resemble elephants, as locals will not tire of insisting.

The train slows to a crawl as it ascends the mountain, clinging to its side, until it reaches a high viewpoint which

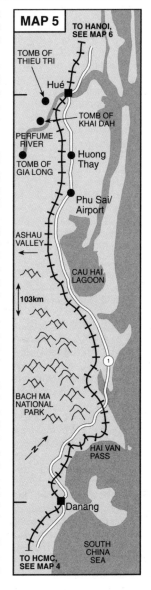

looks down onto a broad curved bay with a populated beach. Look out for the tiny divine unspoilt beach protected by the picturesque cliffs which render it entirely inaccessible except by sea. The vegetation now surrounding the train is thick and lush, officially making it a zone of sub-equatorial monsoon forest. The beautiful layers of mountains which can be glimpsed to the west are part of the Kon Tum Indosinian mountain mass which covers lower Laos, Cambodia and Thailand. For the following delightful half hour you are taken high above wide views of the sea dotted with idyllic coves and with views of the Truong Sen mountain range in the north, through tunnels of up to two minutes long, and then swept along rocky or jungly shores right down at water level.

As the train makes a rocketing descent to the invariably blue waters of **Cau Hai lagoon**, populated with numerous small boats and Chinese fishing nets, look out for the people waiting at the level crossing who wave joyously if you do. The train rounds a bend and suddenly faces the habitation at the very end of a long peninsula with the Bach Ma mountain range framing the view in the background.

The gentle waters of the lagoon mark the end of Hai Van pass, but delightful views of life on the lagoon continue for the next hour of the journey. Upon crossing Highway 1 just before a village on the lagoon's shore the (inferior!) route the road takes can be seen behind you. Be sure at least to look behind at some point in order to catch the spectacular views of the steep dark forested mountains of the Hai Van pass plunging into the sea.

The vegetation around the train is different now that you are back in the lowlands with palm trees, birch trees, rice paddies and water buffaloes. To the west the steeply forested Bach Ma mountains rise suddenly from the flat ground, less than 1km from the tracks, signalling the beginning of the **Bach Ma national park**. This is the start of the narrowest strip of Vietnam which stretches between here and Vinh, 300km to the north.

Marshes now separate the tracks from the lagoon, marshes which are home to some of Vietnam's rare birds. When the marshes are visible only from a distance look to the west to see the mountains surrounding **Ashau valley** 40km away, the scene of heavy fighting in the American war, which is better known to cinema-goers as *Hamburger Hill*.

From here on, it is rice paddies all the way until you reach the outskirts of Hué, distinguishable by settlements in the pine-clad hills which surround the **emperors' tombs** scattered around the south of Vietnam's extravagant 19th-century capital, Hué. The beautiful **Perfume river** which the train crosses before entering **Hué** (see p217) is a foretaste of the picturesque delights of the city and its tombs. But, tombs aside, don't expect too much in the way of ancient buildings – Hué was the scene of very heavy fighting during the American war and little of the emperor's purple city remains.

HUE TO DONG HA [MAP 6]

It takes 1½-2 hours to cover the 66km between Hué and Dong Ha. Leaving Hué's well-kept station the train passes through its poorer suburbs before breaking into open country.

Beyond Hué the railway runs near Highway 1 but does not cut through the many little settlements which line the road. Half way to Dong Ha the train crosses over the huge deep blue **Thuc Ma river** which is full of wooden boats housing fishermen and their families. This traditional scene is marred only by the sight of South Vietnamese and American bunkers along the banks of the river which incongruously provide shelter for modern-day Vietnamese. Vegetation beyond the Thuc Ma river gives way to eucalyptus trees fed by the many rivers which flow from the Truong Sen mountain range to the west.

Fourteen kilometres before Dong Ha the train crosses the wide **Quang Tri river** which runs from the Lao border 40km to the west. On the river's journey from the border it passed the Khe Sanh combat base, one of the most famous sites of the demilitarized zone (DMZ) (see p235). Despite its name, the 5km either side of the Ben Hai river near the 17th parallel (just north of Dong Ha) which was called the DMZ was perhaps the most heavily bombed and bombarded area of the country.

Beyond the Quang Tri river the most dominant vegetation is scrubland, interspersed with carefully irrigated rice paddies and then rubber plants, coconut trees and again eucalyptus trees. All this serves as a foretaste of the sights and sounds of the DMZ, and the train then pulls into **Dong Ha**'s shabby station.

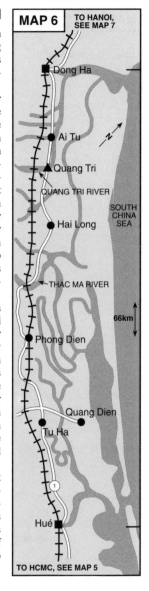

MAP 6 — TO HANOI, SEE MAP 7

Dong Ha

Ai Tu

Quang Tri

QUANG TRI RIVER

SOUTH CHINA SEA

Hai Long

THAC MA RIVER

66km

Phong Dien

Quang Dien

Tu Ha

1

Hué

TO HCMC, SEE MAP 5

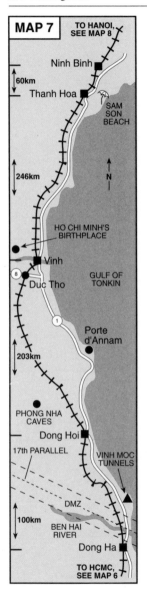

MAP 7

TO HANOI,
SEE MAP 8

Ninh Binh

60km

Thanh Hoa

SAM
SON
BEACH

246km

N

HO CHI MINH'S
BIRTHPLACE

Vinh

8

GULF OF
TONKIN

Duc Tho

1

Porte
d'Annam

203km

PHONG NHA
CAVES

Dong Hoi

17th PARALLEL

VINH MOC
TUNNELS

DMZ

100km

BEN HAI
RIVER

Dong Ha

TO HCMC,
SEE MAP 6

DONG HA TO NINH BINH   [MAP 7]

It takes 9-12 hours to cover the 508km
between Dong Ha and Ninh Binh which
takes in the DMZ, the towns of Dong Hoi
and Thanh Hoa and the ghastly city of
Vinh before arriving in the beautiful
countryside of Ninh Binh.

Leaving behind the town and road-
ways of Dong Ha the train enters the
demilitarized zone itself. Villages thin
out, until the train crosses the **Ben Hai
river** almost exactly on the **17th parallel**
and you enter what was once officially
called the Democratic Republic of
Vietnam.

The 10km around the line of the Ben
Hai river is the territory of Vietnam which
suffered the huge bombardment of the
war, rather than the many, but small-
scale, battles which characterized the
south. If you did not stop to investigate
closely the sites of the DMZ you can still
have a flavour of the experience from the
train with sights of bridges still showing
bomb damage and fields with large dips
in – bomb craters.

After leaving the northern extremity
of the DMZ the land around the railway
gradually returns to the coastal plain
norm of rice paddies. About 101km and
around 1½ hours out of Dong Ha the train
reaches the small town of **Dong Hoi**,
which is an undistinguished fishing port.
Tourists are not a common sight in Dong
Hoi, but that is not a reason to visit the
town. The only reason to do so is to see
the interesting **Phong Nha caves**, 43km
north-west of Dong Hoi, with their huge
underwater canals and glistening stalactites and stalagmites.

Beyond Dong Hoi the railway track
breaks away from the route of the road as
it was built inland to avoid the rocky

coastline at **Porte d'Annam**. The track now bifurcates the thinnest section of Vietnam (50km wide) where Laos is only 20km to the west and visible – the border runs along the highest points of the mountain range. The vegetation here is lush but the land is hard to cultivate as the mountains to the west grow increasingly close to the railway track.

As the railway passes through the small settlement of **Duc Tho** 20km short of Vinh it crosses Highway 8 which leads to Laos over Keo Nua Pass, a possible crossing point into Laos; on a clear day you can see the mountains rising either side of the pass in the distance.

Industrial activities build up as the train approaches the large industrial conurbation of **Vinh** which you reach after six hours and 303km from Dong Ha. Few find much to say in recommendation of Vinh; indeed one traveller from Germany described it as 'the most depressing place I have ever seen'. This region also has some of the worst soil in the country, making life hard for the peasants, and the worst weather – the coast is frequently lashed by severe storms. Vinh does boast being the nearest city to **Ho Chi Minh's birthplace**, 14km to the west at Kim Lien. Here the small farmhouse he spent some time growing up in (when he wasn't at school in Hué) is maintained for (mostly Vietnamese) tourists, and there is also a fairly painful museum.

As Vinh recedes, the railway line stays close to Highway 1 for some 60km, passing through roadside towns and habitations, with rice paddies to either side. The scenery becomes most interesting within an hour and a half's arrival of Ninh Binh. Passing through the town of **Thanh Hoa**, notable only for the acceptable and very popular **Sam Son beach** 15km to the east, the vegetation increases in variety to include maize and the distinctive scenery which characterizes the fabulous region of **Ninh Binh** rises out of the ground in great limestone outcrops. With verdant rice paddies nestling beneath the cliffs backed by distant blue mountains you have a taste of the beauty of the 'inland Halong Bay' that is Ninh Binh.

NINH BINH TO HANOI   [MAP 8, p298]

It takes 2-2½ hours to cover the 114km between Ninh Binh and Hanoi. This is a flat stretch of land over which the trains keep a good speed reaching up to the second, smaller, rice basket of Vietnam, the **Red River** basin. For most of the journey the west of the train affords views of small habitations, rice paddies and distant mountains, while the east primarily looks onto roadway settlements.

Directly out of Ninh Binh the railway line forks to the east, diverting from the route of Highway 1, crosses the Nam Dinh river and heads towards **Nam Dinh**, taking a 59km detour. The target of the detour, Nam Dinh, is a small but pleasant industrial town peppered with tree-lined avenues and small lakes. Its increased prosperity relative to regions just

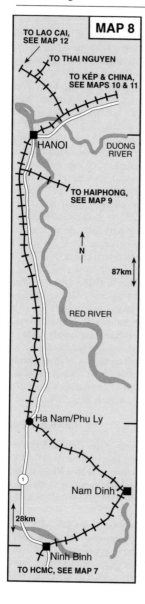

MAP 8

TO LAO CAI, SEE MAP 12

TO THAI NGUYEN

TO KÉP & CHINA, SEE MAPS 10 & 11

HANOI   DUONG RIVER

TO HAIPHONG, SEE MAP 9

N

87km

RED RIVER

Ha Nam/Phu Ly

1

Nam Dinh

28km

Ninh Binh

TO HCMC, SEE MAP 7

south of the town is also a sign of things to come as Hanoi approaches – the proximity to the winding Red River makes this area so much more fertile and the vegetation more lush than the coastal regions.

After the train passes through the town of **Phu Ly** (which is often called Ha Nam on maps) the rising contours of the mountains to the north-west of Hanoi become visible; they stretch into Laos and China but culminate in Vietnam in Dien Bien Phu to the west, and Lao Cai and Sapa to the north-west. Between Phu Ly and Hanoi the scenery from the train alternates between the grimy traffic of Highway 1 which the track runs extremely close to, and fields of lotus flowers which are in bloom in the summer months.

Once the train has entered the suburbs of Hanoi you will know that the main railway station is only five minutes away when the train passes a house on the west side of the tracks manufacturing and selling 2m-high glass statues of the Eiffel Tower! The railway line then runs between some lakes, which are such a feature of this charming city, before arriving at **Hanoi** station, Ga Hanoi.

HANOI TO HAIPHONG   [MAP 9]

It takes around three hours to cover the 94km between Hanoi and Haiphong. The scenery of this journey is not especially notable and bear in mind that when you arrive in Haiphong it is a further three hours by ferry to Halong, or a shorter but hasslesome bus or taxi ride.

Leaving **Gia Lam** station in Hanoi the railway line tracks along by Highway 5 for 15km before reaching the small town of **Hai Duong** after which the road and the railway crosses the **Kinh Thay river**. Highway 5 then crosses the railway line and continues to its north for the rest of the journey to Haiphong, filling the view in this direction and impairing the panorama of paddy fields fed by the many waterways running through the fertile Red River basin.

Between **Hai Duong** and Haiphong the railway line passes through the village of **Phu Thai** and near the settlement of **An Duong**. Industrial activity increases as the city of Haiphong nears, Vietnam's third largest city.

HALONG TO KEP   [MAP 10, p300]

It takes 4³/₄ hours to cover the 120km between Halong Bay and Kep. The journey is a great combination of scenery and the friendly experience of a slow local Vietnamese train which sees almost no foreigners. It is a reward for anyone persevering enough to locate Halong's tiny station, Ga Halong, or Gieng Day. There is only hard-seat accommodation on the train and the track between Halong Bay and Kep runs on 1.435m gauge, rather than the 1m gauge on the Reunification Express line.

It is best to sit on the south side of the train in order to see the Halong Bay-like cliffs – layer upon blue-grey hazy layer – which drift by in the distance rising along by the delta of the **Kinh Thay** river.

On the north side of the river after around two hours (60km) the **Yen Tu** mountain range homes into view and gets ever closer. There are still rice paddies leading to the increasingly foresty vegetation behind. The train runs along extremely thin causeways between the fields around the **Luc Ngan** river (within an hour before Kep); in the summer

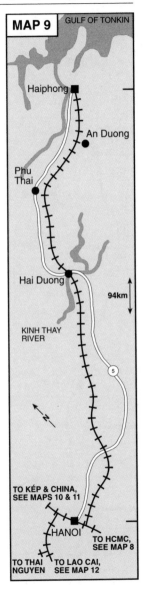

MAP 9 GULF OF TONKIN

Haiphong

An Duong

Phu Thai

Hai Duong

94km

KINH THAY RIVER

5

TO KÉP & CHINA, SEE MAPS 10 & 11

HANOI

TO HCMC, SEE MAP 8

TO THAI NGUYEN TO LAO CAI, SEE MAP 12

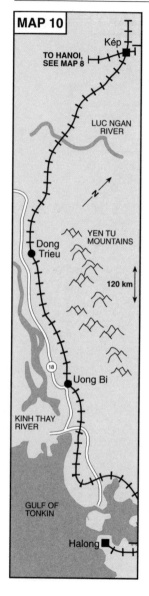

MAP 10

Kép

TO HANOI,
SEE MAP 8

LUC NGAN
RIVER

N

YEN TU
MOUNTAINS

Dong
Trieu

120 km

18

Uong Bi

KINH THAY
RIVER

GULF OF
TONKIN

Halong

months the land round here is often flooded. On this route, and the route from Kep
to Lang Son, you may see a man going
round the train offering drags from what
looks like a mobile opium unit. Although
hill tribes in the north of Vietnam do consume opium this system in fact dispenses
tobacco.

Finally the train rumbles into the tiny
station of **Kep**, with its paddy fields and
gentle lumbering water buffaloes surrounding the few station buildings.

HANOI TO LANG SON VIA KEP
(AND TO CHINA)   [MAP 11]

It takes 2½ hours to cover the 71km from
Hanoi to Kep and four hours between
Kep and Lang Son (85km). The mountain
rail journey from Kep to Lang Son is one
of the most beautiful in the country. The
train crawls up rice-terraced slopes as
colourful hill-tribe people jump on and
off, transporting their (usually animal)
baggage for short distances up the slope.

Leaving Hanoi the train crosses the
Duong river and tracks to the west of the
northern continuation of Highway 1. This
mars the view to the east of the train,
obscuring the fertile fields of Vietnam's
second rice basket. Highway 1 finally
crosses the railway line just before the
tiny centre of **Kep** and diverts from its
path.

The road passes through the **Ai Chi
Lang** – the entrance, or gate, to the very
narrow Chi Lang valley. At this site
Chinese armies through the centuries
have been stopped in their progression
southwards (see p43). The route is particularly beautiful if seen from a bicycle –
bicycles can be transported on the train up
to Lang Son and ridden down, or can be
bought at Lang Son.

It is beyond Kep that the great scenery of the journey begins. The west side of the train is the best for wonderful views of the mountains of Lang Son province which rise behind the coffee and tea plantations. Beyond the Chi Lang valley the train makes a short stop at **Song Hoa** which would be a pleasant place from which to explore the countryside. The craggy scenery comes ever nearer to the tracks until the town of **Dong Mo**, which nestles at their very feet. This area sees very few foreigners and is great to explore, providing you are prepared for basic accommodation.

From Dong Mo to Lang Son the train climbs and winds its way up the mountains, often going as slowly as 10km/hour. This leisurely pace allows you to enjoy the stunning gashes of red clay amidst the luminous green of paddy fields. The train makes a short stop at **Bac Thuy** – a small town in the midst of swirling rice terraces contrasting with low forested hills behind. The train then travels high and slow across this land, hauling itself up the rice-terraced slopes, at times perched high on bridges and causeways way above the tiny settlements below.

The land here is increasingly populated with hill-tribes from the Tay minority group. These montagnards use the train to transport heavy goods short distances between stops by running alongside the train, jumping on, and then a string of people along the tracks provide a relay system handing up baskets of animals or huge bags of rice to the person on the train. Several kilometres later the person on the train throws the cargo onto the ground and then leaps off and walks back to retrieve the precious packages.

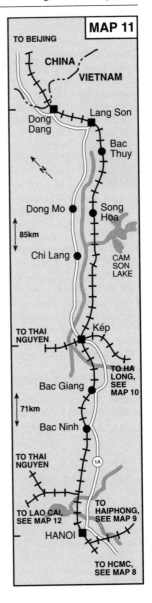

Finally, the train crosses the watershed and descends into the plain of Lang Son.

Trains to China

Trains going into China do not stop at Kep, but you can connect with them by taking a train from Kep north to Dong Mo, Lang Son or Dong Dang.

The through trains are no faster than the local trains.

The trains for China leave Hanoi on Tuesdays and Fridays, and leave Beijing for Hanoi on Mondays and Fridays, meaning that they pass through Vietnam on Wednesdays and Sundays. The China-bound train leaves Dong Mo at 5.35pm, Lang Son at 7.27pm, and Dong Dang at 11pm (having arrived at 8pm). This means that you have option of stopping at Dong Mo and exploring the beautiful scenery around here, or of stopping at Lang Son and exploring the wonderful caves here or sampling the good food on offer.

Continuing to China?
China by Rail is also in this series;
see p320

From Lang Son you can take the train to Dong Dang (which really is a depressing place with nothing to see) and through to China. Or you can take a Honda om or, for around $3, a taxi to the station at Dong Dang and buy a ticket there for the train. Bear in mind, however, that it is cheaper to buy tickets in China so if you can take the hassle it makes sense to buy a ticket in Dong Dang for Pinxiang and then buy a new ticket onwards from there. Be prepared for a wait while you have to change trains, though the change is almost always worth it because Chinese trains are luxurious compared to Vietnamese.

HANOI TO LAO CAI (AND CHINA)   [MAP 12]

It takes $9\frac{1}{2}$ hours to cover the 164km between Hanoi and Lao Cai. The journey from Hanoi to Kunming traverses remarkable mountain scenery, so much so that when it was built it was christened the 'ligne acrobatique'. But you have to enter the Chinese section of the line to witness this picturesque tour de force.

Ten kilometres out of Hanoi's Long Bien station the train passes through **Dong An**. From here there is a train line up to **Thai Nguyen**, an industrialized centre, which connects to the east to Kep, but is a roundabout route that has not found favour with many. Sixty two kilometres out of Hanoi, when the road to Lao Cai crosses the railway line, is **Viet Tri** station. From here it is 24km up a small road to the swirling clouds of **Tam Dao hill station**.

Beyond Viet Tri the train line tracks alongside the **Red River** all the way up to Lao Cai. The views of this often fast-flowing river are continuous and unvarying so if you do not find the thought thrilling you may be best off travelling by night. To the east Highway 70 passes alongside the huge **Thac Ba lake** and traverses the northern side of the **Con Voi mountain range**. This area is populated with hill tribers.

There are as yet no through trains from Hanoi to Kunming, so you are obliged to travel to Lao Cai, cross the border on foot and then pick up a train on the Chinese side at the border town of Hekou. But as the train draws into **Lao Cai** (see p277), you should see this as a force for good, as it encourages you to take the hour's drive winding up into the clouds of **Sapa** (see p278) from where you can visit the beautiful Sapa valley. Here you can spend several days in cheap, but charming, accommodation in this former French hill station delighting in the beautiful surrounding mountains and taking in the costumes and customs of different montagnard tribespeople.

Lao Cai is also the jumping off point for the whole of the little explored northwest area but to journey to Dien Bien Phu or elsewhere you need to hire a decent 4WD (an expensive project) or submit to the vagaries of buses and their conductors (see p93).

Reaching China

It is the section of the railway on the Chinese side for which the Hanoi–Kunming line is justly famed for its beauty. This part of the journey begins in the border town of Hekou (which although not pretty has a reasonable share of decent accommodation and services). To reach Hekou you need to cross the land border at the northern end of Lao Cai on foot. From Hekou the rather more comfortable Chinese trains depart at 2.45pm daily for a spectacle of glorious views, and for Kunming.

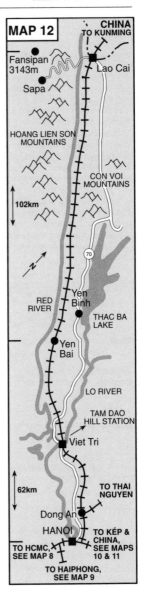

APPENDIX A: LANGUAGE

PRONUNCIATION AND INTONATION

In trying to learn some Vietnamese the three most important things to know are:

1. Vietnamese is a **tonal language** – ie the meaning of words entirely depends on the way they are pronounced, for example with a rising voice or a descending one. This is totally different from Western languages and makes Vietnamese very difficult for Westerners to master (and of course makes Western languages difficult for Vietnamese to pick up).

2. If you **make an effort to speak a little Vietnamese** as you travel around you will instantly earn respect and often win people over.

3. You should **expect to be ripped off if you can't bargain in Vietnamese** – thankfully the numbers are easy to learn (see the box on p306).

Bearing these points in mind here is an explanation of the tones followed by a collection of some of the most crucial (and easiest!) phrases for getting around and making friends. And when you are trying to pronounce Vietnamese the most important thing to do to try to make yourself understood is to really open your mouth while you talk and get your whole jaw round the vowels.

The tones which apply to words are shown by the accents marked on the letters, for example:

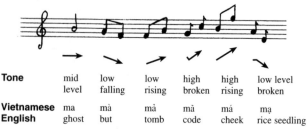

Tone	mid level	low falling	low rising	high broken	high rising	low level broken
Vietnamese	ma	mà	mả	mã	má	mạ
English	ghost	but	tomb	code	cheek	rice seedling

In addition there are accents on vowels which affect the vowel sound but are independent of the tone.

A	'ar' as in father		o	'o' as in hot
ă	'u' as in hut		ô	'aw' as in awful
â	'uh', as in hut but longer		ơ	'ur' as in fur
e	'e' as in bed		ư	'oo' as in boo
ê	'ay' as in pay		ư	'oo' as in French 'tu'
i	'i' as in ing		y	'i' as in ing

r and gi are pronounced like z when they begin a word
đ is pronounced like d
d is pronounced like z (S) or like y in young (N)
th is pronounced as a strong t
tr is pronounced ch

nh is pronounced like the ny in canyon
ng is pronounced like the final ng in thing
kh is pronounced as a gutteral sound like that made by clearing your throat

Just to further complicate things you will find as you travel around that pronunciation varies a lot. The main variation is that in the south the language is more clipped and certain vowels become eclipsed, whereas in the north words are pronounced more exactly (see goodbye, for example).

GREETINGS

There are five main ways to say 'hello', and only by using the correct one can you be polite. They are all easy to learn because the first word is like the Italian ' ciao'.

Hello (to an old or senior man)	chào ông (pronounced ciao ong).
(to a man your age)	chào anh (pronounced ciao ang – literally meaning brother).
(to an old/senior women)	chào bà (pronounced ciao baah).
(to a young woman)	chào chị (pronounced ciao ji).
(to a child of either sex)	chào em (pronounced ciao em)

I	tôi (pronounced doy).
Goodbye	chào (ciao), tạm biệt (tam beet in the south, tam bee-ette in the north)
Please	làm ơn (lam urn) followed by ong/anh/bà/chị/em
Thank you	cảm ơn (gam urn) followed by ong/anh/bà/chị/em
Excuse me (to attract attention)	ong/anh/bà/chị/em oi (oy!)
Excuse me (sorry)	xin lỗi (sin loy) followed by ong/anh/bà/chị/em
Sorry, I don't understand	xin lỗi tôi khổng hiểu (sin loy doy kong heeyoo)
How much is it?	bao nhiêu tiền? (boa ni-yoh di-ayn)
Can I have.....	ong/anh/bà/chị/em làm ơn cho tôi (lam urn jo doy)
Go away	di di (dee dee)
Oh my God! (Amiable)	trời oi (choy oi!)
Don't worry about it/no problem	khổng có chi (kong go zee)
Cheers!	Yo! (Hyo!)

Yes and no are unfortunately difficult as there are no words directly meaning yes or no, rather you have to attach a positive (vang in the north, da in the south) or a negative (khong) to a verb. For example:

I don't want to buy that	khổng mua (kong mwaw) (This is an amazingly useful phrase.)
Yes I am going to Hanoi	vâng/dạ (north/south) tôi đi Hanoi (vuhng/ya, doi dee Hanoi)

Sometimes simply to show agreement the word meaning 'sure' is used – phai (fai)

A lot of misunderstandings arise from the fact that in Vietnamese if you say yes to a negative question it means, as we would say, no. So if you were to ask the question: 'So is $10 not possible then?' and were to receive a nod of the head and the answer yes it would mean 'Yes, that is right, $10 is not possible.' This means that you should avoid asking negative questions as much as you can, but if you do find yourself asking one you need to judge how good the English of your respondent is in order to interpret their answer!

NUMBERS

Numbers are fairly easy to master. For bargaining, it often makes a big difference whether you are dealing in dollars or dong! One way to be sure is to follow the number you say with Do (pronounced Doh) for dollars or nghin (pronounced nghing), which means thousand and therefore denotes all transactions in dong. If you need extra clarity say Vietnam after the nghin – don't bother with saying dong.

0	không (kong)	23	hai mười ba
1	một (mawd)	24	hai mười bốn
2	hai	25	hai mười năm
3	ba	26	hai mười sáu
4	bốn (bawn)	27	hai mười bảy
5	năm (nahm in S, lam in N)	28	hai mười tám
6	sáu (sa-oo)	29	hai mười chín
7	bảy (bai)	30	ba mười
8	tám (dam)	40	bốn mười
9	chín (jin)	50	năm mười
10	mười (moo-uh-i in N,	60	sáu mười
	sometimes me in S)	70	bảy mười
11	mười một	80	tám mười
12	mười hai	90	chín mười
13	mười ba	100	một trăm (mawd jum)
14	mười bốn	101	một trăm một
15	mười năm	102	một trăm hai
16	mười sáu	200	hai trăm
17	mười bảy	300	ba trăm
18	mười tám	1000	một nghin (mot nghing)
19	mười chín	10,000	mười nghin
20	hai mười	100,000	một trăm nghin
21	hai mười một	500,000	năm trăm nghin
22	hai mười hai		

DAYS, DATES AND TIME

today	hom nay (hawm nay)
tomorrow	mai
tomorrow morning	mai sáng
tomorrow afternoon	mai chiều (mai jiayoo)
yesterday	hôm qua (hawm gwa)
Monday	thứ Hai (too hai)
Tuesday	thứ Ba (too ba)
Wednesday	thứ Tư (too too)
Thursday	thứ năm (too num)
Friday	thứ sáu (too sa-oo)
Saturday	thứ bảy (too bai)
Sunday	chú Nhật (joo n-yuhd)

Dates in Vietnamese are expressed as:

day date month year	thứ ngày tháng năm
thứ Nam ngày 14 tháng 2001	Thursday 14 January 2001

Time is also very simply expressed:

am (midnight to noon)	sáng
pm (noon to sunset)	chiều (jiayoo)
sunset to midnight	tôi (doy)
When's the train to Hanoi?	khi nào cóó xe lửả đi Hanoi (kee nao go seh loo-a dee Hanoi)
Hour	giơ (yur)
10 am	mười giơ sáng (moo-uh-i yur sang)
3 pm	bà giơ chiều (ba yur ji-ayoo)
9 pm	chin giơ tôi (jin yur doy)

Times past the hour are expressed in the form of 2.20, where the direct translation is two hours twenty, unless the time is very near the next hour, eg 2.55 which becomes three hours less (kém) five minutes.

twenty past two, 2.20	hai giơ hai mười (hai yur hai moo-uh-i)
half past three, 3.30	ba giơ ba mười (ba yur ba moo-uh-i)
a quarter to five, 4.45	bốn giơ bốn mười năm (bawn yur bon moo-uh-i nahm)
ten to six	sáu giơ kém mười (sa-oo yur gem moo-uh-i)
five to ten	mười giơ kém năm (moo-uh-i yur gem nham)

MAKING CONVERSATION

What is your name?	tên ban là gì? (dayn bahn la yi)
My name is	tên tôi là .... (dayn doy ....)
How old are you?	bạn bao nhiêu tuổi? (ban bao ni-yoh dwoy)
I am 28 years old	tôi hai mười tám tuổi (doy hai tam dwoy)
Are you married? (to man)	anh có vợ chưa? (ang go vur joo-a)
Are you married? (to woman)	chị có chồng chưa? (ji go jawng joo-a)
No, I am not married/not yet	chưa/chưa? đến (joo-a/joo-a dayn)
Yes I am married	tôi đã cuối (doy da gwoy)
How many children do you have?	bạn có mấy người con? (ban gomai ngwoy con)
Where do you come from?	bạn tư đâu đến? (ban doo doh dayn)
I am from England/America	tôi tư nước Anh nước My den (doy doo noo-urg ang/noo-urg mi dayn)
Canada/Australia	Ca-na-da/nước Uc (ca-na-da/noo-urg)
France/Holland	nước Pháp/nước Hoa Lan (fap/hwa-lan)
New Zealand/Japan	nước Tan Tây Lan/nước Nhật (duhn day-ilan/nhaat)
Germany/Sweden	nước đức/nước Thụy điển/(doog/too-i di-ayn)
Norway/Denmark	nước Nauy/nước Dan Mach (nah-wee/dan maj)
Where do you live?	bạn sống ởđâu·(ban song ur doh)
How far is it to Danang?	từ đây tơi Danang bao xa? (doo day doy Danang bao sa)
It is 20km to Danang.	khoảng hai mười ki lo mét đi Danang (kwang hai moo-uh-i kilomet dee Danang)
Do you speak Vietnamese?	bạn có nói tiếng Việt Nam khong? (ban go noi diayng Vietnam không)
Only a little	tôi nói được một it (doy noi doo-urg mawd eet)

USEFUL WORDS AND PHRASES

To attract attention	chị/anh/em oi! (oi). This is very effective and is polite, despite the way it sounds in English!
See you again	Hẹn gập lại (hang gap lie)

Directions

Where is ....?	ở đâu (ur doh)
a hotel	khách sạn (kaj san)
guest-house	nhà khách /nha nghi
Where is ....?	ở đâu (ur doh)
the airport	sân bay (suhn bay)
the train	xe lửa (seh loo-a)
the train station	bên xe lửa(bayn see loo-a)
the ticket	vé (veh)
the bus	xe buyt (seh bweed)
the bus station	bên xe buyt (bayn seh bweed)
a restaurant	nhà hàng (n-ya hang)
a toilet	nhà vệ sinh (n-ya vay sing)
open/closed (of shop)	mở cửa (mur goo-a)/ đóng cửa (dong goo-a)
left/right	bên trái (bayn jai)/bên phải (bayn fai)

Snacks

bread	bánh mì (bang mi)
ham sandwich	bánh mì i kẹp thịt hun khoi (bang mi gep tid hoon koy)
cream, ice cream	kem (gem)
natural yoghurt without sugar	sữa chua không đường (soo-a jwaw kawn doo-urng)
yoghurt with honey	sữa chua với mật ong (soo-a jwaw vuh-i muhd ong)

Drinks

black coffee	cà phê đen (ga fay den)
white coffee (hot)	cà phê sữa (ga fay soo-a)
mineral water	nước khoáng (noo-urg kwang)
coconut milk	nước dừa (noo-urg yoo-a)
fruit juice (fresh fruit purée)	sinh tố (sing daw)
Coca-cola without ice	coca cola đung bỏ đá (coca cola doong bo da)
beer	bia (beer)
333 (the cheapest local beer)	ba ba ba (baa baa baa)
gin and tonic	gin nước tonic (gin noo-urg tonic)
rum	rượu rum (roo-uroo rom)
vodka	rượu vot-ca (roo-uroo vawdga)

Fruit

pineapple	thơm (tohm)
apple	bom (bawm)
custard apple	mân cầu (mahn kow)
dragon fruit	thanh long (tang long)
watermelon	duả đơ (zooah daw)
orange (green!)	cam (kahm)
mango	xoài (swye)

lemon	chanh (chan-h)
durian	sầu riêng (soh ri-ayng)
rambutan	chôm chôm (jawm jawm)
avocado	quâ bơ (gwa bur)
bananas	chuối (choo-ee)
papaya	đu đư (doo doo)

Vegetables

vegetables	rau cơ (z-ow go)
beansprouts	giá (ya)
morning glory (water spinach)	rau muống (z-ow muuong)
tomatoes	cà tô mát (kah toh maht)
potatoes	khoai tây (kwyetey)
cabbage	cải bắp (gai bup)
salad	xà lách (sa laj)

Rice and noodles

rice (also means food)	cơm (kuhm)
beef soup noodles	phở bò (fur baw)
round rice noodles	bún (buhn)
vermicelli	miến (meyeen)

Meat, poultry and fish dishes

meat	thịt (teet)
pork	heo (teet he-yo) (S), lon (lurn) (N)
beef	bò (teet baw)
chicken	gà (gah)
duck	vịt (veet)
fish	cá (kah)
crab	cua (koo-ah)
frog	ếch (eck)
shrimp	tôm (tohm)
lobster	tôm hùm (tohm hohm)
mussels	hgêu (ngeh-oo)
eel	lươn (loo-on)
squid	mực (mwurck)
snails	ốc (awg)
dog	chó (jo) or cày (gay)

Ways of cooking

fry	chiên (ji-ayn) (S), ran (ran) (N)
stir-fry	xào (zow)
roasted	quay (kway)
steamed	hap
grilled	nướng (noo-ong)
clay pot	kho tộ (co tho)
steamboat	lẩu (lao)

Condiments

salt	muối (moo-woy)
pepper	tiêu (tee-yew)
garlic	tơi (doy)
chilli	ớt (urt)

fish sauce	nước mam (nurck mahm)
sweet and sour sauce	chua ngọt (choo-ah ngoht)
soy sauce	xì dầu (see dow)
lemongrass	xà (zaa)
basil	rau răm (ra-oo ram) *or* rau é (ra-oo eh)
MSG	bột ngọt (boht ngoht)

You now can decipher many dishes on Vietnamese menus, eg:

bò xào giá	beef stir-fried with beansprouts
lươn nướng xà ớt	grilled eel seasoned with lemongrass and chilli
ếch ran bơ tơi	frogs fried with butter and garlic

Desserts

crème caramel	kem caramel (kem caramel)
chocolate	sô-cô-la (soh co la)
gâteau	gâto (gaatoh)

Miscellaneous

butter	bơ (bur, as in the French burre)
cheese	phô-mát (fo-mad, as in the French fromage)
eggs	hột gộ (hoht ga)

Emergency

Please can you help me?	xịn ông vui lòng giúp tôi
This is an emergency!	khẩn cấp
Call the police (wiser to use as a threat than actually in the hope of getting some help)	hãy gọi công an
Please find someone who speaks English	Vui lòng tìm ai đó có the nói tiếng anh
I feel ill	tôi cảm thấy mệt
Please call a doctor	vui lòng gọi bác sĩ
Take me to a hospital	đưa tôi đến bệnh viện
I am allergic to	tôi hị đị ảng vơi
peanuts	đậu phọng
penicillin	thuôc
I've been robbed	tôi đã hi cuỏ
I've had a crash	tôi đã hi trâỳ

APPENDIX B: TIMETABLES

HANOI TO HO CHI MINH CITY AND VICE VERSA

	S1 (32 hours)		S3 (39hrs)		S5 (41 hours)		S7 (41 hours)	
	Arr	Dep	Arr	Dep	Arr	Dep	Arr	Dep
Hanoi		21.00		19.00		11.00		14.00
Phu Ly			20.10	20.11	12.14	12.15	15.13	15.15
Nam Dinh			20.43	20.46	12.51	12.56	15.51	15.56
Ninh Binh			21.15	21.16	13.27	13.29	16.27	16.29
Thanh Hoa			22.25	22.28	14.46	14.51	17.45	17.50
Vinh	02.28	02.36	01.05	01.20	17.33	17.53	20.32	20.52
Dong Hoi			05.38	05.53	23.03	23.23	01.57	02.17
Dong Ha			07.42	07.44	01.23	01.25	04.12	04.15
Hué	09.22	09.30	09.46	09.57	02.46	03.01	05.36	05.51
Danang	12.09	12.24	12.54	13.14	06.16	06.41	09.06	09.31
Tam Ky					08.18	08.20	11.06	11.07
Quang Ngai			16.01	16.03	09.31	09.33	12.31	12.34
Dieu Tri	17.36	17.44	18.53	19.08	13.05	13.25	15.40	16.00
Tuy Hoa			21.02	21.04	15.32	15.34	18.02	18.04
Nha Trang	21.37	21.45	23.31	23.43	18.09	18.29	20.32	20.52
Thap Cham			01.15	01.16	20.37	20.45	22.45	22.47
Muong Man			03.57	03.58	23.47	23.49	02.33	02.48
HCMC	05.00		08.00		04.00		07.00	

Ho Chi Minh City to Hanoi

	S2 (32 hours)		S4 (39hrs		S6 (41 hours)		S8 (41 hours)	
	Arr	Dep	Arr	Dep	Arr	Dep	Arr	Dep
HCMC		21.00		19.00		11.00		22.00
Muong Man			23.01	23.02	15.37	15.39	02.45	02.46
Thap Cham			01.42	01.43	18.25	18.40	05.29	05.31
Nha Trang	14.10	04.18	03.13	03.25	20.38	20.58	07.07	07.27
Tuy Hoa			05.42	05.43	23.34	23.36	10.08	10.10
Dieu Tri	08.12	08.20	07.36	07.51	01.35	01.55	12.14	12.34
Quang Ngai			11.24	11.26	04.53	04.55	15.58	16.05
Tam Ky					06.05	06.07	17.16	17.17
Danang	13.27	13.42	14.06	14.26	07.53	08.18	18.54	19.19
Hué	16.21	16.24	17.34	17.39	11.37	11.42	22.32	22.37
Dong Ha			18.52	18.53	13.30	13.33	00.06	00.07
Dong Hoi	19.13	19.21	20.40	20.55	15.35	15.55	02.37	02.57
Vinh	23.15	23.20	01.16	01.31	20.50	21.10	07.53	08.13
Thanh Hoa			04.25	04.30	00.03	00.09	11.00	11.05
Ninh Binh			05.45	05.48	01.32	01.34	12.20	12.21
Nam Dinh			06.19	06.24	02.06	02.11	12.54	12.59
Phu Ly			07.00	07.03	02.46	02.47	13.36	13.39
Hanoi	05.00		08.30		04.00		15.00	

Note that Chinese time is an hour ahead of Vietnamese time – all times are in local time.

HANOI TO BEIJING AND VICE VERSA

M1 km	arr	dep	Station	Fare (Swiss Francs)	M2 km	arr	dep
		14.00	Hanoi			11.30	
167	20.00	23.00	Dong Dang			03.30	06.00
181	00.56	03.20	Ping Xiang	25.34		00.04	03.34
401	07.12	10.30	Nan Ning	47.70		17.39	20.23
	14.19	14.35	Lin Zou			13.25	13.45
832	17.24	17.32	Guilin	74.25		10.52	11.04
	17.42	17.50	Gui Lin Bei			10.26	10.43
	20.49	20.58	Yong Zhou			07.00	07.19
1194	23.04	23.12	Heng Yang	92.86		04.57	05.05
1379	01.10	01.15	Chang Sha	102.08		02.52	02.58
	04.59	05.07	Wu Chang			23.02	23.10
1757	05.26	05.28	Han Kou	108.54		22.41	22.43
2271	10.37	10.44	Zheng Zhou	130.81		17.25	17.31
	14.34	14.36	Shi Jia Zhuang			13.32	13.34
2966	17.18		Beijing	147.26			10.51

HANOI TO LAO CAI AND VICE VERSA

Train	Depart Hanoi	Arrive Lao Cai
LC1	22.00	07.10
LC3	05.20	15.10
LC5 (Friday and Sunday)	21.30	06.10

Train	Depart Lao Cai	Arrive Hanoi
LC2	18.45	04.20
LC4	10.10	20.10
LC6 (Saturday and Monday)	09.40	20.20

Notes

LC5 and LC6 go to and from Kunming, China

Fares for trains LC1, 2, 3, 4: Hard seat 125,000d; Hard sleeper top 175,000d; Hard sleeper middle and bottom 207,5000d; Soft sleeper air-con 244,000d

HANOI TO KUNMING AND VICE VERSA

LC5 km	arr	dep	Station	Fare (Swiss Francs)	LC6 km	arr	dep
		21.30	Hanoi		765	20.20	
293	06.10	09.20	Lao Cai	20.59	472	07.40	09.40
297	09.30	13.20	Hekou	21.21	468	07.20	07.30
517	21.32	21.50	Kai Yuan	36.03	248	22.45	23.05
695	03.31	03.43	Yi Luang	41.91	70	16.50	17.00
765	06.00		Kunming	44.85			14.45

Notes

LC5 departs Hanoi every Friday and Sunday and LC6 departs departs Kunming every Friday and Sunday

The International Booking Office in Ga Hanoi is open 07.00-12.30 and 13.00-20.50

Fares from Hanoi are payable in Swiss Francs. Fares from Kunming are not given.

HANOI TO HAIPHONG AND VICE VERSA

Train	Station	Dep	Arr (Haiphong)
HP1	Hanoi	06.15	07.40
HP3	Long Bien	09.20	11.55
LP9	Long Bien	16.10	18.55
LP11	Long Bien	17.45	20.00

Train	Dep (Haiphong)	Arr	Station (Hanoi)
HP2	18.10	20.20	Hanoi
LP2	06.10	08.50	Long Bien
LP4	08.15	10.00	Long Bien
LP6	14.40	17.00	Long Bien
LP8	05.05	09.40	Long Bien
LP10	14.40	17.00	Long Bien
LP12	16.25	18.55	Long Bien

Notes

Fare 52,000d in hard seat

HANOI TO DONG DANG AND VICE VERSA

Train	Station	Depart	Arr Dong Dang
M1 (Tue and Fri)	Hanoi	14.00	20.00
DD1	Gia Lam	14.17	20.00
DD3	Hanoi	06.00	12.05
HD3	Hanoi	05.30	15.05

Train	Depart Dong Dang	Arr	Station
M2 (Wed and Sun)	06.00	11.30	Hanoi
DD4	14.00	20.35	Hanoi

Notes

Fare 75,000 hard seat

Trains to Lang Son arrive 20 minutes before arrival in Dong Dang

Fare to Lan Son 70m000 hard seat

APPENDIX C: FARES

Fares (in thousands of dong) for the Reunification Express Hanoi–Ho Chi Minh City (HCMC)

Trains S1 (32 hours southwards)/S3 (39 hours)/S5 & S7 (41 hours)

Hanoi to	Km	Hard seat S3/S5 & S7	Soft seat S1/S3/S5 & S7	Soft seat Air-con S1/S3	Hard sleeper (bottom) S1/S3/S5 & S7	Hard sleeper (middle) S1/S3/S5 & S7	Hard sleeper (top) S1/S3/S5 & S7	Soft sleeper S1/S3 (air-con) S5 & S7 (hot air-con)
Nam Dinh	87	43/40	-/46/43	-/67	-/73/67	-/67/62	-/62/56	-/97/69
Ninh Binh	115	54/50	-/58/53	-/85	-/92/85	-/84/78	-/78/71	-/122/88
Thanh Hoa	175	75/70	-/81/75	-/124	-/135/124	-/124/113	-/113/102	-/185/128
Vinh	319	128/119	158/139/128	237/217	256/237/217	237/217/197	217/197/178	352/328/224
Dong Hoi	522	202/187	251/220/202	381/348	412/381/348	381/348/316	348/316/283	568/530/360
Dong Ha	622	239/221	-/260/239	-/413	-/451/413	-/413/374	-/374/336	-/629/427
Hué	688	263/244	327/286/263	498/455	540/498/455	498/455/413	455/413/370	746/695/471
Danang	791	301/278	375/327/301	571/522	619/571/522	571/522/473	522/473/424	856/797/540
Tam Ky	865	-/303	-/-/328	-/-	-/-570	-/-516	-/-463	-/-590
Quang Ngai	928	351/325	-/382/351	-/610	-/668/610	-/610/553	-/553/495	-/933/632
Dieu Tri	1098	412/381	515/449/412	787/719	854/787/719	787/719/651	719/651/583	1182/1100/744
Tuy Hoa	1198	449/416	-/490/449	-/785	-/859/785	-/785/711	-/711/636	-/1202/812
Nha Trang	1315	537/497	672/586/537	1029/940	1117/1029/940	1029/940/851	940/851/762	1547/1440/973
Thap Cham	1408	573/530	-/625/573	-/1003	-/1098/1003	-/1003/907	-/907/812	-/1537/1038
Muong Man	1551	604/-	-/659/-	-/1058	-/1159/—	-/1058/	-/958-	-/1622/-
HCMC	1726	643/594	805/701/643	1233/1126	1338/1233/1126	1233/1126/1019	1126/1019/912	1854/1819/1166